Risk and Reason

Safety, Law, and the Environment

What should be done about airplane safety and terrorism, global warming, polluted water, nuclear power, and genetically engineered food? All over the globe, risks to safety, health, and the environment are a subject of intense interest. Unfortunately, too much of the time we fear the wrong things. Sometimes we make the situation even worse. Rather than investigating the facts, we respond to temporary fears. The result is a situation of hysteria and neglect – and unnecessary illness and death.

Risk and Reason explains the sources of these problems and explores what can be done about them. It shows how individual thinking and social interactions lead us in foolish directions. Offering sound proposals for social reform, it explains how a more sensible system of risk regulation, embodied in the idea of a cost–benefit state, could save many thousands of lives and many billions of dollars – and protect the environment in the process.

Cass R. Sunstein is the Karl N. Llewellyn Distinguished Service Professor at the University of Chicago. He has written many books, the most recent of which are *Republic.com* and *Designing Democracy*. Professor Sunstein has worked in the U.S. Department of Justice, advised on law reform and constitution-making in many nations, and testified before Congress on numerous questions, often involving environmental protection and regulation of risk. A member of the American Academy of Arts and Sciences, he has won many awards, including the Goldsmith Book Prize and the award for the best scholarship in administrative law from the American Bar Association (three times).

Risk
and
Reason

Safety, Law, and the Environment

CASS R. SUNSTEIN

University of Chicago Law School

PUBLISHED BY THE PRESS SYNDICATE OF THE UNIVERSITY OF CAMBRIDGE
The Pitt Building, Trumpington Street, Cambridge, United Kingdom

CAMBRIDGE UNIVERSITY PRESS
The Edinburgh Building, Cambridge CB2 2RU, UK
40 West 20th Street, New York, NY 10011-4211, USA
477 Williamstown Road, Port Melbourne, VIC 3207, Australia
Ruiz de Alarcón 13, 28014 Madrid, Spain
Dock House, The Waterfront, Cape Town 8001, South Africa

http://www.cambridge.org

First published 2002
First paperback edition 2003
Reprinted with corrections 2004

Printed in the United States of America

Typefaces Centaur MT 11.25/13 pt. and Cochin   *System* LATEX 2$_\varepsilon$ [TB]

A catalog record for this book is available from the British Library.

Library of Congress Cataloging in Publication Data

Sunstein, Cass R.
    Risk and reason : safety, law, and the environment / Cass R. Sunstein.
        p.   cm.
    Includes bibliographical references and index.
    ISBN 0-521-79199-5 (hardback)
    ISBN 0-521-01625-8 (paperback)
    1. Risk management.   2. Risk assessment.   3. Decision making.   I. Title.
    HD61 .S86   2002
    368–dc21   2002020166

ISBN 0 521 79199 5 hardback
ISBN 0 521 01625 8 paperback

For Ellen

We are all Expressionists part of the time. Sometimes we just want to scream loudly at injustice, or to stand up and be counted. These are noble motives, but any serious revolutionist must often deprive himself of the pleasures of self-expression. He must judge his actions by their ultimate effect on institutions.

Herbert Simon[1]

The American people are suffering from what can be called "a syndrome of paranoia and neglect" about potential dangers to their health, safety, and the environment. This leads to a paradox that is becoming increasingly recognized. Large amounts of resources are devoted to slight or speculative dangers while substantial and well-documented dangers remain unaddressed.

John Graham[2]

We overreact to some risks and virtually ignore others. Often too much weight is placed on risks of low probability but high salience (such as those posed by trace carcinogens or terrorist action); risks of commission rather than omission; and risks, such as those associated with frontier technologies, whose magnitude is difficult to estimate. Too little effort is placed ameliorating voluntary risks, such as those involving automobiles and diet.... We need to acknowledge that risks to life and limb are inherent in modern society – indeed in life itself – and that systematic strategies for assessing and responding to risks are overdue.

Richard Zeckhauser and W. Kip Viscusi[3]

[1] *Models of My Life 281* (New York: Basic Books, 1991).
[2] Making Sense of Risk: An Agenda for Congress, in *Risks, Benefits, and Lives Saved 183*, Robert Hahn, ed. (New York: Oxford University Press, 1996).
[3] Risk Within Reason, in *Judgment and Decision Making: An Interdisciplinary Reader 465, 476*, Terry Connolly et al., eds. (Cambridge: Cambridge Univ. Press, 2000).

Contents

Preface to the Paperback Edition
Fear Itself

In fall 2002, a pair of snipers killed ten people in the Washington, D.C., area. The victims were randomly chosen. They included men and women, young and old, whites and African-Americans. Each of these murders was a tragedy, of course; but the actions of the snipers affected millions of others as well. Many citizens were afraid that they could be next. Fear, sometimes dull and sometimes very sharp, gripped the area. People's behavior was radically altered. Consider just a few examples:

- Many school districts placed their classes under a "code blue," requiring students to stay inside school buildings and forbidding them from leaving campus for lunch or outdoor activities. Nearly one million children were affected.
- Many people dramatically reduced their public activities. Numerous citizens stopped going to health clubs with large front windows; others took to wearing body armor while pumping gas or shielding themselves with a car door to keep safe.
- At several area schools, scholastic aptitude testing was canceled.
- Numerous sports events – including recreational league soccer for six-year olds, high school girls' tennis, field hockey, and baseball – were canceled or postponed.
- In Winchester, Virginia, all school field trips were canceled.
- Dozens of Starbucks stores removed their outside seating.
- The school system in Prince George's County, Maryland, canceled all athletic events indefinitely.

There is something very odd about the extraordinary effects of the snipers' actions. For people in the area, the snipers caused a minuscule increase in risk. Suppose that five million people were at risk and that the sniper was planning to kill one person every three days. If so, the daily statistical risk was less than one in one million, and the weekly statistical risk was less than three in one million. These are trivial risks, far lower than the risks associated with many daily activities about which human beings do not express even the slightest concern. The daily risk, for example, was smaller than the one in one million risk from drinking thirty diet sodas with saccharin, from driving 100 miles, from smoking two cigarettes, from taking ten airline trips, from living in a home with a smoker for two weeks, from living in Denver rather than Philadelphia for forty days, and from eating thirty-five slices of fresh bread. The real risk could not possibly have been enough to justify the high levels of anxiety and fear – which bordered, for many people, on the edge of hysteria. The extent of alarm could not possibly be justified by the extent of the risk.

This little tale of excessive fear is an illustration of a pervasive phenomenon. I could have picked many other examples: fear of the abduction of young children, the SARS epidemic, genetically altered food, mad cow disease, abandoned hazardous waste sites, terrorist attacks. In all of these cases, people's fears have often outrun reality. In fact unjustified fear is one of the most serious problems facing modern societies and the world as a whole. One reason is that for each of us, such fear can cause big problems in our own lives. Fear also has huge ripple effects, producing economic and other losses. For governments, unjustified fear leads to policies and laws that do far more harm than good. And unjustified fear has a cousin, or a mirror-image: neglect of real hazards – such as those stemming from poor diet, obesity, indoor air pollution, and sun exposure – that create significant threats to people's health and longevity.

One of the major goals of this book is to understand unjustified fear and to see what might be done about it. If we focus on the snipers' attacks in Washington, we can get two clues about the sources of fear. When people lack information about the likelihood of actual harm, they tend to rely on what psychologists call the *availability heuristic*. In using the availability heuristic, people answer the question of probability by seeing whether examples readily come to mind. Instead of investigating reality, they ask: "Can I think of an example?" For those who lack accurate information, it isn't irrational to use the availability heuristic; this heuristic can lead to big mistakes. If an incident is readily available to the mind but statistically rare, people will overestimate risk; if examples do not come to mind but the statistical risk is high, the heuristic can give people an unjustified sense of security. Undoubtedly the fear of sniper attack, in the Washington area, was increased by the high salience of the few attacks and thus by the availability heuristic. So, too, for excessive fear of certain diseases and crimes. (There is a lesson here about why terrorism works.)

There is another explanation. When strong emotions are triggered, people tend to focus on the worst case and not to think much about issues of probability at all. The phenomenon of *probability neglect* occurs when people are highly responsive to the outcome and when significant variations in its likelihood do not much affect thought and behavior. If emotions are running high, the question of probability is especially likely to be neglected. To say the least, the idea of being killed by a sniper, at a gas station or on a playground, is highly emotional. Many of those who altered their behavior in response to the snipers' killings appeared to focus on the bad outcome and to neglect probability altogether.

Unjustified fear is often produced by some combination of the availability heuristic and probability neglect. But an account of this kind, focusing only on how individuals think, is missing something important. Countless risks are, in principle, "available"; and countless risks might, in theory, have the kind of salience that would lead to probability neglect. The risks associated with nuclear power are available to Americans, but much less so to citizens of France, who are largely unconcerned about those risks. In many communities, the risks associated with unsafe sex (which kills tens of thousands of Americans each year) lack much salience. But in some communities, those risks are salient indeed. Americans do not fear the risks associated with genetic modification of food, even though in principle such risks might be "available," as they are in many places in Europe.

Obviously the availability of risks and the risks to which probability neglect attaches, are variable from place to place. Abandoned hazardous waste sites were not a salient source of risk until about 1980, when the Love Canal controversy converted such sites into a strong basis of concern. Hence, availability varies over time. Some statistically large risks do not cause a great deal of fear. In many communities, the risks associated with tobacco smoking (a killer of hundreds of thousands of Americans annually) are not salient at all. Why is this?

To answer this question, we need to know something about social interactions, about how people learn, and about how information is transmitted. In many cases of high-visibility, low-probability risks, the behavior and preoccupations of the media play a large role. Many perceived "epidemics" are in reality no such thing, but instead a product of media coverage of gripping, unrepresentative incidents. Attention to those incidents is likely to ensure availability and salience, promoting an inaccurately high estimate of probability and at the same time some degree of probability neglect. (Consider shark attacks or the abduction of young children.) In the context of the sniper attacks, intense media coverage was the central source of social fear, helping to ensure that large amounts of private and public resources were devoted to risk reduction. And knowing the importance of media coverage, well-organized private groups – some entirely self-interested, others altruistic and pursuing a social cause – often work extremely hard to promote public attention to particular risks. Hence a common tactic is to publicize an incident that might trigger both availability and salience. Of course terrorists themselves are the most extreme and vicious example, using high-visibility attacks to convince people that "they cannot be safe anywhere."

There is a major warning here. When newspapers, magazines and news programs stress highly improbable risks, people's concerns will be out of proportion to reality. And in the face of close media attention, the demand for legal responses will grow. Government is likely to respond. If public officials cater to unjustified concerns, we will spend too much of our time and money on pointless precautions. We might take steps that actually increase the risks we face. In some contexts, including protection against terrorism, those steps will compromise liberty itself. And those very steps will make us more fearful still. At the same time, we will fail to attend to genuinely serious hazards in our daily lives – and government will rest on the sidelines.

For those interested in staying healthy and lengthening their lives, the lesson is simple: Focus on the likelihood that the harm will actually occur. The millions of Americans who have been worrying about terrorism would be far better advised to lose weight, to stay out of the sun, to drive carefully, and to stop smoking. For those interested in policy and law, the lesson is a bit more complex. Public fear is a real problem, even if it is unjustified, and a government does its citizens a grave disservice if it ignores their concerns. But in a democracy, both citizens and leaders know that government can do much better than to rely on human intuitions about fear. The central goals of this book are to see how and why those intuitions go wrong and to explore how both individuals and nations can improve on them.

Preface

All over the world, nations are attempting to reduce risks, to improve safety, and to extend lives. Indeed, risk reduction has become a principal goal of modern governments. What should be done about global warming? How should nations handle the risks associated with terrorism, including risks associated with chemical weapons and safety in airplanes? Should governments regulate or ban genetic modification of food? Should arsenic be removed from drinking water? What is the relationship between energy policy and environmental protection? Should government require cars to meet fuel economy standards? Might such requirements make cars less safe? Questions of this kind are preoccupying public institutions, not only nationally but internationally as well.

Too much of the time, however, governments are making stabs in the dark. Often they devote resources to little problems rather than big ones. Sometimes they react to short-term public outcries. Sometimes they are unaware of the harmful, unintended side-effects of what they do. Sometimes they make the situation worse. In regulating risks, they impose high costs, which create risks of their own – including the risks of higher prices, lower wages, unemployment, and even illness and death. Nations do not place sufficient emphasis on science. Rather than investigate the facts, they tend to react on the basis of intuition or in response to temporary fears. This is a special problem in a time when leaders must confront risks of catastrophe, whether from technology or from terrorism; it is also a problem in an era in which environmental quality, or the health of workers, becomes a serious public issue.

Above all, this book is an effort to link people's ordinary thinking about risk to recurring issues in law and politics. As we shall see, people often think poorly about dangers. Sometimes they fear the wrong things. Their errors are far from innocuous. They lead to problems in daily life, including illness and death. The same errors help account for problems in policy and law, my principal concern here. When people are fearful, government is likely to respond, even when public fear is baseless. When people are indifferent, government is likely to be indifferent too, even when people are facing serious risks. As we will see, a more sensible system of risk regulation could save thousands of lives, and billions of dollars as well.

Among other things, I will suggest a direct and simple response to the problems catalogued here: Before government acts, it should, if feasible, attempt to produce a cost–benefit analysis, understood as a detailed accounting of the consequences of the alternative courses of action. The cost–benefit analysis should allow people to see if the problem at issue is small or large. It should explore the expense of reducing the problem and explain who will bear that expense. It should place a high premium on science. It should ensure that experts, or technocrats, will have a large role in government policy. What I shall call the cost–benefit state is only beginning to emerge. It remains to be built on proper foundations. I will argue for a kind of cost–benefit state, not fundamentally on economic grounds, but as a corrective to cognitive limitations and a response to democratic needs.

Some people think of cost–benefit analysis as a form of cold, barely human calculation, treating health and life as mere commodities and envisioning government as some kind of huge maximizing machine. On the contrary, I urge that cost–benefit analysis should be seen as a simple pragmatic tool, designed to promote a better appreciation of the consequences of regulation. A government that uses cost–benefit analysis is certainly entitled to consider who is helped and who is hurt. It might believe, for example, that special steps should be taken to protect children, poor people, or members of minority groups. A government that uses cost–benefit analysis should also attempt to ensure qualitative as well as quantitative descriptions of the various effects of regulation. Properly understood, cost–benefit analysis is no theology. It is instead an effort to assist both government and citizens, in the hope of ensuring that risk regulation will actually promote its purposes. If, for example, proposed fuel economy standards will significantly reduce greenhouse gases but also lead to smaller and less safe cars – and thus produce over a thousand extra deaths each year – officials and citizens should be aware of that fact.

It would, however, be insufficient simply to ask government to conduct detailed analyses of risks and their regulation. I will argue for institutional reforms, from all branches of government, designed to overcome the problems catalogued here. Congress should take steps to ensure that the system of risk regulation makes overall sense. Regulatory agencies should be authorized to refuse to regulate risks if regulation would create new, and significant, risks of its own. The executive branch should create a publicly available website, containing information about what is known about existing risks and allowing people to compare risks against each other. Courts should not permit government to act when risk regulation will make things worse rather than better. Perhaps most importantly, I will also argue that government should use "smart tools" – methods of reducing risk that will actually work, that will not cost a great deal, that will not overload government's own capacities, and that will permit us to obtain more protection than we otherwise could hope to get. Some of the smartest tools move far beyond cost–benefit analysis at the governmental level and attempt to take advantage of market forces, which can pool information far better than public officials. Hence I will explore how economic incentives, risk reduction contracts, and "free market environmentalism" can avoid some of the problems associated with risk control from the center.

Much of the promise of a cost–benefit state lies in its ability to identify ways of protecting health, and extending lives, that ordinary intuition would neglect. An effort to go well beyond intuition and to explore the consequences of our options ought not to be seen as an effort to reduce social purposes to some arithmetic formula. It is instead a way that human beings, aware of their own limitations, can increase the likelihood that law and policy will actually promote human goals.

Introduction: Magnitudes, Tradeoffs, and Tools

The German psychologist Dietrich Dorner has designed some fascinating experiments to see whether people can reduce social risks.[1] Dorner's experiments are run via computer. Participants are asked to relieve suffering and reduce risks faced by the inhabitants of some region of the world. The problems and risks may involve pollution, poverty, poor medical care, inadequate fertilization of crops, sick cattle, insufficient water, or excessive hunting and fishing. Through the magic of the computer, many policy initiatives are available – improved care of cattle, childhood immunization, drilling more wells. Participants are able to choose among them. Once particular initiatives are chosen, the computer projects, over short periods and then over decades, what is likely to happen in the region.

In these experiments, success is entirely possible. Some initiatives will actually make for effective and enduring improvements. But many of the participants – even the most educated and professional – produce calamities. They do so because they fixate on isolated problems and do not see the complex, systemwide effects of particular interventions. For example, they may appreciate the importance of increasing the number of cattle, but once they do that, they create a serious risk of overgrazing, and they fail to anticipate that problem. They may understand full well the value of drilling more wells to provide water, but they do not anticipate the energy and environmental effects of the drilling, which then endangers the food supply. Only the rare participant is able to see a number of steps down the road – to understand the multiple effects of one-shot interventions into the system and to assess a wide range of consequences from those interventions. The successful participants seem to take small, reversible

---

[1] Dietrich Dorner, The Logic of Failure: Recognizing and Avoiding Error in Complex Situations (New York: Metropolitan Books, 1996).

1

steps or to see the full set of effects at once, and thus to protect themselves against major blunders.

Dorner's experiments are somewhat artificial. They involve computers, rather than real-life problems, lived in real time. But consider an illuminating episode in Britain in 2000, when a train crashed at Hatfield, injuring dozens of passengers and killing several of them. After the crash, railway travel suddenly seemed "unsafe" to many people, and no less than one-third of rail travellers in Britain started using the highway instead. As it happens, Britain's roads are more than ten times as dangerous as its railways. It has been estimated that the increase in automobile traffic led to five additional deaths in the first thirty days after the Hatfield crash – nearly equal the total number of deaths from train accidents in the previous thirty years.

People's behavior in the aftermath of the Hatfield crash tells us a great about our reactions to risks. It shows, for example, that a salient example can greatly influence what we do, even if the example does not reveal anything about the statistical reality. As I will emphasize, salient, vivid examples can make people overreact to small risks. When examples are not salient and vivid, people may be indifferent to real dangers. Equally important, the episode also says something about social influences on behavior. After the crash, people undoubtedly spoke with one another about their fears, creating a kind of cascade of concern about train safety. We shall also see that cascade effects can lead people to large-scale errors about risks. But government regulation, my principal topic here, was not involved. Turn now to an ambitious, entirely well-intentioned governmental effort to control risks – in particular, certain risks associated with air pollution from cars. Unfortunately, the effort was a Dorner-style failure. As we shall see, the failure offers many lessons for the future.

Motor vehicles and gasoline contribute to many air pollution problems. If the United States, or any other industrialized nation, could reduce pollution from cars and trucks, it would also decrease the health risks associated with dirty air. In the process, it would do something about global warming as well. Many policies, in the United States and elsewhere, have been extremely successful in this vein. But this is not a tale of success.

In the early 1980s, American environmentalists became interested in what was, at the time, a radical new step: governmentally mandated "clean fuels." These are motor fuels that consist, in whole or in part, of substitutes for gasoline. The most popular clean fuels come from two sources: ethanol, an alcohol fuel usually made from corn, and methanol, an alcohol fuel usually made from natural gas or coal. According to many environmentalists, clean fuels promised to reduce motor vehicle emissions of numerous sources of air pollution, including carbon monoxide, which contributes to ozone. Because tens of millions Americans lived (and continue to live) in areas that exceed federal standards for ozone, any step that would reduce carbon dioxide emissions could be a big help.

At first clean fuels seemed like an exotic and strange idea, urged only by a small group of like-minded individuals. But as the 1980s drew to a close, a bandwagon effect was well underway. People seeking better ways to control air pollution came to believe that clean fuels were both desirable and feasible. It did not hurt that the influential "corn lobby" had much to gain from the widespread use of ethanol. Various industry groups joined environmentalists to spread the news: clean fuels would be good for the environment. The pressure for action was rapidly becoming irresistible. Public officials, including high-level appointees in the first Bush Administration, took interest in the bandwagon.

As Congress began to debate the question, the oil and gas industry, much threatened by the effort to replace its product, suggested an intriguing compromise: "reformulated gasoline," consisting of a mixture of ordinary gasoline and additives that would reduce harmful emissions. Oil company executives urged that reformulated gasoline could provide the benefits of clean fuels at a fraction of the cost – and far more quickly. Environmental groups rapidly agreed, seeing reformulated gasoline as a chance to move in the direction that they had been seeking all along.

In 1990, the movement for reformulated gasoline spread like wildfire. As the year drew to a close, Congress imposed new legal mandates, requiring reformulated gasoline to be sold in areas suffering from significant air pollution – mostly big cities like Los Angeles, New York, and Chicago. Congress did not specify the oxygenate that must be used, but most companies chose a methanol derivative, methyl tertiaty butyl ether (MTBE) – an oxygen-boosting additive that improves combustion, thus reducing carbon dioxide emissions.

So far, perhaps, so good. But there were early indications that MTBE might also produce serious health risks. As compared with conventional gasoline, MTBE increases formaldehyde emissions. MTBE is also far more toxic than gasoline and highly soluble in water. When it leaks from underground gasoline tanks, or is spilled, it travels readily to wells. A few years after the inauguration of the government's program, MTBE was found to have polluted the water in many areas in which reformulated gasoline is sold – enough to have been detected in no less than 20 percent of the groundwater in such areas. Thousands of groundwater sites in California were contaminated. By the mid-1990s, MTBE was found in drinking water in at least forty-one states.

This is not good news. Even at low levels, MTBE is dangerous to drink, frequently causing nausea, vomiting, headaches, and disorientation. Many scientists believe that MTBE is a human carcinogen. Citing contamination by MTBE, water-well operators have brought lawsuits against gasoline distributors. Things got even worse. In the late 1990s, an independent study suggested that MTBE had only a modest effect in reducing ozone levels. At the same time, it is not costless, adding to the price of gasoline.

In March 1999, the Environmental Protection Agency (EPA) called on Congress to phase out MTBE, citing water pollution and urging, "Americans deserve both clean air and clean water, and never one at the expense of the other." To replace MBTE, the EPA argued that gasoline should include ethanol and "other safe biofuels." The corn lobby loves ethanol and continues to argue on its behalf. But ethanol seems to be an ambiguous blessing too. Importantly, it decreases carbon monoxide emissions, and it does not contribute to water pollution. But it also increases emissions of both hydrocarbons and volatile organic compounds. In any case, new technology in motor vehicles might well be mooting the whole idea of reformulated gasoline. As the debate rages, state and federal issues are spending a lot of money to clean up water pollution from MTBE.

In some ways, this is an unusual episode, but it tells us a great deal about the control of risks. For air pollution, laissez-faire, or reliance on the free market, is not a sensible course. Urban air pollution from motor vehicles creates serious health problems, and aggressive steps have been necessary in response. Many of those steps have succeeded, and there is much more to be done. But it was never clear that the reformulated gasoline program is an especially effective way of reducing air pollution from cars. The government never made a serious effort to compare the reductions from this program with the reductions from many other possibilities. Worse still, the very steps chosen by government were also responsible for the creation of a health risk, one probably more serious than the one that the government was seeking to solve.

When push came to shove, the EPA's recommendation must have turned on a form of balancing. Everyone agreed that it was necessary, at a minimum, to weigh the environmental benefits of regulation against the environmental costs of regulation. But the EPA left that weighing process in a mind-numbing fog, with its unhelpful claim that "Americans deserve both clean air and clean water." The claim is unhelpful because as this very episode reveals, clean air is a matter of degree; no on–off switch separates "clean" from "unclean." What were the particular grounds for the EPA's proposal? And how do we know that "ethanol and other safe biofuels" are the best approach to reducing the risks associated with air pollution from motor vehicles? To both questions, the EPA offered silence. One of the major goals of this book is to criticize that silence and to outline the issues that EPA should have tried to resolve instead.

Gradually and in fits and starts, the American regulatory state, and indeed regulatory states all over the globe, are becoming cost–benefit states. By this

4

I mean that government regulation is increasingly assessed by asking whether the benefits of regulation justify the costs of regulation. For arsenic in the water and ozone in the air, for global warming and clean-up of hazardous waste dumps, for safety in the workplace and in cars, for genetically modified food and regulation of cellular telephones, for airline safety and for risks from contaminated water, governments are making decisions after making an effort to quantify and balance both benefits and costs. In many ways, this counts as a genuine revolution, especially in the control and reduction of risks. The revolution is indeed worldwide,[2] and I shall have something to say about practices in various nations. But my focus here is on American practice, with a hope that the discussion will have more general implications.

I believe that the United States is rapidly reaching the end of an intense "first-generation" debate about whether to base regulatory choices on cost–benefit analysis at all. This debate is now ending, with a substantial victory for the proponents of cost–benefit analysis. In fact, a bipartisan consensus has emerged in favor of the basic approach. The consensus features three points.

First, government should attempt to assess the *magnitude* of any problem that it is attempting to solve, through quantitative assessments to the extent possible. Government should explore whether the problem is large or small. It should try to see if many or few lives are at stake. Where scientific knowledge does not allow for specific estimates, government should try to identify ranges. If it is issuing a new regulation of arsenic in drinking water, for example, government should try to specify how much it is gaining, in terms of deaths and illnesses prevented.

Second, government should attempt to assess *tradeoffs*, by exploring the costs of regulation, also in quantitative terms if possible. Those tradeoffs include a consideration of the extent to which air quality regulation (for example) would compromise water quality goals, automobile safety, and energy requirements. Suppose, for example, that fuel economy standards for cars would significantly reduce air pollution, including emissions of carbon dioxide, which contributes to global warming. Suppose too that fuel economy standards are likely to make cars smaller and less safe, and hence would result in some number of additional deaths each year. The tradeoff should be made explicitly and self-consciously. Indeed, an appreciation of the need for tradeoffs might produce creative solutions that avoid the most serious risks on either side.

Third, government should attempt to use *tools* that are both effective and inexpensive. The most important of the emerging "smart tools" involve dis-closure requirements, economic incentives, risk reduction contracts, and free

---

[2] See Robert Hahn, Global Regulatory Reform (Washington, D.C.: American Enterprise Institute, 2001).

market environmentalism. Because these tools ensure that regulation will be cheaper, they promise to soften resistance to risk reduction policies, and in that sense they are a great friend of such policies. A special benefit of smart tools is that they minimize the burdens placed on government itself – and thus reduce risks in a way that also reduces the need for government planning.

These three principles are simple but also quite powerful. If they were taken seriously, and implemented in the right way, they would have an extremely important effect on risk regulation, potentially saving billions of dollars and tens of thousands of lives. Understood in light of this pragmatic goal, the movement toward cost–benefit analysis should be seen as an effort to ensure, not that companies "save money," and not that regulation is "scaled back," but that regulation is undertaken with a firm sense of its consequences for those who are subject to it. I will therefore urge that the antonym of cost–benefit balancing is not "regulation," but uninformed stabs in the dark. I will also urge that this form of balancing should play a central role in a genuinely deliberative democracy, one that aspires to combine political accountability with a large measure of reflection.

The consensus in favor of cost–benefit balancing has been enshrined in the formal law of the executive branch. In a series of executive orders, Presidents Ronald Reagan, George Bush, Bill Clinton, and George W. Bush have strongly and specifically endorsed the three principles outlined here. But it would be a big mistake to think that cost–benefit balancing has been firmly reflected in the law. Whatever presidents have said, regulatory agencies have sometimes gone off on their own. And a number of important laws, generally enacted by Congress in the 1970s, reject cost–benefit balancing and indeed all three of these principles. A major current question involves the relationship between the new consensus and the old laws, under which most regulatory activity takes place.

Equally important, we are beginning to enter a "second-generation" debate, and here the key questions remain unresolved. The second-generation debate involves the *nature* of cost–benefit analysis – the question of what, in particular, cost–benefit analysis entails. It also raises questions about the limits of cost–benefit analysis – about whether, and why, there are domains in which cost–benefit analysis has no place. A special issue here involves the rights and interests of future generations. How, if at all, should they be counted in the overall calculus?

This book has two major goals. The first is to explore people's difficulties in thinking well about risks and to connect those difficulties to issues of legal and institutional reform. I suggest that an effort to specify consequences, in as much detail as possible, is an excellent response to the cognitive limitations of individual human beings and of the governments that they create. As we shall see, people rely on mental shortcuts that often work well but that can also produce big mistakes. People embrace a form of "intuitive toxicology" that leads to unsupportable fears. Their emotions can lead them astray. Too much of the time, they do not see the need for tradeoffs. They are vulnerable to social influences, leading to "cascades" of both fear and neglect. Well-organized interest groups, from industry and the public interest community, are all too willing to exploit cognitive limitations and social influences to their advantage.

In these circumstances, the chief advantage of cost–benefit analysis is that it can get the effects of various approaches on the table, helping to spur government action where the problem is genuinely large and helping to dampen intrusive regulation where there is little reason for concern. Above all, I make a *cognitive* argument for cost–benefit balancing. I try to show that the emergence of cost–benefit balancing has been a sensible response to some of the problems associated with existing regulation. In its ideal form, an assessment of costs and benefits would prevent the sorts of problems associated with government mandates of MTBE. And in its ideal form, cost–benefit balancing is not opposed to democratic self-government, but instead is one of its best allies. For democracy to work well, people must be reflective about what, exactly, should be done. To know whether government should impose more stringent controls on arsenic in drinking water, it is necessary to have some sense of the costs of those controls (will water bills double? triple?) and also of the benefits (will fewer people get cancer? how many fewer?).

If people choose to proceed even though the costs outweigh the benefits, they are certainly entitled to do that, certainly if they can identify some reason for proceeding. At least cost–benefit analysis will help show them what they are doing. Because I will place a high premium on technical expertise and sound science, this book is, in many ways, a plea for a large role for technocrats in the process of reducing risks. In my view, we need far less in the way of intuitions and interest groups, and not a great deal of pure populism, but far more in the way of science, peer review, and informed public deliberation.

We can sharpen this point with the suggestion that from the inception, the United States has aspired to be a deliberative democracy, one that combines electoral control with a large measure of reflection and reason-giving.[3] A deliberative democracy does not simply respond to people's fears, whether or not those fears are well-founded. Indeed, participants in a deliberative democracy are alert to the fact that people might be frightened of risks that are actually quite small and indifferent to risks that are extremely serious. In these circumstances, a quantitative analysis of risks, to the extent that it is possible, is indispensable to a genuinely deliberative democracy. Deliberative democrats also know that "costs" are no mere abstraction. When the costs of regulation are high, real

---

[3] See William Bessette, The Mild Voice of Reason (Chicago: Univ. Chicago Press, 1993).

Table I.I Deaths from preventable risks in the United States

Risk	Percent of Total Deaths	Range	Total Deaths Per Year
Tobacco	19	14–19	400,000
Diet/activity	14	14–27	300,000
Alcohol	5	3–10	100,000
Microbial	4	—	90,000
Toxic agents	3	3–6	60,000
Firearms	2	—	35,000
Sexual behavior	I	—	30,000
Motor vehicles	I	—	25,000
Illicit drugs	<I	—	20,000

people will be hurt, through increased prices, decreased wages, and even greater unemployment. The key point is that the costs should be placed "on-screen," so that if they are to be incurred, it is with knowledge and approval rather than ignorance and wishful thinking. An understanding of costs, no less than an understanding of benefits, is crucial to democratic deliberation.

My second goal is to establish the meaning and limits of cost–benefit analysis, and in the process to set out a range of reforms for law and policy. By itself, the ideas of "costs" and "benefits" tell us too little. We need to have some sense of how to specify these ideas. We also need to have some sense of institutional reforms, from Congress, the executive, and the courts. I try to provide some guidance on these issues. I urge, for example, that Congress should authorize agencies to use smart tools, designed to increase the benefits and to reduce the costs associated with regulation, in large part by minimizing government's burden. I also urge that agencies should be required to be alert to health–health tradeoffs, which arise when regulation of one risk ends up increasing another risk. I urge as well that an executive office should publicize risk-related information, put risks in a comparative context, spur private and public attention to serious risks, and discourage costly expenditures on small risks. With minor adjustments, proposals of this sort could be used in any nation. Most generally, I attempt to show how a mature democracy, alert to its own failures, attempts to create institutions and tools to ensure that the law will not merely express the right values, or make the right statements, but actually promote human welfare.

Properly understood, a cost–benefit state attempts to make people's lives better. The effort to quantify and to balance is designed not to assess everything in terms of money but to promote close attention to the actual consequences of what government does. As we shall see, that is no small feat, and it holds out considerable promise for the practice of democracy itself.

BIG RISKS THAT CAN ACTUALLY BE PREVENTED

By way of preparation for what follows, it will be useful to close with some numbers that might make the problem more vivid (see Table I.I).[4] What is illuminating about this table is its demonstration of the truly extraordinary gains that could be obtained from a sustained effort to reduce the risks associated with smoking, poor diet and exercise, and alcohol abuse. By contrast, many of the risks that excite public attention are small, even infinitesimal. I shall devote considerable attention to explaining how and why this is so and to exploring what might be done about the situation.

[4] J. Michael McGinnis & William H. Foege, Actual Causes of Death in the United States, 270 JAMA 2207 (1993).

1

Beyond 1970s
Environmentalism

What sets the new synthetic insecticides apart is their enormous biolog-
ical potency. They have immense power not only to poison but to enter
into the most vital processes of the body and change them in sinister and
often deadly ways.[1]

Americans may disagree about a lot of things, but arsenic isn't one of
them. When you turn on the kitchen sink, you ought to be able to drink
what comes out, without worrying about being poisoned.[2]

To many people, it seems entirely obvious that risk regulation should not be
rooted in intuitions and fears and should be based instead on an assessment
of the consequences. To such people, cost–benefit analysis seems extremely attractive, as a way of getting the consequences on the table. On what other basis
could government possibly act? But to others, the judgments of ordinary people
seem to be a good starting point for policy, and the very idea of cost–benefit
analysis seems quite preposterous. Should the government hesitate to prevent
environmental degradation merely because prevention would cost polluters a
great deal? If people are genuinely fearful, shouldn't government try to protect people's safety and health, whatever the numbers might say? Don't people
have rights, and shouldn't those rights "trump" the outcome of cost–benefit
balancing? Why should the numbers matter in any case? Aren't any numbers
based on controversial assumptions, and shouldn't the assumptions be revealed
as such? Why should policy be made by a technocratic elite, consisting mostly
of scientists and economists?

[1] Rachel Carson, Silent Spring 16 (Boston: Houghton Mifflin, 1962).
[2] Rep. David Bonior, quoted in the Chicago Tribune, July 28, 2001, at p. 1.

PRINCIPLES AND PROGRESS

To come to terms with these questions, it is necessary to identify the commitments that originally helped to spur national risk regulation in United States (and elsewhere). Though they extended well beyond the environmental movement, those commitments were embodied in what might be called 1970s environmentalism.

What were the sources of 1970s environmentalism? Undoubtedly the civil rights movement provided both a model and an inspiration, helping to breed distrust of established institutions and to suggest the possibility of large-scale change through law. One of the key contributions of the civil rights movement was to expand the possibilities of conceiving of certain interests as "rights," to the extent that President Richard Nixon himself proclaimed, "Clean air, clean water, open spaces — these should again be the birthright for every American."[3] In this period, it became increasingly common to think that "freedom from risk" consisted of a kind of right, properly guaranteed by government. Of course this notion was bound to run into difficulty once it became clear that safety is a matter of degree, and that no "on–off" switch can tell whether we are in the domain of safety or danger.

Without offering anything like a full account of a complex social movement, I emphasize two additional points here. The first involves the nature of risk-related judgments, in the 1970s, within the public at large. The second involves the response by public officials. As we shall see, environmental commitments arose through a kind of "call to arms," one that accomplished a great deal of good, but one that did not (to say the least) involve anything like a careful analysis of the consequences of different approaches to regulation. As we shall also see, the response of public officials involved a quest for public credit and acclaim, not an assessment of the scientific and economic variables involved. In short, it is important to see that the "initial successes of the environmental movement in securing passages of laws . . . were not the result of normal group politics. Rather, these laws emerged from a period in which mass attention had been drawn to environmental concerns through the media and the activities of politicians and policy entrepreneurs who worked from relatively narrow organizational bases."[4] The same is true for much risk-related legislation.

[3] Annual Message to the Congress on the State of the Union; reprinted in Public Papers of the President: Richard M. Nixon 8, 13 (Washington, D.C.: GPO, 1970).

[4] David Trubek & William Gillen, Environmental Defense, II: Examining the Limits of Public Interest Advocacy, in Public Interest Law, B. Weisbrod et al., eds. (Berkeley: Univ. California Press, 1978).

THE RISE OF PUBLIC COMMITMENTS: CHAINS OF EVIL, ELIXERS OF DEATH

In the 1960s and 1970s, shifts in public opinion had many sources. To understand those shifts in a manageable space, we can do no better than to take a glimpse at Rachel Carson's extraordinary book, *Silent Spring*, published in 1962. *Silent Spring* qualifies as a genuine classic of environmental thinking, and it says a great deal about the relationship among technology, nature, and risk. In the twentieth century, it is the most influential book of its kind; and it had a large effect on environmental thought throughout the world. In many circles it is credited with starting the modern environmental movement, with producing the ban on DDT, even with creating the Environmental Protection Agency, for which Carson argued in congressional testimony shortly after her book was published.

Carson was a specialist in environment issues. For many years, she had been a marine biologist for the U.S. Fish and Wildlife Service. She was also a renowned nature writer. In fact, Carson was also something of a poet. In memorable terms, *Silent Spring* drew attention to the risks associated with pesticides and insecticides.

> For the first time in the history of the world, every human being is now subjected to contact with dangerous chemicals, from the moment of conception until death. In the less than two decades of their use, the synthetic pesticides have been so thoroughly distributed throughout the animate and inanimate world that they occur virtually everywhere. . . . For these chemicals are now stored in the bodies of the vast majority of human beings, regardless of age. They occur in the mother's milk, and probably in the tissues of the unborn child.[5]

Carson was especially concerned with the adverse effects of DDT. Her attack on that chemical was particularly important because DDT had been hailed as a health-care miracle, saving millions of lives by stopping the spread of insect-carried diseases, above all malaria. During World War II, *Newsweek* proclaimed, "One of the three greatest medical discoveries to come out of the war (plasma and penicillin are the others), DDT has enormous possibilities as an insecticide. A representative of the Surgeon General's office said last week: 'DDT will be to preventative medicine what Lister's discovery of antiseptic was to surgery.'" But Carson saw things quite differently. It is worthwhile to spend some time on her account because it tells us a great deal about the virtues and vices of 1970s environmentalism.

---

[5] Rachel Carson, supra note 1 in this chapter, p. 10.

Carson warned of a situation in which human intervention into natural processes was creating significant threats to all living creatures. "The most alarming of all man's assaults upon the environment is the contamination of air, earth, rivers, and sea with dangerous and even lethal materials. This pollution is for the most part irrecoverable; the chain of evil it initiates not only in the world that must support life but in living tissues is for the most part irreversible. In this now universal contamination of the environment, chemicals are the sinister and little-recognized partners in changing the very nature of the world – the very nature of life."[6] It is worth pausing over those words. Thus Carson referred to the "500 new chemicals to which the bodies of men and animals are required somehow to adapt each year, chemicals totally outside the limits of biologic experience," and representing a kind of human "war against nature."[7]

Carson focussed particularly on DDT, which she described as an "elixir of death":

> One of the most sinister features of DDT and related chemicals is the way they are passed on from one organism to another through all the links of the food chain.... The poison may also be passed on from mother to offspring.... This means that the breast-fed human infant is receiving small but regular additions to the load of toxic chemicals building up in his body.... There has been no such parallel situation in medical history. No one yet knows what the ultimate consequences may be.[8]

These ominous words had real consequences. They helped spur an international movement to prohibit the use of DDT. In the United States, DDT was banned in 1972.

AFTERMATH

Carson's argument, and the banning of DDT, tell us a great deal about 1970s environmentalism, which it helped to inspire. Congressman John V. Lindsay inserted whole paragraphs of *Silent Spring* into the *Congressional Record*. Having read the book personally, President John F. Kennedy ordered the Science Advisory Committee to study the effects of pesticides. On May 15, 1963, the Committee vindicated much of Carson's argument, calling for decreased use of toxic chemical and emphasizing that "until the publication of *Silent Spring*, people were generally

---

[6] Id. at 6.

[7] Id. at 7.

[8] Id. at 23.

unaware of the toxicity of pesticides." In the words of the Natural Resources Defense Council, the

> most important legacy of *Silent Spring* ... was a new public awareness that nature was vulnerable to human intervention. ... [T]he threats Carson had outlined – the contamination of the food chain, cancer, genetic damage, the deaths of entire species – were too frightening to ignore. For the first time, the need to regulate industry in order to protect the environment became widely accepted, and environmentalism was born.

And there can be no doubt that Carson was, in many ways, sounding an appropriate alarm: Insecticides can harm all living creatures, including human beings, and it is important to have regulatory institutions in place. (See "The Story on *Silent Spring*," available at *www.nrdc.org/health/pesticides/hcarson.asp.*)

But in the particular case of DDT, there is another side to the story. In 2001, a number of poor nations began to use DDT as the cheapest and most effective way to prevent the spread of malaria. Officials in all these nations, most prominently South Africa, are alert to the risks associated with DDT but insist that those risks are worth incurring in order to counteract the growing death toll from malaria. In fact, the use of DDT has contributed to substantial declines in malaria-related deaths. Although millions of people have been exposed to DDT, the World Health Organization contends that "the only confirmed cases of injury" from DDT "have been the result of massive accidental or suicidal ingestion."[9] It does appear that DDT is a human carcinogen, but this point is not entirely clear, and there is no clear evidence that DDT has produced a significant number of cancers or other adverse effects in human beings.

Carson was entirely correct to say that DDT is toxic to birds and can cause serious reproductive problems for many bird species. But at least in its early years, the ban on DDT itself had significant harmful consequences, for human beings and animals alike. Some substitutes were highly toxic; some were quite expensive; some failed to work. Sweden was the first country to ban DDT, in 1969, but it lifted its ban after it found that alternative pesticides were less effective, risking losses of at least $15 million annually. In some domains, the substitutes themselves produced toxic effects. One analysis concludes: "The health loss from the ban has been much greater than the health gain ... completely banning DDT did more harm than good."[10] This is a controversial conclusion, but at least it raises some questions about Carson's analysis and about 1970s environmentalism

---

[9] Aaron Wildavsky, But Is It True? A Citizen's Guide to Environmental Health and Safety Issues 61 (Cambridge, Mass.: Harvard Univ. Press, 1995).
[10] Id. at 79.

in general – the same sorts of questions that I will be pressing throughout this book.

POLITICIANS

By the late 1960s and early 1970s, it was clear that the public would support aggressive steps to protect the environment, and indeed to reduce risks in general. But legislation often depends on the existence of well-organized interest groups, and in this period, the young movement for environmental protection lacked many such groups. Instead the relevant statutes seem to have arisen through a form of "competitive credit-claiming" by politicians.[11] In this process, public officials try to obtain public credit by proclaiming their commitment to environmental protection or to some other form of risk reduction. To obtain that credit, the particular content of the resulting law does not greatly matter. What matters is that politicians seem especially or unusually committed to the environment.

The National Environmental Policy Act, enacted in 1969, was a case in point. This ambitious statute required all agencies of the federal government to produce "environmental impact statements" before engaging in action that might harm the environment. The statute was spearheaded by officials treating it as a kind of "motherhood" bill, without much consideration of its concrete consequences. Still more remarkable were the Clean Air Act Amendments of 1970, which imposed a range of stringent regulations in the interest of health and environmental protection. For example, the amendments required car manufacturers to reduce pollution by no less than 90 percent within five years, in the process telling the EPA to ignore the economic and technological feasibility of the reductions.

How did these astonishing amendments become law? The answer is that they arose not from a careful analysis of the air pollution problem, but in large part from a contest between President Richard M. Nixon and Senator Edmund Muskie, both of whom sought to claim, before the public, the mantle of leading environmentalist. As each submitted his preferred version, and each sought to demonstrate a "stronger" commitment to risk reduction, the content of the proposed law began to change fundamentally. The original Muskie bill was a genuine shift in the law, but quite tepid in comparison to the subsequent Nixon proposal. Trying to obtain public approval, Nixon submitted an aggressive bill that would call for 90 percent reductions in emissions from new cars within ten years, would require compliance with national standards "within the limits of

---

[11] See the excellent discussion in E. Donald Elliott et al., Toward a Theory of Statutory Evolution: The Federalization of Environmental Law, 1 J. L. Econ. & Org. 313 (1985).

existing technology," and would require states to submit plans to comply with federal air quality requirements within a year.

The original Muskie proposal was sharply challenged by a task force led by Ralph Nader. The highly publicized task force report described Muskie as being soft on industry and as supporting "a 'business-as-usual' license to pollute for countless companies across the country." Evidently stung by the Nader criticism, Muskie's subcommittee came to support a dramatically revised bill, going well beyond Muskie's original proposal or even Nixon's counterproposal. As revised, the Muskie bill would require states to comply with federal standards within nine months, rather than one year; would require compliance regardless of whether it was technologically feasible; and would require a 90 percent reduction in emissions from new cars within five years, rather than ten. Seeking not to be outdone, Nixon signed a bill very much like the Muskie proposal – not because of any kind of analysis of its contents, but because of the political dynamics. "The result was the passage of the Clean Air Act of 1970 in a form which was more stringent than either of them would have preferred."[12]

One of the most striking features of this contest, and the new legislation, is the absence of sustained congressional attention to what would appear to be the key questions. Should the limitations of existing technology be taken into account when the EPA sets standards? Why and why not? Congress did little to explore this question. Perhaps this silence is excusable in light of the fact that the Environmental Protection Agency was asked to set federal standards, and perhaps it could be assumed to be reasonable, forcing companies to go beyond existing technology only when that step made overall sense. But even if so, why did Congress ask car companies to cut pollution by 90% in five years? Why not 75% in three years, or 50% in four years, or 95% in six years, or 50% in three years and 90% in ten? Only slightly more subtly: Is there a risk that antipollution technology will make cars less safe or compromise a national need, actual or perceived, for low-cost energy? Might such technology prove expensive, and if so, might consumers be led to keep old, dirty cars on the road longer, thus aggravating air pollution problems?

Congress did not investigate these crucial questions. Ironically, the Clear Air Act Amendments of 1970 nonetheless produced far more good than harm, as we shall see. More ironically still, a congressional effort to ask and answer the key questions might have led Congress to inaction – a point that contains a large lesson about the danger of "paralysis by analysis." Nonetheless, good questions and good answers would have undoubtedly led to a better clean air act. But to say this is to get ahead of the story.

[12] Id. at 335.

Table I.1 Risk regulation in the 1970s:
New institutions

Environmental Protection Agency (1970)
National Highway Traffic Safety Administration (1970)
Consumer Product Safety Commission (1972)
Occupational Safety and Health Administration (1973)
Mine Safety and Health Administration (1973)
Nuclear Regulatory Commission (1975)
Department of Energy (1977)

WHAT HAPPENED

Whatever we may think of congressional performance, it is hard to overemphasize the great significance of the period, in which much of federal regulation has its origin. The Environmental Protection Agency, for example, was created in 1970; so too for the National Highway Traffic Safety Administration. The Consumer Product Safety Commission was created in 1972. It was followed the next year by the Occupational Safety and Health Administration. Many of the most important federal statutes were enacted in the same years, and government continues to do much of its work under those statutes. Tables I.1 and I.2 give a sense of the period.

The basic commitments of 1970s environmentalism are captured in many of these statutes. In this period, legislators and regulators

(a) placed a high premium on the need for immediate, large-scale responses to long-neglected problems;

(b) favored aggressive regulatory controls, often in the form of federal "command and control" via strict emissions limitations or technological requirements;

(c) emphasized the *existence* of problems rather than their *magnitude*, and for that reason did not much attend to the whole question of priority-setting;

(d) were indifferent to, or at least not focused on, the costs of achieving regulatory goals;

(e) seemed to see regulatory statutes as promoting *distributional* goals, as in the view that occupational safety and health regulation would promote worker safety at the expense of corporate profits; and

(f) often showed moral indignation against the behavior of those who created pollution and other risks to safety and health.

17

Table 1.2 Risk regulation circa the 1970s: New laws

Endangered Species Act (1969)
National Environmental Policy Act (1969)
Clean Air Act Amendments (1970)
Occupational Safety and Health Act (1970)
Federal Insecticide, Fungicide, and Rodenticide Act (1972)
Marine Mammal Protection Act (1972)
Marine Protection, Research, and Sanctuaries Act (1972)
Noise Control Act (1972)
Coastal Zone Management Act (1972)
Federal Water Pollution Control Act (1972)
Endangered Species Act (1973)
Safe Water Drinking Act (1974)
Toxic Substances Control Act (1976)
Resource Conservation and Recovery Act (1977)
Federal Mine Safety and Health Act (1977)
Black Lung Benefits Revenue Act (1977)
Safe Drinking Water Act Amendments (1977)
Clean Air Act Amendments (1977)
Federal Water Pollution Act Amendments (1977)
Soil and Water Resources Conservation Act (1977)
National Ocean Pollution Planning Act (1978)
Port and Tanker Safety Act (1978)
Fish and Wildlife Conservation Act (1980)
Comprehensive Environmental Response, Compensation, and Liability Act (1980)

The basic commitments of 1970s environmentalism can be found in many places. Consider, for example, the key provisions of the Clean Air Act,[13] which require air quality standards to be set without reference to cost; provisions of the Clean Air Act and Water Pollution Control Act, which require emission levels that would come from use of the best available technology, without a careful balancing of costs against benefits[14]; and the Occupational Safety and Health Act's provisions, which require employers to provide safe workplaces "to the extent feasible." And 1970s environmentalism is very much with us today, especially in the form of the widespread view that companies should be required to do "whatever they can" to reduce risks to safety and health.

---

[13] 42 USC 7409(b).
[14] See, for example, 33 USC 1311(b)(1) (A), 42 USC 7411(a)(1), 7412(d)(2), 7475(a)(4), 7502(c)(1).

THE RISE OF COST–BENEFIT BALANCING

I have noted that the last two decades have seen increasing enthusiasm for cost–benefit analysis of regulatory problems. As we will see, federal courts have taken a keen interest in disciplining regulation by ensuring a kind of proportionality between costs and benefits. Congress has hardly been on a steady path, but national legislators have shown some enthusiasm for ensuring a public accounting. But it is within the executive branch that the cost–benefit state has really started to emerge. A crucial step came with a cost–benefit executive order in 1980, from President Reagan, but President Reagan's order had important precursors. To understand what is happening, it is worthwhile to offer a brief overview of these developments.[15]

Notably, the interest in cost–benefit balancing began not through interest in the technique itself but through efforts to assert greater presidential control over administration and regulation. An initial step was the system of "Quality of Life" reviews initiated in the Nixon Administration. Nixon's response to the expanding administrative bureaucracy was to create a "counterbureaucracy" in the White House. He doubled the executive office staff, created the modern Office of Management and Budget (OMB), and established the Domestic Council (chaired by a top aide, John Ehrlichman). The council met with representatives of different departments having jurisdiction over a problem and tried to develop coordinated policy positions for presidential approval.[16] In the "Quality of Life" review process, agencies were required to submit significant rules to OMB in advance of publication in the Federal Register. OMB's principal duty was to circulate the agency draft to other agencies for review and comment. OMB's function was rarely substantive; it served instead a coordinating function.

President Ford continued the interagency review process and added an initial step toward cost–benefit balancing: a process designed to control the effects of regulation on inflation. The Council on Wage and Price Stability (CWPS) was asked to review regulations for their effects on inflation. In addition, OMB promulgated an important circular to agencies, arguing that the inflationary impact of a proposed rule could best be assessed through a quantitative cost–benefit comparison. But the council's role was principally technical, consultative, and advisory. It was understood that the relevant agency might well

---

[15] This overview draws heavily from Richard Pildes & Cass R. Sunstein, Reinventing the Regulatory State, 62 U. Chi. L. Rev. 1 (1995).

[16] Richard Nathan, The Administrative Presidency 28–38 (New York: Wiley, 1983).

persist in the face of CWPS disagreement. Congress ultimately enacted a statute allowing CWPS to participate in rulemaking and to explore adverse effects on inflation.

President Carter built directly on the Ford precedent through a successor to CWPS, the Regulatory Analysis Review Group (RARG). RARG consisted of representatives from major agencies, OMB, CWPS, and the Council on Economic Advisors. The purpose of this fifteen-agency group was to conduct interagency review of cost-effectiveness analyses, which were required of "significant" rules from relevant agencies. Notably, the executive order establishing the RARG review process did not require cost–benefit analysis. In fact, RARG reviewed relatively few rules, though the president did resolve a few highly controversial issues.

All these efforts were designed to increase interagency dialogue, coodination, and analytical precision, as well as to reduce regulatory costs. But the decisive step came within a week of President Reagan's inauguration in 1980, with the formal creation of a mechanism for OMB review of major regulations. The most important of the new innovations, contained in Executive Order 12291, were (1) a set of substantive principles for all agencies to follow, "to the extent permitted by law," including a commitment to cost–benefit analysis; (2) a requirement that a Regulatory Impact Analysis, including cost–benefit analysis, accompany all "major" rules; and (3) a formal mechanism for OMB oversight, with a general understanding that OMB had some (undefined) substantive control. President Reagan considered subjecting the independent agencies to the new order but ultimately declined to do so, partly because of concerns about legal authority but mostly because of fears of an adverse congressional reaction. The independent agencies were asked voluntarily to comply with Executive Order 12291; all of them declined.

Executive Order 12291 proved extremely controversial. Nonetheless, President Reagan expanded on the basic idea four years later with Executive Order 12498. That order established a requirement that agencies submit "annual regulatory plans" to OMB for review. The result was an annual publication, the Regulatory Program of the United States, which contained a discussion of all proposed actions that might be either costly or controversial. Executive Order 12498 served to increase the authority of agency heads over their staffs by exposing proposals to top-level review at an early stage. But it also increased the authority of OMB by allowing OMB supervision over basic plans and by making it hard for agencies to proceed without OMB preclearance.

Under the first President George Bush, the principal innovation was the Council on Competitiveness, chaired by the vice president. The council engaged in occasional review of agency rules, operating as a kind of supervisor of OMB itself. It also set out a number of principles and proposals for regulatory reform. In essence, however, the Bush Administration followed the basic approach of its predecessor, with OMB review under the two Reagan executive orders.

The election of President Clinton raised a number of questions about whether cost–benefit balancing would continue to have a role within the executive branch. Many environmentalists have been skeptical of the idea, and environmentalists were expected to have a significant influence in the Clinton Administration. But in a significant and dramatic step, President Clinton endorsed the essential features of the Reagan–Bush orders in his Executive Order 12866.[17] The crucial point about Clinton's order is that it accepted the basic commitments of the two Reagan–Bush orders, by requiring agencies to assess both costs and benefits and to proceed only when the latter exceeded the former. At the same time, President Clinton offered several changes to the Reagan–Bush processes. First, he attempted to diminish public concerns about interest-group power over regulation by providing a process to resolve conflicts and procedures for greater openness. Second, he included references to "equity," to "distributive impacts," and to qualititative as well as quantitative factors, evidently to ensure that agencies could make adjustments in the process of decision and abandon the cost–benefit assessment where this seems sensible.

All in all, Executive Order 12866 did not seem to have much impact under President Clinton. The office in charge of administering the order – the Office of Information and Regulatory Affairs (OIRA) – was largely passive and toothless, serving a coordinating function without trying to steer regulation in any particular direction. Cost–benefit analysis operated not as a sharp constraint on agency action but as a technique for gathering information about the effects of government policies. The real source of activity in the Clinton Administration was the series of "reinventing government" initiatives designed to shift attention to governmental performance and to increase flexibility for the private sector. We will return to these initiatives in Chapter 10. For present purposes, the key point is that the idea of "reinvention" was designed to focus on results and to allow the private sector more flexibility in deciding how to achieve those results – and that to the extent, there was a real effort to ensure that the costs of compliance would be as low as possible.

What about Congress? Several statutes expressly require agencies to compare costs against benefits before issuing regulations. The Federal Insecticide, Fungicide, and Rodenticide Act (FIFRA) calls for such balancing, as does the Toxic Substances Control Act. A key provision of the Safe Water Drinking Act allows the EPA to soften health-based regulations if it concludes that the health benefits do not justify the expense (see Chapter 7 for details). But most

---

[17] 58 Fed. Reg. 51735 (1993).

federal statutes do not call for cost–benefit balancing, and many of them seem to preclude it. At most, Congress tends to incorporate costs through a requirement that agencies "consider" costs alongside other variables.

For years, however, Congress has been considering more aggressive "super-mandates" cutting across all existing legislation in order to require all agencies to balance costs against benefits.[18] Some of the proposed mandates would be more substantive: They would make cost–benefit balancing the basis for the decision. An enactment of this kind would be extremely dramatic. It would alter the full universe of provisions described earlier, converting them all into cost–benefit provisions. To date, however, no such legislation has been enacted. Thus Congress has restricted itself to more particular procedural requirements, asking for an accounting of costs and benefits to ensure that the public has relevant information. The Unfunded Mandates Reform Act takes some modest steps in the direction of statutory cost–benefit requirements for all regulations. In cases in which a federal mandate "may result" in an aggregate expenditure of $100 million or more, that act requires the government to provide "a qualitative and quantitative assessment of the anticipated costs and benefits of the Federal mandate," alongside an estimate of its "future compliance costs" and of its "effect on the national economy, such as the effect on productivity, economic growth, full employment, creative of productive jobs, and international competitiveness of United States goods and services." But this assessment seems to be only procedural; it has not affected the judgments of regulatory agencies, and indeed it lacks any legal authority at all.

THE RECORD

No one should deny that 1970s environmentalism has done an enormous amount of good. The resulting regulation has helped to produce dramatic improvements in many domains, above all in the context of air pollution, where ambient air quality has improved for all major pollutants.[19] Consider some numbers. EPA's own estimates suggest that as a result of the Clean Air Act, there were no less than 206,000 fewer premature deaths among people thirty years of age or older in 1990 – and also that there were 39,000 fewer cases of congestive heart failure, 89,000 fewer cases of hospital admissions for respiratory

---

[18] See the outline in Cass R. Sunstein, Congress, Constitutional Moments, and the Cost–Benefit State, in Cass R. Sunstein, Free Markets and Social Justice 348 (Oxford: Oxford Univ. Press, 1997).

[19] See Economic Analyses at EPA: Assessing Regulatory Impact 455–6, Richard Morgenstern, ed. (Washington, D.C.: Resources for the Future, 1998); Paul Portney, Air Pollution Policy, in Public Policies for Environmental Protection 77, 101–5, Paul Portney & Robert Stavins, eds. (Washington, D.C.: Resources for the Future, 2000).

problems, 674,000 fewer cases of chronic bronchitis, 850,000 fewer asthma attacks, and 22,600,000 fewer lost work days.[20] Indeed, 1970s environmentalism appears, by most accounts, to survive cost–benefit balancing, producing aggregate benefits sometimes estimated in the trillions of dollars, and in any case well in excess of the aggregate costs.[21] EPA finds annual costs of air pollution control at $32 billion, hardly a trivial number, but less than 4 percent of the annual benefits of $1.1 trillion.[22] Even if the EPA's own numbers show an implausibly high ratio, significant adjustments still reveal benefits far higher than costs.[23]

More generally, the Office of Management and Budget has, for the last several years, engaged in an extensive accounting of the costs and benefits of regulation.[24] In general, the report shows benefits in excess of cost. Even though the government's own numbers should be discounted – agency accounts may well be self-serving and OMB's reports leave much to be desired – at least they provide a place to start. I will say a great deal later about what the dollar figures specifically represent; for now let us use them as a shorthand way to get a sense of the consequences of regulation, with the knowledge that if the benefits are high, there are likely to be large savings in terms of fatalities and illnesses prevented. In its 2000 report, OMB finds total regulatory benefits ranging from $254 billion to $1.8 trillion, with total costs ranging from $146 billion to $229 billion, for net benefits ranging from $25 billion to $1.65 trillion. A more disaggregated picture is also encouraging. In the transportation sector, for example, the benefits range from $84 billion to $110 billion, with the costs from $15 billion to $18 billion, for net benefits of $66 billion to $95 billion. A great deal of the uncertainty stems from scientific doubt about the extent of environmental benefits and costs, producing a possible range from −$73 billion in net benefits to over $1.5 trillion in net benefits.

For most government action, however, the benefits seem to exceed the costs. As especially good examples, consider the regulations listed in Table 1.3, all of which are from recent years.

But even though the overall picture provides no cause for alarm, a closer look at federal regulatory policy shows a wide range of problems. Perhaps foremost is exceptionally poor priority-setting, with substantial resources sometimes going to small problems, and with little attention to some serious problems. There are also unnecessarily high costs, with no less than $400 billion being

---

[20] Portney, id. at 102–3.

[21] Id.

[22] Id. at 109.

[23] Id. at 113 (showing a benefit–cost ratio of 3 to 1).

[24] Available at *www.whitehouse.gov/omb/inforeg/index.html.*

Table 1.3 Net benefits of selected regulations ($ millions)

Regulation	2000	2005	2010	2015
Head impact protection	310–370	1,210–1,510	1,210–1,510	1,210–1,510
Conservation reserve program	1,100	1,100	1,100	1,100
Restriction on sale and distribution of tobacco	9,020–9,820	9,020–9,820	9,020–10,220	9,020–9,820
Acid rain controls	260–1,900	260–1,900	260–1,900	260–1,900
Energy conservation standards for refrigerators	330	330–360	510–580	440–500
New surface water treatment	50–1,200	50–1,200	50–1,200	50–1,200
Emission standards for new highway heavy-duty engines	0	110–1,200	110–1,200	110–1,200
Disposal of PCBs	136–736	136–736	136–736	136–736
Particulates standard	0	0	12,000–113,000	20,000–86,000

attributable to compliance costs each year,[25] including $130 billion on environmental protection alone.[26] It is worthwhile to pause over this number, and to note that the dollar figures should not be taken as meaningless abstractions or as reflecting lower profits for "companies." If the cost of regulation is high, it is likely to be translated into higher prices, lower wages, fewer jobs, and greater poverty, or some combination of these things.

OMB's own report shows some disturbing numbers: For the next fifteen years, OSHA's methylene chloride regulation will have annual costs of $100 million and annual benefits of $40 million[27]; a regulation calling for

[25] Thomas Hopkins, The Costs of Federal Regulation, 2 J. Reg. & Soc. Costs 5, 25 table 2 (1992).
[26] Paul Portney & Robert Stavins, Regulatory Review of Environmental Policy: The Potential Role of Health–Health Analysis, 8 J. Risk & Uncertainty 111, 119 n. 1 (1995).
[27] Id., table 12.

Table 1.4 Net benefits of questionable regulations ($ millions)

Regulation	2000	2005	2010	2015
Exposure to methylene chloride	−60	−60	−60	−60
Roadway worker protection	0	0	0	0
Financial assurance for municipal solid waste landfills	−100	−100	−100	−100
Pulp and paper effluent guidelines	−150 to 0	−150 to 0	−150 to 0	−240 to 0
Ozone standards	0	−235 to 240	−840 to 1,190	−9,200 to −1,000
Child restraint system	−40 to 40	−40 to 40	−40 to 40	−40 to 40
Vessel response plans	−220	−220	−220	−220
Nitrogen oxide emission from new fossil fuel fired steam generating units	−57 to 29	−57 to 29	−57 to 29	−57 to 29

roadway worker protection has benefits of $30 million but equivalent costs; the cost–benefit ratio for airbag depowering regulation seems pretty bad, though there is uncertainty in the data[28]; EPA's regulation for financial assurance for municipal solid waste landfills has monetized benefits of $0, but costs of $100 million, and this is expected for the next fifteen years.[29] By way of general illustration, consider Table 1.4,[30] all drawn from recent regulations.

These figures, drawn from regulations in a single year, show a less than coherent pattern of regulation, especially when Table 1.3 is put together with Table 1.4. According to one study, better allocations of health expenditures could save, each year, 60,000 additional lives at no additional cost – and such allocations could maintain the current level of lives saved with $31 billion in

[28] Id.
[29] Id.
[30] Id.

annual savings.[31] The point has been dramatized by repeated demonstrations that some regulations create significant substitute risks[32] – and that with cheaper, more effective tools, regulation could achieve its basic goals while saving billions of dollars.[33]

In these circumstances, the most attractive parts of the movement for cost–benefit analysis have been rooted not in especially controversial judgments about what government ought to be doing, but instead in a more mundane search for pragmatic instruments designed to reduce some central problems, many of them the social counterpart of difficulties we all face in thinking about risk: poor priority-setting, excessively costly tools, and inattention to unfortunate side-effects. I will connect cost–benefit balancing to problems in ordinary intuition in Chapter 2. For the moment, note simply that by drawing attention to costs and benefits, it should be possible to spur the most obviously desirable regulations, to deter the most obviously undesirable ones, to encourage a broader view of consequences, and to promote a search for least-cost methods of achieving regulatory goals.[34] Notice here that so defended, cost–benefit analysis is an obstacle to unjustified regulation, but it should be a spur to government as well, showing that it should attend to neglected problems. And indeed the Office of Information and Regulatory Affairs, charged with overseeing cost–benefit balancing, issues "prompt letters," asking agencies to initiate regulation, as well as "return letters," asking agencies to rethink the question whether regulation is really warranted. If cost–benefit balancing is supported on these highly pragmatic grounds, the central question is whether that form of balancing is actually producing what can be taken as policy improvements by people with diverse views about appropriate policy.

On these counts, the record of cost–benefit analysis, at least within the EPA, is generally encouraging.[35] Assessments of costs and benefits have, for example, helped produce more stringent and rapid regulation of lead in gasoline; promoted more stringent regulation of lead in drinking water; led to stronger controls on air pollution at the Grand Canyon and the Navaho Generating Station; and produced a reformulated gasoline rule that promotes stronger controls on

---

[31] Tammy Tengs et al., Five Hundred Life-Saving Interventions and Their Cost-Effectiveness, 15 Risk Analysis 369 (1995).

[32] See John Graham & Jonathan Wiener, Risk vs. Risk: Tradeoffs in Protecting Health and the Environment (Cambridge, Mass.: Harvard Univ. Press, 1995).

[33] See, for example, A. Denny Ellerman et al., Markets in Clean Air (New York: Cambridge Univ. Press, 2000); Robert Stavins, Market-Based Environmental Policies, in Public Policies for Environmental Protection, supra note 19 in Chapter I.

[34] For many examples, see Economic Analyses at EPA, supra note 19 in Chapter I.

[35] See id.

air pollutants.[36] In these areas, cost–benefit analysis, far from being only a check on regulation, has indeed spurred governmental attention to serious problems.

Cost–benefit analysis has also led to regulations that accomplish statutory goals at lower cost or that do not devote limited private and public resources to areas where they are unlikely to do much good. With respect to asbestos, for example, an analysis of benefits and costs led the EPA to tie the phase-down schedules to the costs of substitutes and also to exempt certain products from a flat ban.[37] With respect to lead in gasoline and control of CFCs (destructive of the ozone layer), cost–benefit analysis helped promote the use of economic incentives rather than command-and-control regulation[38]; economic incentives are much cheaper and make more stringent regulation possible in the first place. For regulation of sludge, protection of farmworkers, water pollution regulation for the Great Lakes, and controls on organic chemicals, cost–benefit analysis helped regulators produce modifications that significantly reduced costs.[39] For modern government, one of the most serious problems appears to be, not agency use of cost–benefit analysis, but frequent noncompliance with executive branch requirements that agencies engage in such analysis.[40]

If we take all these points together, we can see that the cost–benefit state is attentive to the three themes I have emphasized, all of which were overlooked by 1970s environmentalism. To recapitulate: The first is the need to assess magnitudes, if possible through numbers. It is hard to know whether a risk is worth reducing unless we have a sense of its size. The second is the need to take account of tradeoffs. It is hard to know what should be done about a risk, even a large one, without also knowing the consequences of trying to reduce it. The third is the importance of using sensible regulatory tools – instruments of protection that minimize rather than maximize costs, that maximize rather than minimize effectiveness, and that undermine rather than promote the influence of self-interested private groups with their own agendas. These three themes, each involving an effort to go beyond unreliable intuitions, will play a major role in the discussion to follow.

[36] See id. at 458.

[37] Id. at 458.

[38] Id. at 49–86; 131–69.

[39] Id. at 458.

[40] See Hahn, supra note 2 in the Introduction.

2

Thinking About Risks

The American people have no doubt that more people die from coal dust than from nuclear reactions, but they fear the prospect of a nuclear reactor more than they do the empirical data that would suggest that more people die from coal dust, having coal-fired burners. They also know that more lives would be saved if we took that 25 percent we spend in the intensive care units in the last few months of the elderly's lives, that more children would be saved. But part of our culture is that we have concluded as a culture that we are going to rightly or wrongly, we are going to spend the money, costing more lives, on the elderly. . . . I think it's incredibly presumptuous and elitist for political scientists to conclude that the American people's cultural values in fact are not ones that lend themselves to a cost–benefit analysis and presume that they would change their cultural values if in fact they were aware of the cost–benefit analysis.[1]

The nation is quickly buying up stocks of gas masks, shelves are being stripped of antibiotics, and bottled water may not be far behind. Many travelers have canceled trips by air and taken trains or cars instead, even across the country. New Yorkers fearful of an attack on the subways insist on riding in cars on traffic-choked streets. Doctors in Boston report that patients with minor ailments like colds and sore throats have been calling out of fear that they may have been sickened by a toxic chemical or lethal germ introduced by terrorists. Meanwhile, business at McDonald's and Haagen-Dazs is thriving. What does this say about how people respond to threats to their health and lives?[2]

[1] Joseph Biden, Confirmation Hearings for Stephen G. Breyer, to be an Associate Justice of the United States Supreme Court, Senate Committee on the Judiciary, 103d Cong., 2d Sess. 42 (July 14, 1994) (Miller Reporting transcript).
[2] Jane E. Brody, Don't Loss Sight of Real, Everyday Risks, New York Times, Oct. 9, 2001, at F6.

In this chapter I bring an understanding of ordinary thinking about risk in contact with the law of risk regulation. My central goal is to show how ordinary thinking goes wrong, and how the errors are especially important, and pernicious, in the design of public policy. I show that people's intuitions about risks are highly unreliable. Some of those intuitions do serve us well in ordinary life.[3] But even so, they lead to ineffective and even counterproductive law and policy. In the process of discussing this point, I offer a new argument for cost–benefit analysis. I suggest that cost–benefit analysis is best defended as a means of overcoming predictable problems in individual and social cognition. Cost–benefit analysis should be understood as a method for putting "on screen" important social facts that might otherwise escape private and public attention.

It would be fully possible to accept the cognitive points and to agree that people are likely to err in thinking about risks, while also rejecting cost–benefit analysis as a tool for policymakers. Certainly I do not mean to embrace the controversial and implausible proposition that all regulatory decisions should be made by aggregating private willingness to pay, as if economic efficiency is or should be the goal of all regulation. I will eventually attempt to produce an *incompletely theorized agreement* on a certain understanding of cost–benefit analysis – an agreement on a form of cost–benefit analysis to which many different people, with diverse and competing views, should be willing to subscribe. I will offer many more details in Chapter 5. For present purposes, the important point is that people tend to make many mistakes in thinking about risks. It would be extremely valuable to find correctives, perhaps above all by getting a better sense of the consequences of both risks and risk reduction.

A TALE OF TWO TABLES

Let us begin with two simple tables, Tables 2.1 and 2.2. It is well known that there is a great deal of variability in national expenditures per life saved. Consider Table 2.1, which has come to define many discussions of these problems.[4]

The particular numbers in this table should be taken with many grains of salt.[5] The table does not contain nearly all the benefits from regulation,

---

[3] The point is emphasized in Gerd Gigenzerer et al., Simple Heuristics That Make Us Smart (Oxford: Oxford Univ. Press, 1999), and noted in much work involving heuristics and biases. There is a continuing debate over the extent to which heuristics, of the sort emphasized in this chapter, work well in ordinary life. I am not intending to take a stand on that debate here. My only claim is that the heuristics and biases that I discuss are an inadequate basis for public policy, and that a sensible government can do better.

[4] Based on data from Office of Management and Budget, Budget of the United States Government Fiscal Year 1992 Pt 2, 370 table C-2 (Washington, D. C.: GPO, 1991).

[5] See Lisa Heinzerling, Regulatory Costs of Mythic Proportions, 107 Yale L. J. 1981 (1998).

Table 2.1 Cost per life saved of selected regulations

Regulation	Agency	Cost Per Premature Death Averted ($ millions 1990)
Unvented space heater ban	CPSC	0.1
Aircraft cabin fire protection standard	FAA	0.1
Auto passive restraint/seat belt standards	NHTSA	0.1
Steering column protection standard	NHTSA	0.1
Underground construction standards	OSHA-S	0.1
Trihalomethane drinking water standards	EPA	0.2
Aircraft seat cushion flammability standard	FAA	0.4
Alcohol and drug control standards	FRA	0.5
Auto fuel-system integrity standard	NHTSA	0.5
Standards for servicing auto wheel rims	OSHA-S	0.5
Aircraft floor emergency lighting standard	FAA	0.6
Concrete & masonry construction standards	OSHA-S	0.6
Side-impact standards for autos (dynamic)	NHTSA	0.8
Children's sleepwear flammability ban	CPSC	0.8
Auto side door support standards	NHTSA	0.8
Low-altitude windshear equipment & training standards	FAA	1.3
Electrical equipment standards (metal mines)	MSHA	1.4
Trenching and excavation standards	OSHA-S	1.5
Traffic alert and collision avoidance (TCAS) systems	FAA	1.5
Hazard communication standard	OSHA-S	1.6
Arsenic/copper smelter	EPA	2.7
Grain dust explosion prevention standards	OSHA-S	2.8
Rear lap/shoulder belts for autos	NHTSA	3.2
Benzine NESHAP (original: fugitive emissions)	EPA	3.4
Ethylene dibromide drinking water standard	EPA	5.7
Benzene NESHAP (National Emission Standard for Hazardous Pollutants) (revised: coke byproducts)	EPA	6.1
Asbestos occupational exposure limit	OSHA-H	8.3
Benzene occupational exposure limit	OSHA-H	8.9
Electrical equipment standards (coal mines)	MSHA	9.2
Arsenic emission standards for glass plants	EPA	13.5
Ethylene oxide occupational exposure limit	OSHA-H	20.5
Arsenic/copper NESHAP	EPA	23.0
Hazardous waste listing for petroleum refining sludge	EPA	27.6
Cover/move uranium mill tailings (inactive sites)	EPA	31.7
Benzene NESHAP (revised: transfer operations)	EPA	32.9
Cover/move uranium mill tailings (active sites)	EPA	45.0
Acrylonitrile occupational exposure limit	OSHA-H	51.5
Coke ovens occupational exposure limit	OSHA-H	63.5
Lockout/tagout	OSHA-S	70.9
Asbestos occupational exposure limit	OSHA-H	74.0
Arsenic occupational exposure limit	OSHA-H	106.9

Regulation	Agency	Cost Per Premature Death Averted ($ millions 1990)
Diethylstilbestrol (DES) cattlefeed ban	FDA	124.8
1,2-Dichloropropane drinking water standard	EPA	653.0
Hazardous waste land disposal ban (1st 3rd)	EPA	4,190.4
Atrazine/alachlor drinking water standard	EPA	92,069.7

including those that fall short of mortalities averted (including illnesses averted, benefits for animals, and aesthetic and recreational gains). An adequate cost–benefit analysis would certainly take those benefits into account. There is good reason to focus on "life years saved" rather than "lives saved"; other things being equal, a regulation that protects small children is far more attractive than a regulation that saves elderly people who will die shortly in any event. We will also see that the table depends on many contentious assumptions, above all involving the appropriate discount rate, meaning the treatment of future benefits; modest changes in the discount rate can greatly reduce the expenditures and the disparities.

But at the very least, Table 2.1 creates a presumption that the current system of regulation suffers from serious misallocation of resources. It also suggests that with better allocations, we could obtain large gains. Recall the finding that it would be possible to save the same number of lives that we now save with tens of billions of dollars left over – and that better priority-setting could save 60,000 lives, and 636,000 life-years, annually at the same price.[6] Here too the particular numbers are too crude to be taken seriously, but the general point – that resources are being badly misallocated – is unquestionably correct.

What is the source of the misallocations? Interest-group power undoubtedly plays a substantial role: Well-organized groups are able to obtain measures in their interest or to fend off measures that would harm them, but poorly organized ones typically fail. Indeed, cost–benefit analysis might be defended partly as a corrective to interest-group power, operating as it might as a kind

---

[6] See Tammy O. Tengs & John D. Graham, The Opportunity Costs of Haphazard Social Investments in Life-Saving, in Risks, Costs, and Lives Saved: Getting Better Results from Regulation 167, 172–4, Robert W. Hahn, ed. (New York: Oxford Univ. Press, 1996).

Table 2.2 Rating health risks

Public	EPA Experts
1. Hazardous waste sites	Medium-to-low
2. Exposure to worksite chemicals	High
3. Industrial pollution of waterways	Low
4. Nuclear accident radiation	Not ranked
5. Radioactive waste	Not ranked
6. Chemical leaks from underground storage tanks	Medium-to-low
7. Pesticides	High
8. Pollution from industrial accidents	Medium-to-low
9. Water pollution from farm runoff	Medium
10. Tap water contamination	High
11. Industrial air pollution	High
12. Ozone layer destruction	High
13. Coastal water contamination	Low
14. Sewage-plant water pollution	Medium-to-low
15. Vehicle exhaust	High
16. Oil spills	Medium-to-low
17. Acid rain	High
18. Water pollution from urban runoff	Medium
19. Damaged wetlands	Low
20. Genetic alteration	Low
21. Nonhazardous waste sites	Medium-to-low
22. Greenhouse effect	Low
23. Indoor air pollution	High
24. X-ray radiation	Not ranked
25. Indoor radon	High
26. Microwave oven radiation	Not ranked

Note: Medium-to-low means between medium and low.

of technocratic check on measures that would do little good or even produce net harm (and also on measures that do much less good than they should).[7] But officials are, of course, responsive not only to interest groups but also to general public pressures, and thus part of the answer must lie in the distinctive judgments of ordinary people, who do not assess risks through a well-informed cost–benefit lens. Indeed, divergences between expert and lay assessments of risks have been demonstrated in many places. Consider the comparison in Table 2.2.[8]

[7] Of course it is possible that the content of the cost–benefit test will reflect interest-group power.
[8] Reprinted by permission from Stephen G. Breyer, Breaking the Vicious Circle: Toward Effective Risk Regulation 21 (Cambridge, Mass.: Harvard Univ. Press, 1993).

The EPA itself has found that EPA policies are responsive not to expert judgments but to lay assessments of risks.[9] EPA policies track ordinary judgments extremely well.

If we put Tables 2.1 and 2.2 together, we can suggest a general hypothesis. The government currently allocates its limited resources poorly, and it does so partly because it is responsive to ordinary judgments about the magnitude of risks. A government that could insulate itself from misinformed judgments could save thousands of lives and billions of dollars annually. Let us attempt to be more specific about the cognitive problems that help account for current problems.

PROBLEMS AND INTUITIONS

It is obvious that people, including government officials, often lack risk-related information. They might not know much about the nature and magnitude of the risks at issue, and they might know little about the various consequences of risk reduction. The public demand for regulation is often based on misunderstandings of facts. But why, exactly, might people's judgments about risk and risk regulation go badly wrong?

THE AVAILABILITY HEURISTIC

The first problem is purely cognitive: the use of the *availability heuristic* in thinking about risks. It is well established that people tend to think that events are more probable if they can recall an incident of their occurrence.[10] Consider the fact that people typically think that more words, on any given page, will end with the letters "ing," than have "n" as the second-to-last letter (though a moment's reflection shows that this is not possible).[11] With respect to risks, judgments are typically affected by the availability heuristic. For example, whether people will buy insurance for natural disasters is greatly affected by recent experiences. If floods have not occurred in the immediate past, people who live on flood plains are far less likely to purchase insurance. In the aftermath of an earthquake, insurance for earthquakes rises sharply – but it declines steadily from that point, as vivid memories recede.

[9] See id.

[10] See Amos Tversky & Daniel Kahneman, Judgment Under Uncertainty: Heuristics and Biases, in Judgment Under Uncertainty: Heuristics and Biases 3, 11, Daniel Kahneman, Paul Slovic & Amos Tversky, eds. (Cambridge: Cambridge Univ. Press, 1982) (describing the availability heuristic).

[11] Amos Tversky & Daniel Kahneman, Extensional Versus Intuitive Reasoning: The Conjunction Fallacy in Probability Judgment, 90 Psychol. Rev. 293, 295 (1983).

Do people know which risks led to many deaths, and which risks lead to few? They do not. In fact they make huge blunders. In one study, people were told the annual number of deaths from motor vehicle accidents in the United States (at the time about 50,000) and then were asked to estimate the number of deaths from forty other causes of death.[12] In another study, people were given two causes of death and asked to say which produced more fatalities. People tended to make large mistakes, and when they did so, the availability heuristic was partly responsible. "In keeping with availability considerations, overestimated items were dramatic and sensational whereas underestimated items tended to be unspectacular events which claim one victim at a time and are common in non-fatal form."[13] Specifically, people significantly overestimated highly pub- licized causes of death, including tornadoes, cancer, botulism, and homicide. By contrast, they underestimated the number of deaths from stroke, asthma, emphysema, and diabetes. At the same time, people tend to think that the number of deaths from accidents is higher than the number of deaths from disease, whereas the opposite is true. In the same vein, people mistakenly believe that more people die from homicides than from suicides. Availability can also lull people into complacency, as when certain risks, not easily accessible, seem invisible, and what is out of sight is effectively out of mind.

These points suggest that highly publicized events are likely to lead people to be exceedingly fearful of statistically small risks. Much of the concern with nuclear power undoubtedly stems from its association with memorable events, including Hiroshima, Chernobyl, and Three Mile Island. As we shall see, emo- tions play a large role here; if people can visualize the "worse case," they are likely to be quite alarmed, and assessments of probabilities will be crowded out by fear. Public officials, no less than ordinary people, are prone to use the availability heuristic; in a democracy, officials, including lawmakers, will be highly reactive to public alarm.

If people are extremely concerned about the risk of airplane accidents, we should expect aggressive regulation of airlines, perhaps to the point of diminishing returns. If people are worried about abandoned hazardous waste dumps, we might well expect a large amount of resources to be devoted to cleaning them up, even if the risks are relatively small.[14] Similar problems will

---

[12] See Paul Slovic, The Perception of Risk pp. 106–7 (London: Earthscan, 2000).

[13] See id. p. 107.

[14] For evidence, see James Hamilton & W. Kip Viscusi, Calculating Risks: The Spatial and Political Dimensions of Hazardous Waste Policy (Cambridge, Mass.: MIT Press, 1999); Timur Kuran & Cass R. Sunstein, Availability Cascades and Risk Regulation, 51 Stan. L. Rev. 683 (1999).

appear in courts, with juries and judges taking "phantom risks" quite seriously.[15] There is also a lesson here about how to attract public attention to a risk: *Make a vivid example of its occurrence highly salient to the public.* This way of proceeding, far more than statistical analysis, is likely to activate public concern. Unfortunately, terrorists appear to understand this lesson very well.

To the extent that people lack information, or base their judgments on mental shortcuts that produce errors, a highly responsive government is likely to blunder. Cost–benefit analysis is a natural corrective, above all because it focuses attention on the actual effects of regulation, including, in some cases, the existence of surprisingly small benefits from regulatory controls. To this extent, cost–benefit analysis should not be taken as undemocratic but, on the contrary, should be seen as a means of fortifying democratic goals, by ensuring that government decisions are responsive to well-informed public judgments. Note that I have not suggested that a democratic government must refuse to act if the monetized costs exceed the monetized benefits. The only point is that an accounting of the costs and benefits, both qualitative and quantitative, can overcome public ignorance. If the public wants to proceed after it has received that accounting, nothing here suggests that it is prohibited from doing so.

INTUITIVE TOXICOLOGY

Are ordinary people toxicologists? Paul Slovic et al colleagues have uncovered the content of "intuitive toxicology" by comparing how experts (professional toxicologists) and ordinary people think about the risks associated with chemicals.[16] The result is a fascinating picture. It is not clear that any identifiable heuristics are at work in intuitive toxicology. But it is clear that people are using mental shortcuts, and that these lead to errors.

Consider the views of toxicologists and ordinary people on the following kinds of propositions:

(a) There is no safe level of exposure to a cancer-causing agent.
(b) If you are exposed to a carcinogen, then you are likely to get cancer.
(c) If a scientific study produces evidence that a chemical causes cancer in animals, then we can be reasonably sure that the chemical will cause cancer in humans.

---

[15] See Peter Huber et al., Phantom Risk: Scientific Influence of the Law, 425–8 (Cambridge, Mass.: MIT Press, 1999) (discussing scientifically unsupportable outcomes involving "traumatic cancer" and harm to immune systems); id. at 137–46 (discussing lawsuits with unclear scientific basis).

[16] See Slovic, supra note 12 in Chapter 2, pp. 285–98, from which I borrow throughout this section.

(d) The land, air, and water around us are, in general, more contaminated now than ever before.

(e) Natural chemicals, as a rule, are not as harmful as man-made chemicals.

(f) Residents of a small community (30,000 people) observed that several malformed children had been born there during each of the past few years. The town is in a region where agricultural pesticides have been in use during the last decade. It is very likely that these pesticides were the cause of the malformations.

(g) All use of prescription drugs must be risk-free.

Ordinary people agree with such statements, by pluralities or even majorities. In contrast, toxicologists disagree with such statements, usually by overwhelming majorities. What are ordinary people thinking? Can we discern some structure to their judgments? Three beliefs seem to be playing a large role. *First,* many people believe that risk is an "all or nothing" matter. Something is either safe or dangerous, and there is no middle ground. *Second,* many people are committed to a belief in the benevolence of nature. They think that the products of human beings, and human activities, are more likely to be dangerous than the products of natural processes. *Third,* many people subscribe to the "zero risk" mentality, at least in some domains. Such people believe that it is both possible and appropriate to abolish risk entirely, a belief that appears closely connected with the notion that risk is a matter of "all or nothing."

Experts believe that all three beliefs are false. Moreover, it seems clear that with respect to risks, experts are thinking far more sensibly than are ordinary people. Why do people think this way? It might well be that at least some of these ideas work well in most contexts in which nonspecialists find themselves. People want, for example, to know whether an activity is "safe," not to know about the statistical probability of harm; and the excessively simple category of "safe" can tell them essentially what they need to know. The problem is that ideas of this kind misfire in contexts in which regulatory choices, and some daily decisions, have to be made. Of course, ordinary people do not have the time to investigate the statistics, and nonspecialists may do well to rely on such principles. But policymakers should do a good deal better.

To be sure, experts do not entirely agree among themselves. Most interestingly, toxicologists employed by industry are far more optimistic about chemical risks than toxicologists employed by government or academic institutions; there is also a large "affiliation bias" so that people tend to believe what their institution would want them to believe. But the differences among toxicologists are dwarfed by the differences between toxicologists and ordinary people. We should conclude that people's social role will move their judgments in predictable directions and that experts are likely to be biased if they are working with someone having a stake in the outcome – but also that even acknowledging this point, experts are, on many fundamental issues, in basic accord with one another.

Cost–benefit analysis can be an important corrective to intuitive toxicology. People tend to think that if a substance is carcinogenic, it should be banned. But what if this particular carcinogen produces little harm at low levels, or perhaps even benefits? And what if the result of the ban would be to increase, by hundreds of dollars, the annual water bill faced by poor people? People may think that it is risky to tamper with nature; but what if genetically modified food is cheaper, more nutritious, and safer than the alternatives? One of the primary virtues of cost–benefit analysis is that it can weaken the hold of intuitive toxicology, giving people a real sense of the consequences of different courses of action.

AGGRAVATING SOCIAL INFLUENCES: SOCIAL CASCADES

The availability heuristic and intuitive toxicology do not, of course, operate in a social vacuum. They interact with emphatically social processes, and in particular with informational and reputational forces. When one person says, through words or deeds, that something is or is not dangerous, he creates an *informational externality*.[17] A signal by some person A will provide relevant data to others. When there is little private information, such a signal may initiate an *informational cascade*, with significant consequences for private and public behavior, and with possibly distorting effects on regulatory policy. I shall discuss these points in some detail in Chapter 4; for now, a brief outline will be useful.

Imagine that A says that abandoned hazardous waste sites are dangerous, or that A initiates protest activity because such a site is located nearby. B, otherwise skeptical or in equipoise, may go along with A; C, otherwise an agnostic, may be convinced that if A and B share the relevant belief, the belief must be true; and it will take a confident D to resist the shared judgments of A, B, and C. The result of these set of influences can be social cascades, as hundreds, thousands, or millions of people come to accept a certain belief simply because of what they think other people believe.[18] There is nothing fanciful to the idea. Cascade effects help account for the existence of widespread public concern

---

[17] See Andrew Caplin & John Leahy, Miracle on Sixth Avenue: Information Externalities and Search, 108 Econ. J. 60 (1998).

[18] See David Hirshleifer, The Blind Leading the Blind: Social Influence, Fads, and Informational Cascades, in The New Economics of Human Behavior 188, Mariano Tommasi & Kathyrn Ierulli, eds. (Cambridge: Cambridge Univ. Press, 1995).

about abandoned hazardous waste dumps (not the most serious environmental hazard), and in more recent years, they spurred excessive public fears of the pesticide Alar, of risks from anthrax, and of dangers of shootings in schools in the aftermath of the murders in Littleton, Colorado. Such effects recently helped produce massive dislocations in beef production in Europe in connection with "mad cow disease"; they are currently giving rise to European fear of genetic engineering of food.

On the reputational side, cognitive effects may be amplified as well. If many people are alarmed about some risk, you may not voice your doubts about whether the alarm is merited, simply in order not to seem obtuse, cruel, or indifferent. And if many people believe that a certain risk is trivial, you may not disagree through words or deeds, lest you appear cowardly or confused. The result of these forces can be cascade effects, mediated by the availability heuristic. Such effects can produce a public demand for regulation, even though the relevant risks are trivial. At the same time, there may be little or no demand for regulation of risks that are, in fact, quite large in magnitude. Self-interested private groups can exploit these forces, often by using the availability heuristic. Consider the fact that European companies have tried to play up fears of genetically engineered food as a way of fending off American competition – a reason for special concern in light of the likelihood that genetically engineered food might be a huge boon for poor nations.

These are tales of excessive and insufficient concern with risk. At the individual level, risk-taking behavior is also a product, much of the time, of similar forces. People often take risks, even foolish ones, simply because other people are doing the same thing. Suppose that Johnson is unsure whether to smoke, or drive drunk, or use dangerous drugs; if other people are doing these things, Johnson might choose to do so as well. The choice to take the relevant risks might be based on informational influences; if everyone else is smoking, how foolish can it be to smoke? Or the choice might be based on reputational considerations; if everyone else thinks that it is right to smoke, then your reputation might be enhanced if you smoke, and damaged if you fail to smoke. Cigarette companies are entirely aware of these points. An executive at R. J. Reynolds emphasized, "If a majority of one's closest associates smoke cigarettes, then there is strong psychological pressure, particularly as a young person, to identify with the group, follow the crowd, and avoid being out of phase with the group's value system even though, paradoxically, the group value system may esteem individuality. This provides a large incentive to begin smoking."[19]

---

[19] Quoted in Jon Hanson & Douglas Kysar, The Joint Failure of Economic Theory and Legal Regulation, in Smoking: Risk, Perception, and Policy 229, 255, Paul Slovic, ed. (New York: Sage 2001).

There is a close associated between cascade effects and *group polarization*. Group polarization is the typical result of deliberation, which moves people toward in a more extreme point in the direction that they were already heading. People who tend to think that global warming is a nonexistent problem, fabricated by environmentalists to promote their own parochial ends, are likely to think, after discussion with one another, that this is entirely true. People who fear that genetic engineering of food will cause severe agricultural damage, or dangers to human beings, might well be led, by discussion, to think that genetic engineering of food should be banned. Group polarization helps explain why some people, in some communities, become terrified of tiny risks (electromagnetic fields, in some areas; crimes, in others), while some people, in some communities, remain indifferent to significant risks (skin cancer, indoor air pollution). I will say much more about social effects of this sort in Chapter 4.

If government is deciding what to do, cost–benefit analysis has a natural role in these circumstances. If that analysis is made relevant to decision, it can counteract cascade effects induced by informational and reputational forces, especially when the availability heuristic is at work. The effect of cost–benefit analysis is to subject a public demand for regulation to a kind of technocratic scrutiny, to ensure that the demand is not rooted in myth, and to ensure as well that government is regulating risks even when the public demand (because insufficiently informed) is low. And here too there is no democratic problem with the inquiry into consequences; a governmental effort to "cool" popular reactions is hardly inconsistent with democratic ideals. Similarly, there is nothing undemocratic about a governmental effort to divert resources to serious problems that have not been beneficiaries of cascade effects.

SYSTEMIC EFFECTS AND "HEALTH–HEALTH TRADEOFFS"

Often people focus on small pieces of complex problems, and causal changes are hard to trace. A decision to impose fuel economy standards on new cars may cause a "downsizing" of the fleet, and in that way increase risks to life. A decision to ban asbestos may cause manufacturers to use less safe substitutes. A decision to regulate nuclear power may increase the demand for coal-fired power plants, with harmful environmental consequences. Regulation of tropospheric ozone may control the health dangers of ozone, but ozone has various benefits as well, including protection against cataracts and skin cancer; hence regulation of ozone may cause health problems comparable to those that it reduces.[20] Indeed,

---

[20] See Randall Lutter & Christopher Wolz, UV-B Screening by Tropospheric Ozone: Implications for the NAAQS, 31 Env. Sci. & Tech. 142A, 144A (1997) (estimating that the EPA's

regulation of ozone will increase electricity prices, and because higher electricity prices will deprive poor people of air conditioning or lead them to use it less, such regulation may harm or literally kill people.

These are simply a few examples of situations in which a government agency is inevitably making "health–health tradeoffs" in light of the systemic effects of one-shot interventions. Indeed, any regulation that imposes high costs will, by virtue of that fact, produce some risks to life and health, since "richer is safer."[21] A virtue of cost–benefit analysis is that it tends to overcome people's tendency to focus on parts of problems, by requiring them to look globally at the consequences of apparently isolated actions. I will discuss these issues in detail in Chapter 6.

DANGERS ON-SCREEN, BENEFITS OFF-SCREEN

Why are people so concerned about the risks of nuclear power, when experts tend to believe that the risks are quite low – lower, in fact, than the risks from competing energy sources, such as coal-fired power plants, which produce relatively little public objection? Why do they believe that small risks from pesticides should be regulated, even if comparatively small risks from X-rays are quite tolerable?

Suggestive answers come from research suggesting that for many activities that pose small risks but that nonetheless receive public concern, people perceive low benefits as well as high risks.[22] For example, nuclear power itself is seen as a low-benefit, high-risk activity. Similar findings appear for some activities

new ozone NAAQS could cause 25 to 50 more melanoma skin cancer deaths and increase the number of cataract cases by 13,000 to 28,000 each year). See also Ralph L. Keeney & Kenneth Green, Estimating Fatalities Induced by Economic Impacts of EPA's Ozone and Particulate Standards 8 (Reason Public Policy Institute, Policy Study No. 225, June 1997) (calculating that if attainment of the new standards costs $10 billion annually, a number well within EPA's estimated cost range, it will contribute to 2,200 premature deaths annually). On the general phenomenon, see Graham & Wiener, supra note 32 in Chapter 1.

21 John D. Graham, Bei-Hung Chang, & John S. Evans, Poorer Is Riskier, 12 Risk Analysis 333, 333–5 (1992); Frank B. Cross, When Environmental Regulations Kill: The Role of Health-Health Analysis, 22 Ecol. L. Q. 729 (1995); Ralph L. Keeney, Mortality Risks Induced by the Costs of Regulations, 8 J. Risk & Uncertainty 95 (1994); Aaron Wildavsky, Richer Is Safer, 60 Pub. Interest 23 (1980); Aaron Wildavsky, Searching for Safety 59–75 (New Brunswick, N. J.: Transaction Books, 1988).

22 See Ali Siddiq Alhakami & Paul Slovic, A Psychological Study of the Inverse Relationship Between Perceived Risk and Perceived Benefit, 14 Risk Analysis 1085, 1088 (1994).

that have in fact a relatively high risk: a judgment of low risk accompanies a judgment of high benefits. The very fact that activities are known to have high benefits skews judgment in their favor, and hence makes people understate the costs as well.

The obvious conclusion is that sometimes people favor regulation of some risks because the underlying activities are not seen to have compensating benefits. Thus for some activities, tradeoffs are not perceived at all. Dangers are effectively on-screen, but benefits are off-screen. Note that this is not because such activities do not, in fact, have compensating benefits. It is because of a kind of perceptual illusion, a cognitive problem. Consider in this regard Howard Margolis's basic account of the different judgments of experts and ordinary people.[23] Margolis thinks that in some cases, ordinary people are alert to the hazards of some activity but not to its benefits, which are cognitively off-screen. In such cases, people will tend to think, "better safe than sorry," and they will have a highly negative reaction to the risk. In such cases, they will demand aggressive and immediate regulation. In other cases, the benefits of the activity, but not the hazards, will be very much on people's minds – in which case they will tend to think, "nothing ventured, nothing gained."[24] In such cases, they will think that regulators are overzealous, even fanatics. In still other cases – in Margolis' view, the cases in which observers are being most sensible – both benefits and risks will be on-screen, and people will assess risks by comparing the benefits with the costs.[25]

It is reasonable to think that for experts, benefits and costs are usually on-screen, and that when ordinary people are much more alarmed than experts, it is sometimes because the risks are apparent but the benefits are not. How else are we to make sense of the fact that the very small risks associated with X-rays do not occasion much concern, while the very small risks associated with pesticides and herbicides frequently appear on the list of most feared risks? A sensible conjecture is that people know that on balance, a world with X-rays is safer, and better, than a world without them. For pesticides and herbicides, by contrast, the benefits seem far less tangible, if they are visible at all. It is safe to predict that if people were told, by a reliable source, that eliminating pesticides would lead to serious health problems – for example, because pesticide-free fruits and vegetables carried special dangers[26] – the perceived risk of pesticides would decline dramatically. Indeed, I predict that if people were informed that

---

[23] Howard Margolis, Dealing with Risk, 75–92 (Chicago: Chicago Univ. Press, 1997).

[24] Id. at 91–92.

[25] Id. a 73–79.

[26] See the discussion of organic food in Alan McHughen, Pandora's Picnic Basket (Oxford: Oxford Univ. Press, 2000).

eliminating pesticides would lead to a significant rise in the price of applies and oranges, the perceived risk would go down as well.

Margolis offers a nice example to support this prediction. The removal of asbestos from schools in New York City was initially quite popular, indeed demanded by parents, even though experts believed that the risks were statistically small. (As it happens, the risk of a child getting cancer from asbestos insulation was about one-third the risk of being struck by lightning.) But when it emerged that the removal would cause schools to be closed for a period of weeks, and when the closing caused parents to become greatly inconvenienced, parental attitudes turned right around, and asbestos removal seemed like a really bad idea. When the costs of the removal came on-screen, parents thought much more like experts, and the risks of asbestos seemed like the risks of X-rays: statistically small and on balance worth incurring.

An important factor here is *loss aversion*. People tend to be loss averse, which means that a loss from the status quo is seen as more undesirable than a gain is seen as desirable.[27] In the context of risk regulation, the consequence is that any newly introduced risk, or any aggravation of existing risks, is seen as a serious problem, even if the accompaying benefits (a gain from the status quo and hence perceived as less salient and less important) are considerable.[28] Thus when a new risk adds danger, people may focus on the danger itself and not on the benefits that accompany the danger. And an important problem here is that in many cases where dangers are on-screen and benefits off-screen, the magnitude of the danger is actually quite low. Of course, it is possible that a new risk is worse than an old risk, perhaps because it is larger in degree, perhaps because people will have a hard time in adjusting to it. The problem is that loss aversion operates in an automatic, insufficiently reflective manner so that preoccupation with new risks cannot possibly be justified in these terms.

[27] See Richard H. Thaler, The Psychology of Choice and the Assumptions of Economics, in Quasi Rational Economics 137, 143, Richard H. Thaler, ed. (New York: Russell Sage Foundation, 1991) (arguing that "losses loom larger than gains"); Daniel Kahneman, Jack L. Knetsch & Richard H. Thaler, Experimental Tests of the Endowment Effect and the Coase Theorem, 98 J. Pol. Econ. 1325, 1328 (1990); Colin Camerer, Individual Decision Making, in The Handbook of Experimental Economics 665–70, John H. Kagel & Alvin E. Roth, eds. (Princeton, N. J.: Princeton Univ. Press, 1995).

[28] For some policy implications of loss aversion, see Jack L. Knetsch, Reference States, Fairness, and Choice of Measure to Value Environmental Changes, in Environment, Ethics, and Behavior: The Psychology of Environmental Valuation and Degradation 52, 64–5, Max H. Bazerman, David M. Messick, Ann E. Tenbrunsel & Kimberly A. Wade-Benzoni, eds. (San Francisco: New Lexington Press, 1997).

Cost–benefit analysis can be a corrective here by placing the various effects on-screen.

EMOTIONS, THE AFFECT HEURISTIC, AND ALARMIST BIAS

Thus far the discussion has focused on individual and social *cognition*. Indeed, most psychological work on risk has been highly cognitive in orientation, asking whether mental heuristics produce errors, and how people frequently depart from what is generally considered to be rational behavior. But something is missing in thinking about perceived risks only in these terms. With respect to risks, many of our ordinary ways of speaking suggest strong emotions: panic, hysteria, terror.[29] Vivid mental pictures of widespread death or catastrophe can drive a demand for risk regulation. Consider, for example, the motivations of those who press for regulation of airplane safety in the aftermath of an airplane crash – even though such regulation may increase travel risks on balance (by driving up the price of flying and causing a shift to driving, the more dangerous form of transportation).[30] How do people's *feelings* affect their reactions to risks?

Return to the remarkable finding mentioned earlier: When asked to assess the risks and benefits associated with certain items, people tend to think that risky activities contain low benefits, and that beneficial activities contain low risks. In other words, people are likely to think that activities that seem dangerous do not carry benefits; it is rare that they will see an activity as *both* highly beneficial and quite dangerous or as *both* benefit-free and danger-free. This is extremely odd. Why don't people think, more of the time, that some activity is both highly beneficial and highly risky? Why do they seem to make a kind of general, gestalt-type judgment, one that drives assessment of both risks and benefits? Aware that risk and benefit are "distinct concepts," the psychologist Paul Slovic thinks that "affect" comes first and helps to "direct" judgments of both risk and benefit.[31] Hence Slovic suggests an "affect heuristic," by which people have an emotional, all-things-considered reaction to certain processes and products, and that heuristic operates as a mental shortcut for a more careful evaluation.

[29] See George Loewenstein et al., Risk As Feelings, 127 Psych. Bull. 267 (2001).

[30] See Robert W. Hahn, The Economics of Airline Safety and Security: An Analysis of the White House Commission's Recommendations, 20 Harv. J. L. & Pub. Policy 791 (1997).

[31] See, for example, Paul Slovic, supra note 12 in Chapter 2, at 413–28; Paul Slovic et al., The Affect Heuristic, in Intuitive Judgment: Heuristics and Biases, Tom Gilovich et al., eds. (New York: Cambridge Univ. Press, 2002).

Consider one of the most interesting tests of the role of the affect heuristic.[32] The test is designed to provide new information about the *risk* associated with some item and then to see if the information altered people's judgments about the *benefit* associated with it – and also to provide new information about the benefit of some item and to test whether that information would alter people's judgments about the accompany risk. The motivation for this study is simple. If people's judgments were purely cognitive, information about the great *benefits* of (say) food preservatives should not produce a judgment that the *risks* are low – just as information about the great risks of (say) natural gas should not make people think that the benefits are low.

Strikingly, information about benefits alters judgments about risks, and information about risks alters judgments about benefits. When people learn about the low risks of an item, they are moved to think that the benefits are high, and when they learn about the high benefits of an item, they are moved to think that the risks are low. It seems that people assess products and activities through affect, and that information that improves people's affective response will improve their judgments of all dimensions of those products and activities. When presented with a risk, people have a general emotional attitude to it – hence an "affect" – and this general attitude operates as a heuristic, much affecting people's judgments about both benefits and dangers. The point is further supported by the finding that when people are forced to make decisions under time pressure, the inverse relationship between benefits and risks is even more clearly established.[33] When people have little time, affect seems to do a lot of the work. If people like an activity or a product, they see high benefits and low risks, whereas dislike produces a judgment of low benefits and high risks.

It is important to be careful with the relevant categories here. There is no sharp distinction between "cognition" and "emotion."[34] Emotions are generally the products of beliefs, and hence an emotional reaction to risk – terror, for example – is generally mediated by judgments.[35] But this is not always true; sometimes the operation of the brain allows intense emotional reactions with minimal cognitive activity. Some scientific work suggests that the brain has special sectors for emotions, and that some types of emotions, including some

---

[32] See id.

[33] See id.

[34] See Dan M. Kahan & Martha C. Nussbaum, Two Conceptions of Emotion in the Criminal Law, 96 Colum. L. Rev. 269 (1996); Jon Elster, Alchemies of the Mind: Rationality and the Emotions (Cambridge: Cambridge Univ. Press, 1999).

[35] See Martha Nussbaum, Upheavals of Thought (New York: Cambridge Univ. Press, 2001); Elster, supra note 34 in Chapter 2.

fear-type reactions, can be triggered before the more cognitive sectors become involved at all.[36] Whether or not this is so, the judgments that fuel fear-type emotions are not always reliable, especially when probability is ignored.

We need not venture into controversial territory to urge that some risks seem to produce extremely sharp, largely visceral reactions. These reactions are sometimes largely impervious to argument. Indeed, experience with "mass panics" has shown exactly this structure, as assurances based on statistical evidence have little effect in the face of vivid images of what might go wrong.[37] "If someone is predisposed to be worried, degrees of unlikeliness seem to provide no comfort, unless one can prove that harm is absolutely impossible, which itself is not possible."[38] Some fears even seem to have a genetic foundation; consider, as a possible example, fear of snakes, which appears in people who have no reason to think that snakes are dangerous. Perhaps more to the point, existing experiments suggest that when it comes to risk, a key question is whether people can imagine or visualize the "worst case" outcome – and that surprisingly little role is played by the stated probability that that outcome will occur.[39] In other words, people's reactions to risks are often based mostly on the badness of the outcome and the vividness of that outcome rather than on the probability of its occurrence. Consider also these points:

1. When people discuss a low-probability risk, their concern rises even if the discussion consists mostly of apparently trustworthy assurances that the likelihood of harm really is infinitesmal.[40]
2. If people are asked how much they will pay for flight insurance for losses resulting from "terrorism," they will pay more than if they are asked how much they will pay for flight insurance from all causes.[41]
3. People show "alarmist bias." When presented with competing accounts of danger, they tend to move toward the more alarming account.[42]

---

[36] See Joseph LeDoux, The Emotional Brain: The Mysterious Underpinnings of Emotional Life (New York: Simon & Schuster, 1996).

[37] See the discussion of Love Canal in Timur Kuran & Cass R. Sunstein, Availability Cascades and Risk Regulation, 51 Stan. L. Rev. 683, 691–8 (1999).

[38] See John Weingart, Waste Is a Terrible Thing To Mind 362 (Newark, N. J.: Center for Public Issues, 2001).

[39] See Yuval Rottenstreich and Christopher Hsee, Money, Kisses, and Electric Shocks: On the Affective Psychology of Risk, 12 Psych. Sci. 185, 186–8 (2001).

[40] See Ali Siddiq Alha kami & Slovic, supra note 22 in this Chapter.

[41] See George Loewenstein et al, supra note 29 in this Chapter at 275.

[42] W. Kip Viscusi, Alarmist Decisions With Divergent Risk Information, 107 Econ. J. 1657, 1657–9 (1997).

4. Visualization or imagery matters a great deal to people's reactions to risks. When an image of a bad outcome is easily accessible, people will become greatly concerned about a risk, holding probability constant.[43]
5. If the potential outcome of a gamble has a great deal of associated affect (a kiss with a favorite movie star, an electric shock), its attractiveness or unattractiveness is remarkably insensitive to changes in probability, even changes as large as from .99 to .01.[44]

A possible conclusion is that, with respect to risks, vivid images and concrete pictures of disaster can "crowd out" other kinds of thoughts, *including the crucial thought that the probability of disaster is really small*. With respect to hope, those who operate gambling casinos and state lotteries play on the emotions in the particular sense that they conjure up palpable pictures of victory and easy living. With respect to risks, insurance companies and environmental groups do exactly the same. With respect to products of all kinds, advertisers try to produce a good affect to steer consumers into a certain direction, often through the use of appealing celebrities, through cheerful scenes, or through the creation of an association between the product and the consumer's preferred self-image.

The role of cost–benefit analysis is straightforward here. Just as the Senate was designed to have a "cooling effect" on the passions of the House of Representatives, so cost–benefit analysis might ensure that policy is driven not by hysteria or alarm but by a full appreciation of the effects of relevant risks and their control. If the hysteria survives an investigation of consequences, then the hysteria is fully rational, and an immediate and intensive regulatory response is entirely appropriate. Nor is cost–benefit analysis, in this setting, only a check on unwarranted regulation. It can and should serve as a spur to regulation as well. If risks do not produce visceral reactions, partly because the underlying activities do not yield vivid mental images, cost–benefit analysis can show that they nonetheless warrant regulatory control. The elimination of lead in gasoline is a case in point.[45]

An additional lesson follows: If government is seeking a method to ensure that people will take a more rational approach to risk, it might well attempt to appeal to their emotions. With respect to a cigarette smoking, abuse of alcohol, reckless driving, and abuse of drugs, this is exactly what government occasionally attempts to do. It should be no surprise that some of the most effective efforts to control cigarette smoking appeal to people's emotions, by making them feel

---

[43] See Paul Slovic et al., Violence Risk Assessment and Risk Communication, 24 Law and Human Behavior 271 (2000).

[44] See Rottenstreich and Hsee, supra note 39 in Chapter 2.

[45] See Economic Analyses at EPA, supra note 19 in Chapter I.

that if they smoke, they will be dupes of the tobacco companies or imposing harms on innocent third parties.[46] I will return to this point in Chapter 10.

THE PROPORTIONALITY EFFECT

Suppose that 200 million people face a statistically small risk, so that government intervention would save a quite small percentage of those 200 million people – say, one in a million. Now suppose that 1,000 people face a statistically large risk, so that government intervention would save a nontrivial percentage of those 1,000 – say, one in a hundred. Evidence suggests that people would be far more inclined to support the second intervention than the first; people "worry more about the proportion of risk reduced than about the number of people helped."[47] A moment's reflection should show that the intuitive inclination is not easy to defend. In the cases just given, the first intervention would save 200 lives, whereas the second would save just 10. On what theory should the government prefer the second? It is not easy to answer this question, but people generally seek to save a high proportion of people in the relevant population, and focus less than they might on absolute savings of lives. Indeed the proportionality effect seems to explain the fact that people are willing to pay an enormous amount to protect an identifiable victim, such as a child trapped in a well – but much less to protect "statistical lives," as when a hundred or more people, not identifiable in advance, will die as a result of exposure to carcinogens.[48]

A striking study of the proportionality effect asked people how much they were willing to pay to reduce existing risks by 20 percent, and compared the answers to actual government practice.[49] The upshot of the study is that both absolute numbers and proportionality are important, and that people's intuitions map onto actual policy choices. Not surprisingly, the study found that people are willing to spend more to reduce absolutely larger risks. For example, the mean willingness to pay was $161 to reduce by 20 percent 10,000 deaths from automobiles per year, whereas the mean willingness to pay was merely $46 to reduce by 20 percent 40 deaths from aviation each year. But at the same time, the proportionality effect plays a large role, as demonstrated by the fact that

---

[46] Lisa Goldman & Stanton Glantz, Evaluation of Antismoking Advertising Campaigns, 279 JAMA 772 (1998).

[47] See Jonathan Baron, Thinking and Deciding 500–2 (Cambridge: Cambridge Univ. Press, 3d ed., 2000).

[48] See K. E. Jenni & George Loewenstein, Explaining the Identifiable Victim Effect, 14 J. Risk & Uncertainty 235 (1997).

[49] See T. L. McDaniels, Comparing Expressed and Revealed Preferences for Risk Reduction, 8 Risk Analysis 593 (1988).

per life saved, people's willingness to pay is much higher for the smaller risks, with a national willingness to pay $103 million per life saved in the context of aviation, but just $1.3 million per life saved in the context of automobiles. All this is survey evidence. But actual government expenditures show the same effect. Government does not allocate its resources to save as many lives as possible but shows a willingness to spend far more, per life saved, when the risk is faced by a relatively small population. It is reasonable to think that the proportionality effect accounts for many of the anomalies shown in Table I.I.

Of course, there are some complexities here. Interest group pressures, and not merely intuitions, are an important factor behind government practice. When a small population faces a risk, perhaps it will be well-organized and be in a position to press vigorously for governmental help. In addition, there may be a sound moral principle at work, and not merely a confused intuition. It is reasonable to think that government should care, not only about the total number of people at risk, but also about the statistical danger faced by particular people. Perhaps everyone has a right, under normal circumstances, not to be subject to a risk of death of, say, 1 in 100. Perhaps it is much worse for 10,000 people to face a fatality risk of 1 in 100 than for 2 million people to face a fatality risk of 1 in 100,000, even though more people will die in the later case. I do not mean to resolve the theoretical complexities here. The only point is that the proportionality effect seems to operate as an automatic, unreflective intuition, and it almost certainly helps to produce policies that no one, after reflection, would support. A chief advantage of cost–benefit analysis is that it promotes that very reflection, by drawing attention to the actual numbers and ensuring that if people really do not want to increase the absolute number of lives saved, they will know that this is what they are doing.

SEPARATE EVALUATION AND INCOHERENCE

Suppose that you are asked to say, without reference to any other problem, how much you would be willing to pay to protect certain threats to coral reefs. Now suppose that you are asked to say, without reference to any other problem, how much you would pay to protect against skin cancer among the elderly. Suppose, finally, that you are asked to say how much you would be willing to pay to protect certain threats to coral reefs and how much you would be willing to pay to protect against skin cancer among the elderly. Empirical evidence suggests that people's answers to questions, taken in isolation, are very different from their answers to questions when they are asked to engage in cross-category comparisons.[50] It

[50] See Cass R. Sunstein, Daniel Kahneman, David Schkade & Ilana Ritov, Predictably Incoherent Judgments, p. 54 Stan. L. Rev. (forthcoming 2002).

appears that when people assess problems in isolation, they do so by reference to other problems in the same basic category – and that this intuitive process is dramatically altered when people are explicitly told to assess problems from other categories as well. The result of assessing individual problems, taken in isolation, is to produce what people would themselves consider a form of incoherence.

The forms of regulatory spending shown in Table I.I undoubtedly reflect, in part, the kinds of irrationality that follow from judgments that are made without close reference to other problems from different categories. Incoherence is the natural result of the relevant cognitive processes. The argument for a form of cost–benefit analysis is straightforward: It operates as a built-in corrective to some of the distortions that come from taking problems in isolation. The point applies to "contingent valuation" assessments, but it operates more broadly with respect to expenditure decisions that otherwise risk incoherence, simply by virtue of the fact that they operate without looking at other problems, including those from other categories.

GENERAL IMPLICATIONS

Two arguments are now in place. The first is that for a variety of identifiable reasons, people make mistaken judgments about risks. Their intuitions lead them astray. To be sure, some of the heuristics that people use are well-suited for daily life, especially for busy people who do not have the time or inclination to investigate the details. But government should do a good deal better, and it is not likely to do so if it is simply responding to what people fear and do not fear. The second argument is that cost–benefit analysis can operate not as a rule for decision but as a useful tool, helping to correct the various risks to which all of us are susceptible.

In this light, it is true but obvious to say that people lack information and that their lack of information can lead to an inadequate or excessive demand for regulation, or a form of "paranoia and neglect."[51] What is less obvious is that predictable features of cognition will lead to a demand for regulation that is unlikely to be based on the facts. When people ask for regulation because of fears fueled by availability cascades, and when the benefits from the risk-producing activity are not registering, it would be highly desirable to create filters on their requests. When interest groups exploit cognitive mechanisms to create unwarranted fear or diminish concern with serious problems, it is desirable to have institutional safeguards. When people fail to ask for regulation for related

---

[51] See John D. Graham, Making Sense of Risk: An Agenda for Congress, in Risks, Costs, and Lives Saved: Getting Better Results from Regulation 183, Robert W. Hahn, ed. (New York: Oxford Univ. Press, 1996).

reasons, it would be desirable to create a mechanism by which government might nonetheless act if the consequences of action would be desirable.

A caveat: It is entirely possible that the public demand for regulation will result from something other than cognitive errors, even if the relevant risk seems low as a statistical matter. Interest groups are exceedingly important. As we have seen, they use their power to produce regulation that they favor. Sometimes they enlist the very forces discussed here. To say the least, moral judgments are exceedingly important as well. People may think, for example, that it is especially important to protect poor children from a certain risk in a geographically isolated area, and they may be willing to devote an unusually large amount to ensure that protection. What seems to be a cognitive error may turn out, on reflection, to be a judgment of value, and a judgment that can survive reflection. I will return to this point in the next chapter. For the moment, note two simple points. Whether an error is involved is an empirical question, subject, at least in principle, to empirical testing. And nothing in cost–benefit analysis would prevent people from devoting resources to projects that they consider worthy, even if the risk is relatively low as a statistical matter.

THE PSYCHOLOGICAL LOGIC OF TERRORISM: A CONCLUDING NOTE

People's mistakes in thinking about risks bear a great deal on catastrophes in general and on terrorism in particular. Indeed, terrorism has an unmistakable psychological logic, and we can bring many of my themes together if we identify that logic.

I have emphasized that people tend to use the availability heuristic, in accordance with which probability is measured by asking whether a readily available example comes to mind. In the aftermath of a terrorist act, and for a period thereafter, the act is likely to be readily available – and thus to make people think that another such act is likely, whether or not it is in fact. The result is that one or two highly publicized incidents will have a significant and potentially huge impact on both thought and behavior. In these ways, terrorist acts are no different from floods, earthquakes, and other catastrophes, all of which have immediate effects. In the aftermath of the attacks of September 11, 2001, many Americans were afraid to travel in airplanes and even to appear in public places. If we know how people think about risks, we will find this level of fear entirely unsurprising.

People also show disproportionate fear of risks that seem unfamiliar and hard to control (a point discussed in more detail in Chapter 3). A new risk is likely to receive far more attention than is warranted by the sheer numbers. A large disparity between reactions to old risks and new risks characterizes both individual judgment and law itself, which treats new hazards far more aggressively than old ones. For individual judgments, the disparity may result partly from the fact that people have become accustomed to existing risks, and hence are less disturbed by them than the data may warrant. But for both individuals and societies, serious problems can emerge from the disproportionate fear of risks that seem unfamiliar and hard to control. For present purposes, the key point is that the risks associated with terrorism are likely to seem new, unfamiliar, and apparently hard to control – and a terrorist act will therefore produce widespread and intense public fear.

I have also suggested that people are prone to *probability neglect*, especially when their emotions are intensely engaged. If a bad outcome is very vivid, people are not likely to think much about whether it is likely to come to fruition. When probability neglect is at work, people's attention is focussed on the bad outcome itself, and they are inattentive to the fact that it is unlikely to occur. Almost by definition, an act of terrorism will trigger intense fear, and hence people will focus on the awfulness of the potential outcomers, not on their probabilities.

All these forces are likely to be aggravated by social influences. After an act of terrorism, people will be talking to one another about that act, and cascades of fear will undoubtedly develop. It is almost inevitable that baseless rumors will spread rapidly and widely. In these circumstances, it should be unsurprising that the harms and costs of a single terrorist act can be felt for a long time and reflect "ripple effects" far beyond the act itself.[52] The attacks of September 11 are an obvious case in point. A comprehensive account will take a long time to produce, but consider, for illustrative purpose, the following facts and projections, developed shortly after those attacks: New York City was expected to forfeit between $1 billion and $3 billion in lost revenue; global airline losses were projected to exceed $10 billion; total "big company" layoffs were about 200,000, with British Airways laying off 12.5 percent of its employees and American Airlines and Boeing each laying off at least 20,000 people; car rental companies were projected to lose 50 to 60 percent of their business with in the months following the attacks.[53] Of course this is just the beginning: the ripple effects of the attacks – financial, material, and psychological – extend to countless domains.

All these points suggest that acts of terrorism show an acute appreciation of the psychological phenomena I have discussed. Of course, it is difficult to do any kind of cost–benefit analysis of measures to reduce the risks of terrorism, especially because of the level of uncertainty involved. But at least we can say that

---

[52] See Paul Slovic, supra note 12 in Chapter 2, at 232–45.

[53] See Cass R. Sunstein, The Laws of Fear, 115 Harv. L. Rev. 1119, 1130–21 (2002) for support and discussion.

government should not react hysterically to people's fears – not least because a hysterical response would give terrorists a large additional victory. I will turn to this issue in due course. For now the important point to notice is that people's approach to the risks of catastrophe, including the risks associated with terrorism, can be better understood if we have a working knowledge of how people assess risks in general.

3

Are Experts Wrong?

With the deaths of two people from shark attacks over the Labor Day weekend, the summerlong fascination with these fear-inducing creatures of the deep has turned into a near-obsession as Americans wonder whether the oceans are safe for recreation and sport. But to scientists who study sharks and their occasionally tragic interactions with humans, the numbers of shark attacks and fatalities appear well within the range of the normal. What is out of the ordinary is the amount of attention being paid to them.... A person is 30 times more likely to be struck by lightning than bitten by a shark.[1]

In the late 1980s, the Environmental Protection Agency embarked on an ambitious project, designed to compare the views of "the public" and "EPA experts" on the seriousness of environmental problems.[2] The project revealed some striking anomalies, for the two groups sharply diverged on some crucial issues.

With respect to health risks, the public's top concerns included radioactive waste, radiation from nuclear accidents, industrial pollution of waterways, and hazardous waste sites. But in the view of EPA experts, not one of these problems deserved a "high" level of concern. Two of the public's top concerns (nuclear accident radiation and radioactive waste) were not even ranked by EPA experts. Of health risks considered by the public, the very lowest ranked were indoor air pollution and indoor radon – both ranked high by experts. EPA concluded that there was a remarkable disparity between the views of the public and the views of its own experts. It also noted, with evident concern, that EPA policies and appropriations seemed to reflect the public's preoccupations, not its own.

[1] Stevenson Swanson, High-profile attacks feed shark fears, experts say, Chicago Tribune, September 5, 2001, at pp. I, 20.
[2] Leslie Roberts, Counting on Science at EPA, 249 Science 616 (1990).

53

With respect to risks, the persistent split between experts and ordinary people raises some of the most interesting problems in all of social science. For purposes of understanding these disputes, we might distinguish between two approaches: the *technocratic* and the *populist*. Good technocrats tend to think that ordinary people are frequently ill-informed and that the task of regulators is to follow science, not popular opinion.[3] On the technocratic view, the central question is what the facts really show, and when people are mistaken on that point, they should be educated so that they do not persist in their errors. Of course, technocrats acknowledge that science will often leave gaps. They know that the proper course of action cannot be determined by science alone. But they urge that facts are often the key issue, and that when they are, government should follow the evidence, rather than public beliefs. Technocrats also insist that when people know the facts, they will, much of the time, have a clear sense of what to do.

For their part, populists tend to distrust experts and to think that in a democracy, government should follow the will of the citizenry rather than a self-appointed technocratic elite.[4] On this view, what matters, for law and policy, is what people actually fear, not what scientists, with their own, inevitably fallible judgments, urge society to do. Populists insist that the very characterization of risks involves no simple "fact," but a host of normative judgments. Experts look at the number of fatalities involved, but they could as easily choose alternative measures, such as the number of life-years at risk, or the percentage of people at risk, or the percentage of the exposed population at risk. In the populist view, risks do not exist "out there," and any judgment about risk is subjective rather than objective in character. If expert judgments are inevitably value judgments, it seems only sensible to use popular opinion as a central ingredient in law and policy. For populists, ordinary intuitions have normative force and deserve to count in the democratic arena.

To make progress on the disagreement, it would be very valuable to have a clearer sense of what, exactly, accounts for the split between experts and ordinary people. Is one or another group biased? Are intuitions likely, as I have suggested thus far, to reflect mistaken judgments of fact, or instead worthy judgments of value? Once we answer these questions, there will remain other problems, raising questions about what should be done in the face of the relevant divisions. Perhaps

---

[3]   This view is represented, in various ways, by Stephen Breyer, supra note 8 in Chapter 2; Howard Margolis, Dealing with Risk: Why the Public and the Experts Disagree on Environmental Issues (Chicago: Univ. Chicago Press, 1997).

[4]   This view is represented in Elizabeth Anderson, Value in Ethics and Economics (Cambridge, Mass.: Harvard Univ. Press, 1993); Lisa Heinzerling Political Science, 62 U. Chi. L. Rev. 449 (1995) (reviewing Stephen Breyer, Breaking the Vicious Circle (1995)).

what matters is not whether people are right on the facts, but whether they are frightened. Perhaps ordinary people have a kind of "thick" rationality, as worthy in its own way as that of experts. Certainly experts can have their own biases and agendas. Perhaps the real issue is how to increase the public's role in risk regulation so that government will respond to their concerns.

As a result of some influential studies, it has become commonplace to think that, in an important sense, experts are wrong and ordinary people are right. On this view, ordinary people have a kind of "rival rationality" that is far "richer," and better, than the rationality of experts.[5] With respect to risks, people's "rival rationality" makes good sense of their judgments. When people are especially concerned about pesticides, and not so much concerned about indoor air pollution, it is because they make qualitative judgments about diverse risks. These qualitative judgments, it is said, deserve respect.

I believe that this common view is too simple. When they disagree, experts are generally right, and ordinary people are generally wrong. Certainly experts are more often right than ordinary people are. When ordinary people make mistakes, it is usually for three now-familiar reasons: They rely on mental shortcuts; they are subject to social influences that led them astray; and they neglect tradeoffs. As a general rule, people often want to reduce the most serious risks, where seriousness is measured statistically, but they do not know how to do that. A rapid, intuitive judgment operates as a substitute for the more careful inquiry.

In this chapter I have two goals. The first is to argue that ordinary people do not, in general, have a richer rationality and to explain why expert judgments are far more likely to be right. The second goal, in some tension with the first, is to show that legitimate judgments of value can lead government to be concerned not only with statistics, but also with whether the risks at issue are especially hard to avoid, accompanied by special pain and suffering, and unfairly distributed. Of course, the full story is more qualified and complicated than this. To understand it, we need to back up a bit.

STATISTICS, BUT BEYOND STATISTICS

There are qualitative differences among statistically identical risks. People often say they have a special fear of certain deaths, including those from cancer and AIDS. Many people insist that it is best to die quickly, quietly, and in one's sleep at night. All deaths are bad. But some deaths seem worse than others.

Ideas of this kind do help account for the disparities in government's treatment of different risks. People are not always subject to heuristics that lead

---

[5] This view plays a large role in Paul Slovic, supra note 12 in Chapter 2; for discussion, see Cass R. Sunstein, The Laws of Fear, 113 Harv. L. Rev. 1119 (2002).

them to error or to social influences that make otherwise sensible people go wrong. Tradeoff neglect is not always what is at issue. When ordinary people disagree with experts, it is sometimes because of their values, not because of less expertise. People's beliefs about the special badness of certain deaths have consequences for selection of consumer products, occupational choice, style of life, and government regulation. If deaths from automobile accidents involve minimal suffering, and elicit relatively little public concern, manufacturers and regulators will be under correspondingly less intense pressure to make cars safe. If, by contrast, AIDS deaths, and deaths from airplane accidents, are especially abhorrent, we can predict a strong demand for AIDS prevention programs and for regulation of airlines. And if some risks and some deaths are particularly bad, government should devote additional resources to preventing them.

Ordinary people are indeed concerned with "qualitative" factors aggravating certain deaths, and in this chapter, I will show how this concern helps explain some apparent anomalies in current government regulation. More particularly, I argue that four sources of public concern do and should play a role in regulatory policy: (1) risks accompanied by unusual pain and suffering, (2) risks concentrated among socially disadvantaged groups, (3) risks that are hard to avoid except at high cost, and (4) risks that produce unusually high externalities, in the form of "ripple effects" on people not directly involved. But I also believe that the public concern reflects serious confusions, and that when ordinary people disagree with experts, it is often because ordinary people are confused. I try to suggest an approach to risk reduction that could overcome the confusion, and reflect a sound understanding of the facts, while also incorporating judgments of value that deserve respect.

DIFFERENT DEATHS, DIFFERENT PREFERENCES AND JUDGMENTS

There is considerable evidence that when voting, responding to questions, or engaging in ordinary behavior in the marketplace, people evaluate different deaths differently. Many studies suggest that people are especially averse to some risks and some kinds of death.

One such study finds that Americans are willing to pay significantly more to contribute to lowering the risks of cancer than they are willing to contribute to lowering other risks of death.[6] In terms of willingness to pay, cancer ranks first, followed in order by automobile accidents, home fires, and aviation. A national survey in England offers suggestive evidence on how people compare

---

[6] Ian Savage, An Empirical Investigation into the Effect of Psychological Perceptions on the Willingness to Pay to Reduce Risk, 6 J. Risk & Uncertainty 75 (1993).

Table 3.1 Ratings of serious conditions
by cause of death

Cause of Death	% Ranking Disutility Highest
Motor accidents	11
Heart disease	13
Cancer	76

Table 3.2 Mortality values by cause of death

Category (per statistical life)	Value Estimates (million $),		
	Low	Medium	High
Unforeseen instant death	1	2	5
Asthma/bronchitis	1.3	2.5	5.5
Heart disease	1.25	2.75	6
Emphysema	1.4	3.5	9
Lung cancer	1.5	4	9.5

deaths from cancer, heart disease, and motor vehicle accidents.[7] People were asked whether they would prefer to save 100 lives from one or another of these three causes. Nearly three-quarters of people ranked a cancer death as worse than a death from heart disease or motor vehicle accidents. Consider the summary in Table 3.1. The authors conclude that people "would be willing to pay very substantial sums to avoid the protracted period of physical and psychological pain prior to cancer death."[8]

Other studies suggest that people are willing to pay nearly twice as much to reduce heart disease deaths as motor vehicle deaths, and that they are willing to pay nearly three times as much to prevent a death from cancer as a death from motor vehicle accidents.[9] Private willingness to pay to avert cancer deaths has been found to be systematically higher than private willingness to pay to avert unforeseen instant deaths. More specifically, consider the results in Table 3.2.[10]

---

[7] M. W. Jones-Lee, M. Hammerton & P. R. Phillips, The Value of Safety: Results of a National Sample Survey, 95 Econ. J. 49 (1985).

[8] Id. at 68.

[9] George Tolley, Donald Kenkel & Robert Fabian, Valuing Health for Policy 339 (Chicago: Univ. Chicago Press, 1995).

[10] Id. at 342.

These findings strongly suggest that people view some deaths as worse than others, but they should be taken with many grains of salt. It is not clear that people in good health have adequate information from which to assess deaths from diverse causes. The notion of a "cancer death" may produce irrational and ill-considered fear – perhaps because people call to mind especially stressful periods of pain and suffering that are not representative (the availability heuristic again), or perhaps because those incidents may assume undue salience, dwarfing the very fact of death itself. In answering survey questions, people have a great deal of difficulty in coming up with reliable dollar amounts to capture their willingness to pay to reduce certain risks. I will return to these points later.

For more subtle evidence, consider a study of 1,000 randomly chosen American citizens, revealing significant differences in peoples' preferences among programs that would save exactly the same number of lives at exactly the same cost.[11] Thus, for example, 55% of respondents chose a program controlling industrial air pollution over one involving smoking education; 54% chose one controlling auto emissions over one involving colon cancer screening; 63% chose one involving industrial air pollution over one involving pneumonia vaccination; 65% chose a smoking ban in the workplace over controls on radon in homes; and 72% chose a program banning pesticides in fruit over one regulating radon in homes. Definite patterns emerge from these choices. Important variables in the disparity appear to be (a) the ease with which the risk can be avoided and (b) the extent to which beneficiaries of the program were to blame for their deaths. These are the very factors that are said to show that people have a "richer rationality" than experts, a possibility to which I now turn.

RICHER RATIONALITY?

Consider, on the basis of the foregoing evidence, a hypothesis. In evaluating risks. experts tend to focus on numbers – on the aggregate lives or life-years at stake. But ordinary people are much more subtle. They look at a range of more qualitative variables. They care not simply about number of lives at risk but also about whether the risk is equitably distributed, potentially catastrophic, controllable, voluntarily incurred, and so forth. On this view, ordinary people have a "richer" conception of rationality. According to the influential psychologist Paul Slovic, people's "basic conceptualization of risk is much richer than that of experts and reflects legitimate concerns that are typically omitted from expert risk

[11] Maureen Cropper & Uma Subramanian, Public Choice Between Lifesaving Programs 6 (World Bank Policy Research Working Paper 1497, 1995).

Table 3.3 Qualitative factors affecting risk judgments

Factors	Aggravating	Mitigating
Familiarity	New	Old
Personal control	Uncontrollable	Controllable
Voluntariness	Involuntary	Voluntary
Media attention	Focused on by media	Ignored by media
Equity	Unfairly distributed	Fairly distributed
Children	Children at special risk	Children not at risk
Future generations	At risk	Not at risk
Reversibility	Irreversible	Reversible
Dreadedness	Especially dreaded	Not especially dreaded
Identifiability of victims	Victims known	Victims not identifiable
Accompanying benefits	Benefits clear	Benefits not visible
Human or natural origin	Human origin	Created by nature
Trust in applicable institutions	Lack of trust	Good deal of trust
Timing of effects	Delayed	Immediate
Understanding	Meachanisms or process not understood	Mechanism or process understood
Past history	Major or minor accidents	No past accidents

assessments."[12] This is the basis for the claim that experts and ordinary people display "rival rationalities" and that "each side must respect the insights and intelligence of the other."

Table 3.3 provides a compilation of factors that affect risk judgments.[13] From this table, it might be suggested that experts are obtuse, at least insofar as they focus exclusively on lives or life-years at stake. We might well conclude that a sensible person would be alert not just to statistics but to a wide range of other variables as well. The effort to vindicate ordinary judgments, by reference to considerations of this sort, is part of a long tradition – one that is skeptical of scientists and technocrats and that insists that ordinary understandings have a kind of complexity and denseness that specialists lack.

There is much wisdom in the tradition, and indeed the "richer rationality" view has started to become highly influential, not least within the federal government (see Chapter 7, which notes the EPA's consideration of factors of this kind). And in some ways, it is clearly correct. The risks associated with voluntary activities (skiing, horseback riding) receive less public concern than statistically smaller risks from involuntary activities (food preservatives, pesticides, herbicides, certain forms of air pollution). But in the context of risks, I believe

---

[12] Slovic, supra note 12 in Chapter 2, p. 238.

[13] Margolis, supra note 3 in this chapter, provides an overview.

that the richer rationality claim is overstated. To be sure, some of these factors do justify special concern with some risks. But there is no "rival rationality" in the minds of ordinary people.

Offhand, it should be readily apparent that some of these factors are not at all helpful in supporting the idea that people have different values from experts. In several cases, the factor is simply an indicator that the risk is statistically large. Media attention, for example, is a heuristic for determining whether the problem is serious. If people are especially concerned about risks that preoccupy the media, it is probably because what concerns the media is likely, other things being equal, to be worthy of concern. Especially in light of the availability heuristic and social influences, ordinary people, trying to reduce large risks, will naturally be concerned about hazards that are receiving attention from newspapers and television stations. The point helps explain why people have sometimes been excessively fearful of shark attacks, air travel, and new diseases. The same point also helps explain why different cultures, and different subcultures, are frightened of different things: They hear, from relevant media, different reports of what is dangerous.

Past history also works as a heuristic. What has happened before is a (rough) proxy for what will happen again. Sensible people who want to reduce large risks, and to ignore tiny ones, will care about history. Similar things can be said about trust. If people do not trust an institution's assurances, they are thinking that the risk is more serious than they are being told. Nor is any special puzzle posed by the fact that public concern is heightened when children and future generations are at risk. When this is so, more life-years are at stake, and in the case of future generations, more lives. Of course, people want to save more lives, and more life-years, rather than fewer. On all these counts, experts and ordinary people seem to be on exactly the same page – with the qualification that ordinary people sometimes use simplifying devices, such as media attention, to test whether a risk is really large or small.

But some of these factors do seem to suggest that people are not concerned only with numbers of lives at stake. For example, deaths that are particularly "dreaded" may have aggravating characteristics, to which ordinary people are alert but which experts neglect. The notions of voluntariness and control may also be relevant insofar as they suggest that some risks are more freely run, and therefore deserving of less public concern.

DO THE QUALITATIVE FACTORS ACTUALLY EXPLAIN EVALUATIONS? A CAUTIONARY NOTE

Notwithstanding these points, I want to question the claim that qualitative factors of this kind explain all or even much of people's disagreement with experts. In brief, I will suggest that people's judgments are based on some combination of an affective judgment and a rapid, largely intuitive assessment of the relevant costs and benefits. Of course, it would be desirable to be able to explain the ingredients of the affective judgment itself. I will not be able to do that here. But I will suggest that the affective judgment is based in part on an intuitive, uninformed statistical assessment, involving both the benefits and the risks associated with products and activities; and I will mention some evidence that supports that suggestion. The upshot is that experts are more likely to be right than are ordinary people.

Let us look at the evidence first. How do we know that ordinary people think that these qualitative factors are so important? The answer is *not* that people spontaneously point to such factors in explaining their assessments of risk. We do not have data to suggest that ordinary people have an accurate sense of the number of lives at stake, and that their assessments stem from qualitative judgments. Instead the answer is that experimenters *expressly* identify these factors and set them before experimental subjects, asking people to rate certain risks along specific dimensions, including their catastrophic potential, their dreadedness, their threat to future generations, their controllability, and so forth. Is it at all surprising, or even informative, that the risks that people most fear tend to be rated most severely along these dimensions?

Consider the fact that in one study, the most feared risks include DDT, pesticides, herbicides, and smoking, whereas X-rays, microwave ovens, nonnuclear electric power, marijuana, and sunbathing are ranked far lower.[14] The most feared risks do worse, along several of the "qualitative" dimensions, than those risks that are least feared. But this finding does not establish that the qualitative dimensions are the *grounds* for people's rankings of these risks. People's evaluations of risks might well be explained by their general "affect" toward the product or activity in question (see Chapter 2). When people say that they fear DDT and pesticides, but do not fear microwave ovens or sunbathing, it is probably because they have a rapid, intuitive response to these sources of risk, producing fear in some cases but not in others. If so, people are not making some richly rational judgment that some of these risks are controllable and others not, or that some of the relevant risks are inequitably distributed.

It remains to explain the existence of a good or bad "affect." With respect to most risks, any affective response is mediated by judgments. I believe that for most people, reactions to risks are a product of a rapid, largely intuitive assessment, not based on a careful sorting of the consequences of exposure. Of course that assessment depends in significant part on what concerns experts, the

[14] See id.

61

statistical magnitude of the risk at issue. A rough sense of the magnitude of the risk certainly plays a role in producing affect. And indeed nothing in the data is inconsistent with the possibility that people fear certain risks because they have a general impression that they are statistically large, and that this fear helps to explain their rankings. If so, people will naturally rank the risks they most fear as worse, on the qualitative dimensions, than risks that they fear least. Notice that on this view, people's rankings on the qualitative judgments are not the reason for their relative rankings of risk. On the contrary, their general impression of statistical magnitude is doing most of the work. The rankings on the qualitative dimensions are explained by, and do not themselves explain, people's concern about the large statistical risks associated with certain products and practices. To the extent that people are not thinking much about statistics, it is reasonable to think that their overall affective response helps explain their judgments on all or almost all of the qualitative dimensions. Recall that people's judgments about risks and benefits tend to be inversely related (see Chapter 2), and hence when people think something is dangerous, they believe that it has low benefits too – a finding that testifies to the role of affect in producing judgments. There is no reason to doubt that affect helps explain qualitative judgments as well.

Certainly it is puzzling to find that people treat as quite serious dangers that are microscopically small as a statistical matter, while risks that are statistically much larger are treated as "just a part of life." No doubt it is *possible* that people's judgments about risk severity are a product of some of the more qualitative considerations listed in Table 3.3. But it is also possible that an apparently rich judgment that a certain risk is severe, or not severe, depends not on well-considered judgments of value, but instead on a rapid intuitive judgment, on a failure to see that tradeoffs are inevitably being made, on heuristic devices that are not well-adapted to the particular context, or instead on a range of confusing or confused ideas that people cannot fully articulate. When people say, for example, that the risk of nuclear power is very serious, they might be responding to their intense visceral concern. The affect associated with nuclear power is, for many people, quite negative, and that affect operates as a heuristic for a judgment of the seriousness of the risk.

As I have said, the affect, and the judgment, might well be based, at least in part, on (uninformed) statistical judgments about likely lives at risk and on people's failure to see (as they do in other contexts) that that risk is accompanied by a range of social benefits. In fact people seem to think that both nuclear power and pesticides have few benefits, and only costs.[15] I have mentioned evidence that when people are shown that some product or activity has high benefits,

---

[15] See Alhakami & Slovic, supra note 22 in Chapter 2, at 1085.

they tend to think that it poses lower risks than they previously thought; and when told that some product or activity poses high risks, they tend to think that it offers lower benefits than they previously thought.[16] This evidence strongly supports the view that affect is produced by rapid assessments of both risks and benefits because changes on either side of the equation tends to change affect, too.

Consider some other examples. It is clear that the risk of cancer death from the use of X-ray technology does not now produce an intense public outcry, probably because people know that the technology contains benefits as well. The example shows that it is false to say that cancer-related risks always produce intense public concern. The same is true for the use of cell phones as a possible cause of cancer – probably because people really do not want to ban the use of cell phones, which have obvious benefits, and hence will require strong evidence of harm. Ordinary people are not greatly exercised about the risks of automobile accidents. Here there are no visceral judgments of great concern, partly because people are well aware that automobile travel produces high benefits as well as costs.

I suggest that, in many cases, people's judgment that a certain risk is unusually bad is not a rich qualitative assessment but is based on some combination of affect, rooted partly in an unreliable intuition about the likely *facts*. The intuition is rapid, statistically ungrounded, and often not even conscious. When, for example, nuclear power "codes" as a serious risk, this is often because the benefits are off the viewscreen, and the potential for catastrophe looms large, perhaps because of heuristic devices such as availability. True, people frequently say, when prompted to do so, that the risks about which they are most concerned are "involuntary," or "uncontrollable." But it is important to emphasize here that when people are asked to say *why* they believe that some risk is especially bad, their answers may not truly explain their beliefs, but instead represent post hoc rationalizations of more visceral judgments (based partly on faulty quantitative assessments).[17] In other words, the reasons given may not actually lie behind the judgments; people are not always good at giving accounts of what underlies their judgments.

All this raises the possibility that people's references to "control" and "involuntariness" do not explain the actual basis of their judgments. I believe that people are really concerned, most of the time, with the magnitude of the risk – and that ideas like control and voluntariness, although relevant, do not explain much about the difference between ordinary people and experts.

[16] See Slovic, supra note 12 in Chapter 2, pp. 421–6.

[17] Margolis, supra note 3 in this chapter.

A MIXED VERDICT

I have been claiming, not that qualitative factors are irrelevant to ordinary perceptions of risk, but that the same evidence said to support "rival rationality" might reflect simple errors of fact. An interesting way to test my claims would be to see whether people are able to generate statistically accurate judgments about certain risks. When specifically asked about the number of expected deaths from various sources, do people make roughly the same judgments that experts do? If so, then it might indeed be that when ordinary people diverge from experts, it is because of the qualitative factors. But if ordinary people err in estimating the number of lives at risk, and if their perceptions of risk severity are correlated with their estimates, then their errors might well explain the divergences. Actually there is much evidence on this point.[18] On the purely factual issues, ordinary people make systematic mistakes.[19]

Where does this leave us? Many of the disagreements between experts and ordinary people stem from the fact that experts have more information and are also prepared to look at the benefits as well as the risks associated with controversial products and activities. To the extent that experts focus *only* on the number of lives at stake, they are genuinely obtuse. It is reasonable to devote special attention to dangers that are hard to avoid, or accompanied by special suffering, or faced principally by children. But there is no "rival rationality" in taking these factors into account. On the positive side, what is needed is more empirical work to determine the extent to which ordinary risk perceptions are based on errors or instead on values. On the normative side, we need to think more clearly about the nature of concepts like "dread," "involuntary," and "uncontrollable." With respect to policy, what is needed is incorporation of people's values, to the extent that they can survive a process of reflection. Let us now turn to that issue.

DELIBERATIVE DEMOCRACY

By itself the fact that people perceive certain risks and deaths as especially bad should not be decisive for purposes of law and policy. Suppose, for example, that ordinary judgments stem from heuristic devices that produce predictable factual mistakes, so that both private behavior and the demand for regulatory protection are affected. Certainly government should not incorporate judgments based on mistakes. The appropriate response is not to capitulate but to inform people

[18] Slovic, supra note 12 in Chapter 2, at 105–7.

[19] W. Kip Viscusi, Jurors, Judges, and the Mistreatment of Risk by the Courts, 30 J. Legal Stud. 107, 130–2 (2001).

of the real facts. This general point suggests that it is important to examine not simply what deaths people especially abhor, but also *why* those deaths are abhorrent and whether the underlying reasons can survive scrutiny. Along with many others, the American political system aspires to be a deliberative democracy, in which citizen preferences are supposed to be subject to a process of reflection. They are not to be automatically translated into law.

Thus the question becomes whether citizen judgments that certain deaths are especially bad can survive a process of reflection. My conclusion is that, understood in a certain way, the special concerns about dreaded deaths and unfairly distributed deaths are fully reasonable and deserve a role in policy. But the special concerns about deaths stemming from involuntarily run and uncontrollable risks raise many hard questions. I do not believe that those concerns justify according additional concern to deaths that "code" as a product of involuntary or uncontrollable risks. At most, they suggest that government might spend more resources on deaths where the cost of risk-avoidance is especially high and devote less attention to deaths where the cost of risk-avoidance is especially low. Let us now turn to some details.

DREAD

Some risks are said to be "dreaded," whereas other risks are not. Deaths from cancer and AIDS seem particularly dreaded, and it is often said that the risk of such deaths deserves special attention. But what does this mean? In the abstract, to say that a risk is dreaded seems to say that people fear it, which suggests that the idea of dread is just a synonym for perception of risk, not an explanation for it. If so, it is no surprise that there is a correlation between risks perceived as serious and risks deemed to be dreaded. (Is it surprising that people are afraid of things that they find frightening?) It is even possible that when people say that a risk is dreaded, what they mean, in part, is that the risk is large in magnitude. People do not dread being attacked by unicorns or Martians. But they do dread cancer, partly because the risk of getting cancer is not so low.

If progress is to be made here, perhaps we can assume that a dreaded risk is one that is accompanied by significant pain and suffering before death. This is certainly an intelligible idea. The underlying point is probably that the relevant deaths are especially grueling; hence, there is a kind of "pain and suffering premium" — not merely a life lost, but an antecedent period of intense emotional and physical difficulty as well. This period of intense difficulty might be especially difficult for those with the illness and for friends and family members as well. Sudden, unanticipated deaths can be dreaded, too — consider the extremely unpleasant idea of dying in an airplane crash. But the dread here stems from some factor (perhaps terror) different from and much shorter than the extended period of suffering that precedes some deaths. Thus we might conclude that dreaded deaths deserve special attention in accordance with the degree of suffering that precedes them.

Deaths preceded by pain and suffering do seem to deserve extra attention. But some qualifications are necessary. First, people can adapt to suffering much better than they think they can. Recent work in psychology has shown that people often fear certain risks before the fact, but when those risks come to fruition, they are able to adapt much better than they believed possible, and the experience is less bad than they anticipated.[20] Notably, people think that they will respond much more negatively to a positive result for HIV than they do in fact.[21] Thus people may dread certain diseases more than they "should" in the sense that the lived experience of the disease is less horrible than was thought before the fact. If true, this point makes it necessary at least to question whether before-the-fact fear justifies the degree of attention that uninformed people seek from government, if after-the-fact adaptation is possible.

Second, some pain and suffering may well be an inevitable part of a desirable period in which people, including families, can plan and adapt themselves to the fact of death and achieve a measure of peace with it. On this count, a sudden unanticipated death may be worse. The desirable features of a death that is not sudden, and for which planning becomes possible, may not register when people are asked, in surveys, to compare an automobile death with a cancer death.

Third, it seems sensible to say that the period of pain and suffering that precedes death ought – in all but the most unusual cases – to be far less important, relatively speaking, than the fact of death itself. Thus something appears to have gone wrong if people say that they would like to devote (say) three times as much to preventing cancer deaths as they would like to devote to preventing deaths from automobile accidents. Maybe they are focusing too intensely on certain vivid instances of intense suffering. Maybe the valuation would not survive a modest degree of information and critical reflection. Perhaps the fact that the relevant scale is unbounded produces distortions in dollars.

These points suggest the possibility of relying not on responses to survey questions, and perhaps not even on market behavior, but instead on a kind

---

[20] Daniel Kahneman, New Challenges to the Rationality Assumption, in The Rational Foundations of Economic Behaviour, Kenneth Arrow et al., eds. (New York: St. Martin's Press, 1996); Daniel Kahneman, Peter Wakker & Rakesh Sarin, Back to Bentham? Explorations of Experienced Utility, Q. J. Econ. 375 (1997).

[21] See E. M. Sieff, Robyn Dawes & George Loewenstein, Anticipated Versus Actual Reaction to HIV Test Results, 112 Am. J. Psych. 297 (1999).

of "deliberative opinion poll" that seeks to inform answers and to allow an exchange of opinion.[22] On this view, it is important not to ask people to offer their quick, likely uninformed reactions to hypothetical questions (how much worse is death from cancer than death from a heart attack?), but instead to offer underlying facts and to take into account informed answers. Much better responses might be expected after people are given a solid basis for assessing the relevant deaths, for making comparisons, and for putting the period that precedes death in context with the death itself.

VOLUNTARINESS

People seem to perceive voluntarily incurred risks as less troublesome than involuntarily incurred risks. Consider diverse public reactions to airplane crashes and automobile crashes. Or consider the fact that tobacco is by far the largest source of preventable deaths in the United States, producing more than 400,000 fatalities each year. Reduction of smoking is of course a priority, but it is not an especially high one in light of the enormous risks; why do we not devote much more of our regulatory efforts to reducing smoking? The reason seems to lie in a judgment that smoking is a voluntary activity and hence the resulting deaths are less troublesome than other sorts of deaths. Here people have voluntarily assumed the relevant risks.

PUZZLES: HIGH COST OF AVOIDANCE RATHER THAN INVOLUNTARINESS?

There are many puzzles here. The most important problem is that it is not simple to know when a risk is voluntarily incurred. "Voluntariness" may be entirely absent in the case of an unforeseeable collision with an asteroid; but voluntariness is not, in the cases under consideration, an all-or-nothing matter. Instead, it is a matter of degree. There is no on–off switch to distinguish between voluntary and involuntary exposure to risks.

Return to the conventional thought that airplane crashes are "involuntary" and automobile crashes more "voluntary." Does this thought make any sense? Actually it would be possible to see the risks from air travel as voluntarily run; people have a choice about whether to fly, and when they do fly, they pay a certain amount for a certain package, including risks of various sorts. The same is true of automobile safety. In both cases, people make a range of voluntary choices, including the choice of whether and how to travel, and of the amount to pay for additional safety. Why are the risks from cars more voluntary?

---

[22] See James Fishkin, The Voice of the People (New Haven, Conn.: Yale Univ. Press, 1995).

Maybe people are responding to the perceived fact that they have no control over the pilot's behavior, whereas they have considerable control over automobile safety because they are themselves drivers. In fact drivers are pervasively (and not rationally) optimistic about the risks that they face; about 90 percent of drivers think that they are safer than the average driver and less likely to be involved in accidents.[23] But drivers do not have as much control as they think; many people injured in automobile accidents are not at fault, and thus along the dimension of voluntariness there is hardly a crisp distinction between air travel and automobile travel. Nor is airline safety entirely out of people's control. Airlines respond to market forces, including the market for safety, and of course you can always refuse to fly. The difference between the two risks is hardly so categorical as to justify an assessment that they fall on poles of some voluntariness–involuntariness divide. Indeed, it is not clear even what is meant by the suggestion that one is voluntary and the other is not. Something else appears to underlie that suggestion.

I think that what is true for the division between flying and driving is true for many oppositions between risks that are voluntarily and involuntarily run. By reframing the situation and by broadening our viewscreen, we can see apparently involuntarily incurred risks as a product of perfectly free choices. People choose to live in places with bad air quality; they choose to live in high-crime areas; they voluntarily take jobs where the risks are high. In some cases, but not in others, people will fail to reframe. What is going on here?

Three Cases

To shed some light on the issue, let us consider three classes of cases. First, consider the question whether workers exposed to cancer risks are voluntarily or involuntarily so exposed. If workers do not know about such risks – if they lack relevant information – we seem to have an easy case of involuntariness. Thus it makes sense to say that risks are run involuntarily when the people running them do not know about them. Lack of adequate information provides a perfectly legitimate case for a judgment of involuntary exposure to risk. But of course information itself can be obtained at some cost, pecuniary or otherwise. If people do not have information, they have chosen, in a sense, not to do so. (Of course, their choices might be constrained in multiple ways, as through a lack of education.) We are thus dealing, in cases of this kind, with high costs of risk avoidance – in the distinctive form of high costs of acquiring relevant information.

[23] See Shelley Taylor, Positive Illusions: Creative Self-Deception and the Healthy Mind 10 (New York: Basic Books, 1993).

Second, suppose that people who are exposed to a certain risk are aware of the risk but are not in a contractual relation with the risk-producer. Many victims of pollution are in this position; recall that in surveys, air pollution is a particular source of public concern. People in Los Angeles may well know that they face high levels of smog. Are they exposed involuntarily? If we conclude that they are, we might mean that a risk is incurred involuntarily when and in the sense that it is typically very expensive for people to avoid it – and when and in the sense that someone else can reduce the risks more cheaply. Here a claim that the risk is faced "involuntarily" may mean that those who "run" the risk can reduce it only at very high cost, at least compared to those who "produce" the risk. Or it is possible that we mean that on nonutilitarian grounds, the people exposed to the risk have a moral entitlement to be free from it, at least if they have not explicitly agreed to it.

But turn now to a third class of cases, involving a wage package or contract that does include compensation for the relevant risks. A worker might, for example, receive a higher salary just because the job contains risks. Assuming that point, we might want to distinguish between two different possibilities. In the case of a high-level scientist, knowledgeable about the relevant risks and involved in work that he finds rewarding, people may well conclude that we have an instance of voluntariness. (In the same category can be found the case of an astronaut.) But people might not say the same about a low-level worker who does not like his work at all. What distinguishes the two cases? If knowledge is present, or if the compensation package includes payment for the relevant risk, it is not clear how the two differ. The underlying judgment must be that the compensation for the risk is inadequate, perhaps because social inequality has produced a wage package that seems unfair even if voluntarily chosen by the parties. When we say that the risk is not voluntarily run, we must mean that people do not have adequate options from which to make a truly free choice.

From this discussion it seems reasonable to speculate that any judgment that a risk is run "involuntarily" is probably based on (1) a lack of knowledge of the risk, or, more accurately, high costs of obtaining information about the risk; (2) a belief that information to one side, it would be very costly for people to avoid the risk; or (3) a belief that people who run the risk lack enough options to do so freely, notwithstanding their belief that the contract is in some sense worth signing. What emerges is a simple point. The question whether a risk is run voluntarily or not is often not a categorical one but instead a question of degree – associated with information cost, risk-reduction cost, and the existence or not of accompanying benefits. Of course there are interesting background questions about why and when a risk "codes" as voluntary or involuntary; undoubtedly the answer depends a great deal on heuristic devices and selective attention.

WHY THE RISK IS INCURRED AND PROBLEMS
OF RESPONSIBILITY AND BLAME

Risks might seem voluntarily run when people do not approve of the *reason* that people are running those risks and involuntarily run when people think that the reason for which the risk is run is laudable. It is predictable that people will not want to pour enormous taxpayer resources into lowering the risks associated with sky-diving, even if the dollars/life-years saved ratio is quite good. By contrast, it is doubtful that people think that it is wrong to spend enormous resources on the prevention of death from childbirth or being a police officer, even though the decision to have a child is usually voluntary, and so too with the decision to become a police officer.

People might reasonably think that when the appeal or purpose of the activity is associated with its very riskiness, resources should not be devoted to risk reduction. At least this is plausible when the risk is an independent good or part of the benefit of the activity. And it is easy to imagine a belief that some activities – unsafe sex, cigarette smoking – are like the sky-diving case, perhaps because the risk is sometimes part of the benefit, perhaps because the risks are not incurred for a purpose that observers find worthy or valuable.

It might seem that this consideration – the reason that the risk is incurred – overlaps with or is even identical to the question whether there are high costs of risk avoidance. But on reflection the two ideas are hardly the same. It may well be that failing to sky-dive, or sky-diving with some safety-increasing technology, really would impose high costs on sky-divers. There seems to be an objective judgment, not necessarily connected with subjective costs, when it is claimed that some risks are voluntary, and deserve less attention, because they are run for inadequate purposes.

Relatedly, airplane accidents may seem different from automobile accidents not because the former are less voluntary, and not because of diverse costs of risk avoidance, but because the victims of airplane accidents are less blameworthy than the victims of automobile accidents, in the sense that the death is not a product of their own negligence or misconduct. In the case of an airplane disaster, weather conditions, mechanical failure, or pilot error are likely causes; in the case of an automobile accident, it is more likely (though not of course certain) that the victim could have avoided death through more careful driving. The point is crude, since many victims of automobile accidents are not drivers, and many drivers in accidents do not behave negligently. But the perceived difference, in a significant number of cases, may underlie an apparent judgment of "voluntariness" that is really a judgment about responsibility and blameworthiness.

UNDERLYING QUESTIONS AND ASSUMPTION OF RISK

We might therefore conclude that whether a risk qualifies as involuntary raises many of the questions raised by the question whether government should try to regulate the market at all. A risk might be characterized as involuntarily run for the following reasons:

1. because affected people lack relevant information;
2. because the risks are imposed on third parties;
3. because the costs of bargaining are high;
4. because some motivational or cognitive problem makes it hard for people to reduce risks through bargaining.

These of course are among the conventional grounds for risk regulation in the first instance. When a risk seems voluntary, and not worthy of substantial regulatory resources, the term "voluntary" serves as a placeholder for an argument that there is no sufficient ground for government action because the accompanying benefits are high or the risk-reduction costs are low, and because market arrangements take adequate account of these facts.

Should voluntarily run risks receive no governmental attention on the ground that the relevant people are fully informed and have already received compensation? Let us suppose that a risk is incurred voluntarily when an informed person decided to incur it in light of its costs and benefits. Suppose, for example, that someone freely purchases a small car with fewer safety features or decides to become a boxer, an astronaut, or a police officer in a dangerous neighborhood. If a death results from such a choice, it might seem that the chooser has no legitimate ground for complaint. In a sense, there has been compensation for the risk. But even in such cases, it is far from clear that government lacks a role. If government can reduce a serious risk at low cost, and thus eliminate deaths, it should do so even if there was ex ante compensation for the relevant risk.

There is a general point here. Sometimes people confuse two quite different questions: (1) Should people be banned from running a certain risk, when they have run that risk voluntarily? (2) Should government attempt to reduce a certain risk, when people have run that risk voluntarily? A negative answer to question (1) does not answer question (2).

From this point, we should conclude that for purposes of policy and law, a judgment that a risk is "voluntary" should not be decisive. A better understanding of what factors underlie and support that judgment should be used for purposes of regulatory policy. The simplest lesson is that we might give special attention to risks when those in danger lack relevant information or when the costs of risk avoidance are especially high – or give less attention to risks when those in danger have the information and when the costs of risk avoidance are low.

CONTROL

People find uncontrollable risks especially unacceptable. Automobile accidents may seem less troublesome than airline disasters partly for this reason. But what does it mean to say that a risk is "uncontrollable"?

The reference to control is probably based above all on the perceived possibility of avoiding death altogether though one's own acts. But this idea links control with voluntariness, and it should be clear from the previous discussion that the question is not whether risks can be controlled, but how difficult or expensive it is for individuals to control them. People can control airplane-related risks by refusing to fly; people can control risks from coal-fired power plants by living in areas served by solar energy. The question is not whether a risk can be controlled or not, but at what cost it is controllable, and with what benefits it is hard to control. Individuals tend to frame risk control in all-or-nothing terms, depending on the particular temporal event on which they focus. But this is a form of selective attention. As with voluntariness, "controllability" is a conclusion more than it is an analytic tool. The real question is the cost of preventing the risk – a matter of degree, not of kind.

HIGH EXTERNALITIES, CATASTROPHES, AND "MEANING"

The psychological evidence suggests, though it does not squarely identify, an important and relevant fact: Some deaths produce unusually high "externalities," in the sense that they generate widespread losses, including those stemming from empathy and fear, in a way that leads to predictable pecuniary and nonpecuniary costs.[24] Consider, for example, the death of the president of the United States, a death that imposes a wide range of costs and that taxpayers invest significant resources to prevent. A parallel can be found in the relatively large level of resources devoted to prevent the assassination of many important public officials.

But the point is hardly limited to these cases. An airplane hijacking or crash, partly because it is likely to be well-publicized, may produce large ripple effects in the form of widespread empathy and fear. It will even deter air travel by making people unusually frightened of air travel, simply because of heuristic devices (availability) and other predictable factors that make people's probability assessments go awry. An airplane crash might be especially disturbing because the

[24] See the treatment of the social amplification of risk in Slovic, supra note 12 in Chapter 2, pp. 232–45.

sudden loss of dozens or hundreds of people seems so unusually and senselessly tragic, in a way that produces large empathetic reactions, or because it signals the further possibility of random, apparently inexplicable events in which large numbers of people die. The resulting fear may be damaging because it is itself a harm to the people concerned, and because it may lead people to use less safe methods of transportation, such as automobiles. We saw these very points in connection with the terrorist attacks in the United States on September 11, 2001, where the burdens, harms, and costs were hardly limited to the admittedly massive losses on the day itself.

Some catastrophes are especially disturbing because they appear to produce pointless and especially unnatural deaths. A 1997 airplane crash in Israel, killing over seventy soldiers, is an example. It produced an extended period of national mourning — stemming from the youth of those who were killed, the fact that they were serving their country, and the highly unusual character of the accident, apparently stemming from preventable human error. These considerations suggest that special attention is justifiably devoted to air safety in the time following a crash even if the relevant precautions do not cause a significant drop in deaths. The same idea may justify special safeguards of nuclear reactors. Even a minor and harmless accident may produce a kind of day-to-day fearfulness that properly places a role in an official calculus, at least if educative efforts cannot work against public fears to the extent that they are irrational or based on an error-producing heuristic.

Special public concern about catastrophic events may thus reflect a judgment that certain kinds of deaths have many harmful effects, extending well beyond the deaths themselves. Consider in this regard the "Buffalo Creek Syndrome," documented several times in the aftermath of major disasters. Nearly two years after the collapse of a dam that left 120 dead and 4,000 homeless, psychiatric researchers continued to find significant psychological and sociological changes; survivors were characterized by a loss of direction and energy, other disabling character changes, and a loss of communality.[25] One evaluator attributed this loss of direction specifically to "the loss of traditional bonds of kinship and neighborliness."[26] When ordinary people are especially concerned with catastrophes, it may be because they appreciate these points. To the extent that this is so, differences between lay and expert assessments rest on genuine value differences (four times as many deaths may be much more than four times as bad) rather than on factual errors in cognitive processes of ordinary people.

[25] Daniel Fiorino, Technical and Democratic Values in Risk Analysis, 9 Risk Analysis 293 (1989).

[26] J. Robinson, M. Higgins & P. Bolyard, Assessing Environmental Impacts on Health: A Role for Behavioral Science, 4 Env. Impact Assessment Rev. 41 (1983).

Another way to explain this point is to say that the socially perceived "meaning" of a death, or a series of deaths, may affect and form part of public judgments about appropriate responses. Some deaths are taken to be part of life, whereas others seem disruptive and terrifying. If the social meaning of an airline disaster is that air travel has "become unsafe," government may have an obligation to respond with special intensity because the social perception will produce significant social losses in various spheres (including, as noted, net mortality itself, if people shift to more dangerous forms of travel).

Perhaps the public's concern here reflects irrationality; perhaps it can be reduced through low-cost strategies. For example, some of the fear that follows certain widely reported deaths is based on confusion or ignorance about actual probabilities; if it is possible to dispel the confusion, the fear should dissipate as well. Here the question is whether government can legitimately spend extra resources to avert the harms associated with irrational public attitudes. Information-based strategies would be preferable to allocating additional resources to deaths whose occurrence produces widespread panic. I have said that after the terrorist attacks of September 11, President Bush used an interesting strategy. Instead of assuring people that the statistical risks were low, he emphasized that flying was a patriotic act — a way of ensuring that terrorists would not win. This was an attempt to give a special meaning of the act of flying so that those who flew would think, not that they were acting recklessly, but that they were attempting to ensure that the business of the nation would continue.

INEQUITABLE DISTRIBUTION

Some risks might be, or be thought to be, inequitably distributed, above all because the victims are disproportionately members of socially disadvantaged groups. Certain deaths might, for example, be concentrated among poor people, African Americans, or homosexuals. Consider the risk of lead paint poisoning suffered by inner city children, or the risk of AIDS, faced disproportionately by African Americans as well as by homosexual men. Citizens or elected representatives may think that inequitably distributed risks of death deserve special attention from government. Here the relevant deaths are bad not because each one is especially bad to experience, but because there is social concern about the fact that a certain cause of death falls disproportionately on members of certain social groups.

When such social concern exists, and when it is not objectionable on constitutional or other grounds, it is entirely legitimate for officials to respond. Thus regulators should be permitted to give *distributional weights* to risks whose distributional incidence is especially troublesome. The point supports special efforts to control AIDS; environmental risks like asthma, which are concentrated among inner city children; and perhaps the spread of diseases whose incidence is concentrated among women. In fact there is a sense in which current policies already embody an effort to give distributional weights. Agencies tend to use "willingness to pay" as the basis for valuing risks of death and so on. But they use a uniform number, without lowering it for poor people or raising it for rich people. For example, agencies do not use a lower number when the risks are borne mostly by those with little money, such as farm workers. Nor do agencies use a higher number when the risks are borne mostly by wealthy people. Of course poor people are willing to pay less than wealthy people, if only because they have less money. The government's refusal to use a lower number for risks faced by poor people is, in an important sense, a distributional weight; it reflects a decision to weigh risks faced by poor people above their willingness to pay and to weigh risks faced by rich below theirs. Should this approach be extended by giving a high priority to environmental dangers faced by poor communities?

It is tempting, and not unreasonable, to say that it should be. But the proposal raises some questions. Most importantly, risk regulation may not be an effective way to pursue distributional justice. A risk policy with distributional weights is an "in-kind" redistributive scheme – that is, an attempt to redistribute resources not through transferring money directly but through the indirect route of giving priority to dangers faced by certain people. As a general rule, redistribution through regulation is a notoriously unreliable way to help the most disadvantaged; a high minimum wage, for example, does not transfer resources directly from "employers" to "employees." The costs of a high minimum wage are borne partly by consumers, who will have to pay higher prices, and partly by people who are frozen out of the job market.

Similar things can be said about efforts to redistribute resources through occupational safety and health regulations. If government makes the workplace safer, that is all to the good, standing by itself. But it does not stand by itself. There is good evidence that efforts to make the workplace safer will result in diminished wages for workers, and it is not clear that workers are better off as a result.[27] I do not mean to suggest that occupational safety and health regulation cannot be justified. Because workers, like everyone else, have problems in processing information, the government deserves to have a large role here. All I mean to suggest is that if government wants to ensure more equality in the distribution of resources, regulation is not the most effective strategy. If government wants to help people who need help, the best approach is to give them help directly.

---

[27] See the discussion of workers' compensation programs in Price Fishback & Shawn Everett Kantor, A Prelude to the Welfare State: The Origin of Workers' Compensation (Chicago: Univ. Chicago Press, 1998).

But we are now dealing with regulation accompanied by distributional weights, and there is some hope for success here. In terms of redistribution, this approach will be less effective than redistribution via cash, but at least it is possible that a government that is attentive to risks faced by the least well-off will be able both to reduce hazards and to improve the distribution of wealth. Unfortunately, it is also possible that any distributional weighting will subject the political market to pressures from well-organized groups, which will predictably offer equitable arguments for their preferred outcome, perhaps at the expense of the weakest and least organized members of society. There is good evidence that this happens.[28]

Finally, it is not clear that in-kind benefits should *generally* be distributed in a way that benefits the less well-off. It does not seem to make sense to say that homosexuals and women, for example, should receive better transportation, better dental care, more food stamps, and better housing than heterosexuals and men. Redistributive efforts are already being made through other, better routes. For example, the earned income tax credit is an effective way of helping the working poor; it is far more effective than efforts to reduce risks faced by lower income workers. But I do not mean to resolve all these complexities here. My minimal claim is that if there is a public judgment in favor of according a distributional weight to a certain death-reduction policy, and if that judgment is not unconstitutional or otherwise illegitimate, policymakers should not be barred from respecting that judgment.

BEYOND POPULISM, BEYOND TECHNOCRACY

Ordinary people do not show a richer rationality. They use heuristics that lead them astray. When they are thinking well, they are generally concerned with the extent of the danger – both its severity and its probability. Nonetheless, people do not consider statistically equivalent risks to be the same. Some risks, and some deaths, are especially bad.

Some such judgments do not really treat some deaths as worse, *in themselves*, than other deaths. They are based on the fact that deaths of some kinds occur very early, and thus a large number of life-years are lost. This point can easily be incorporated in regulatory policy, by focusing on how many years, not only how many lives, are at stake. When a death is preceded by a period of pain and suffering, it is appropriate to make special efforts to guard against it. When people believe that deaths are inequitably distributed, it may well be sensible to make particular efforts to prevent them, at least if the judgments about what is inequitable are legitimate. Finally, and perhaps most importantly, it is

---

[28] See Hamilton & Viscusi, supra note 14 in Chapter 2.

appropriate to devote unusually high levels of resources to preventing deaths accompanied by high externalities, at least if those externalities cannot be reduced through education and information. Harder puzzles are posed by the widespread idea that some deaths are especially bad because they involve a lack of control and involuntariness. Perhaps the central ideas are that people do not know about some risks, and that some risks are especially hard, or costly, to avoid. It makes sense to say that government should devote special attention to risks of this kind. Of course experts make mistakes, and they may even be biased, especially if they have economic ties to one or another side.[29] But precisely because they are experts, they are more likely to be right than ordinary people. Brain surgeons make mistakes, but they know more than the rest of us about brain surgery; lawyers make mistakes, but they know more than most people about the law.

Where does this leave us? It suggests that many of the disagreements between experts and ordinary people stem from the fact that experts have more information and are also prepared to look at the benefits as well as the risks associated with controversial products and activities. Ordinary people often make judgments on the basis of a quick, intuitive assessment, in which affect plays a large role. To the extent that experts focus only on the number of lives at stake, they are genuinely obtuse. It is reasonable to devote special attention to dangers that are hard to avoid or accompanied by special suffering or faced principally by children. It is wrong to say that all statistically identical risks should be treated the same. But if they are to be treated differently, it must be for reasons. We now have a sense of what those reasons might be. The question is whether it is possible to devise government solutions that can respond to them.

[29] For a colorful presentation, see Sheldon Rampton and John Stauber, Trust Us, We're Experts (New York: Putnam, 2001).

4

This Month's Risk

(with Timur Kuran)

Learning by observing others can explain the conformity, idiosyncrasy, and fragility of human behavior. When people observe one another's behavior, they very often end up making the same choices; thus, localized conformity. If the early movers erred, followers are likely to imitate the mistake; hence idiosyncrasy. If later on a few people start behaving differently for whatever reason, then a sudden phase change can occur in which the old convention is swept away by the new; hence fragility. Such imitation can explain either transient fads or permanent choices among alternative products, sexual and marital options, scientific theories, and religious beliefs.[1]

At the Siting Board's open houses, people would invent scenarios and then dare Board members and staff to say they were impossible. A person would ask, "What would happen if a plane crashed into a concrete bunker filled with radioactive waste and exploded?" We would explain that while the plane and its contents might explode, nothing in the disposal facility could. And they would say, "But what if explosives had been mistakenly disposed of, and the monitoring devices at the facility had malfunctioned so they weren't noticed?" We would head down the road of saying that this was an extremely unlikely set of events. And they would say, "Well, it could happen, couldn't it?"[2]

I have said that senseless policies for risk reduction, in daily life and in law, often come from our use of the availability heuristic, by which risks seem more

[1] David Hirshleifer, The Blind Leading the Blind, in the New Economics of Human Behavior 188–9, Mariano Tommasi and Kathryn Ierulli, eds. (Cambridge: Cambridge Univ. Press, 1995).
[2] John Weingast, Waste Is A Terrible Thing To Mind (Newark, N.J.: Center for Analysis in Public Issues, 2001).

likely to come to fruition if salient examples come readily to mind. I have also suggested that senseless policies result from social influences, though which some risks come to seem serious and others trivial, only because of what other people seem to think.

The goal of this chapter is to connect these points to the "risk-of-the-month" syndrome that afflicts the law in many nations, emphatically including the United States. An understanding of social influences, combined with an understanding of the availability heuristic, helps explain the broader public fixation on this month's risk, at the expense of a system that would ensure a sensible overview of real hazards, grounded on the actual evidence. To summarize the argument: The availability heuristic interacts with social processes, producing *availability cascades.* Such cascades occur when people's expressions of fear trigger chains of individual responses, which make these perceptions appear increasingly plausible through their rising availability in public discourse. The rise in availability is ordinarily driven by a hybrid mechanism driven by two motives: information seeking and reputation building. Availability cascades can generate persistent *social availability errors*, in the form of widespread but mistaken beliefs. Whether or not the availability heuristic is involved, cascade effects can lead people to believe that a risk is much greater, or much smaller, than it is in fact. The resulting mass delusions may last for a long time, and they may produce wasteful or even harmful laws and policies.

Let us begin with some examples.

LOVE CANAL

Between 1942 and 1953, the Hooker Chemical Company filled Love Canal, an abandoned waterway that feeds into the Niagara River in New York State, with more than 21,000 tons of chemical waste.[3] It then covered the waste with dirt and sold it to the Niagara Falls Board of Education for $1. The local government developed the area, turning it into a neighborhood of more than 200 houses. The neighborhood was settled in 1957, and the site of the old canal, which many of the new homes bordered, became a school and a playground.

After several years of unusually heavy rain, the canal overflowed its banks in 1976. In that year a joint American–Canadian commission responsible for monitoring the Great Lakes found the insecticide Mirex in Lake Ontario fish. Shortly thereafter the New York Department of Environmental Conservation

---

[3] This account draws on independent research and on Lois Marie Gibbs, Love Canal: The Story Continues (Gabriola Island: New Society Publishers, 1998); Wildavsky, supra note 9 in Chapter 1; Marc Landy et al., The Environmental Protection Agency: Asking the Wrong Questions, 2nd ed. (New York: Oxford Univ. Press, 1994).

identified Love Canal as a major contributor. The local press began reporting that area residents were worried about the health effects of Love Canal, as reflected in a front-page story published by a local newspaper in October 1976. Frightening tales spread quickly: children being burnt, omnipresent odors inducing nausea, undrinkable water, black sludge everywhere. Residents feared that the buried chemicals had resurfaced, making their neighborhood unlivable. Here was an informational cascade in action, with group polarization to boot; as people expressed their fears, anxiety began to intensify.

At this stage no public official, state or federal, attempted to reassure the public about the dangers, perhaps because any attempt at reassurance would have been met with considerable distrust. Newspapers continued to fuel fears. ("If it bleeds, it leads" is a familiar slogan in the press room; the slogan helps explain media attention to the risk of the month.) A key development was a set of alarming stories in the *Niagara Falls Gazette* in June 1978. Those stories came to the attention of Lois Marie Gibbs, who came to become a central figure in publicizing residents' fears of cancer and other adverse health effects and in mobilizing public attention. Indeed, Gibbs, a housewife who eventually appeared on national television programs and was invited to both the state capitol and the White House, ended up becoming one of the "availability entrepreneurs" behind the eventual passage of the Superfund statute.

Initially, Gibb's reaction to the newspaper articles led her to go door-to-door in the area, organizing a petition and eventually developing "a set speech."[4] The local health department attempted to provide reassurance, on the basis of detailed studies, that there was no evidence of leukemia of even low or fluctuating white–blood cell counts. But the "numbers had no meaning" and did not dampen citizen concern.

The stakes grew dramatically when New York State Health Commissioner Robert Wheelen declared a public health emergency in the area. Characterizing Love Canal as a "great and immediate peril," he urged area residents to stay out of their basements and to avoid eating anything from their gardens. Wheelen sought the temporary relocation of twenty-five pregnant women and children under two, whereupon residents whom the plan would leave behind inquired why their health would be treated as "less important." A month later, Wheelen published a report, "Love Canal: Public Health Time Bomb," which described Love Canal as a "modern day disaster, both profound and devastating." The federal government, too, responded to the growing sense of crisis. The director of the Federal Disaster Assistance Administration toured the area very visibly around the same time, and two days later President Jimmy Carter declared a national emergency.

[4] Gibbs, id. at 19.

Mounting public concern appeared to prevent any public official, or for that matter any private citizen, from questioning the reality of the danger; information was flowing rapidly from one group to another, and anyone who challenged the mounting concern risked attack. In early 1980, at a time when Love Canal was prominently featured in network newscasts almost every day, Governor Carey established a blue-ribbon panel to review the scientific evidence. The panel endorsed none of the reports of serious health effects. But its evaluation had no appreciable influence on subsequent events. In May of the same year, a group of Love Canal residents held two EPA officials hostage at the headquarters of the Homeowners Association. The next day President Carter decided to relocate an additional 700 families at a cost of at least $3 million.

The Love Canal "time bomb," as press reports called it, was not the original source of government concern about abandoned hazardous waste dumps. But there is no doubt that publicity about Love Canal was crucial to enactment of a new law in 1980. In that year, *Time* magazine made the topic of waste sites a cover story, and new network documentaries followed suit. Congress responded quickly with the Comprehensive Environmental Response and Liability Act (CERCLA), generally known as "Superfund." The act called for $1.6 billion in expenditures over five years.

The social transformation that occurred between 1978 and 1980 has proved enduring. Since that period, Americans have consistently ranked waste sites among the country's top environmental problems. In a highly publicized study, the EPA found that Americans rank hazardous waste sites *first* among all environmental problems – above pesticides, acid rain, indoor air pollution, radioactive waste, water pollution, exposure to work-site chemicals, tap-water contamination, and thinning of the ozone layer, among many others.[5] This preeminence was confirmed by subsequent public opinion polls.[6] To this date, moreover, American presidents and serious presidential candidates of both major parties invoke abandoned waste dumps as a leading environmental problem. And Congress has continued to spend vast sums on clean-up campaigns. By now it has allocated well over $20 billion to the cause.

Yet it remains unproven that the contamination of Love Canal ever posed significant risks to anyone. No subsequent study discovered any link between the identified chromosome alterations and the contamination in question. An exhaustive 1982 study by the EPA, based on 6,000 samples of soil, air, and groundwater from the evacuated area and other sampling regions, found

---

[5] Table 2.4 in W. Kip Viscusi, Rational Risk Policy: The 1996 Arne Ryde Memorial Lectures 22 (Oxford: Clarendon Press, 1998). See also Breyer, supra note 8 in Chapter 2, at 21.

[6] See Breyer, id. at 21.

"no evidence of environmental contamination" at Love Canal.[7] And in the same year the Department of Health and Human Services found that the emergency zone was "as habitable as the control areas with which it was compared."

ALAR

The pesticide Alar has long been used on apples. About 1 percent of Alar is composed of UDMH, a carcinogen. Alar's manufacturer, the Uniroyal Company, embarked on a two-year study of its effects, completing the initial year of investigation in January 1989. The preliminary indicated a greater incidence of tumors in rodents exposed to high levels of UDMH. On the basis of these tentative findings, the Natural Resources Defense Council (NRDC) made a series of extrapolations, which it interpreted as implying that between 4,700 and 6,200 preschool children, or about one out of every 4,200 exposed to Alar, will develop cancer by age six.

The television show *60 Minutes* publicized the allegation against a background consisting of a red apple overlaid with a skull and crossbones. The program instigated a public outcry, complete with protests from many celebrities, including the actress Meryl Streep, who founded an activist group called Mothers and Others for Pesticide Limits. The NRDC's self-conscious agenda was "to create so many repetitions of [its] message that average American consumers (not just the policy elite in Washington) could not avoid hearing it – from many different media outlets in a short time. The idea was for the 'story' to achieve a life of its own, and continue for weeks and months to affect policy and consumer habits."[8] This was a self-conscious effort to create a cascade effect.

The EPA reviewed the evidence, concluding that the risk was vastly exaggerated: one in 111,000 rather than in 4,200. Now a risk of one in 111,000, if it exists, is worthy of concern, especially if children are involved. The EPA did not, however, reach any conclusion about the proper course of regulation. But by the time the EPA made its announcement, the demand for apples had plummeted. In desperation, the nation's apple growers asked Uniroyal to withdraw Alar from the market. And before the year was out, but after the EPA announcement, Uniroyal agreed to stop producing Alar, evidently to avoid the costs of contested cancellation proceedings.

By its own lights, the EPA's initial risk estimate has turned out to be too high. According to its subsequent analyses, only one in 250,000 children exposed

[7] See Wildavsky, supra note 9 in Chapter I, at 149.
[8] See id. at 204.

to Alar will develop cancer, doubtless a nontrivial risk, but less than half the initial EPA figure, and lower than that of the NRDC by a factor of 600. Thus a 1991 editorial in *Science* argues that "a clearly dubious result about possible carcinogenicity by a special interest group was hyped by a news organization without the most simple checks on its reliability or documentation."[9] A United Nations panel, along with others who have investigated the data, found that even the EPA's revised figure is too high. Alar does not cause cancer in mice, it concluded, and it is not dangerous to people.[10] One observer has concluded: "Words fail on Alar. The most charitable interpretation is that an environmental group . . . decided to take matters into its own hands by writing a report and orchestrating its release to the media in so forceful a manner as to compel governmental action. The syndrome its report played out is by now distressingly familiar: a few suggestive tests involving tiny quantities raised way above the actual amount by extreme assumptions about children's eating habits, expanded further by statistical manipulations, extrapolated against huge populations to create row-upon-row of child cancer victims."[11]

These claims should not be taken for more than they are worth. Under the EPA's current analysis, 1 in 250,000 children exposed to Alar will develop cancer. It is not clear that the removal of Alar from the market was a bad thing, all things considered. But it is clear that people were much more frightened than they should have been. Their fear resulted from an availability cascade.

THE SUMMER OF THE SHARK

On July 6, 2001, Jesse Arbogast, eight years old, was swimming in shallow waters in Pensacola, Florida. A bull shark attacked Jesse and bit off his arm. Jesse's uncle rushed into the water and wrestled the shark to the shore, where it was shot. Jesse's arm was retrieved from the mouth of the shark, which was reattached during the twelve hours of surgery that saved Jesse's life.

In the United States, was the summer of 2001 "the summer of the shark"? *Time* magazine so announced in a cover story of July 30.[12] In the story's words, "Sharks come silently, without warning. There are three ways they strike: the hit-and-run, the hump-and-bite, and the sneak attack." After vividly describing

---

[9] See Daniel Koshland, Credibility in Science and the Press, 254 Science 629 (November 1, 1991).

[10] Wildavsky, supra note 9 in Chapter I, at 221.

[11] Id. at 222.

[12] Terry McCarthy, Why Can't We Be Friends? A Horrific Attack Raises Old Fears, Time, July 30, 2001, at 34.

the attack on Jesse Arbogast, the story announced, "Suddenly reports of shark attacks – or what people thought were shark attacks – began to come in from all around the U.S." The reports were disturbing, for sharks "lurk in the vast, mysterious ocean, an element that still stirs mythic fear." Together with an apparent fixation on Jesse's progress, shark attacks received extraordinary national attention in August 2001, sharply increasing public fear. Indeed, a computer search of news sources found over 1,000 references to shark attacks between August 4 and September 4 – and 126 references to "the summer of the shark." National television programs devoted a great deal of attention to shark attacks and to Jesse Arbogast, often with vivid pictures.

But did shark attacks actually increase in 2001? To its credit, the *Time* story noted that "for all the terror they stir, the numbers remain minuscule" – and that people are thirty times more likely to be killed by lightning than to be killed by a shark. In fact there was no reliable evidence of an increase in shark attacks in the summer of 2001. But in light of all the attention, new legal reforms were proposed and even enacted, designed to prevent people from feeding and approaching sharks and otherwise to protect against the apparent epidemic of attacks. But in the exasperated words of George Burgess, the director of the International Sharks Attack file: "What has happened is that we had a very high-profile attack on the eight-year-old boy which made headline news. And those attacks are happening in places where there is a lot of media, as opposed to the Third World. There ha[ve] been some hysterical headlines."[13] There is no reason to believe that the legal remedies have saved a single life.

SOCIAL ANIMALS AND CASCADE EFFECTS

What explains widespread public fixations on unthreatening waste dumps, relatively harmless chemicals, and shark attacks, when for years on end far more serious health hazards, such as cigarette smoking, indoor air pollution, "junk food" consumption, and asthma in the inner city have commanded comparatively little attention? At first blush, the episodes in question confirm an essential finding of cognitive psychology: Being "boundedly rational," people rely on mental shortcuts that leave them misinformed in many contexts, even seriously wrong. The episodes are consistent also with a central theme in modern economics, namely, that citizens of a large polity have incentives to remain "rationally ignorant." Why should most residents of Love Canal, or the rest of us, devote time and effort to learning the full truth about the alleged contamination when as individuals

---

[13] Andrew Buncombe, How Sharks Became the Story of the Summer, The Independent, August 7, 2001, at 11.

we each have only one voice and one vote to influence policies that the choices of many millions will help shape?

It would be a mistake, however, to treat these episodes merely as additional manifestations of bounded rationality and rational ignorance. Both interpretations raise the question of why, in each case, millions of Americans fell victim to exactly the *same* delusion. People evidently formed their perceptions interdependently, with each individual's expressed perceptions helping to shape those of others. Equally important, invoking bounded rationality or rational ignorance sidesteps the challenge of explaining why people came to believe *what* they did. What people "knew" depended, in the first instance, on their predispositions to believe certain claims more readily than others.

The availability heuristic, obviously central to the incidents just described, can produce substantial distortions whenever some dangers are easier to imagine than others. It is undoubtedly true that, in certain contexts, the availability heuristic is helpful for people who lack the time and inclination to investigate complex issues on their own. But the availability heuristic also produces major errors. Return, for example, to the fact that people systematically err in assessing the number of lives lost as a result of various risks. Grossly underestimating dangers that are not highly publicized (heart disease, strokes, asthma), they grossly overestimate risks to which the media pays a great deal of attention (accidents, electrocution).

In contexts subject to availability cascades, the same objective information may be capable of sustaining very different patterns of belief, depending on whether a cascade occurs and, if so, which of many possible cascades is initiated. Thus, one risk may gain salience, receive an enormous amount of attention, and become the object of stringent regulation, while another risk, which experts deem equivalent, is treated as "part of normal life."

Against this background, it is unsurprising that culturally and economically similar nations display dramatically different reactions to identical risks. Whereas nuclear power enjoys widespread acceptance in France, it arouses considerable fear in the United States. Whereas genetic engineering of food causes immense concern in Europe, it has been a nonissue in the United States, at least until recently. It is also unsurprising that a public assessment of any given risk may change suddenly and dramatically even in the absence of a major change in the relevant scientific evidence. Over a short time, people convinced that their environment is perfectly livable may come to think, because everyone else seems to be getting alarmed, that it is replete with dreadful carcinogens. And insofar as people lack their own means for judging a claim's validity, there is a danger that the beliefs generated by a cascade will be factually incorrect. Millions of individuals may develop erroneous beliefs simply by giving each other reasons to adopt and preserve them.

INFORMATIONAL AND REPUTATIONAL CASCADES

As suggested in Chapter 2, social influences can be divided into two kinds: informational and reputational. These two influences produce two different types of cascade effects.

INFORMATIONAL CASCADES

An informational cascade occurs when people with little personal information about a particular matter base their own beliefs on the apparent beliefs of others. Imagine, for example, that Alan says that abandoned hazardous waste sites are dangerous, or that Alan initiates protest activity because such a site is located nearby. Betty, otherwise skeptical or in equipoise, may go along with Alan; Carl, otherwise an agnostic, may be convinced that if Alan and Betty share the relevant belief, the belief must be true. It will take a confident Deborah to resist the shared judgments of Alan, Betty, and Carl. The result of these set of influences can be social cascades, as hundreds, thousands, or millions of people come to accept a certain belief simply because of what they think other people believe.[14]

The example is artificial and stylized, but there is nothing artificial to the basic idea. Cascade effects help account for the existence of widespread public concern about a number of sources of risk, including those discussed earlier. Under the right conditions, many of a society's members, even most, will end up with essentially identical beliefs, which may well be fanciful. Insofar as a society is socially fragmented, it may exhibit *local informational cascades*. A local informational cascade is one limited, for example, to a geographical area, a demographic subgroup, or a core of activists who share a political objective. In the recent past, local informational cascades have developed with respect to the risks posed by AIDS, skin cancer from sun, and shark attacks. Of these, the first two have been based on solid evidence and largely salutary, helping to encourage people to protect themselves against serious problems. As we have seen the shark attack scare was grossly exaggerated, amounting to a kind of hysteria. Nor is this an isolated case. When people are participating in informational cascades – local, national, even international – it is fully possible that they will become fearful of something that carries small risks. Extremist groups, fearful of an imagined attack by government or some adversary, are often prone to informational cascades of this sort. Indeed, cultural variation can often be best

---

[14] See David Hirshleifer, The Blind Leading the Blind: Social Influence, Fads, and Informational Cascades, in The New Economics of Human Behavior 188, Mariano Tommasi & Kathyrn Ierulli, eds. (Cambridge: Cambridge Univ. Press, 1995).

explained by the fact that certain information is, for largely arbitrary reasons, able to spread quickly in one place but not in another.

REPUTATIONAL CASCADES

Like an informational cascade, a reputational cascade is driven by interdependencies among individual choices.[15] It differs, however, in the underlying personal motivations. In the case of a reputational cascade, people do not subject themselves to social influences because they think that others are more knowledgeable. Their motivation is simply to earn social approval and avoid disapproval. Even the most confident people sometimes adjust their expressions in the interest of building or preserving their reputations; they go so far as to silence themselves. The phenomenon is common in social discussions of risks.

If many people are alarmed about some risk, you might not voice your doubts about whether the alarm is merited, simply in order not to seem obtuse, cruel, or indifferent. And if many people believe that a certain risk is trivial, you might not disagree through words or deeds, lest you appear cowardly or confused. Sometimes people take to speaking and acting as if they share, or at least do not reject, what they view as the dominant belief. As in the informational context, the outcome may be the cleansing of public discourse of unusual perceptions, arguments, and actions. Such effects can produce a public demand for regulation even though the relevant risks are trivial. Lawmakers, even more than ordinary citizens, are vulnerable to reputational pressures; that is part of their job. They may even support legislation to control risks that they know to be quite low. In the context of regulation of hazardous waste dumps, it is clear that reputational factors actually helped to fuel a cascade effect, eventually leading to the Superfund statute.

At the same time, there may be little or no demand for regulation of risks that are, in fact, quite large in magnitude. And just as informational cascades may be limited in their reach, there can be *local reputational cascades* — ones that reshape the public pronouncements of particular subgroups without affecting those of the broader group. I believe that, with respect to risk, informational influences are the most important factors in altering citizen behavior, as individual fear grows with a sense that other (reasonable) people are frightened, but reputational

---

[15] Timur Kuran, Ethnic Norms and Their Transformation Through Reputational Cascades, 27 J. Legal Stud. 623 (1998). For a more detailed treatment, see Timur Kuran, Private Truths, Public Lies (Cambridge, Mass.: Harvard Univ. Press, 1995). On the mechanisms through which momentous social transformations may catch the world by surprise, see Timur Kuran, Sparks and Prairie Fires: A Theory of Unanticipated Political Revolution, 61 Pub. Choice 41 (1989).

influences are also pertinent. Consider the suggestion of a medical researcher who questions a number of Lyme disease diagnoses: "Doctors can't say what they think anymore.... If you quote me as saying these things, I'm as good as dead."[16] Or consider the remarks of a sociologist who has publicly raised questions about the health threats posed by mad-cow disease, suggesting that if you raise those doubts publicly, "You get made to feel like a pedophile."[17]

GROUP POLARIZATION

When like-minded people are talking mostly to one another, especially interesting things are likely to happen. If members of a group tend to think that global warming poses a significant danger, their discussions will move them, not to the middle, but to a more extreme point in line with their original tendencies.[18] If neighbors are really worried about the dangers of electromagnetic lines and have little concern with indoor air pollution, their internal discussions will increase their fear of electromagnetic lines and dampen their concern with indoor air pollution. If people tend to be concerned about global warming, their exchange of opinions will make them still more concerned. If members of a group tend to believe that for cancer, the serious dietary problem lies in the use of pesticides, those same people will tend, after discussion, to have a heightened fear of pesticide use. All these are examples of *group polarization* – a process by which people engaged in process of deliberation end up thinking a more extreme version of what they already thought.

Group polarization is central to the cascade-like processes discussed here. If like-minded people are speaking mostly with one another, they can end up with intensely heightened concerns about small risks. And if they do not speak with others, they may remain entirely unaware of risks that are, in fact, quite serious.

When risks are involved, group polarization is highly likely to interact with the availability heuristic. If a particular incident is well-known among a certain group, discussion can move people to ever more extreme positions, eventually producing significant social mobilization. Sometimes the result is social fragmentation, as when some groups seem concerned about risks toward which other groups are indifferent. This is itself an unhealthy state of affairs. Sometimes the result is a more widespread pattern of panic and neglect. Sometimes, of course,

---

[16] David Grass, Stalking Dr. Steele, New York Times, July 17, 2001 (magazine), at 56.

[17] Andrea Higgins, It's a Mad, Mad, Mad-low World, Wall Street Journal, March 12, 2001, at A13.

[18] See Roger Brown, Social Psychology 2d ed. (New York: Free Press, 1986); Cass R. Sunstein, Deliberative Trouble? Why Groups Go To Extremes, 110 Yale L. J. 71 (2000).

the result is to produce significant concern about a problem that really deserves attention. In the context of cigarette smoking and skin cancer from sun exposure, group polarization has led people to protect themselves from substantial dangers.

In this chapter, all the major illustrations of availability cascades involve the regulation of risks. But the general framework can be applied to other domains. Illustrations include the rise and decline of McCarthyism; the struggle for civil rights; the spread of affirmative action and the spread of public opposition to it; the emergence of feminism, the anti-tax movement, and the religious right; ongoing campaigns against pornography and hate speech; campaigns for safe sex; the persistence and sudden fall of communism; the global turn toward market-friendly government policies; terrorism; and finally, the spread of ethnic and religious separatism across the world. Anyone interested in fueling public concern about a public problem would do well to take advantage of the mechanisms discussed here. And even though the underlying mechanisms can make things worse, by focusing attention on small or nonexistent problems and concerns, they can also make things much better, by ensuring that serious problems, or neglected grievances, receive public attention.

PUBLIC UPHEAVALS

An analysis of any mass upheaval that triggers political and legal responses to perceived risks must take account of two sets of influences. The first consists of the effects that social variables have on personal ones. The social variable of greatest interest here is *public discourse*, which is the ensemble of publicly expressed or conveyed sentiments, ideas, and information that individuals use as gauges of what others know and want. Policy initiatives and enactments, including steps taken by official agencies, are also relevant: A law that regulates hazardous waste dumps might well lead people to think that hazardous waste dumps pose a serious problem. The different sets of influences form a circular process. Public discourse shapes individual risk judgments, risk preferences, and policy preferences, and the reshaped personal variables then transform the public discourse that contributed to their own transformations.

Strictly speaking, a private characteristic, such as a private perception of the risk associated with a chemical spill, is known only to the person who holds it. Because of its visibility, the transformation of a public variable can have sudden and direct effects on individual thoughts and dispositions. If a newspaper report suggests that a water supply is unsafe, thousands of readers may instantly feel frightened. By contrast, the immediate effects of private variables are necessarily limited. If an official investigates scientific reports about a waste dump and becomes convinced that worries are unjustified, this knowledge itself will have no impact on the information available to concerned residents. What will influence the perceptions of residents is what he says publicly.

Note that the public pronouncements of public officials are especially important, partly because those pronouncements are made to many people at the same time. The pronouncements of public officials are also highly susceptible to social influences because such officials are subject to public control, through elections and otherwise. Public officials know that they might be severely punished for downplaying a risk that is perceived as serious or for calling attention to a hazard that is perceived as trivial. Indeed, an official's pronouncements can diverge from the thoughts that he carries within his head and from the knowledge he conveys to a close friend. To avoid charges of insensitivity, even to avoid having to justify an unpopular position, he may make speeches and promote policies that convey deep concern about the very waste spill that he actually considers harmless. Or the official might publicly reassure the public, suggesting that the risk of terrorism is trivial, when he is privately unsure or even much alarmed. Just as an official may tailor his public pronouncements to protect his reputation, so, too, may the other individuals who contribute to public discourse and public activity.

We have seen that a strictly informational cascade occurs when people start attaching credibility to a proposition (e.g., a certain abandoned waste dump is dangerous) merely because other people seem to accept that proposition. Ordinarily, individuals differ in their preconceptions, their openness to public discourse, and their sensitivity to changes in the apparent views of others. In the absence of such variations, everyone would adjust simultaneously to new information, producing not a cascade but a sudden shift by independent actors. With a cascade, adjustments come at different times, with some individuals becoming convinced of a serious danger at the earliest sign of adverse health effects, but others remaining skeptical to varying degrees until more information becomes available. Eventually a "tipping point" is reached, when many people suddenly fall into line.[19] The ultimate outcome can be a widely shared judgment based on little information. Although widely shared, the judgment can also be quite fragile, in the sense that it may shift as a result of small shocks. Thus people might be fearful, for a time, about some risk – consider shark attacks, or air travel in the aftermath of a disaster – that produces no concern at all after a few months.

But only rarely are cascades *purely* informational. In practice, each public signal or communication will differ from its private counterpart insofar as people seek to protect or improve their social standing by refusing to depart

---

[19] See Kuran, supra note 15, this Chapter. For a popular discussion, see Malcolm Gladwell, The Tipping Point (New York: Little Brown, 2000).

from the official orthodoxy. As a result of the apparent social pressures, a group of officials may endorse reports that Love Canal poses a huge threat to nearby residents, when they know of data that make the reports suspect. They might even feign approval of a relocation plan even though they consider the step ludicrous.

Together, these factors give individuals and groups extraordinary opportunities to advance their agendas merely by expressing approval of individuals who lend them public support and disapproval of those who deny them support. A related means of earning the affection, support, and goodwill of a group is to help punish its enemies and reward its friends. For instance, a citizen who is aware of the lack of scientific evidence for serious danger may, in the interest of bolstering her reputation, intimate that an official who counsels calm should be reprimanded or even removed from office, perhaps on the ground that he is lamentably "weak on the environment." Through such actions, actions that reflect reputational influences will contribute to the very social pressures that produce and reproduce them.

Group polarization is especially likely when people are talking about risks. As the Love Canal example suggests, those who are fearful of a particular danger often speak mostly with like-minded others. In the environmental context, groups who seek to downplay certain risks, or to treat environmentalists as unscientific zealots, are often moved to these positions by internal discussions. In the same vein, large social movements can arise in just this way, as those who are concerned about an actual or supposed hazard do not merely reinforce but actually heighten one another's fears. Group polarization owes a great deal to the informational and reputational incentives discussed earlier. In some forms, it can even produce a form of "group-think," in which large numbers of people believe or say that they believe the same thing, even if they are wrong. It is important to emphasize that this process can be benign, even indispensable. The enactment of much environmental legislation would not have been possible without it. But when imperfectly informed people push one another toward extremes, the fear might well be unjustified, leading government to waste large levels of resources on small problems.

Fear itself is not all we have to fear. Sometimes we should fear fearlessness. But baseless fear is itself a serious problem for a democratic society.

INTEREST GROUPS AND AVAILABILITY CAMPAIGNS

Self-interested private groups are entirely willing to exploit the underlying forces, frequently by publicizing certain examples or incidents and by encouraging deliberation among like-minded people. Often the financial stakes involved in risk regulation are very high, and selfish interests, including corporations, fuel public fears by emphasizing the dangers posed by the products of their competitors. For example, European companies have tried to play up fears of genetically engineered food as a way of fending off competition from American farmers. Public interest groups take a similar approach. In the case of Alar, the Natural Resources Defense Council self-consciously attempted to start a cascade. In seeking regulation of cell phone use in cars, activists have mostly emphasized particular tragedies, not statistical evidence. Indeed the phenomenon is quite general. In trying to attack punitive damage awards from juries, corporations have seized on particular cases involving apparently absurd awards, such as a multimillion dollar award for burns resulting from a hot coffee cup at MacDonald's. (This is not, of course, to deny that punitive damage awards raise problems, in part because jurors are vulnerable to the cognitive problems emphasized here.[20])

People who have some understanding of the dynamics of availability cascades, and seek to exploit those dynamics, may be characterized as *availability entrepreneurs*. Located anywhere in the social system, including the government, the media, nonprofit organizations, the business sector, and even households, these entrepreneurs attempt to trigger availability cascades likely to advance their own agendas. They do so by fixing people's attention on specific problems, interpreting phenomena in particular ways, promoting group polarization, attempting to raise the salience of certain information, encouraging the statement of views favorable to their preferred options, and discouraging the statement of unfavorable views. Once initiated by groups with a financial or ideological stake in policy control, social pressures may grow through the assistance of the broader population. For this reason, such groups confer reputational benefits on individuals who support particular positions and impose reputational costs on those who oppose them. They make individuals seem altruistic or selfish, virtuous or vicious, depending on what preferences and beliefs they express.

The resulting *availability campaigns* often produce social benefits by overcoming public torpor and fueling debates on long-festering though rarely articulated social problems; return to the risks associated with cigarette smoking and skin cancer from exposure to the sun. At the same time, availability campaigns sometimes do great harm by fueling widespread availability errors. As we shall see, this danger points to a need for institutional safeguards designed to ensure better priority-setting and fuller use of scientific knowledge.

Imagine, then, that when a waste spill is reported, journalists seeking a career break that will make them famous or politicians aiming to build up their proenvironmental credentials take to denigrating the responsible industry. Sensing

---

[20] See Cass R. Sunstein et al., Punitive Damages: How Juries Decide (Chicago: Univ. Chicago Press, 2002).

an opportunity to appear virtuous, the first people to witness this campaign participate in the denunciations. In so doing, they raise the volume of criticism, which makes additional people aware of ongoing transformation in public discourse. They join the chorus of criticism to build their own reputations, which raises the volume further, and in this manner the vilification campaign grows through a reputational cascade. The cascade completes its course when news of the campaign has reached everyone who cares sufficiently about maintaining a good reputation.

In the environmental context, a common tactic is to produce a headline-grabbing uproar by dramatizing and publicizing a few related problems, even a single one. Recent examples of dramatized problems include, in addition to Love Canal, Alar, and other problems already mentioned, the plight of the giant panda, which the World Wildlife Fund has used to dramatize the plight of endangered species, and the Exxon Valdez disaster, which the Sierra Club and other environmental organizations have invoked to promote more stringent safeguards against oil spills. For their part, groups that would bear the costs of the requested policy measures, such as oil and shipping companies in the case of Exxon Valdez, respond in kind. In particular, they draw attention to claims that have turned out to be baseless ("the-boy-who-cried-wolf" phenomenon) and highlight the environment-friendly aspects of their operations. At least implicitly, the actors who participate in these contests understand how availability cascades work. Moreover, it is clear that they understand the reputational and the informational processes at work.

Showing a working knowledge of the availability heuristic, cascade effects, and group polarization, availability entrepreneurs seize on selected incidents and publicize them to make them generally salient to the public. They play on people's emotions, activating the affect heuristic. They also draw associations that trigger painful memories, as when environmentalists proclaim that nuclear reactors currently in operation are setting the stage for "another Three Mile Island," or when they characterize a toxic spill as "a new Love Canal." The entrepreneurs who coin such phrases sometimes act strategically. But most consider their claims of danger to be quite accurate. After all, they themselves are subject to the availability heuristic, and the fact that they move in circles within which the claim seems to be believed may have convinced them of the existence of a tremendous danger. Thus, an antinuclear activist may believe passionately in the necessity of eliminating nuclear power because all her friends are themselves opponents of nuclear power, and they make the danger in question very salient to her. Of course none of this is meant to deny the possibility that availability entrepreneurs are entirely right.

A common method for triggering availability cascades is for a group to pass carefully sifted information to selected journalists, who then rush to release hot stories that justify the group's work. The information will often contain grains of truth, but it may also harbor biases, even outright fabrications. We saw an example of the spread of misleading information in discussing the Alar incident. For another such example, consider that during the Christmas season the media typically feature stories about holiday suicides. These stories give the impression, and sometimes say explicitly, that the risk of suicides rises during the holiday season for people living alone (who feel especially lonely), for the financially strapped (who realize that the presents they want to purchase lie beyond their reach), and for sundry other categories of troubled people. In fact, the suicide rate usually *declines* between Thanksgiving and New Year's.[21] The reason why this period sees a rush of suicide stories is that the reporters receive their information from organizations that run suicide hotlines, and they do not bother to check all their facts. The organizations receive most of their donations around Christmas, which coincides with the end of the tax year, a time when taxpayers develop greater awareness of tax deductions and, hence, become readier to make charitable donations. The common belief that suicides rise during the holiday season serves, then, the fundraising goals of the suicide hotlines.[22]

Reports of suicides tend to fuel new suicides through processes akin to those discussed here.[23] Through the availability heuristic, well-publicized suicides foster an awareness of suicide as a vehicle for alleviating pain; they also reduce the stigma attached to suicide whenever the victims are celebrities who evoke sympathy. (The phenomenon is related to the general one of "copycat crimes," which is also explicable in terms of availability cascades.) But to identify certain adverse effects of publicizing the commonness of suicides is not at all to say that the availability campaigns in question constitute cases of cynical, self-serving manipulation. The suicide hotlines are run by people with honorable goals: prevention of despair and preservation of life. Nor does the analysis here mean that the campaigns are counterproductive on the whole. The lives saved by virtue of the funds raised may well outnumber those lost as a result of the added Christmas publicity.

Even when cognitive deception is involved, availability cascades can serve a socially beneficial purpose. Indeed, the entrepreneurs who set them in motion may well be exploiting psychological biases as a response to private ignorance and public torpor. As with anyone seeking to provide a public good, people trying

---

[21] The monthly variations in the suicide rate are typically minor, although the rate usually peaks in summer. See the Monthly Vital Statistical Report, 1994–5.

[22] Katherine Dunn, Fibbers: The Lies Journalists Tell, New Republic, June 21, 1993, at p. 18.

[23] See David Cutler et al., Explaining the Rise in Youth Suicide, in Risky Behavior Among Youths 219, Jonathan Gruber, ed. (Chicago: Univ. Chicago Press, 2001).

to lessen a social risk face the familiar obstacles to collective action. Availability entrepreneurs help to overcome those obstacles. In acting as manipulative sales-people, they perform vital social services.

Journalists help spread the messages of availability entrepreneurs, partly through leaks that they receive from private or public sources. Citizens join the fray through letters, phone calls, and participation in talk shows, thus contributing to the heightening of awareness about the identified problem, as happened in the Love Canal and Alar cases. Eventually, laws or regulations are adopted that give the instigating group opportunities for new uproars to maintain, and even strengthen, the achieved public consciousness.

When the mass media often report carelessly, an important reason is that few people realize the extent to which reporters use slanted press releases and strategic leaks. The typical citizen has no time to investigate whether a story about an environmental hazard or an industrial safety problem has come from a trade association, a fundraising operation, or a regional group that stands to benefit disproportionately from resources allocated to solving the problem. When we watch film clips on television, read statistics in the newspaper, or hear an interview over the radio, we frequently presume that the information reflects the findings of disinterested journalists. But far more often than is generally known, the media are simply using videotapes, audiotapes, and reports prepared by a party driven to enhance the availability of certain perceptions and viewpoints and expecting this transformation to start a cascade.

ENDURING PROBLEMS, RAPID SHIFTS, AND UNCOORDINATED LAW

To be sure, availability cascades eventually come to a stop. A central reason is that some learning takes place independently of social forces, as when a person who accidentally drinks a few glasses of water from Love Canal senses, when he remains healthy, that the Canal's toxicity may have been exaggerated. Learning can break, or brake, a cascade. Another reason is that reducing small risks can impose significant burdens and inconveniences. People who complain about actually harmless waste sites endure big costs when the government orders their relocation. But even if a cascade can stop, people might reach a consensus on a certain belief even if it is false. The continuing fear of abandoned hazardous waste dumps is a case in point. Once a consensus and a policy are in place, both may endure even if subsequent scientific evidence discredits the information that triggered the cascade responsible for their emergence. Individuals who, whether through study, experience, or exposure to dissent, develop doubts about the prevailing conventional wisdom may be reluctant to challenge the consensus, perhaps because they lack self-confidence (can so many people be wrong?), partly because of a reluctance to make themselves unpopular. By keeping quiet, even paying lip service to the new conventional wisdom, they will help to preserve the prevailing public discourse.

Of course the public discourse shaped by the cascade will contribute to the perceptions of new generations. Insofar as young generations form their beliefs on the basis of informational availability, what they learn will reflect the distortions of the prevailing public discourse. Even today, two decades after scientists found the alleged health hazards of Love Canal essentially unfounded, references to the region evoke thoughts of profit-hungry industrial bosses destroying a gorgeous countryside and risking the lives of helpless men, women, and children for the sake of a few more dollars. People who have never been to the Niagara Falls region, and who were not even born when Love Canal made the headlines daily, know of the episode through a public discourse still controlled by an availability cascade that ran its course twenty years ago.

But there is also a possibility of variability over time. Even a small social shock can cause the public consensus to unravel as hidden doubts come out in the open and unarticulated knowledge gets expressed. In fact, the initial unraveling of the consensus may lead people to change sides, create a cascade effect, and eventually usher in a new consensus. A quarter century ago, few people considered second-hand smoke a health hazard, and the few who did could not ask smokers to move elsewhere without risking ridicule or angry reactions. Now most Americans consider secondhand smoke harmful, many seriously exaggerate the risk, and it is the minority of smokers who risk ostracism if they argue publicly that secondhand smoke poses no risk. Likewise, only a short time ago nonscientists showed little concern about the thinning of the ozone layer. Now millions of people are alarmed. These two transformations took place over periods much shorter than it took for the relevant scientific evidence to accumulate.

THE SELF-REINFORCEMENT OF AVAILABILITY

In choosing to join the chorus of concern over an environment's safety, individuals make the signs of environmental degradation increasingly available to others. An availability cascade will thus feed on itself. Every person who reacts to changes in the availability of information on the risk makes such information more available to others. But there are some important wrinkles here.

To make a risk claim and the supportive data *more* available is to make information pointing to the absence of this risk *less* available. An availability cascade is necessarily accompanied, therefore, by an *unavailability cascade* that progressively frees public discourse of those voices that are out of tune with the evolving chorus. This concurrent cascade makes it increasingly difficult for people with stated or unstated reservations about the developing consensus to retain their misgivings. Making their private knowledge increasingly insecure and their private preferences seem unusual, the ongoing cascade weakens their resistance and facilitates their participation in the evolving consensus.

Imagine a Love Canal resident who, when the story breaks, feels that the press is overreacting and that her neighbors are acting irrationally. At first, she is able to share her doubts and misgivings with other skeptical residents, and she notices skeptical commentaries and editorials in the press. But as the cascade unfolds, open skepticism becomes less and less common. She runs into fewer neighbors prepared to express reservations, and she encounters fewer press accounts that call for calm and caution. She begins wondering, therefore, whether she has been blind to facts obvious to almost everyone else. This self-doubt weakens her resistance to the mounting pressures against questioning the spill's gravity. At some point, her threshold of resistance is reached, and she joins the availability cascade. Dissenting voices become fainter still, making it that much harder for the dwindling number of open skeptics to hold out as critics. In the late 1970s, as Love Canal became a top news story, many commentators likened the episode to an industrial Vietnam by noting that dioxin is one of the chemicals in Agent Orange, which American forces used in the Vietnam War. Others described the problem of dumping chemicals to "Gypsy hauling" and "midnight dumping," which gave the impression that no one is safe from deadly chemicals, that "new Love Canals" could be unfolding in anyone's backyard. These images created an intellectual climate that made it difficult to maintain a feeling of security.

Similar processes can produce little public concern, and little governmental activity, with respect to quite serious dangers. Even if a teenager suspects that cigarette smoking, air travel, reckless driving, and sun exposure are risky, he may suppress his concerns, in order to reduce the danger of disapproval from his relevant peer group. (Cognitive factors might operate here: "I don't know anyone who died of lung cancer, and I know plenty of smokers," or "My friends drive fast, and none of them has ever been in an accident.") He might even smoke or drive fast. The resulting "unavailability errors" can lead to hundreds or even thousands of premature deaths. Consider in this regard the fact that many experts said, before the terrorist attacks of September 11, 2001, that in the United States, airport security was lax, and that the system was highly vulnerable to terrorist attacks. Notwithstanding these warnings, people felt entirely secure, in large part because no such attack was cognitively available, or at least salient enough to produce fear. This is a vivid illustration of how cognitive processes can produce neglect as well as hysteria.

Availability cascades create serious problems for the theory and practice of democracy. They suggest the possibility that apparently democratic outcomes will be both misinformed and unrepresentative, in any normatively attractive sense, of citizens' beliefs, desires, and judgments. As a result of the underlying processes, both individuals and governments focus on some risks that do not deserve such attention and disregard some risks that are actually quite serious. What might be done in response?

5

Reducing Risks Rationally

Often it is possible to resolve hard questions of law and policy without resolving deeply contested issues about justice, democracy, or the appropriate aims of the state. Often it is possible for people who disagree on many topics to agree on a social practice. In many areas of law and public policy, people can reach closure about what they should do despite their disagreement or uncertainty about why, exactly, they should to do it. When closure is reached in this way, we might say that people find their way toward *incompletely theorized agreements.*[1]

Thus people who sharply disagree about the purposes of the criminal law can agree that rape and murder should be punished, and punished more severely than theft and trespass. People can support an Endangered Species Act even if they disagree about whether the protection of endangered species is desirable for theological reasons; because of the rights of animals, plants, and species; or because of the value of animals, plants, and species for human beings. Incompletely theorized agreements are hardly foreign to government regulation. In the area of regulatory reform, deregulation of the trucking and airlines industry commanded agreement from many diverse people; in fact, it was spearheaded by Senator Edward M. Kennedy, who was enthusiastically joined by many conservatives. A great advantage of incompletely theorized agreements is that they allow people of diverse views to live together on mutually advantageous terms. An even greater advantage is that they allow people of diverse views to show one another a high degree of both humility and mutual respect.

In this chapter, I attempt to outline, in a preliminary and general way, government responses to the problems discussed thus far. The basic tasks are to find ways to ensure against cascade effects based on insufficient evidence; to promote governmental responses to significant risks even if the public has

---

[1] I discuss this point in detail in Cass R. Sunstein, Legal Reasoning and Political Conflict (New York: Oxford Univ. Press, 1996).

shown little interest in reducing them; and to place tradeoffs on-screen, including the risks that are created by risk regulation. Three principles, sketched in the introduction, provide the basic orientation. First, government should attempt to assess the magnitudes of risks; it should not concern itself with risks that are statistically small. Second, government should examine all the effects of risk reduction, including costs and additional hazards created by risk reduction itself. Third, government should explore alternatives to any proposed action, including alternatives that involve less intrusive tools for achieving the same basic ends. To adopt these principles is to move much of the way toward cost–benefit analysis, and to do so without saying anything especially controversial about the proper ends of government.

But let us begin with some ideas that, while extremely influential, seem to me quite inadequate: pollution prevention, the precautionary principle, and sustainable development. Each of these ideas is often proposed as an alternative to the analytical techniques of cost–benefit analysis – an alternative that is less "cold," more attuned to potential harms to real people, and more friendly to the environment. Despite their popularity, and their extraordinary international prominence, I think that the three ideas are unhelpful, sometimes even ludicrous. An understanding of why this is so helps to prepare the way for the more affirmative discussion that follows.

POLLUTION PREVENTION, RISK PREVENTION

Should pollution be "prevented" rather than "cured"? With respect to many problems, including illness, prevention does indeed seem best – cheapest and most effective. It is usually better to have a flu shot than to treat flu after the fact. For most people, a good diet and exercise, alongside a refusal to smoke, are a lot better than heart surgery and chemotherapy. Perhaps prevention should be the preferred approach in the domain of social risks.

Barry Commoner, a well-known scientist and environmentalist, has urged that government regulation of risks should be fundamentally remodeled, with the idea of "prevention" at its core.[2] The idea has been influential in many circles. In fact Congress has enacted a statute – unimaginatively but informatively named the Pollution Prevention Act – that puts a premium on pollution prevention.[3] The goal of pollution prevention is to ensure that regulators prevent pollution before it even enters the system. As real-world examples, consider the phaseout of lead in gasolines, the use of solar power, and the substitution of electric cars for cars powered by gasoline. According to Commoner and many others, this

---

[2] See Barry Commoner, Making Peace with the Planet (New York: Pantheon Books, 1990).
[3] 42 USC 13101.

approach is far more promising than "end-of-the-pipe" controls imposed on polluting technologies. Advocates of pollution prevention argue that pollution prevention promises larger and more dramatic pollution reductions and does not rely on imperfectly reliable, after-the-fact technological "fixes."

Thus Commoner contends that the "real improvements have been achieved not by adding controls or concealing pollutants but by simply eliminating them. The reason there is so much less lead in the environment – and in children's blood – is that lead has been almost entirely eliminated from the manufacture of gasoline. The reason why DDT and related pesticides are now much less prevalent in wildlife and our own bodies is that their use has been banned."[4] Prevention works "because it is directed at the *origin* of the pollutant in the production process itself." By contrast, controls "yield little or no improvement" because they "are only one element in a larger system that can readily counteract their apparent efficiency." For Commoner, the overall lesson is that if "you don't put something in the environment, it isn't there." To take one illustration, Commoner urges that if we would really like to reduce nitrogen oxide emissions from cars, we will build "smogless engines that do not produce nitrogen oxides," rather than relying on catalytic converters.[5] It would be easy to build on the idea of pollution prevention to suggest that in many contexts, regulators should move toward "risk prevention." Instead of managing risks that are already in the system, they should attempt to eliminate enterprises and activities that produce (unacceptably high?) risks.

Often pollution prevention makes sense. The EPA was right to eliminate lead from gasoline; the government was also right to stop the use of CFCs, which contribute to destruction of the ozone layer. If asbestos is a potent carcinogen, and if it can be eliminated without causing serious problems, there is a good argument for eliminating asbestos. But sometimes pollution prevention would be extremely unappealing, even ridiculous, simply because it is not worthwhile, all things considered. Consider some examples. The best way to prevent automobile pollution would be to eliminate the internal combustion engines that power most trucks and cars. The best way to prevent pollution from current power sources would be to stop relying on fossil fuels, now used by utility power plants. The best way to prevent the risks of genetically modified plants would be to ban the genetic modification of plants. Should the EPA be told to ban the internal combustion engine and coal combustion? Should national legislatures forbid the genetic modification of plants? If these would be ridiculous conclusions – as I think they would be – it is because the costs of the bans would dwarf the benefits. Pollution prevention is not worthwhile as such; it is worthwhile when it is better, all things considered, than the alternatives.

---

[4] Commoner, supra note 2 in this chapter, at 42.

[5] Id. at 99.

There is a further point. In many contexts, the idea of pollution prevention, or risk prevention more generally, is literally paralyzing because no approach will actually "prevent" pollution or risk. If the internal combustion engine is banned, substitutes will have to be introduced, and electric cars cause pollution of their own, above all because they currently require considerable energy use. Perhaps electric cars are, on balance, better from the environmental point of view. But if they are better, it is because they produce less (not no) pollution; and that is a different claim from the claim that "prevention" is always or generally best. As we have seen, a ban on the genetic modification of plants might increase overall risks, if it is the case that genetically modified plants reduce risks compared to the alternative.

In fact the strongest argument for pollution prevention rests, at bottom, on cost–benefit balancing. Those who urge pollution prevention are thinking of instances where this approach has large benefits and small costs. In the context of eliminating lead from gasoline, cost–benefit analysis firmly supported pollution prevention, because the benefits dwarfed the costs. The same is true for banning CFCs. But where the balance does not support regulation, pollution prevention is a mistake. Properly understood, pollution prevention is what is recommended by cost–benefit analysis – but only sometimes.

None of this is to deny that sometimes projections of the future will involve a degree of guesswork and speculation. As we have seen, guesswork and speculation are the rule rather than the exception. But when this is so, good cost–benefit analysis calls for attention to the range of possibilities. What is not justified is to "prevent" pollution without an inquiry into the consequences, good and bad, of prevention. The most that can be said is that pollution prevention should always be considered as a possible option and that in some cases, it will turn out to be preferred. But as a general approach to environmental protection, or to the reduction of social risks, it is obtuse. In many contexts, pollution prevention would be literally dangerous, in fact a disaster.

THE PRECAUTIONARY PRINCIPLE

All over the world, there is increasing interest in a simple idea for the regulation of risk: In the case of doubt, follow *the precautionary principle.*[6] Avoid steps that will create a risk of harm. Until safety is established, be cautious. In a catch-phrase: Better safe than sorry. In ordinary life, pleas of this kind seem quite sensible. People buy smoke alarms and insurance. Shouldn't the same approach be followed by regulators as well?

[6] Protecting Public Health & the Environment: Implementing the Precautionary Principle, Carolyn Raffensberger & Joel Tickner, eds. (Washington, D.C.: Island Press, 1999).

Many people believe so. The Ministerial Declaration of the Second International Conference on the Protection of the North Sea, held in London in 1987, states: "Accepting that in order to protect the North Sea from possibly damaging effects of the most dangerous substances, a precautionary principle is necessary which may require action to control inputs of such substances even before a causal link has been established by absolutely clear scientific evidence."[7] The closing Ministerial Declaration from the United Nations Economic Conference for Europe in 1990 asserted, "In order to achieve sustainable development, policies must be based on the precautionary principle.... Where there are threats of serious or irreversible damage, lack of full scientific certainty should not be used as a reason for postponing measures to prevent environmental degradation."[8] The widely publicized Wingspread Declaration, from a meeting of environmentalists in 1998, went further still: "When an activity raises threats of harm to human health or the environment, precautionary measures should be taken even if some cause and effect relationships are not established scientifically. In this context the proponent of the activity, rather than the public, should bear the burden of proof."[9]

There is some important truth in the precautionary principle. Sometimes it is much better to be safe than sorry. Certainly we should acknowledge that a small probability (say, 1 in 100,000) of a serious harm (say, 100,000 deaths) deserves extremely serious attention. It is worthwhile to spend a lot of money to eliminate that risk. The fact that a danger is unlikely to materialize is hardly a good objection to regulatory controls. But everything depends on the size of the investment and the speculativeness of the harm. Unless the harm would be truly catastrophic, a huge investment makes no sense for a harm that has a one in one billion chance of occurring. Taken literally, the precautionary principle would lead to indefensibly huge expenditures, exhausting our budget well before the menu of options could be thoroughly consulted. If we take costly steps to address all risks, however improbable they are, we will quickly impoverish ourselves. This is no less true for nations than for individuals.

But there is a larger problem. The precautionary principle can provide guidance only if we blinker ourselves and look at a subset of the harms involved. In real-world controversies, a failure to regulate will run afoul of the precautionary principle because potential risks are involved. But regulation itself will cause potential risks, and hence run afoul of the precautionary principle too; and

[7] Quoted in Rethinking Risk and the Precautionary Principle 3, Julian Morris, ed. (Oxford: Butterworth-Heinemann, 2000).

[8] Id. at 5.

[9] Id.

the same is true for every step in between. Hence the precautionary principle, taken for all that it is worth, is literally paralyzing. It bans every imaginable step, including inaction itself.

A failure to allow genetic modification might well result in many deaths, and a small probability of many more. Hence the precautionary principle seems to argue both for and against banning genetic modification of food. The point is very general. An expensive regulation can have adverse effects on life and health, and hence a multimillion dollar expenditure for "precaution" has – as a worst case scenario – significant adverse health effects, with perhaps many tens of lives lost. If this is so, the precautionary principle seems to argue against the regulation. If the precautionary principle argues against any action that carries a small risk of significant harm, then we should be reluctant to spend a lot of money to reduce risks because those expenditures themselves carry risks. Like the idea of pollution prevention, the precautionary principle, understood in an extreme form, stands as an obstacle to regulation and nonregulation, and to everything in between. Indeed the most sensible understandings of the precautionary principle emphasize the need for an overall assessment and insist on exploring all of the risks at stake, including low-probability, potentially catastrophic risks.[10]

Perhaps this argument is missing something. In some contexts, regulation is indeed a form of insurance, or a way of placing special locks on a door. Consider the following choice. Would you rather have

(a) a sure loss of $20 or
(b) a 1 percent chance of losing $1,980?

In terms of expected value, (b), representing a statistical loss of $19.80, is a bit less bad than (a); but most people would gladly choose the sure loss of $20. People do not like to run a small risk of a large or catastrophic loss; this is why we buy insurance and take special precautions against serious harms. Where a risk would be very high, and when we can reduce or eliminate it with cash, it makes sense to endorse the precautionary principle.

If we speak in these terms, however, we are substantially qualifying the precautionary principle, treating it less like a dogma and more as the beginning of a serious analysis of how to approach risks. A competent cost–benefit analysis (CBA) takes good account of the precautionary principle by asking regulators to attend to low-probability risks of significant harms. CBA subsumes this risk, as it does all others, into the overall assessment. A special advantage of CBA is that it incorporates all risks, on all sides of the equation; it therefore prevents

[10] See Indur Goklany, The Precautionary Principle (Washington, D.C.: The Cato Institute, 2001).

the kinds of myopia and tunnel vision that are threatened if we take precautions against some risks and thereby fail to take precautions against others. (Consider bans on the use of cell phones in cars, which may increase risks by, for example, preventing people from making or receiving calls in emergencies.) Because CBA is a source of information, and not something to be used mechanically as the basis for decisions, good regulators will often buy the equivalent of insurance. Nothing in CBA precludes a policymaker from concluding that we should suffer a sure loss of, say, $200,000 to prevent a I percent risk of $19,800,000 in monetary and other losses. Nor does CBA prevent regulators from deciding that a I/I0,000 risk of I00,000 deaths is worse, or less bad, than a I/I,000 risk of I0,000 deaths. This is a political judgment, not a technical one to be decided by mechanical use of the numbers.

Aaron Wildavsky, a political scientist with a special interest in risk regulation, attacks the precautionary principle on grounds similar to those I have used here.[11] Wildavsky convincingly argues that often risks are on both sides of the equation, and hence the idea of "precaution" senselessly guards against one set of risks while ignoring the others. In Wildavsky's view, the notion of "precaution" should not merely be disregarded; it should also be replaced. It should be replaced with a principle of "resilience," based on an understanding that nature, and society, are quite able to incorporate even strong shocks, and that the ultimate dangers are therefore smaller than we are likely to fear. Unfortunately, the principle of "resilience" is no better than that of "precaution." Some systems are resilient, but many are not. Whether an ecosystem, or a society, is "resilient" cannot be decided in the abstract. In any case resilience is a matter of degree. Everything depends on the facts. As we will see, cost–benefit balancing is to be preferred, not because resilience is unlikely, but because it is necessary to inquire into the particular problem to know.

SUSTAINABLE DEVELOPMENT

The notion of "sustainable development" has had an extraordinary influence in international environmental debates, so much as that it now serves as a kind of symbol for any serious commitment to environmental protection. But the notion is highly ambiguous. What kind of development counts as sustainable? What counts as "unsustainable"? In a standard formulation, the idea of sustainable development is said to refer to "development that occurs on a scale that does not exceed the carrying capacity of the biosphere."[12]

---

[11] See Wildavsky, supra note 9 in Chapter I.
[12] See Robert Percival et al., Environmental Regulation: Law, Science, and Policy II82 (Boston: Little, Brown & Co., 2000).

To the extent that endorsement of sustainable development is meant as a criticism of approaches that are literally "unsustainable" in the sense that future generations will lack environmental goods – clean air and water, for example – everyone should support sustainable development. Any minimally sensible policy will ensure decent lives and options for future generations. No sane person is opposed to that. Indeed, cost–benefit analysis itself calls for sustainable development, because a competent analyst incorporates the interests of members of future generations. But outside of the easy cases for environmental protection, the real question is not "sustainable" development or "unsustainable" development; it involves what level of resources to commit to environmental protection. Often there is no simple line to divide the sustainable from the unsustainable. If certain regulatory steps would increase "sustainability" but cause a great deal of suffering and misery, simply by virtue of their expense, a sensible administrator will take that point into account. And if the sensible administrator is thinking in this way, he is balancing the various considerations, very much in the way that cost–benefit analysis helps to do. In the international context, the administrator might even ask for financial help from wealthier countries, help that is required from the standpoint of justice.

Because cost–benefit balancing requires consideration of the interests of future generations, the goal of sustainable development is in no conflict with that form of balancing. Indeed, cost–benefit analysis strongly supports the idea that sustainability is a desirable goal. It also helps give content to the hard question, which is how much should be done to improve environmental quality in poor as well as wealthy nations.

To conclude: Pollution prevention can be a good idea, but it would sometimes lead to disaster, not least because it would increase serious risks. Sometimes it is better to be safe than sorry, and here the precautionary principle makes sense. People do, and should, buy insurance. But sometimes the precautionary principle leads to paralysis, and in any case some precautions are simply not worthwhile. Everyone should support sustainable development. But support for sustainable development does not answer any of the hard questions. It is important to ensure that policies are sustainable rather than the opposite. But in poor nations as well as rich ones, regulators need much better guidance than that.

WHAT IS COST–BENEFIT ANALYSIS?
WHY FAVOR IT?

For the moment, let us understand cost–benefit analysis to entail a *full accounting of the consequences of risk reduction, in both quantitative and qualitative terms.* Officials should have this accounting before them when they make decisions. They should not be bound by the "bottom-line" numbers. But if they are to proceed, they should be prepared to explain how the benefits justify the costs, or if not, why it is nonetheless worthwhile to go forward. I am therefore understanding cost–benefit analysis to require a certain procedure: a quantitative and qualitative accounting of the effects of regulation, together with a duty to explain the grounds for action unless the benefits justify the costs. On this view, the antonym to regulation guided by cost–benefit analysis is regulation undertaken without anything like a clear sense of the likely consequences – or regulation that amounts to a stab in the dark.

The most basic argument for cost–benefit balancing, thus understood, is cognitive. The goal is to overcome cognitive limitations by ensuring that people have a full, rather than limited, sense of what is at stake. People often miss the systemic effects of risk regulation; cost–benefit analysis is a way of putting those effects squarely on-screen. At the same time, cost–benefit analysis helps overcome the problems created by the availability heuristic, by allowing an accounting of the actual consequences of current risks, and of the effects of reducing then. If people are fearful of a risk that is actually quite small, cost–benefit analysis will supply a corrective. If people are indifferent to a risk that is actually quite large, cost–benefit analysis will help to stir them out of their torpor. One of the primary advantages of cost–benefit analysis, properly understood, is that it promotes an understanding of health–health tradeoffs, but it also does much more. To the extent that people's emotions are getting the better of them, by producing massive concern abut small risks, cost–benefit analysis should help put things in perspective and at the same time might help to calm popular fears. To the extent that people's perspective is distorted by seeing problems in isolation, cost–benefit analysis can help to put isolated problems in the context of a full range of dangers, thus preventing the kinds of distortions that come from a narrow perspective. The result should be to help with cognitive distortions and to produce sensible priority-setting.

There are democratic advantages as well. As I have emphasized, interest groups often manipulate policy in their preferred directions, sometimes by exaggerating risks, sometimes by minimizing them, sometimes by using heuristics and biases strategically, so as to mobilize public sentiment in their preferred directions. An effort to produce a fair accounting of actual dangers should help to diminish the danger of interest-group manipulation. More generally, cost–benefit analysis should increase the likelihood that citizens generally, and officials in particular, will be informed of what is actually at stake. By itself this is a large democratic gain.

Of course interest groups will also try to manipulate the numbers in their preferred directions. Industry, which is typically well funded, will exaggerate the costs and minimize the risks. Public interest groups will do the opposite.

(I explore this point later in connection with the regulation of arsenic in drinking water.) A government that attempts to produce cost–benefit analysis will face a formidable task; it is possible that government will lack the information necessary to do this task well. But if there is a degree of accuracy, and if ranges are specified where there is uncertainty, cost–benefit analysis can be seen, not as some antidemocratic effort to tyrannize people with numbers, but instead as an indispensable tool of democratic self-government.

Of course, it is possible that in practice cost–benefit analysis will have excessive influence on government decisions, drowning out "soft variables."[13] Since the numbers are not all that matters, any such effect would be a point against cost–benefit analysis. But to date, the actual record does not support this concern. To take just one example, the EPA's decision to go forward with new controls on arsenic in drinking water was supported partly on the ground that nonquantifiable variables tipped the balance.[14] The risk that cost–benefit analysis will drown out relevant variables is not a reason to abandon the analysis, but to take steps to ensure against any such effect.

ARE RISKS SOCIALLY CONSTRUCTED?
OF SCIENCE AND ITS DISCONTENTS

A large goal of cost–benefit analysis is to increase the role of science in risk regulation. This is a controversial goal. Many diverse people have been skeptical of the idea that risk regulation should be grounded, first and foremost, in an understanding of scientific fact. Some of these groups purport to be inspired by democratic, even populist ideals. They suggest that the underlying issues should be resolved by ordinary people, not by a technocratic elite.[15] Some of these critics are skeptical of the whole idea of scientific objectivity. They doubt that risk is an objective concept, measuring something "out there" in the world.[16] Others urge that scientists have values and agendas of their own, and that the effort to strengthen the role of science is actually an effort to fortify the place of those values and agendas. They insist that questions of risk regulation are questions of value, not of fact, and that the real issue is whose values will prevail.

---

[13] Lisa Heinzerling, Clean Air and the constitution, 20 St. Louis U. Pub. L. Rev. 121, 151 (2001) ("cost–benefit analysis tends to underrate those things that cannot be so quantified and monetized"); Laurence H. Tribe, Ways Not to Think About Plastic Trees: New Foundations for Environmental Law, 83 Yale L. J. 1315, 1318–19 & n. 25 (1974).

[14] See Chapte 7; see also Corrosion Proof Fittings v. EPA, 947 F. 2d 1201 (5th Cir., 1991).

[15] Kristin Shreder-Frechette, Risk and Rationality (Berkeley, Calif.: Univ. California Press, 1991).

[16] See Slovic, supra note 12 in Chapter 2, at p. 392.

Respect for "science" is said to be a smokescreen here. Some of these critics include powerful industries purporting to respect the facts but fearful that a careful look at the facts will compromise their economic self-interest; tobacco companies are only the most visible example. In a more theoretical vein, some people insist that risks are "socially constructed," and that any judgment about the magnitude or even the existence of a "risk" is a matter of social judgments, not of something external to what people think.[17]

Some of these objections are easy to handle. Of course there is a problem if some groups are manipulating science to promote their own selfish agendas. At the level of principle, little needs to be said, except perhaps that manipulation of this sort is deplorable. The real task is to ensure that any efforts at manipulation will fail. But some of the critiques of scientific objectivity, and some claims about "social construction," raise hard questions. For the moment let us simply insist that, with respect to risks, there really are facts, and it is crucial to know the truth as best we can. Some risks are genuinely serious, in the sense that many people are going to get hurt, get sick, or die as a result. Some risks are not serious, in the sense that few people, or no people, are in danger. Whether a risk is serious, in the sense that many people will be hurt or die, is a question of fact, not of values. Of course values affect any evaluative judgment about the seriousness of risks, but the factual questions are crucial and should be identified and evaluated as such.

Risks are "socially constructed" in the sense that the categories that we use to perceive them are our own. Moreover, both individuals and societies will be greatly concerned about some hazards but treat others as inevitable aspects of life, worth acknowledging but no more. There is a great deal to be said about the relationship between risk and culture, and I will deal very little with that important issue here.[18] What is important for present purposes is that risk is not socially constructed, in any interesting sense, when a certain number of people will (actually) be injured or killed as a result. As best we can tell, hundreds of thousands of people will die each year, in the United States alone, as a result of cigarette smoking. To argue on behalf of cost–benefit analysis, it is necessary only to say that numbers of this sort have real meaning.

Now these points are not meant to deny that scientists have their own values, and that with different assumptions, risks can be estimated as large or small. It is easy to show that with small variations in assumptions, we will come up with dramatically different projections about the future, and that in the face of scientific uncertainty, reasonable people can come up with widely

---

[17] See id.

[18] For an influential discussion, see Mary Douglas & Aaron Wildavsky, Risk and Culture (New York: The Free Press, 1992).

varying judgments about the seriousness of risks. Indeed, Chapter 6 is devoted to an exploration of exactly this issue. Of course the assumptions that produce different judgments will sometimes be a product of values, not simply science. What is the discount rate for future benefits and costs? How should we proceed if we lack knowledge about the rate or nature of climate change? What is the level of risk from exposure to low levels of arsenic, when we have evidence only for high exposure levels? It is extremely important to ensure that assumptions are identified as such, not least to ensure public oversight of how to proceed in the face of uncertainty.

But none of this justifies skepticism about the role of science in risk regulation. There really are facts, whether or not we are able to identify them. Of course we should sometimes be skeptical of scientists' ability to get the facts right; scientists are themselves sometimes skeptical of their ability to get the facts right. When skepticism is justified, the best approach is not to do nothing, to let companies do whatever they wish, to adopt the precautionary principle, to regulate to the hilt, to flip a coin, or even to defer to public values, whatever they happen to be. The best approach is instead to specify the range of possible outcomes, with some sense of the likely probabilities. If there is a small chance of a catastrophic outcome, inaction is hardly the obvious course; people buy insurance, and risk regulation is a form of (preventative) insurance. In some cases, it might not be possible even to specify a range. Here science will leave us at sea. But many cases are not like that.

It bears emphasizing that science cannot by itself resolve normative questions. An understanding of likely consequences cannot resolve issues of value. But democratic judgments should be made with reference to the best understandings of the facts, rather than short-term panics and scare tactics. People should be allowed to see the range of legitimate uncertainty. For these purposes, cost–benefit analysis is an excellent place not to end but to start.

EIGHT PROPOSITIONS

Recall that by cost–benefit analysis, I mean a full accounting of the effects of regulation, both qualitative and quantitative, along with descriptions in both monetary and nonmonetary terms. My basic suggestion is that government should offer that accounting and also make it relevant for purposes of decision. To make these ideas more concrete, here are eight propositions, offered in the hope that they might attract support from diverse theoretical standpoints.

I. Agencies should not only identify the advantages and disadvantages of proposed efforts to reduce risks but also attempt to quantify the relevant effects to the extent that this is possible. When quantification is not possible, agencies should discuss the relevant effects in qualitative terms. The statement should include the full range of beneficial effects.

2. The quantitative description should supplement rather than displace a qualitative description of relevant effects. Both qualitative and quantitative descriptions should be provided. It is important to know not only raw numbers but also the nature of the relevant effects (e.g., lost workdays, cancers averted, respiratory problems averted). To the extent possible, the qualitative description should give a concrete sense of who is helped and who is hurt (e.g., whether the beneficiaries are mostly or partly children, whether the regulation will lead to lost jobs, higher prices, more poverty, and so forth). Where the only possible information is speculative, this should be noted, along with the most reasonable speculations.

3. To improve the overall evaluation, agencies should attempt to convert nonmonetary values (involving, for example, lives saved, health gains, and aesthetic values) into dollar equivalents. There is nothing magical or rigid about the dollar equivalents. The conversion is simply a pragmatic tool to guide analysis and to allow informed comparisons.

4. Agencies entrusted with valuing life and health should be controlled, by statute or executive order, via presumptive floors and ceilings. For example, a statute might say that a statistical life will ordinarily be valued at no less than $2 million and no more than $10 million. Evidence of worker and consumer behavior, suggesting a valuation of between $5 million and $8 million per statistical life saved, is at least relevant here. The willingness to pay numbers are in this range, which is certainly relevant if not decisive. Similar numbers appear to represent the midpoint of agency practice. Thus both market and governmental measures point in the same basic direction. It is important in this regard that as the expenditures get very far above $10 million, regulations threaten to become counterproductive. An expenditure of $15 million per life saved threatens to take as many lives as it protects.

If Congress does not act, OMB should establish presumptive floors and ceilings for various regulatory benefits. If an agency is going to spend (say) no more than $500,000 per life saved, or more than $20 million, it should have to explain itself.

5. Agencies should be permitted to make adjustments in the analysis on the basis of the various "qualitative" factors. For example, agencies might add a "pain and suffering premium" or increase the level of expenditure because children are disproportionately affected or because the victims are members of a disadvantaged group. It would be reasonable to conclude that because AIDS has disproportionate adverse effects on homosexuals and poor people, special efforts should be made to ensure against AIDS-related deaths. To the extent possible, agencies should be precise about the nature of, and grounds for, the relevant adjustments, especially in light of the risk that interest-group pressures will convert allegedly qualitative adjustments in illegitimate directions. Agencies might incorporate these considerations in a "sensitivity analysis," showing how the numbers are sensitive to changes in assumptions.

6. Agencies should be required to show that the benefits justify the costs. If they do not, they should be required to show that the action is nonetheless reasonable, on the basis of a publicly articulated explanation. In most cases, the tabulation of costs and benefits should be accompanied by a showing that the benefits justify the costs. If the benefits do not justify the costs, the agency should explain itself. Perhaps the agency could claim that those who bear the costs can easily do so, whereas those who receive the benefits have a special claim to public help. The principal danger here is that well-organized groups will be able to use equitable arguments on behalf of their preferred adjustments. It is important to ensure a degree of discipline here. Perhaps the dangers of interest-group manipulation are serious enough to suggest that uniform numbers or ranges might be used.

7. Under ordinary circumstances, the appropriate response to social fear not based on evidence, and to related ripple effects, is education and reassurance rather than increased regulation. We have seen that public concern about certain risks can be widespread and very intense, even though the concern is not merited by the facts. The best response to unjustified fear is not to capitulate to it but to inform people that the fear is baseless. A government should not expend significant resources merely because an uninformed public thinks that it should. But if education and reassurance fail, increased regulation may be defensible as a way of providing a kind of reassurance in the face of intense fears, which can themselves impose high costs of various kinds. Recall, for example, the possibility that people who are afraid of risks of plane crashes will shift to driving, a more risky method of transportation; consider also the fact that the fear is itself both a problem and a cost. In the aftermath of an actual or apparent terrorist attack, involving airplanes or anthrax, the government might respond quite aggressively, even if it believes that the risk of another attack is very low. One reason for an aggressive response is that a low probability of a significant harm is itself worth addressing. But another reason is that widespread public fear has a wide range of ripple effects, far outrunning the material consequences of the risks themselves.

112

8. **Unless the statute requires otherwise, judicial review of risk regulation should require a general showing that regulation has produced more good than harm, on a reasonable view about valuation of both benefits and costs.** On this view, courts should generally require agencies to generate and to adhere to ceilings and floors. But they should also allow agencies to depart from conventional numbers (by, for example, valuing a life at less than $3 million, or more than $15 million) if and only if the agency has given a reasonable explanation of why it has done so. The ultimate task would be develop a kind of "common law" of cost–benefit analysis, authorizing agencies to be lawmaking institutions in the first instance.

If all this is correct, it should ultimately be possible to produce a convergence on a form of cost–benefit analysis that should be understood as a pragmatic instrument and that ought not to be terribly contentious – a form of cost–benefit analysis that does not take a stand on highly controversial questions about what government ought to do and that promises to attract support from people with diverse views about what is good and what is right. For those who reject proposals of the sort that I have outlined here, the question remains: On what other basis should government choose one or another approach to risk regulation?

Even if we endorse cost–benefit analysis, it is not enough simply to urge agencies to engage in it. Institutional reforms are necessary from each of the three branches of government. I offer a brief sketch here.

CONGRESS

As an institution, Congress is strikingly ill-equipped to place risks in comparative perspective. One reason is that legislators, like everyone else, are subject to cognitive biases. Another reason is that legislators are subject to the public demand for legislation, which is produced by those very biases as well as by well-organized groups that attempt to steer the legislature in their favor. Members of the national legislature are especially vulnerable to availability cascades, partly because they can produce an irresistible demand for legislation, and partly because isolated members often act as availability entrepreneurs, working in concert with private persons to further parochial agendas. Interest groups are in a good position to exploit the underlying mechanisms, heightening or dampening public fears, sometimes by manipulating people's affect about certain products and processes. At the same time, the committee system keeps Congress highly balkanized. It also increases its susceptibility to short-term pressures. Because the activities of committee members are carefully scrutinized by directly affected lobbies, they are often reluctant to publicize information, make statements, or take positions that can be used against them at election time.

An unfortunate consequence is that when an availability cascade, or some other pressure, fuels massive demand for acting on a matter under the committee's purview, committee members may yield, and legislative action may follow without any attempt to coordinate it with existing policies, to place it in a comparative context, or to assess the issue of tradeoffs. *Risk redistribution* becomes at least as likely as *risk reduction*. If the corn lobby has particular influence before the key committee, it might well be able to push for a requirement of ethanol in gasoline, whatever the health consequences. A balkanized Congress is in an excellent position to be giving out gifts to well-organized private groups, in the form of purportedly public-spirited regulation that really helps some groups while hurting others.

In its present form, Congress is entirely illequipped to consider the problem of health–health tradeoffs. Here too committee structure ensures a high degree of fragmentation and does not allow for deliberation on such tradeoffs. On the contrary, that structure makes substitute risks difficult to evaluate or, much worse, even to see; often those risks are thought to be subject to the jurisdiction of another committee, which means, in practice, that coordination is extremely difficult. What can be done? Here are several possibilities.

- *Risk oversight.* Congress should create a risk regulation committee that would be entrusted with compiling information about a wide range of risk levels and helping to produce sensible priorities. This committee would have authority over both substantive statutes and the appropriations process. It would thus operate as a check on short-term pressures by putting particular concerns in a broader context. Its basic goal would be to engage in risk ranking, to publicize misallocations, and to initiate legislative corrections. In its ideal form, the committee would rely heavily on prevailing scientific knowledge. Its essential function would be to ensure against myopic, unduly quick, and poorly reasoned responses, not to insulate risk regulation from social values. This committee should have the power to introduce corrective legislation when a statute, or agency action under a statute, has been shown to increase aggregate risks. Like any government body, the risk regulation committee would most certainly become the target of well-organized private groups seeking to mold policies to their own advantage. But the very acts of comparing risks and publicizing the comparisons would provide a measure of protection against well-organized private interests. If the social costs of accommodating a particular lobby's demands gain widespread recognition, counterlobbying may neutralize the lobby's political effectiveness.
- *Health–health comparisons.* Congress should also address the problem of health–health tradeoffs through a new directive in the Administrative

Procedure Act (APA), the basic law governing the legality of actions by administrative agencies. The new directive could build on a House bill introduced in 1995, which contains a subsection entitled "substitution risks." This subsection says that "each significant risk assessment or risk characterization document shall include a statement of any substitution risks to human health, where information on such risks has been provided to the agency." This would be a strikingly modest initiative. It does not require agencies to investigate substitute risks on their own. Nor does it say that agencies may not proceed unless the regulation yields net benefits. I suggest instead an amendment to the Administrative Procedure Act: *"Agencies shall ensure, to the extent feasible, that regulations do not create countervailing risks that are greater than those of the regulated risk."* A forerunner of this idea can be found in the "clean fuels" provision of the Clean Air Act, which says that the administrator of EPA may not prohibit the use of a fuel or fuel addictive "unless he finds . . . that in his judgment such prohibition will not cause the use of any other fuel or fuel additive which will produce emissions which will endanger the public health or welfare to the same or greater degree than the use of the fuel or fuel additive proposed to be prohibited."[19] This idea should be generalized. (For more details, see Chapter 6.)

- *Peer review*. Recent proposals have put considerable emphasis on requiring executive agencies to corroborate the evidence that underlies regulations through peer review.[20] In fact, many agencies have already experimented with peer review. The arguments thus far strongly support this initiative and suggest that the experiments should be expanded through a general congressional requirement. The most important point is that peer review can serve as a check on the mistakes that come from populist wildfires. Whether an availability cascade is in progress or has completed its course, peer review provides an important safeguard against policy responses that the facts do not justify. This is the basic case for peer review in the context of availability cascades; the Love Canal and Alar scares would have looked quite different if peer review had occurred at various stages. As we will see, peer review helped provide a great deal of information about the risks associated with arsenic. Indeed, peer review can easily be a prod rather than a brake, spurring agencies to deal with serious problem.

- *Cost–benefit mandates*. Congress has debated a number of bills designed to require agencies to engage in cost–benefit analysis. We have seen that

---

[19] 42 USC 7545(c)(2)(C).

[20] See, for example, the bills discussed in Cass R. Sunstein, *Free Markets and Social Justice* chapter 10 (New York: Oxford Univ. Press, 1997).

the dynamics of availability cascades, alongside the risk of tradeoff neglect, provide a new and distinctive reason for some kind of cost–benefit mandate, not as a way of obtaining an uncontroversial assessment of policy options and not because economic efficiency is the only legitimate ground for regulation, but as a commonsensical brake on measures that would do little good and possibly considerable harm.

Because of the risk that a salient event will cause a cascade, there is a good argument for attempting to understand and quantify the magnitude of the risk, and also for putting on-screen the various disadvantages of attempting to counteract it. In particular, cost–benefit analysis might well serve as a check on ill-advised availability campaigns; consider, for example, the very different findings of cost–benefit analysis for a lead phasedown (amply justified) and for eliminating asbestos (a far more mixed picture). An understanding of the relevant social mechanisms certainly does not prove that cost–benefit analysis is a good idea; everything depends on implementation. But such an understanding offers a new and largely institutional basis for a cost–benefit requirement, operating to widen the viewscreen of political actors and to contain availability errors.

THE EXECUTIVE BRANCH

The most effective response to the problems discussed here would probably involve the executive branch, which is in the best position to analyze risks comprehensively. Unlike courts, the executive branch can have a systematic overview of risk regulation; unlike Congress, the executive branch has institutions in place with which to undertake the process of rationalizing regulation. Of course whatever the executive branch does must fit within the law as enacted by Congress; in that sense the legislature has a kind of priority. But here are three complementary proposals.

OFFICE OF INFORMATION AND REGULATORY AFFAIRS

In Chapter I, we saw that President Reagan created the Office of Information and Regulatory Affairs, assigning it the responsibility of overseeing risk regulation to ensure both coordination and rationality. Since that time, OIRA has helped to coordinate regulatory policies. But its functions have varied. Under President Reagan, OIRA operated essentially as a cost–benefit monitor that intervened in an ad hoc way to force the reconsideration of grossly inefficient regulations. President Clinton undertook a number of impressive steps to "reinvent government" to ensure greater attention to results than to processes; but this particular role was deemphasized. In the Clinton Administration, OIRA was a weak institution, doing little of substantive value.

In view of the problems discussed here, OIRA should be reinvigorated, and its powers should be extended and strengthened, so as both to deter unreasonable regulation and to ensure that reasonable regulation is forthcoming. Specifically, OIRA should have, and be known to have, a degree of authority over priority-setting and cost–benefit balancing. It should work to mitigate the most unfortunate effects of cognitive biases, both by diverting resources and attention from small risks and by ensuring that serious but neglected risks receive attention. OIRA has used the idea of the "return letter," to require reconsideration of inadequately justified regulations, alongside the idea of the "prompt letter," to encourage agencies to respond where regulation would do more good than harm. Where experts working under OIRA lack confidence in risk judgments that are spreading and becoming embellished through a cascade, they should conduct fact finding exercises and, where necessary, publicize the inaccuracies of the popular beliefs. Thus OIRA's mission should also include the dissemination of systematic information concerning risks, including changes in what scientists know about the risks and the methods for lessening them. Finally, it should conduct systematic comparisons with other societies with an eye toward finding cross-country differences that might provide clues to misperceptions or policy flaws at home.

OIRA should also see, as one of its central assignments, the task of overcoming governmental tunnel vision, by ensuring that aggregate risks are reduced and that agency focus on particular risks does not mean that ancillary risks are ignored or increased. This is a more modest and particularized version of Justice Stephen Breyer's larger suggestion that government technocrats should have a power to set priorities by diverting resources from smaller problems to larger ones.[21] No body in government is now entrusted with the authority of ensuring that risk regulation is managed so as to ensure global rationality and coherence. OIRA is well situated to take on that role, at least by attending to the possibility that regulation of some risks may make risk levels higher on balance. It is important to underline the complementary features of this proposal: OIRA should block regulations that cannot be justified, but also seek to energize agencies to produce regulations that would do more good than harm. The problem involves paranoia and neglect. Where there are targets of opportunity – areas in which significant risks can be reduced, without imposing unacceptable burdens and costs – OIRA should see, as one of its key missions, the encouragement of agency action. One possibility would be to designate one or more people as having a special responsibility for identifying areas where aggressive regulatory action could do some good.

---

[21] Stephen G. Breyer, Regulation and Its Reform (Cambridge, Mass.: Harvard Univ. Press, 1992).

A New Risk Agency

If it proves infeasible to redesign OIRA along the proposed lines, and OIRA's role remains very limited, one might create a new institution that would publicize the inconsistencies of the prevailing regulatory system and focus attention on the most serious risks. Going well beyond the OIRA model, Justice Breyer has suggested the creation of a group of well-trained risk managers, versed in various disciplines and authorized to divert resources from small problems to large ones.[22] Armed with federal authority, some kind of "Breyer group" would undertake the sort of analyses and educational activities proposed here. The group would have the authority to publicize its findings about the relative seriousness of risks, require agencies to engage in similar priority-setting, and recommend changes in statutes, regulations, and even appropriations. It might even be empowered to engage in some relocating on its own.

The Internet

Why do people turn to nonexperts for information on various risks? One reason is that they have no easy way of finding statistically accurate and scientifically up-to-date judgments. How do the risks of driving compare with the risks of flying? How do the risks of pesticides compare with the risks of not eating a lot of fruits and vegetables? How are the risks of eating peanut butter compared with the risks of smoking cigarettes? Are organic foods healthier than genetically modified foods?

Without information on such questions, people cannot develop the capacity to compare risks and obtain sound understandings of the relative gravity of the risks associated with, for example, air travel, cell phone use, automobile driving, poor diet, and lack of exercise. To be sure, some such information may be found in the books shelved in a good library or bookstore. But people looking for it might have to read dozens of books to make the necessary comparisons; not only that, they would first have to identify the appropriate sources. Information should be made easily accessible in the quickest possible and most up-to-date form. In the modern era, the Internet would serve as the ideal vehicle.

The executive branch might well create a new website, dedicated to the listing of various risks and the identification of the probabilities, or range of probabilities, associated with each of them. The technology of the web allows the nesting of multiple levels of detail.[23] The most elementary level ought to be

[22] See Breyer, supra note 8 in Chapter 2.

[23] The Harvard Center on Risk Analysis provides a great deal of information in this vein. See *www.hcra.harvard.edu/*.

extremely simple to follow – simple enough, perhaps, for high school graduates to check the latest scientific knowledge on, say, the risks associated with Alar or the damage caused by the spill at Love Canal. Where the scientific community is divided on a particular risk matter, as it is on global warming, the website should make the substance of the controversy as clear as possible. If the government fails to act, or if the government's information seems incorrect, such a website could be set up and operated by a nongovernmental organization, along the lines of *Consumer Reports*. It could even be a profit-oriented enterprise; after all, many profit-seeking credit bureaus enjoy a good reputation because they have a stake in its maintenance. Whether or not a nongovernmental entity is willing or able to undertake the task, the federal government could take the lead, though here there are obvious issues of trust.

The website's construction would constitute a substantial educational service. Potentially counteracting the irrational attitudes and decisions caused by cognitive biases and heuristics, it would allow individuals to form their risk judgments more rationally than they currently can. An even more ambitious enterprise would provide information also about the groups that have a stake in the risk judgments that drive regulatory policies. One could publicize analyses of the organized political activity concerning various risk issues. Finally, the website could contain systematic information on any discrepancies between private and public opinion on current risk issues. Such information would identify hidden currents of opinion, thus strengthening individual resistance to the biases of public discourse and pressures rooted in public opinion.

In a world in which all perceived risks are quickly evaluated by trusted scientists, who then post their knowledge in comprehensible form on a website known to everyone, availability errors will be less likely to develop. If a news program claims that apples carry a deadly poison, people can check the website to learn what is known about the identified risk. If scientific tests show the risk is nonexistent, few people will believe the claim, and no cascade will follow. If the claim is groundless, a possibly costly cascade will have been prevented without involving the courts. Of course some people might distrust what a website, private or governmental, has to say. But everything is to be gained by increasing information on risk-related questions.

COURTS

Courts, too, have a role to play in preventing excessive reactions to availability cascades and in ensuring attention to neglected tradeoffs. I will deal with this issue in some detail in Chapter 8; for now consider some basic points.

The most natural route involves the judicial review of administrative actions alleged to be "arbitrary" or "capricious" within the meaning of the

119

Administrative Procedure Act.[24] The ban on arbitrary or capricious action is increasingly being understood to require agencies to show that their action produces "more good than harm."[25] This notion might well be taken to embody a presumptive requirement that costs not be grossly disproportionate to benefits. Simple though it sounds, existing doctrine authorizes courts to invalidate the most extreme and the most poorly conceived regulatory proposals, at least when statutes do not require them. Courts should hardly be expected to identify cognitive errors and to invalidate an outcome for having been produced by them. But if regulations must be shown to make things better rather than worse, taking account of all relevant variables, a safeguard will be in place.

AN IMPORTANT PRAGMATIC QUALIFICATION

The arguments I have made for cost–benefit balancing are highly pragmatic. I have urged that if this form of balancing is done well, regulation is likely to be far more sensible than it now is. But this is not inevitable. Suppose, for example, that the principal effect of cost–benefit analysis is to stall desirable (as well as undesirable) regulation, ensuring that regulations would be more difficult to implement. Suppose too that if regulations would be more difficult to implement, the public would be worse off, simply because serious dangers would not be addressed. Under these assumptions, cost–benefit analysis would not be justified. It would fail cost–benefit analysis. And there can be no doubt that many of those who reject cost–benefit analysis do so on the ground that this "tool" would – in their judgment – simply provide yet another obstacle to desirable protection of safety, health, and the environment. Perhaps the skeptics would favor cost–benefit analysis if it could be done quickly and accurately, without distorting influences. But the skeptics might fear that the likelihood of rapid, accurate cost–benefit analysis is too low to justify the real risk, which is to stall and even block lifesaving interventions.

I have not established that these skeptics are wrong. And if they are right, we should abandon cost–benefit analysis. Whether they are right depends on empirical issues on which we lack clear evidence. In response, I have pointed to cases in which cost–benefit analysis has done considerable good, not least by spurring regulation. But the real burden lies on public officials who seek to use cost–benefit analysis as a tool for improving decisions. If they use the tool properly, and if both lives and dollars are saved as a

[24] 5 USC 706.
[25] See Edward Warren & Gary Merchant, "More Good Than Harm": A First Principle for Environmental Agencies and Reviewing Courts, 20 Ecol. L. Q. 379 (1993); Margolis, supra note 3 in Chapter 3.

result, the skeptics' concerns will be met on their own, sensibly pragmatic grounds.

FOUR OBJECTIONS

The argument made thus far, cautious though it may seem, runs into four immediate objections. The first involves democratic considerations. The second points to the limitations of quantification. The third involves the question of who bears the relevant costs and who gets the relevant benefits. The fourth involves the possibility that some tradeoffs, including some trades of dollars for lives, should be treated as "taboo." I take up these objections in sequence.

POPULISM

The first objection, populist in character, would be that in a democracy, government properly responds to the social "demand" for law. Government does not legitimately reject that demand on the ground that cost–benefit analysis suggests that it should not act. On this view, a democratic government should be accountable. Any approach that uses efficiency, or technocratically driven judgments, as a brake on accountability is fatally undemocratic.

The problem with this objection is that it rests on a controversial and even unacceptable conception of democracy, one that sees responsiveness to citizens' demands, whatever their factual basis, as the foundation of political legitimacy. If those demands are uninformed, or based on unreliable intuitions about risks, it is perfectly appropriate for government to resist them. Indeed, it is far from clear that reasonable citizens want, or would want, their government to respond to their uninformed demands. After the analysis and information have been generated, and public officials have taken them into account, democratic safeguards continue to be available, and electoral sanctions can be brought to bear against those who have violated the public will. At the very least, cost–benefit analysis should be an ingredient in the analysis, showing people that the consequences of various approaches might be different from what they seem.

QUANTIFICATION AND EXPRESSIVE RATIONALITY

In an extensive discussion, Lisa Heinzerling has raised a number of objections to cost–benefit balancing.[26] Heinzerling argues that many of the values depend on controversial judgments of value. Making reference to Table 2.1 in particular, she urges that cost–benefit analysis masks those judgments. Heinzerling contends

[26] See Heinzerling, supra note 5 in Chapter 2, at 1981.

Table 5.1 Corrected (?) table on cost-effectiveness of regulations

Regulation	Adjusted Cost Estimate (thousands of 1995 dollars)
Asbestos (OSHA 1972)	700
Benzene (OSHA 1985)	2,570
Arsenic/glass plant (EPA 1986)	6,610
Ethylene oxide (OSHA 1984)	3,020–5,780
Uranium mill tailings/inactive (EPA 1983)	2,410
Acrylonitrile (OSHA 1978)	8,570
Uranium mill tailings/active (EPA 1983)	3,840
Coke ovens (OSHA 1976)	12,420
Asbestos (OSHA 1986)	3,860
Arsenic (OSHA 1978)	24,490
Arsenic/los-arsenic copper (EPA 1986)	5,740
Land disposal (EPA 1986)	3,280
Formaldehyde (OSHA 1985)	31,100

that many of the key numbers depend on controversial judgments about how to "discount" future benefits, that is, how to treat benefits that will occur in the future. This is indeed a highly disputed issue. The numbers in Table 2.1 depend on a 10% discount rate, whereas the agencies tended to use a lower discount rate, or not to discount at all. Heinzerling also suggests that Table 2.1 depends on downward adjustment of the agency's estimates of risk. Her own estimates result in Table 5.1, which is a corrected risk table, adjusted for inflation.

Table 5.1 may be more accurate than Table 2.1; certainly there are problems with any approach that assumes a 10 percent discount rate, which seems far too high (see Chapter 8 for details). But even if Heinzerling's table is better, it offers an ironic lesson, serving largely to confirm the point that current regulatory policy suffers from poor priority-setting. The disparities here are not as dramatic as in Table 2.1, and they certainly do not establish pervasive overregulation; but they do support the view that resources are being misallocated and that there is a serious problem to be solved.

Heinzerling does not, however, conclude that this revised table is the appropriate basis for evaluating regulatory policy. Her aim is not to come up with a better table from which to reassess government behavior. On the contrary, she takes her argument to be a basis for rejecting cost–benefit analysis altogether. This, then, is a lesson about "the perils of precision."[27] Heinzerling suggests that it "would be better if we left the picture blurry, and declined to connect the dots between all the confusing and sometimes conflicting intuitions

[27] Id. at 2042.

and evidence."[28] She is concerned that "some, probably many, people will be fooled into believing that numerical estimates of risks, costs, and benefits are impartial reflections of factual reality, in which case the likely result of increased reliance on quantification in setting regulatory policy will be that the side that best obscures the value choices implicit in its numbers will prevail."[29]

There is considerable truth here and an important pragmatic warning; but I think that Heinzerling's lesson is greatly overdrawn. Truth first: If an agency says that the cost of regulation is $100 million and the benefit $70 million, we still know much less than we should. It is important to know who bears these costs, and if possible with what consequences. Will wages be lower? Whose wages? Will prices be higher? Of what products? A disaggregated picture of the benefits would also be important; what does the seventy million dollar figure represent? Consider, for example, a recent table explaining that the costs of skin cancer, from health effects of reducing tropospheric ozone, are between $290 million and $1.1 billion, with dollar subtotals for skin cancers and cataracts.[30] By itself, this table is insufficiently informative to tell people what they need to know.

Heinzerling is therefore on firm ground if she means to suggest that the dollar numbers cannot substitute for a fuller inquiry into what is at stake. Any cost–benefit analysis should include more than the monetary values by, for example, showing what the values are about, such as life-years saved and accidents averted. But her own table suggests that the general conclusion – that cost-benefit analysis can illuminate inquiry – remains unassailable. If regulation ranges from tens of thousands to tens of millions per life saved, at least there is an issue to be addressed. One of the functions of cost–benefit balancing is to help show where limited resources should go. In fact, a regulation of particulates is hard to evaluate without knowing, for example, the number of deaths averted and the range of consequences for morbidity: How many work-days will be saved that would otherwise be lost? How many hospitalizations will be avoided? How many asthma attacks will be prevented? It could even be useful to attempt to describe these effects in terms of "quality-adjusted life-years" (see Chapter 9), knowing that here, too, a good analyst will go back and forth between bottom lines and the judgments that go into their creation.

I suspect that theoretical claims lie behind Heinzerling's skepticism about quantification. She may believe that many of the goods at stake in regulation (e.g., human and animal life and health, recreational and aesthetic opportunities)

---

[28] Id. at 2069.

[29] Id. at 2068.

[30] See Lutter & Wolz, supra note 20 in Chapter 2, at 142A, 145. In fairness to the authors, it should be noted that a previous table in their essay describes adverse health effects in quantitative terms by listing the numbers of cases averted.

are not merely commodities, that people do not value these goods in the same way that they value cash, and that cost–benefit analysis, by its reductionism, is inconsistent with people's reflective judgments about the issues at stake. Arguments of this sort have been developed in some philosophical challenges to cost–benefit analysis.[31] Such arguments are convincing if cost–benefit analysis is taken to suggest a controversial position in favor of the commensurability of all goods. Part of what people express, in their daily lives, is a resistance to this form of commensurability, and some goods are believed to have intrinsic as well as instrumental value. The existence of qualitative differences among goods fortifies the claim that any bottom line about costs and benefits should be supplemented with a more qualitative description of the variables involved. But cost–benefit analysis should not be seen as embodying a reductionist account of the good, and much less as a suggestion that everything is simply a "commodity" for human use. It is best taken as pragmatic instrument, agnostic on the deep issues and designed to assist people in making complex judgments where multiple goods are involved.

We should conclude that the final number may provide less information than the ingredients that went into it, and that officials should have and present cost–benefit analysis in sufficiently full terms to enable people to have a concrete sense of the effects of regulation. This is an argument against some overambitious understandings of what cost–benefit balancing entails. But it is not an argument against cost–benefit balancing.

Whose Costs? Whose Benefits?

The third objection, hinted at earlier, is perhaps the most obvious. Suppose that the costs of additional reductions in sulfur dioxide emissions would be $500 million. Suppose that the health benefits of these reductions, once monetized, would be $250 million. Suppose too that we do not have any trouble with the underlying calculations – that we have accurately identified the health benefits and that we have properly "translated" them into monetary equivalents. If the costs are double the benefits, is it clear that government should not go forward? A critic of cost–benefit analysis might think that this is not clear at all. Everything depends on *who* would bear the relevant costs and *who* would enjoy the relevant benefits. Suppose that if the regulation is imposed, companies will lose hundreds of millions of dollars in profits, but a nontrivial number of people will live who would otherwise die. If the costs mean lower profits, and the benefits mean longer lives, it might seem clear that the government should act, even if the costs are higher than the benefits.

---

[31] See Anderson, supra note 4 in Chapter 3.

The basic point is right; we do need to know who would bear the costs and enjoy the benefits. That has been and will continue to be one of my principal themes. Recall that I have not urged that the monetized numbers should be decisive. But for those who seek to reject cost–benefit analysis, things are a bit more complicated. The reason is not that redistribution through regulation is undesirable, or that we should care a lot about the profits of "companies." The reason is that when expensive regulation is imposed, "companies" are not going to be the only ones who pay. Sometimes workers will lose their jobs – and increases in unemployment are associated with a wide range of social ills, including crime and suicide. Sometimes workers will have lower wages – and wage decreases are especially hard on people who are living at the margin. Sometimes prices will go up, and price increases are especially hard on poor people. If regulation is very expensive, some people might even die. When companies are asked to spend hundreds of millions of dollars on risk reduction, ordinary people will inevitably be affected, usually for the worse. The "cost" side of the cost–benefit calculus means much more than a decrease in profits.

Of course, we cannot know, in the abstract, whether the cost of regulation will be borne by consumers, current workers, the unemployed, or companies themselves. Much depends on what the market will allow companies to do. If prices can be increased without significantly reducing sales, companies will increase prices; if wages can be cut without losing good workers, wages will be cut; if companies can do what they have done before with a smaller workforce, employment will be reduced. Inevitably companies will select what is, for them, the cheapest way to respond to the costs of regulation.

This is no mere conjecture. Consider, for example, the fact that workers' compensation programs are an excellent way to increase safety for workers because they increase employers' incentive to maintain a safe workplace – indeed, such programs probably cut workers' fatalities by 30 percent or more.[32] In this way, workers' compensation programs should be counted as a huge success. But there is also evidence that such programs contributed to a substantial decrease in workers' wages – in some sectors, a dollar-for-dollar decrease, meaning that workers lost in salary what they gained in benefits.[33] To take a more recent example outside of the domain of health and safety, there is evidence that the parental leave program has produced a similar wage cut for affected workers.[34] None of this establishes that a workers' compensation program or a parental

---

[32] See W. Kip Viscusi, Reforming Products Liability, p. 178, (Cambridge, Mass.: Harvard Univ. Press, 1995).

[33] See Fishback & Kantor, supra note 27 in Chapter 3.

[34] See Jonathan Gruber, The Incidence of Mandated Maternity Benefits, 84 Am. Econ. Rev. 622 (1994).

leave program or a costly safety regulation is a bad idea. Even if the result is to produce wage reductions or increased unemployment, the effort to reduce risks might be justified on balance. My claim is only that the dollar costs associated with risk reduction are extremely important, and that they are important not because we should care about some abstraction called "dollars" or because company profits are important as such, but because costly regulations are translated, all too often, into harmful consequences for real people. The point is that those harmful consequences should be placed on-screen so that we do produce harmful unintended consequences and, on occasion, real calamities.

TABOO TRADEOFFS AND TRADEOFF AVERSION

For many regulations, there appears to be a relatively simple choice: dollars or risks? When the question is put in this form, many people find it tempting to reject cost–benefit analysis. In fact, rejecting that form of analysis seems, to many, to be the appropriate way to put priorities exactly where they belong – on the protection of life and health. In recent years some intriguing evidence suggests that this is how most people think. Some tradeoffs, between risks and dollars, actually seem to be "taboo," in the sense that some people, some of the time, will absolutely refuse to allow some goods to be traded for money.[35] How much would you have to be paid to allow your daughter, or mother, to suffer for a month, or to lose five years from her life? When a tradeoff is taboo, any proposed deal is not even considered. It would violate a firmly held moral principle.

In any case, people frequently display not merely tradeoff neglect but also *tradeoff aversion*. When a government commission suggests that a certain amount is "too high" to spend to protect human lives, almost three-quarters of subjects, in one experiment, rejected the suggestion – not because the commission was wrong on the numbers, but simply because it was weighing lives against dollars.[36] Jonathan Baron and his collaborators have done a great deal of work on "protected values" – values that people seek to insulate from ordinary tradeoffs.[37] When values are protected, people tend to believe that they are absolute; they deny the need for tradeoffs and show considerable anger at violations of those values. Would you agree with a company's decision to refuse to spend money

---

[35] See Philip Tetlock, Coping With Tradeoffs, in Elements of Reason: Cognition, Choice, and the Bounds of Rationality 239, Arthur Lupia et al., eds. (Cambridge: Cambridge Univ. Press, 2000).

[36] Id. at 255.

[37] Jonathan Baron & Mark Spranca, Protected Values, 70 Org. Behavior Human Decision Processes I (1997).

on improving the safety of the workplace on the ground that a cost–benefit analysis suggests that the improvement simply isn't worthwhile? Studies of jury behavior have shown that most people will not. In fact, jurors will punish, often severely, companies that have engaged in cost–benefit analysis before marketing products that carry a risk of harm.[38]

Suppose, for example, that an automobile company is aware that, in extremely unusual circumstances, its brake system will fail, thus causing injury and death, and that the company could correct the problem with a costly expenditure, one that would, say, cost $15 million per life saved. Suppose that the company refuses to make the expenditure, on the ground that the benefits do not justify it. A jury will likely be aghast at the company's behavior. Indeed, the jury might well award punitive damages. Note that this is not because the company has placed too low a value on human life. Even if the company's willingness to pay is quite high, juries will be unmoved. The problem is the fact that the company has made an explicit tradeoff between risk and cost. This finding is duplicated by others showing that people are extremely unhappy with government decisions to make such explicit tradeoffs, even though they would be willing to approve of the relevant decisions if those decisions are made on less transparent grounds.

I think that this kind of tradeoff aversion is a pernicious form of tradeoff neglect, with harmful effects on risk reduction efforts. But we have to be careful here. It would be far too simple to say that those who oppose explicit tradeoffs of risks and dollars are making some inexplicable "mistake." In ordinary life, anyone who talks explicitly in cost–benefit terms is likely to seem cold and calculating, perhaps even worse. A parent who says, "I will not buy a Volvo because the additional safety for my child just isn't worth $600," would seem a bit strange. It would be much stranger for the parent to claim, "If I am paid enough, I will be willing to subject my child to a small danger." In surveys, a significant percentage of people actually say that they would not accept any amount of money to subject themselves to an small increase in risk, or to allow the environment to be harmed.

But why is this? People, including parents, trade risks for dollars all the time. We choose how much to spend on cars, knowing that safety is expensive; we decide how much to spend on security systems in the home; we choose where to live, knowing that some areas are safer than others; we go out at night, even though we know that by doing so, we increase our risks; when the cost of risk reduction is too high, we will not incur that cost even to protect our own children. What seems forbidden is not behavior that embodies tradeoffs, but rather unduly explicit talk to the effect. The taboo on such talk may well serve salutary social functions by helping to establish and maintain certain attitudes, in which life

---

[38] See W. Kip Viscusi, Corporate Risk Analysis: A Reckless Act?, 52 Stan. L. Rev. 547 (2000).

and health are not seen as simple commodities, qualitatively indistinguishable from money and other things that are simply for use. But we should not be fooled by the fact that people are nervous about explicit talk of reducing safety for money. Tradeoffs of money and risks are exceedingly common.

A more careful look at taboo tradeoffs suggests that when people disapprove of trading money for risks, they are generalizing from a set of moral principles that are generally sound, and even useful, but that work poorly in some cases.[39] Consider the following moral principle: *Do not knowingly cause a human death*. In the key studies, people disapprove of companies that fail to improve safety when they are fully aware that deaths will result – whereas people do not disapprove of those who fail to improve safety while appearing not to know, for certain, that deaths are going to ensue. When people object to risky action taken after cost–benefit analysis, it seems to be because that very analysis puts the number of expected deaths squarely on-screen. Companies that fail to do such analysis, but that are aware that a "risk" exists, do not make clear, to themselves or to jurors, that they caused deaths with full knowledge that this was what they were going to do. People disapprove, above all, of companies that cause death knowingly.

The problem here is that it is not always unacceptable to cause death knowingly, at least if the deaths are relatively few and an unintended byproduct of generally desirable activity. If government allows the marketing of SUVs, or small, fuel-efficient cars, it knows that deaths will occur; indeed, a government that requires small, fuel-efficient cars will produce some deaths as a result. If government allows new highways to be built, it will know that people will die on those highways; if government allows new power plants to be built, it will know that some people will die from the resulting pollution; if companies produce tobacco products, and if government does not ban those products, hundreds of thousands of people will die; alcohol kills people too. Much of what is done, by both industry and government, is likely to result in one or more deaths. Of course it would make sense, in most or all of these domains, to take extra steps to reduce risks. But that proposition does not support the implausible claim that we should disapprove, from the moral point of view, of any action taken when deaths are foreseeable.

The question is whether the statistical risk is worthwhile. Of course, the raw numbers cannot resolve that question. But without the raw numbers, any attempt to provide an answer is a stab in the dark. I believe that taboo tradeoffs and tradeoff aversion, far from being an objection to cost–benefit analysis, are a large part of the reason that it is so important.

[39] See Jonathan Baron, Nonconsequentialist Decisions, 17 Behavioral and Brain Sciences 1 (1994).

CATASTROPHES, TERRORISM, AND UNCERTAINTY

I have been assuming throughout that the numbers can actually be assigned – that government is able to specify a range of possible outcomes, and that this range can help discipline the decision about that to do. Often this is true. But sometimes the range is extremely wide, and government is not able to assign probabilities or to come up with ranges with any confidence. In the aftermath of the terrorist attacks of September 11, 2001, what was the probability of a further attack within a week? A month? Six months? A year? Suppose that government is attempting to control the risks from biochemical attacks, or from the worst-case scenario involving global warming. Is cost–benefit analysis helpful? If not, what kind of analysis might be helpful instead?

Regulators are sometimes acting in a situation of "risk," where probabilities can be assigned to various outcomes, but sometimes they are acting in a situation of "uncertainty," where no such probabilities can be assigned. In a situation of uncertainty, it is exceedingly hard to do cost–benefit analysis.[40] And indeed it would be possible to think that the argument I have made applies only in cases when it is feasible to come up with numbers. But careful analysis will be helpful even when full cost–benefit balancing is impossible. If a catastrophe has a very low probability of occurring, it does not deserve the level of attention that it should command if its probability is higher. And even if cost–benefit analysis is not feasible, it is important to pursue cost-effectiveness, by ensuring that the steps being taken are both the cheapest and the most effective means of producing the goal at hand. This is no less true in the context of risks from terrorism than elsewhere. For global warming, a "cap-and-trade" system (see Chapter 10) seems to be the most promising, in part because it is so much less expensive than the alternatives. Indeed, the administration of George W. Bush is attempting to reduce the risk of global warming not through mandates but through information, moral suasion, and tax incentives. The Bush approach is, in my view, inadequate; but at least it is possible that these steps will produce some good relatively cheaply.

There is a related problem. Prospective estimates of both costs and benefits often turn out to be wrong. This is not merely because of interest-group pressures. One reason is that officials lack the extensive information that would permit them to make accurate predictions; indeed, the informational demand on agencies is overwhelming, especially because technologies change over time.

---

[40] It is standard, in such circumstances, to follow the maximin principle (choose the policy with the best worst-case outcome). See Jon Elster, Explaining Technical Change, 185–207 (Cambridge: Cambridge Univ. Press, 1983), for a helpful discussion.

An enduring problem for regulatory policy is the absence of precise information on the cost or benefit sides. Industry, which typically has the most information about costs, has a strong incentive to overstate its burden. This point should be taken not as a criticism of cost–benefit analysis as such, but as a reason for skepticism about industry's numbers and for continuous monitoring and up-dating. Hence any system for cost-benefit balancing should create a mechanism to ensure that the prospective analysis is not way off – and should allow for correction if, as often happens, things turn out to be very different from what was anticipated.

Of course it is possible that, in practice, cost–benefit analysis will be used to block sensible regulation, and will therefore do more harm than good. If cost–benefit analysis simply makes it harder for agencies to protect the public, and mostly increases the power of regulated groups to block desirable regulation, it is senseless to celebrate cost–benefit analysis. But there are reasons to believe that cost–benefit analysis is not simply an antiregulatory tool. I have mentioned that cost–benefit analysis helped to spur the removal of lead from gasoline and dramatic steps, pushed by the United States, to eliminate CFCs, which contribute to depletion of the ozone layer. More recently, the Office of Information and Regulatory Affairs has pioneered the idea of a "prompt letter" – letters designed to prompt agencies to act in cases in which the benefits of action seem to outweigh the costs. Inspired by tentative cost–benefit analysis, OIRA has asked OSHA to consider requiring automatic defibrillators to be placed in workplaces; has urged the FDA to issue a final rule requiring disclosure of the level of trans fatty acids in foods; and has asked the Department of Transportation to take steps to improve automobile safety by establishing a high-speed, frontal offset crash test. In any case, cost–benefit analysis has often driven policy in more sensible directions by showing the best means of achieving regulatory goals. For those who have enthusiasm for cost–benefit analysis, there is a continuing duty to show that this is a tool for better outcomes and more sensible priority-setting, rather than a recipe for inaction.

BEYOND COST–BENEFIT ANALYSIS:
A HAYEKIAN TURN?

I have suggested that the choice of "smarter tools" remains one of the largest imperatives for risk reduction. Cost–benefit analysis can help to identify those tools, and for that reason governmental acceptance of cost–benefit balancing might well spur the selection of more effective, cheaper means of accomplish-ing regulatory goals. Within EPA, this has happened on many occasions (see Chapter 10). But there are some deeper issues here, and they suggest the need for some fundamental redirection of the cost–benefit state. The basic problem is that an adequate cost–benefit analysis imposes large demands on government, which may well lack the necessary information. What might be done instead?

To answer that question, imagine a small community consisting of farmers, each of whom owns a dozen cows, and all of whom own, jointly, the land on which the cows graze. It is easy to see that the farmers will soon find themselves facing a problem of overgrazing. Because the land is owned in common, each farmer will receive all the benefits of grazing by his cows but will pay only a fraction of the cost of that grazing. If farmers are acting in their rational self-interest, all of them will think that way, and before long the grass will be depleted. This is the famous "tragedy of the commons," and it accounts for many environmental problems.[41]

How might the tragedy be averted? Perhaps the small community could develop certain social norms, which would ensure limitations on grazing activity. Good norms can prevent tragedy and greatly reduce risks. Perhaps the small community could charge people for grazing, so as to ensure that the available stock is not depleted. In the spirit of this chapter, the community might even conduct a cost–benefit analysis of different levels of grazing and mandate levels of grazing, from each farmer, that would be consistent with the outcome of the analysis. It is easily imaginable that the latter approach would be better than unrestricted grazing. But it would also be full of pitfalls. Can the community really make accurate calculations? Won't things change over time? Doesn't the analysis, and then the set of mandates, seem a bit too reminiscent of Soviet-style planning?

Friedrich Hayek, winner of the Nobel Prize and critic of "planning" in all its guises, emphasized government's pervasive lack of information, certainly as compared with the information held by the numerous people who participate in a marketplace.[42] In the context of our farming community, it would be possible to reject planning, even of the sort suggested by cost–benefit analysis, and to urge instead a kind of Hayekian turn: Create private property rights, and let the farmers operate as they wish, within the constraints of those rights. More specifically, each farmer might be given a right to a certain plot of land and be allowed to use the land of others only with permission or as a result of a voluntary agreement. No trespassing would be allowed. The beauty of this solution is that it solves the tragedy of the commons, by ensuring that there is no commons at all. If each farmer is responsible for his own land and his own cattle, he has the right incentive, to use the land in a way that does not deplete it.

[41] Garrett Hardin, The Tragedy of the Commons, 162 Science 1243 (1968).

[42] F. A. Hayek, The Use of Knowledge in Society, 35 Am. Econ. Rev. 519 (1945).

The movement toward "free market environmentalism" is designed to generalize from this tale.[43] The basic claim is that the risks of environmental degradation might best be handled through creating property rights, so as to ensure that people have responsibility for environmental amenities that might otherwise be subject to the tragedy of the commons. If, for example, environmental groups are allowed to purchase a right not to cut timber or to pay ranchers for destruction of property at the hands of wolves, it might be possible to provide far more effective protection than could ever come from interest group struggles over government mandates. I believe that free market environmentalism, although not a panacea, holds out a great deal of promise, and that along with other emerging tools, it suggests the possibility of a general movement in Hayekian directions for risk reduction policies. I will turn to these issues in detail in Chapter 10.

[43] Terry Anderson & Donald R. Leal, Free Market Environmentalism (New York: Palgrave, 2001).

6

Health–Health Tradeoffs

I have referred to a pervasive problem in risk regulation, one that has only started to receive public attention. The problem arises *when the diminution of one health risk simultaneously increases another health risk*. The phenomenon is common in daily life, where risk reduction strategies may produce risks of their own. If you engage in an aggressive program of exercise to lose weight, you should be careful to make sure that the exercise is not itself unduly hazardous. If you change your diet so as to avoid pesticides, you might find yourself eating foods that carry higher risks on balance. The problem can be found in many domains of policy and law.

Thus, for example, fuel economy standards, designed to reduce environmental risks, may make automobiles less safe, and in that way increase risks to life and health.[1] If government bans the manufacture and use of asbestos, it may lead companies to use more dangerous substitutes,[2] and efforts to remove asbestos from schools may cause serious risks to workers. Regulations designed to control the spread of AIDS and hepatitis among health-care providers may increase the costs of health care, and thus make health care less widely available, and thus cost lives.[3] Regulation of nuclear power may make nuclear power safer; but by increasing the cost of nuclear power, such regulation will ensure reliance on other energy sources, such as coal-fired power plants, which carry risks of

---

[1] See Robert W. Crandall, Policy Watch: Corporate Average Fuel Economy Standards, 6 J. Econ. Persp. 171, 178 (1992); Robert W. Crandall & John D. Graham, The Effect of Fuel Economy Standards on Automobile Safety, 32 J. L. & Econ. 97 (1989).

[2] See *Corrosion Proof Fittings v. EPA*, 947 F.2d 1201 (5th Cir. 1991).

[3] See *ADA v. Martin*, 984 F.2d 823, 826 (7th Cir. 1993): "OSHA also exaggerated the number of lives likely to be saved by the rule by ignoring lives likely to be lost by it. since the increased cost of medical care, to the extent passed on to consumers, will reduce the demand for medical care, and some people may lose their lives as a result."

their own.[4] We saw in Chapter I that when government requires reformulated gasoline as a substitute for ordinary gasoline, it may produce new pollution problems.[5] Animal welfare organizations have thought about expanding the liability of veterinarians for malpractice; but they are aware that expanded liability may increase the cost of medical care for animals, and thus discourage people from seeking medical attention for animals in need.

The general problem is ubiquitous. If individuals and governments can be encouraged to take health–health tradeoffs into account, they are likely to make much better decisions. It is even possible that consideration of health–health tradeoffs will lead to innovative solutions, minimizing all the relevant risks.

In this chapter, I discuss the relation between health–health tradeoffs and the law. I also deal with the respective roles of courts, Congress, and the president in managing health–health tradeoffs. I urge that agencies ought to be taken to have legal authority to make such tradeoffs, and that they ought to exercise that authority much more than they now do. I also argue for a modest but far from trivial judicial role in requiring agencies to consider aggregate rather than isolated risks. Thus I claim that agency decisions that increase aggregate risk levels should be found arbitrary or capricious under the Administrative Procedure Act. More generally, I urge that Congress should amend the Administrative Procedure Act to require agencies to consider ancillary risks and to minimize net risks. I also argue that the Office of Information and Regulatory Affairs should see the reduction of overall risk as one of its principal missions. Much more than it now does, it should undertake a coordinating function so as to ensure that this mission is carried out. In these ways, I hope to connect the question of deliberative outcomes with the subject of institutional design.

REGULATED AND ANCILLARY RISKS

To get a handle on this problem, we need to make some distinctions. Call the risks that government is trying to control the *regulated risks*. Call the risks that are increased by regulation the *ancillary risks*. Ancillary risks take many different forms, depending on their relationship to the regulated risk. We might say that the increase in acid deposition is not within the same domain as the risks prevented by regulation of nuclear power plants. This is true in two different ways. First, and most importantly, the law does not consider the risks to be in the

---

[4] See Stephen Breyer, Vermont Yankee and the Courts' Role in the Nuclear Energy Controversy, 91 Harv. L. Rev. 1833, 1835–6 (1978). See generally Peter Huber, Electricity and the Environment: In Search of Regulatory Authority, 100 Harv. L. Rev. 1002 (1987).

[5] See Jonathan H. Adler, Clean Fuels, Dirty Air, in Environmental Politics: Public Costs, Private Rewards 19, 22–4, Michael S. Greve and Fred L. Smith, Jr., eds. (New York: Praeger, 1992).

same domain, for the agency that regulates one of these risks has no authority to regulate the other. Second, the risk of acid deposition (mostly from coal-fired power plants) has a different source from the risk from nuclear power plants. Compare a situation in which the regulation of sulfur dioxide emissions increases emissions of carbon monoxide. If this happens, we are dealing in any event with air pollution, indeed air pollution from largely the same technologies, and the EPA has the statutory authority to regulate both sources. We can easily imagine a complex continuum of relationships between regulated risks and ancillary risks. For some purposes, the best way to define the risk domain will be through the relevant law, which, as we will see, sets constraints on the kinds of risk that might be considered.

A democratic society might well seek a measure of coordination among agencies, so that an agency operating in one risk domain does not increase risks in another domain. Certainly agencies should coordinate their efforts to reduce net risks. But a special problem in this connection is that agencies have quite different standards for deciding when risks require regulation.[6] The International Commission on Radiological Protection, for example, recommends that environmental factors should not cause an incremental cancer risk, for those exposed over a lifetime, of about 3 in 1,000. But American agencies do not follow this recommendation, and their own practices are wildly variable. The Nuclear Regulatory Commission sees 1 in 1,000 as acceptable; the EPA's acceptable range varies from 1 in 10,000 to 1 in 1,000,000. The FDA has tried to use a standard of 1 in 1,000,000, but under the Delaney Clause (now partially repealed), courts have required a standard of essentially 0. OSHA's understanding of the "significant risk" requirement found in its governing statute means that a risk of 1.64 in 1,000 is unacceptable, but a risk of 0.6 in 100,000 may be acceptable; labor groups have said that 1 in 1,000,000 is too high.

These varying standards make health–health tradeoffs quite complex. If one agency is using a standard of 1 in 1,000 for risk A, and doing so lawfully, how should it deal with an increase in risk B, when that risk is regulated by a different agency operating lawfully under a different standard? Matters become even more complex when risks from cancer, which raise special social concerns, are being compared with other sorts of risk. I return to this issue later.

There are many different mechanisms by which risk regulation may increase aggregate risks.[7] First, a regulatory ban or intervention may result in independent health risks coming from ancillary "replacement" risks. If we ban substance A, the replacement substance B may be dangerous, too. I have noted that a ban on

---

[6] See March Sadowitz & John D. Graham, A Survey of Residual Cancer Risks Permitted by Health, Safety, and Environmental Policy, 6 Risk 17 (1995).

[7] See Wildavsky, Searching for Safety, supra note 21 in Chapter 2.

asbestos, actually proposed by the EPA, may lead companies to use still more hazardous substitutes – a special problem in light of the fact that asbestos is used in brake linings. Heavy regulation of nuclear power, justified on safety grounds, may lead people to rely on fossil fuels, which create a number of air pollution problems and increase the problem of global warming. This does not mean that government should not ban asbestos or regulate nuclear power heavily. But when deciding what to do, government should be aware of the fact that it is dealing with systems – and that any isolated action might create a new problem for safety or health.

Second, regulation may force society to lose or forego "opportunity benefits." For example, careful screening procedures that keep out drugs and services may deprive people of health benefits at the same time that they protect people from health risks. This problem has received recent attention in connection with the Food and Drug Administration, especially with its efforts to control the spread of AIDS: If government erects high barriers to the introduction of new medicines, it may end up killing a lot of people. The point applies to barriers to new technologies in general. Regulated substances may have health benefits as well as health risks, and by eliminating those health benefits, regulation may therefore create health dangers on balance. If the government regulates or bans genetically modified foods, it may remove significant health benefits, particularly from poor nations, which have the most to gain from genetically modified foods.

Finally, economic costs imposed by regulation may create indirect health risks. This point is more controversial. But other things being equal, people who are poorer tend to be less safe and less healthy, as we shall now see.

"RICHER IS SAFER"

Thus far we have been discussing cases in which the act of regulating one risk produces ancillary risks through a simple causal chain, but there is a related possibility. Regulations cost money – sometimes a great deal of money. Private expenditures on regulatory compliance may reduce risk, but they also produce less employment and more poverty. As a rule, people who are unemployed or poor tend to be in worse health and to live shorter lives. Nations having high levels of wealth tend, other things being equal, to have citizens who live longer and are less sick.[8] Wealth may not buy happiness, but it does seem

---

[8] See Graham, Chang & Evans, supra note 21 in Chapter 2; Cross, supra note 21 in Chapter 2. The connection should not be exaggerated. It is possible for poor states to ensure relatively long lives for their citizens, and for wealthy states to do relatively poorly on this count. See also the discussion of the connection between income and longevity in Jean Dreze & Amartya Sen,

to buy longevity, at least as a statistical matter. Wealthier people can afford better doctors and medicines; they can afford to spend more on good diet and exercise; perhaps most important, they tend to avoid the sources of the most serious risks.[9] Poorer people have a harder time on all these counts. It follows that if regulations increase poverty, and decrease wealth, they will increase risk as a result.

This point has been reflected in judicial opinions. Consider, for example, Judge Frank Easterbrook's suggestion that a policy designed to protect fetuses from toxic exposures, by excluding women of child-bearing age from certain jobs, might "reduce risk attributable to lead at the cost of increasing other hazards," including the hazards stemming from less income, since "there is also a powerful link between the parents' income and infants' health."[10] Or consider a court's suggestion, in the context of an OSHA regulation designed to reduce the risk of contracting hepatis or AIDS from dentists, that the increased cost of dental care could end up producing harmful health effects for poor people.[11] The more general question is this: Would it be possible to connect, in any systematic way, governmentally required expenditures on risk reduction with increased risks of death? If such a connection could be drawn, we could see, in another way, whether risk reduction policies would improve mortality on balance. And if such a connection could be drawn, but was ignored, we could see an area in which tradeoff neglect would prove literally fatal.

An incipient literature attempts to do precisely this. A 1990 study attempted to develop a model to quantify the view that "richer is safer."[12] According to economist Ralph Keeney, a single fatality might result from an expenditure of from $3 million to $7.5 million. In a concurring opinion in a 1991 case involving occupational safety and health regulation, Judge Stephen Williams invoked this evidence to suggest that OSHA's refusal to engage in cost–benefit

India: Economic Development and Social Opportunity 59–61, 207–10 (Oxford: Clarendon, 1995). Dreze and Sen show that per capita income is linked with longevity but also that fair distribution is important, since a high per capita income that coexists with large pockets of poverty may be accompanied by high mortality rates. Cross correctly emphasizes the importance of distributional considerations and hence the connection between health–health analysis and environmental justice. See Cross, id. at 762–4, 782–3.

[9] Randall Lutter et al., The Cost Per Life Saved Cutoff for Safety Enhancing Regulation, 37 Econ. Inquiry 599 (1999).

[10] *International Union v. Johnson Controls*, 886 F2d 871, 908 (7th Cir., 1989) (J. Easterbrook, dissenting), reversed, 499 US 187 (1991).

[11] See *ADA v. Martin*, 984 F.2d 823 (7th Cir., 1993).

[12] Ralph Keeney, Mortality Risks of Induced by the Costs of Regulation, 10 Risk Analysis 147 (1990). See also Wildavsky, Searching for Safety, supra note 21 in Chapter 2.

analysis might not be beneficial for workers.[13] Judge Williams reasoned in the following way. If a fatality results from an expenditure of $7.5 million, some regulations might produce more fatalities than they prevent. Many regulations, of course, cost more than $7.5 million per life saved. In Judge Williams's view, an agency that fails to measure costs against benefits might be failing to measure mortality gains against losses.

The claimed relationship between wealth reductions and mortality is not uncontroversial.[14] But a number of studies find such a relationship. Consider the summary in Table 6.1.[15] Of course, these are aggregate-level data. We should expect costly regulations to have more serious effects on mortality if poor people bear most of the costs; concentrated costs on poor people are especially likely to increase health and mortality risks. The same effects will be reduced if wealthy people bear most of the burden. If poor people pay more than their share for pollution controls,[16] any estimate of mortality effects, based on aggregate data, will have to be adjusted upward.

These points lead to a broader one with considerable implications for risk reduction policies. Even if agencies are sometimes prevented, by law, from measuring costs against benefits, perhaps they could compare health losses with health gains and conclude that some regulations are not worthwhile because they cost lives on net. In fact, it can be shown that some regulations fail "health–health analysis" whether or not they pass cost–benefit analysis. Consider Table 6.2.[17]

The most systematic recent study has come from economists Robert Hahn, Randall Lutter, and W. Kip Viscusi.[18] The authors conclude that an expenditure of $15 million will create about one statistical death. In their view, the

---

[13] *International Union, UAW v. OSHA*, 938 F2d 1310, 1326–7 (DC Cir., 1991). See also *Building & Construction Trades Department v. Brock*, 838 F2d 1258 (DC Cir., 1988), suggesting that "leaning toward safety may sometimes have the perverse effect of increasing rather than decreasing risk." Id. at 1267. See also *New York State v. Brown*, 854 F2d 1379, 1395 n. 1 (DC Cir., 1988 (J. Williams, concurring): "extravagant expenditures on health may in some instances affect health adversely, by foreclosing expenditures on items – higher quality food, shelter, recreation, etc. – that would have contributed more to the individual's health than the direct expenditures thereon."

[14] See Portney & Stavins, supra note 26 in Chapter 1, at 111, 118 (arguing that adverse health effects from the cost of regulation are possible but unlikely).

[15] Table 6.1 is borrowed from Randall Lutter & John F. Morrall, III, Health–Health Analysis: A New Way to Evaluate Health and Safety Regulation, 8 J. Risk & Uncertainty 43, 49 table I (1994).

[16] See David Harrison, Who Pays for Clean Air? (Cambridge, Mass.: Ballinger, 1975).

[17] Borrowed from Lutter and Morrall, supra note 15 in Chapter 6 at 59, table 6.

[18] See Robert Hahn, Randall Lutter & W. Kip Viscusi, Do Federal Regulations Reduce Mortality (Washington, D.C.: American Enterprise Institute, 2000).

Table 6.1 Is richer safer?

Study	Data	Implicit Income Gains Necessary to Avert One Death ($ millions)	Comments
Keeney (1990)	Used income and mortality correlations from Kitagawa and Hauser (1960) data, and others	12.3	Cited in *UAW v. OSHA*, as $7.25 1980 dollars. Represents an upperbound.
Joint Economic Committee (1984)	Aggregate U.S. income, employment, mortality and morbidity; 1950–80	1.8 to 2.7	Reflects income loss from recession of 1974–5.
Anderson & Burkhauser (1985)	4,878 male workers over 10 years (1969–79)	1.9 (wages); 4.3 (other income)	Older workers aged 58–63. Measures effects of wages and of value of one's home on mortality.
Duleep (1986)	9,618 white married male workers aged 35–64 over 6 years (1973–8)	2.6	Controls for prior disability and educational attainment.
Duleep (1989)	13,954 white married male workers aged 25–64 over 6 years (1973–8)	6.5	Finds income effects at all income levels.
Duleep (1991)	9,618 white married male workers aged 35–64 over 6 years (1973–8)	3.9	Controls for prior disability, educational attainment, and exposre to occupational hazards.
Wolfson (1992)	500,000 Canadian workers, over 10–20 years	6	Investigates longevity rather than mortality. Finds income effects at highest quintiles of income.
National Institutes of Health (1992)	1,300,000 Americans, all ages (1979–85)	12.4	Estimate reflects effect of income changes on family mortaliy. Study does not use multiple regression, does not control for prior health status or education.
Chirikos & Nestel (1991)	5,020 men, aged 50–64 studied during 1971–83	3.3	Uses two measures of health endowments.
Chapman & Hariharan (1993)	5,836 older men over 10 years	12.2	Uses four distinct controls for prior health conditions.
Graham, Hung-Chang & Evans (1992)	38 years of age-adjusted mortality and income data for the United States	4.0	Distinguishes effects of permanent income from those of transitional income.

Table 6.2 Regulations passing *HHA v. BCA* tests

Budgeted Regulations	Year	Agency	Status	Cost Per Life Saved ($ millions 1992)
1. Steering column protection	1967	NHTSA	F	0.1
2. Unvented space heaters	1980	CPSC	F	0.1
3. Cabin fire protection	1985	FAA	F	0.3
4. Passive restraints/belts	1984	NHTSA	F	0.4
5. Fuel system integrity	1975	NHTSA	F	0.4
6. Trihalomethanes	1979	EPA	F	0.4
7. Underground construction	1989	OSHA-S	F	0.4
8. Alcohol & drug control	1985	FRA	F	0.7
9. Servicing wheel rims	1984	OSHA-S	F	0.7
10. Seat cushion flammability	1984	FAA	F	0.8
11. Floor emergency lighting	1984	FAA	F	0.9
12. Crane susp. pers. Platf	1988	OSHA-S	F	1.2
13. Children's sleepware flammability	1973	CPSC	F	1.8
14. Side doors	1979	NHTSA	F	1.8
15. Concrete & masonry construction	1988	OSHA-S	F	1.9
16. Hazard communication	1983	OSHA-S	F	2.4
17. Asbestos	1986	OSHA-H	F	2.8
18. Benzene/fugitive emission	1984	EPA	F	3.8
Regulations failing BCA test				
19. Grain dust	1987	OSHA-S	F	8.8
20. Radionuclides/uranium mines	1984	EPA	F	9.3
Regulations failing HHA (and BCA) test				
21. Benzene	1987	OSHA-H	F	23.1
22. Ethylene oxide	1984	OSHA-H	F	34.6
23. Uranium mill tail./inactive	1983	EPA	F	37.3
24. Acrylonitrile	1978	OSHA-H	F	50.8
25. Uranium mill tail./active	1983	EPA	F	71.6
26. Asbestos	1989	EPA	F	72.9
27. Coke ovens	1976	OSHA-H	F	83.4
28. Arsenic	1978	OSHA-H	F	125.0
29. DES (cattlefeed)	1979	FDA	F	178.0
30. Arsenic/glass manufacture	1986	EPA	F	192.0
31. Formaldehyde	1987	OSHA-H	F	119,000.0

association between income and health stems largely from the fact that poorer people engage in certain risky behavior; to the extent that people have more money, risky behavior tends to decrease. Taking the $15 million as a cutoff, the authors survey all final regulations issued between 1991 and June 1998 and designed to reduce risks of death. The overall news is quite good: eleven regulations decrease mortality risks, and the savings from the beneficial regulations are far larger than the losses from the harmful regulations – so much so that as a whole, the regulations promise to save 6,400 lives each year. But a majority of the studied regulations appear, on balance, to cost more lives than they save. The most sobering conclusion is that *thirteen regulations actually increase mortality risks on balance*. The question is whether it is possible to design a system for controlling risks that does not produce this problem.

The idea that "richer is safer" has not been absent from public deliberations about risk. In a now-celebrated letter written in 1992, James McRae, the acting administrator of OIRA, wrote to the Department of Labor, questioning a proposed OSHA regulation involving air contaminants in the workplace. OSHA had estimated savings of between eight and thirteen lives per year, at an annual cost of $163 million. McRae suggested that there was a significant gap in OSHA's analysis: If a statistical fatality is produced by an expenditure of $7.5 million, the regulation could actually cause twenty-two additional deaths. McRae asked OSHA to investigated the relation between health, wealth, and safety. OSHA responded that existing data seemed speculative but called for more comments from the public.[19]

Eventually a public outcry forced OIRA to retreat. Senator John Glenn in particular complained of OIRA's "Alice-in-Wonderland type claim that health and safety regulations cause harm to workers" and objected that the "richer is safer" view "seems to stand logic on its head – to say that controlling a dangerous substance in the workplace makes an increased health hazard to the worker."[20] But if richer is safer, a concern about the health effects of costly regulations is perfectly logical. Despite the public outcry, increasing research on the issue suggests that lives can indeed be lost through required regulatory expenditures, and that there is reason for government to take the problem seriously. At the very least, there is a serious problem if the danger, and the need for tradeoffs, are entirely neglected.

WHY DOES IT MATTER?

We have now seen enough to know that an impressive body of work attempts to measure health gains from regulation against health risks from regulation. But why should we focus on this particular question? Why would it not be better to attend to the overall gains from regulation and to the overall losses from regulation? What is special about health–health tradeoffs?

---

[19] 57 Fed. Reg. 26002 (1992).

[20] Ralph L. Keeney, Mortality Risks Induced by the Costs of Regulations, 8 J. Risk & Uncertainty 95 (1994), quoting News Release from Senator John Glenn (March 19, 1991).

Part of the answer lies in existing public judgments, taken as simple brute facts. People seem to think that regulation is bad if it causes more deaths than it saves; everyone agrees that a demonstration to this effect counts strongly against regulation. But people do not always know how to compare health gains (fifteen lives gained, for example) with monetary losses (an expenditure of $15 million, for example). As we have seen, this uncertainty stems partly from the fact that lives and dollars are not easily made commensurable, and partly from the fact that the appropriate amount to spend on protection of a (statistical) life depends on context. A deliberative judgment on net health tradeoffs is easier to reach than a deliberative judgment on other sorts of tradeoffs. It may thus be especially simple to obtain an incompletely theorized agreement that a net mortality loss is bad. People can make choices more easily when the tradeoffs involve qualitatively indistinguishable things, like lives, rather than qualitatively diverse things, like lives and dollars. A judgment of this kind undoubtedly underlies the interest in health–health analysis. When it is hard to trade off lives against dollars, the burdens of judgment might be eased when we are trading off lives against lives.

There is considerable truth to this suggestion, but it is a bit too crude. As we shall see, lives are themselves not commensurable, in the sense that a single metric – "lives saved" – is itself too crude to account for considered democratic judgments. Problems of incommensurability cannot be eliminated so easily. They play a large role in health–health comparisons, too.

INCORPORATING HEALTH–HEALTH COMPARISONS

Let us try, in a simple, intuitive way, to identify the factors that should enter into deliberative judgments about health–health tradeoffs. Begin with a simple case in which the costs of information and inquiry are zero. If this is so, all agencies should investigate all risks potentially at stake. Agencies should always take account of ancillary risks and try to limit aggregate risks.

Of course, the costs of investigation and inquiry are never zero; in fact, they are often very high. We can readily imagine that agencies could spend all their time investigating ancillary risks, and never do anything else. (This is a potential problem with cost–benefit analysis: Cost–benefit analysis may itself fail cost–benefit analysis, a topic that I shall take up in due course.) When the costs of inquiry are not zero, the obligation to inquire into ancillary risks might be a function of several factors. *First* is the cost of delay, understood as the cost of not regulating the regulated risk until more information has been compiled. To figure out this cost, it is necessary to know something about the seriousness of the regulated risk and the length of time necessary to investigate the ancillary risk. *Second* is the cost of investigating the ancillary risk, where this cost is understood as a product of the cost of compiling and evaluating the relevant information. *Third* is the benefit of investigating the ancillary risk, with the benefit understood as the likelihood of uncovering information that might help to produce a different and better result.

Under this view, it is, of course, important to know something about the possible extent of the ancillary risks and the burdens involved in discovering it. Before the actual investigation has occurred, there will be a good deal of intuition and guesswork; the full facts cannot be known until inquiries have been completed, and the real question is whether it is worthwhile to complete the inquiries or even to embark on them. But even at an early stage, it is possible to know that some ancillary risks are likely to be high, while others are trivial or low. Moreover, some ancillary risks can be investigated relatively inexpensively, while others depend on scientific and predictive judgments that require an enormous investment of resources. Finally, an agency might be reluctant to inquire into ancillary risks on the theory that if it does so, it will be unable to regulate the risk at issue before it is too late. Thus it seems clear that the extent and nature of the regulated risk are crucial factors for those deciding whether to explore ancillary risks.

On this simple, intuitive view, we might think in the following way: If it would be enormously expensive to investigate whether fuel economy standards would really produce smaller and more dangerous cars, if the fuel economy standards would themselves do a lot of good, and if the likelihood of a high ancillary risk seems small, then it makes sense to proceed with the fuel economy standards without investigating the ancillary risks. On the other hand, it is easy to imagine a scenario in which investigation of ancillary risks is reasonable, or when failure to investigate would be irrational. NHTSA's position with respect to fuel economy standards and safety is that the ancillary risk is indeed worth investigating, and all the evidence suggests that in designing fuel economy standards, the risk of adverse safety effects should be considered and minimized.[21]

Compare the question how to handle ancillary risks created by the prohibited manufacture of asbestos. One ancillary risk arises from the fact that asbestos appears to be the best product for use in brake linings, and existing substitutes are worse. Whether this is true, and how serious the ancillary risk is, can be investigated at the present time. But other ancillary risks involve the substitutes for asbestos in products for which no substitutes are now available. On the view of the Environmental Protection Agency, invalidated by a federal court,[22] the ban on asbestos will force technological innovation, producing new substances that do the work now done by asbestos. This seems to be a reasonable view.

---

[21] See the detailed report, Effectiveness and Impact of Corporate Average Fuel Economy Standards, available at *www.nap.edu/books/0309076013/html/*.

[22] See Corrosion Proof Fittings, 947 F.2d 1201 (9th Cir., 1991).

If so, the government has reason to regulate asbestos now and to wait before evaluating any substitute risks.

EXISTING LAW

How should we understand existing law in light of this first approximation? As we will see, Congress has apparently forbidden health–health analysis in many settings, and questions therefore arise about what understanding, if any, accounts for the prohibition.

Some of the relevant statutes might be seen to reflect *categorical judgments* about calculations of the kind just discussed. Congress might think, for example, that the Nuclear Regulatory Commission (NRC) should not ask whether regulation of nuclear power will make for more acid deposition because the problem of unsafe nuclear power is an especially serious one, because nuclear power regulation is unlikely to lead to significant increases in acid deposition, and because it is very hard for the NRC, given its limited budget and expertise, to make the necessary extrapolations. Under the considerations I have discussed, the NRC might plausibly be exempted from the duty of exploring ancillary risks.

Alternatively, and more promisingly still, the problems posed by ancillary risks might be solved by a *division of labor*. Any effects on automobile safety that come from air pollution regulation might be controlled by the National Highway Transportation Safety Administration. Perhaps NHTSA has the authority to make sure that the ancillary risk does not come to fruition. Any adverse effects of EPA regulation could be prevented by NHTSA. Perhaps the two agencies will coordinate their efforts to ensure that aggregate risks are minimized. The problem of acid deposition might be controlled, not by the NRC, but by the EPA, through its own program dealing with that problem.

Or consider the health risks from regulation inducing employment and poverty. It might be thought that the disemployment effects of regulation are or should be addressed by other governmental institutions, including those entrusted with the power to reduce unemployment and poverty. Of course, there are problems with the division of labor strategy. Coordination of risk regulation is difficult to achieve, and in modern government, it has not been pursued in any systematic way. In any case, it would be surprising if a healthy division of labor accounted for all of existing practice, for there is no evidence that agencies systematically respond to increases in ancillary risk created by regulation.

Another explanation would point to the important role of *interest groups* in the regulatory process. On this view, the disparities in regulatory strategies are attributable to the fact that well-organized groups are able to obtain legislation in their interest or to fend off harmful regulation. It should be unsurprising that the statute regulating agricultural practices allows for a form of open-ended balancing; the agricultural groups are in a good position to fend off draconian legislation. Often risk redistribution, rather than risk reduction, is the effect of government policy. Some environmental groups work very hard to obtain severe restrictions on carcinogenic substances.

Yet another explanation would point to *myopia, selective attention, sensationalism, credit-claiming, and random agenda selection* as important forces in the production of risk regulation. We have seen that some statutes stem from sensationalistic events, like the Love Canal scare, that encourage legislators to hold hearings and claim credit for fixing problems that are really just part of a complex whole. Such statutes are likely to reflect myopia or selective attention. The result may well be a form of random agenda selection that does not adequately reduce risks or that even increases some risks.

Finally, some statutes might reflect *public judgments* about how to conduct health–health tradeoffs. Perhaps the public believes that an increase in a certain risk is not a relevant factor in the assessment of another risk. This could be a product of simple confusion, as in the well-established refusal, on the part of some of the public some of the time, to acknowledge any need for tradeoffs. Such judgments should not be given any weight in law, but Congress appears to disagree with this proposition. Or public judgments might be based on heuristics of certain kinds, producing errors (see Chapter 2), or instead of gripping anecdotes that make draconian regulation of a certain risk seem quite sensible. In these ways, public judgments could be confused, and we might seek a form of expert judgment that would produce more in the way of regulatory rationality.

Some such judgments might, however, result from something other than confusion. Our first approximation has suggested that all risks should be aligned along a single metric – expected annual deaths, aggregate benefits and costs – and hence measured against one another. Both expert and economic approaches attempt to do this, though in interestingly different ways. As we saw in Chapter 3, experts tend to look at expected annual deaths and to assess risks accordingly. But ordinary people base their judgments on something other than this. They look, for example, at whether the risk is faced voluntarily or involuntarily; whether it is equitably distributed; whether it is faced by future generations; whether it is potentially catastrophic; whether it involves a death that is especially dreaded; and whether it is new and poorly understood. If these factors are taken into account, it might well be the case that people would find, say, 300 cases of cancer more acceptable than 325 cases of heart disease, given certain assumptions about what causes each. It is similarly possible that people might therefore accept a regulated risk involving 100 annual fatalities even if the ancillary risk involves 110 annual fatalities; perhaps the ancillary risk is less severe because it is voluntarily run, not especially dreaded, and well understood. The democratic decision to look at something other than quantity is easy to defend. It is also fully rational (see Chapter 3).

We come, then, to a complication for the initial approximation: Risks should be evaluated in accordance with the various qualitative factors deemed relevant by ordinary people who are evaluating risk. Of course, it would be possible to assign numbers to these factors if this step aided analysis.

COURTS AND EXISTING LAW

I now turn to existing law. If an agency takes account of ancillary risks, has it behaved unlawfully? If an agency refuses to consider such risks, should courts require it do so?

CONSIDERATION OF ANCILLARY RISKS

Suppose first that an agency actually considers health—health tradeoffs. Is it permitted to do so? Agencies have considerable flexibility here, since under existing law, ambiguous statutes can be interpreted as agencies reasonably see fit.

Sometimes, however, statutes are unambiguous on this point, and ancillary risks are excluded as reasons for regulatory action or inaction. Under the relevant provisions of the Food and Drug Act, for example, the FDA appears to be banned from considering the possibility that the exclusion of foods with carcinogens will increase risks from, say, heart disease. The FDA is banned from considering this or any other ancillary risk. A similar problem arises under the toxic substances provision of the Occupational Safety and Health Act, which probably bans OSHA from asking whether richer is safer, or even from balancing workplace risks against ancillary risks created by regulation.

But sometimes agencies are given sufficiently broad authority, and they may, if they choose, consider ancillary risks. The Federal Insecticide, Fungicide, and Rodenticide Act provides that agencies must ask whether pesticides produce "unreasonable adverse effects on the environment," and this term requires the agency to take "into account the economic, social, and environmental costs and benefits of the use of any pesticide."[23] Thus FIFRA certainly authorizes EPA to consider the possibility that any regulation would create aggregate harms. The Clean Air Act and the Federal Water Pollution Control Act allow

[23]   7 USC 136(bb).

146

government to consider a broad range of good and bad environmental effects in requiring technologies to reduce air and water pollution.[24] Under the Safe Drinking Water Act, the EPA is allowed to consider the possibility that stringent regulation of lead will lead to control strategies that will actually increase other water pollution problems.[25] Outside of the context of toxic substances, the Occupational Safety and Health Act defines occupational safety and health standards as those "reasonably necessary or appropriate" to the goal of ensuring "safe or health employment and places of employment." OSHA may reasonably decide that a standard is not "reasonably necessary or appropriate" if the effect of the regulation is to lose aggregate lives. It is probably permitted to consider the effects of regulation in causing risks to life and health through poverty and unemployment.

REFUSAL TO CONSIDER ANCILLARY RISKS

Now suppose that an agency refuses to consider, or to make decisive, the fact that its decision to reduce one risk increases another risk. Perhaps a new regulatory initiative from the Nuclear Regulatory Commission would increase the risks from coal-fired power plants. Is the NRC's refusal to consider such risks unlawful? The first question is whether the statute requires consideration of ancillary risks. The second question is whether, if the statute does not do so, the agency's decision is arbitrary or capricious.

As we have seen, many statutes do not require agencies to consider ancillary risks. In any case, courts defer to reasonable agency interpretations of statutes, so in many instances the agency will have the authority to decide whether to consider ancillary risks. If the agency has the statutory authority not to consider ancillary risks, the question is whether the agency's failure to do so is reasonable. In an extreme case, failure to consider risks that are likely to be large, and that are not terribly costly to investigate, might well be seen as arbitrary within the meaning of the APA. Indeed, I believe – for reasons to be elaborated shortly, and investigated in some detail in Chapter 9 – that courts should be less reluctant than they now are to find agency action arbitrary on this ground.

A great deal, of course, turns on existing information. When the data about ancillary risks are speculative or unreliable, agencies are probably not required to consider such risks. OSHA could lawfully conclude – as it has, in fact, concluded – that the evidence that richer is safer is too speculative to be used at this time. Its decision to this effect ought not to be found arbitrary or

---

[24] See, for example, 42 USC §§7411(a)(1), 7521(a)(3)(A) (1994).
[25] *American Water Works Association v. EPA*, 40 F.3d 1266, 1271 (DC Cir., 1994).

capricious unless it can be shown that the evidence is solid and that the costs of incorporating it are reasonable. The relevant provision of the statute – the "reasonably necessary or appropriate" language – gives OSHA discretion to do with this evidence as it chooses. Under FIFRA, by contrast, an agency that fails to consider ancillary risks would probably be violating the statute, at least on a showing that the ancillary risks are real and the costs of investigation are not excessive.

Consider in this regard the principal case involving the issue of health–health tradeoffs, *Competitive Enterprise Institute (CEI) v. NHTSA*.[26] NHTSA establishes fuel economy standards; in doing so, NHTSA is required to consider the issue of "feasibility." In deciding the question of feasibility, NHTSA has taken account of passenger safety, including risks created by regulation, and while there is a possible statutory issue here,[27] everyone in *CEI* accepted NHTSA's views on this point. The question in the case was whether NHTSA had acted lawfully in refusing to relax its fuel economy standards for certain model years. Automobile companies urged that relaxation was required in order to save lives – because the existing standards would lead to downsizing and hence to smaller and more dangerous vehicles – and they presented strong evidence to this effect.

The agency responded that this evidence was unconvincing and that "domestic manufacturers should be able to improve their fuel economy in the future by . . . technological means, without outsourcing their larger cars, without further downsizing or mix shifts toward smaller cars, and without sacrificing acceleration or performance."[28] The court held that this explanation was inadequate. The agency failed to claim or show that, in fact, manufacturers would fail to downsize their cars. In any case, downsizing would be costly, and that "cost would translate into higher prices for large cars (as well as small), thereby pressuring consumers to retain their old cars and make the associated sacrifice in safety. The result would be effectively the same harm that concerns petitioners and that the agency fails to negate or justify."[29] The court therefore remanded to the agency for a better explanation or a change in policy.

---

[26] 956 F.2d 321 (DC Cir., 1992).

[27] The relevant statute required NHTSA to promote fuel economy "to the maximum extent feasible." 15 USC §2002(a)(4) (1988), repealed by Pub L No. 103–272, §7(b), 108 Stat 1379 (1994). It is not clear that this provision allows NHTSA to consider safety effects as part of its judgment about feasibility. Compare *American Textile Manufacturers Institute, Inc. v. Donovan*, 452 U.S. 490, 509 (1981) (interpreting "feasible" in 29 USC §655(b) as not requiring cost–benefit analysis).

[28] *CEI*, 956 F.2d at 324, quoting NHTSA, Passenger Average Automobile Fuel Economy Standard for Model Year 1990, 54 Fed. Reg. 21985, 21966 (1989).

[29] Id. at 325 (citation omitted).

On remand, the agency offered a somewhat better explanation. NHTSA pointed to what it saw as the absence of clear indications that fuel economy standards had caused any manufacturer to price consumers out of the market for larger, safer cars. NHTSA referred as well to an absence of manufacturer claims about the specific design standards that would result from the standards. The court found this explanation sufficient.[30] In doing so, it applied a highly deferential form of review.

In light of the record, however, and the predictable pressures on an agency like NHTSA, the result in the case might well be questioned. NHTSA may well suffer from a form of "tunnel vision," especially in dealing with fuel economy standards, for which there is a powerful constituency. The interests that call for attention to ancillary safety risks are typically poorly organized, and when the claims come from the automobile manufacturers, NHTSA may be too ready to distrust them. To say this is not to say that NHTSA should be required to relax its fuel economy standards. But it is to say that a demonstration of the sort made by the automobile manufacturers might well serve as a kind of warning signal to the court, requiring a solid response from the agency. In *CEI*, the agency's response could not qualify as solid, as the court itself, while affirming the agency, seemed to suggest. A special advantage of requiring agencies to take account of health–health tradeoffs is that such requirements might spur imaginative solutions, minimizing all the relevant adverse effects. Indeed, it seems possible to come up with fuel economy standards that reduce the risk of producing more dangerous vehicles, and solutions of this kind are not likely to be attempted if that risk is not placed on-screen.[31]

A promising model for the future is provided by an important court of appeals decision holding that under a statute that required open-ended balancing of relevant factors, an agency was required to ask whether the risks that would substitute for asbestos would lead to even greater risks.[32] Or consider the question whether EPA is required to consider the beneficial effects of an air pollutant in choosing the optimal degree of regulation. The problem may seem exotic, but ground-level ozone appears to have beneficial effects in counteracting skin cancers and cataracts, even as it has adverse effects in producing respiratory problems. In concluding that the EPA was required to take the beneficial effects into account, the court said it would seem "bizarre that a statute intended to improve human health would...lock the agency into looking at only one

---

[30] *CEI v. NHTSA*, 45 F.3d 481, 484–6 (DC Cir., 1995).

[31] National Research Council, Effectiveness and Impact of Corporate Fuel Economy Standard (Washington, D.C.: National Academy Press, 2001), available at *www.nap.edu/catalog/10172.html?onpi_newsdoc 073001.*

[32] *Corrosion Proof Fittings v. EPA*, 947 F.2d 1201 (5th Cir., 1991).

half of a substance's health effects in determining the maximum level of that substance."[33]

The point I am making here might well be generalized. Agencies ought to be required to show that they are doing more good than harm.[34] This does not mean that courts should engage in independent review of agency judgments on this score, but it does mean that courts should take a "hard look" at agency decisions failing to undertake health–health comparisons. We will return to this point in Chapter 8.

CONGRESS

In its present form, Congress is ill equipped to consider the problem of health–health tradeoffs. Its committee structure ensures a high degree of fragmentation and does not allow for deliberation on such tradeoffs. On the contrary, that structure makes ancillary risks difficult to evaluate or, much worse, even to see; often those risks are thought to be subject to the jurisdiction of another committee, which means, in practice, that coordination is extremely difficult. In these circumstances, I offer two simple suggestions for legislative reform.

The first is that Congress should create a new subcommittee entrusted specifically with the power to assess aggregate risk levels, to compare risks, and to initiate revision of statutes that increase net risks. This committee should have the power to introduce corrective legislation when a statute, or agency action under a statute, has been shown to increase aggregate risks.

My second suggestion is that Congress should address the problem of health–health tradeoffs through a new directive in the Administrative Procedure Act. Notably, initiatives designed to require cost–benefit balancing say relatively little about this problem. To be sure, Congress appears to be learning. Many statutory "consideration" requirements[35] draw attention to health–health tradeoffs, for example by requiring agencies entrusted with reducing air pollution problems to take account as well of "non-air quality health and environmental impact and energy requirements."[36] Here is an explicit recognition that the EPA is allowed to consider the danger that a regulation that decreases air pollution will also create water pollution or some other environmental problem.[37] The

---

[33] *American Trucking Association v. EPA*, 175 F.3d 1027, 1052 (DC Cir., 1999).

[34] See generally Warren & Marchant, supra note 25 in Chapter 5.

[35] 42 USC 7429 (a) (2) (OSHA); 42 USC 300g-1(b)(4)(B) (Safe Drinking Water Act).

[36] 42 USC 7411(a)(1).

[37] See *American Petroleum Institute. v. EPA*, 52 F2d 1113 (DC Cir., 1995) (recognizing this point but also holding that EPA had unlawfully elevated these "consideration" factors).

reformulated gasoline program takes this basic form,[38] as does the provision governing emissions standards for new vehicles, which authorizes the EPA to examine "safety factors" as well as cost and energy issues.[39] Thus the EPA is instructed to ask whether a program designed to reduce air pollution might thereby make cars more dangerous; if so, EPA should reconsider the program. The Toxic Substances Control Act similarly requires the EPA to take account of substitute risks.[40] Under the fuel regulation program of the Clean Air Act, the EPA is not allowed to prohibit a fuel or fuel additive unless "he finds, and publishes such finding, that in his judgment such prohibition will not cause the use of any other fuel or fuel additive which will produce emissions which will endanger the public health or welfare to the same or greater degree than" the prohibited item.[41]

But Congress could go much further. I suggest a proposed amendment to the Administrative Procedure Act: *"Agencies shall ensure, to the extent feasible, that regulations do not create countervailing risks that are greater than those of the regulated risk."* The more modest and particular ideas found in existing law should be generalized.

EXECUTIVE BRANCH

The Office of Information and Regulatory Affairs has been entrusted with the power to coordinate regulatory policy and to ensure reasonable priority-setting. In view of the absence of good priority-setting, and the enormous room for saving costs and increasing regulatory benefits, there is much to be done.

OIRA should see, as one of its central assignments, the task of overcoming governmental tunnel vision, by ensuring that aggregate risks are reduced and that agency focus on particular risks does not mean that ancillary risks are ignored or increased. This is a more cautious version of Justice Breyer's larger suggestion that OIRA should have a power to set priorities by diverting resources from smaller problems to larger ones.[42] No body in government is now entrusted with the authority of ensuring that risk regulation is managed so as to ensure global rationality and coherence. OIRA is well situated to take on that role, at least by attending to the possibility that regulation of some risks may make risk levels higher on balance.

It should be clear that this is a plea for a strong role for technocrats in the process of risk regulation. Ordinary people are not in a good position to see

---

[38] 42 USC 7545(k)(1).

[39] 42 USC 7521(a)(3)(A).

[40] *Corrosion Proof Fittings v. EPA*, 947 F.2d 1201 (5th Cir., 1991).

[41] 42 USC 7545 (c)(2)(c).

[42] See Breyer, supra note 8 in Chapter 2, at 59–72.

the adverse health effects of (some) health regulation. Nor are we ordinarily attentive to the possibility of developing innovative solutions, able to diminish risks on all sides of the equation. I now turn to a case study that, in my view, strongly fortifies the case for expertise, rather than intuition, in the regulatory process.

7

The Arithmetic of Arsenic

Americans may disagree about a lot of things, but arsenic isn't one of them. When you turn on the kitchen sink, you ought to be able to drink what comes out, without worrying about being poisoned.[1]

"What we know is a drop, what we do not know – an ocean" (Isaac Newton). In spite of significant gains in knowledge, we are still moving mainly in the dark when dealing with the quantitative importance of risk factors in chemical carcinogenesis, the mechanisms of action of chemical carcinogens, and hence their detection and the assessment of their risks to human health. The basic understanding ... is still missing.[2]

Because the shape of the dose-response curve in the low-dose region cannot be verified by measurement, there is no means to determine which shape is correct.... [W]hen modeling the risks associated with lower doses, the dose/risk range in which regulatory agencies and risk assessors are most frequently interested, there is a wide divergence in the risk projected by [different models, all of which fit existing evidence.] ... In fact ... the risks predicted by these ... models produce a 70,000-fold variation in the predicted response.[3]

Additional epidemiological evaluations are needed to characterize the dose-response relationship for arsenic-associated cancer and noncancer end points, especially at low doses. Such studies are of critical importance for improving the scientific validity of risk assessment.[4]

[1] Quoted in the Chicago Tribune, July 28, 2001, at p. I.
[2] Toxicology, p. 178, Hans Marquardt et al., eds. (New York: Academic Press, 1999).
[3] Phillip L. Williams et al., Principles of Toxicology 456 (New York: Wiley-Interscience, 2000).
[4] National Research Council, Arsenic in Drinking Water 3 (Washington, D.C.: National Academy Press, 1999).

Anyone who's read an Agatha Christie mystery knows that arsenic is a poison.[5]

What does cost–benefit analysis mean in practice? In this chapter, I attempt to answer that question. I do so by exploring one of the most contested environmental decisions of the Bush Administration: the suspension of the EPA regulation of arsenic in drinking water. Much of the contest over that decision has involved a debate about the relevant costs and benefits. As we will see, it is possible to draw a range of general lessons from the arsenic controversy.

My principal finding is simple: Sometimes the best that can be done is to specify an exceedingly wide "benefits range," one that does not do a great deal to discipline judgment. Much of the discussion will be devoted to establishing this point. At the same time, I suggest that cost–benefit analysis provides an important improvement over the "intuitive toxicology" of ordinary people. This intuitive technology can lead people to large blunders in thinking about risk, as the case of arsenic clearly reveals. More particularly, I urge that an understanding of the arsenic controversy offers seven general lessons.

1. Cost–benefit analysis can often produce an illusion of certainty. Even where, as in the arsenic case, science has a great deal to offer, the most that the agency can be expected to do may be to specify a range, sometimes a wide range, without assigning probabilities to various "points" along the spectrum. This suggestion should be taken as an attack not on CBA but on what might be described as the false promise of CBA: the thought that science and economics, taken together, can produce bottom lines to be mechanically applied by regulatory agencies.

2. With respect to health benefits, plausible assumptions can lead in dramatically different directions. In the case of arsenic, it would be possible to follow most of the EPA's assumptions and to conclude that the annual number of lives saved would be as low as 5 or as high as 112, and that the annual monetized benefits of the proposed standard would be as high as $1.2 billion or as low as $10 million! It is worthwhile to pay special attention to the *dose–response curve*, on which direct information is typically absent; I will make a particular effort to connect the underlying scientific questions to problems in cost–benefit balancing.

3. If literate in some basic science and economics, an adroit lawyer, on either side, might mount apparently reasonable challenges to *any* EPA decision about whether and how to regulate arsenic in drinking water. An industry lawyer should be able to urge, with some force, that any new regulation of arsenic is too

---

[5] Cong. Rec. H4751 (July 27, 2001) (Rep. Anna Eshoo).

severe because the costs exceed the benefits. An environmental lawyer should be able to urge, with some force, that nearly any imaginable regulation of arsenic is too lenient because the benefits of further regulation would exceed the costs. Both challenges would be plausible for a simple reason: It is easy to identify assumptions that would drive the numbers up or down. Hence one of my principal goals is to provide a kind of primer on how informed lawyers can integrate science, economics, and law in order to challenge regulatory outcomes.

4. In part because of point 3, and in light of the scientific and economic complexities, courts should play an exceedingly deferential role in overseeing CBA at the agency level. To say the least, judges are not specialists in the relevant topics, some of which are highly technical, and because good lawyers will be able to raise so many plausible doubts, the best judicial posture is one of deference. In the arsenic case, and in many other contexts, agencies must decide in the midst of considerable scientific uncertainty and on the basis of judgments of value on which reasonable people can differ. If agencies have been both open and reasonable, the judicial role is at an end. The claim for judicial deference is rooted in institutional considerations, and above all a sense of the likely problems of intensive judicial review – not in approval of any particular agency decision.

5. The false precision of CBA is a significant cautionary note, but it should not be taken as a fundamental attack on the method itself, at least if CBA is understand as a way of compiling relevant information. In the arsenic case, an assessment of costs and benefits cannot determine the outcome. Even so, the assessment is indispensable to inform the inquiry and to ensure that discretion is exercised in a way that is transparent rather than opaque. Without some effort to ascertain the effects of regulation, agencies are making a stab in the dark. At the very least, an understanding of the data helps show why the decision about how to regulate arsenic is genuinely difficult – and why, and where, reasonable people might differ. This is itself a significant gain.

6. The Safe Drinking Water Act (SDWA), designed to control pollution in drinking water, has been amended to require cost–benefit balancing, partly to permit the EPA to relax regulatory requirements where the benefits are low and the costs are high. At the same time, however, the SDWA continues to have a high degree of rigidity. The EPA is not authorized to impose regulation selectively and in those areas in which regulation would do the most good; it is required to proceed with a uniform, national regulation. The EPA is also forbidden to create trading programs, which might well make best sense for some pollutants. Statutory amendments would be sensible here, especially under a statute dedicated to cost–benefit balancing. Regulatory statutes generally should authorize agencies to target regulations to areas where the benefits exceed the costs, and should also allow agencies to use market incentives where appropriate.

7. It would be extremely valuable to assemble information about the distributional consequences of regulation. The benefits of some regulations are enjoyed disproportionately by people who are poor and members of minority groups.[6] The burdens of some regulations are imposed disproportionately on exactly the same groups. To assess the arsenic rule, it would be highly desirable to know whether poor people are mostly helped or mostly hurt. Would they bear high costs? Would the regulation operate as a regressive tax? Unfortunately, the EPA has not answered that question, though it would almost certainly be easy for it to do so. Existing executive orders, calling for CBA, should be amended to require a distributional analysis as well.

Throughout the discussion, I will be relying on the record compiled by the EPA at the time that it made its decision; subsequent to that decision, new evidence has been found and discussed, giving rise to increased fears about the risks posed by arsenic.[7] In part as a result of this evidence, the EPA, under President George W. Bush, decided to go forward with the Clinton Administration initiative. Part of the goal of my discussion is to show that this is a fully reasonable decision – but not the only reasonable decision.

ARSENIC AND THE PUBLIC

My principal topic will be the contest over the appropriate analysis of existing data relating to arsenic, but at it will be useful to begin with a puzzle. In April 2001, the Bush Administration suspended the Clinton Administration's arsenic regulation, calling for further study.[8] There seems to be little question that of all the controversial environmental actions of the early Bush Administration, the suspension of the arsenic rule produced the most intense reaction.

A national survey, conducted between April 21 and April 26, 1001, found that 56 precent of Americans rejected the Bush decision, whereas only 34 percent approved of it – and that majorities of Americans opposed the decision in every

---

[6] See Matthew E. Kahn, The Beneficiaries of Clean Air Act Regulation, 24 Regulation 34 (2001).

[7] See Subcommittee to Update the 1999 Arsenic in Drinking Water Report, Arsenic in Drinking Water: 2001 Update (Washington, D.C.: GPO, 2001).

[8] See 66 Fed. Reg. 16,134 (2001) (delaying arsenic rule); 66 Fed. Reg. 20,579 (2001) (ordering subsequent process).

region of the nation.[9] At various points, the public outcry combined concern, certainty, and cynicism. "Arsenic everywhere, and Bush is not helping," according to one newspaper.[10] "You may have voted for him, but you didn't vote for this in your water," wrote the *Wall Street Journal*.[11] In an editorial, the *New York Times* demanded that "Americans should expect their drinking water to be at least as safe as that of Japan, Jordan, Namibia and Laos," all of which impose a 10 ppb standard.[12] A respected journalist asked, "How callous can you get, Mr. Compassionate Conservative?"[13] Ridiculing the Bush Administration in a cartoon entitled, "Safety is for Sissies," *Time* magazine epitomized public sentiment by targeting the arsenic decision as a chief example of several environmental foibles.[14] The public reaction came to a head during the legislative debates on the issue, particularly within the House of Representatives, which voted to reinstate the Clinton rule on the theory that arsenic "is a poison."[15]

Here is the puzzle. With respect to arsenic, the underlying issues are highly technical, and very few people are expert on the risks posed by exposure to low levels of arsenic. What accounts for the public outcry?

I believe that the reason is simple: *Arsenic* was involved, and so was *drinking water*. These two facts made the controversy seem highly accessible, and it seemed easy to be outraged. Why was the Bush Administration allowing dangerously high levels of arsenic to remain in drinking water? This appeared to be a rhetorical question. By contrast, many environmental problems are both obscure and technical, and people do not have an easy or intuitive handle on them. Is carbon dioxide a serious problem? Most people have no idea. But arsenic is well known, and it is well known to be a poison, not least because of the exceedingly popular movie, *Arsenic and Old Lace*. In fact, an influential environmental group, the Natural Resources Defense Council, has exploited exactly this reference with its work on the arsenic problem, under the title, "Arsenic and Old Laws".[16]

---

[9] Mark Barabak, Bush Criticized As Fear of Environment Grows, LA Times, April 20, 1001, available at *latimes.com/news/timespoll/national/lat_poll010430.htm*.

[10] Erik Olson, Arsenic Everywhere, and Bush Is Not Helping, Baltimore Sun, May 14, 2001, at 9A.

[11] John Fialka, Arsenic and Wild Space: Green Activists from Across Spectrum Unite Against Bush, Wall Street Journal, April 11, 2001, at A20.

[12] Robert K. Musil, Arsenic on Tap, New York Times, April 24, 2001, at A18.

[13] Michael Kinsley, Bush Decision on Arsenic Tough to Swallow, Times Union, April 16, 2001, at A9.

[14] Bruce Handy & Glynis Sweeny, Safety Is for Sissies, Time, April 16, 2001, at 88.

[15] Cong. Rec. H4751 (July 27, 2001).

[16] Natural Resources Defense Council, Arsenic and Old Laws: A Scientific and Public Health Analysis of Arsenic Occurrence in Drinking Water, Its Health Effects, and EPA's Outdated Arsenic Tap Water Standard (2001), available at *www.nrdc.org/water/drinking/arsenic/exesum.asp*.

In Chapter 2, we saw that ordinary people are "intuitive toxicologists," with a set of simple rules for thinking about environmental risks. Among those simple rules is a belief that substances that cause cancer are unsafe and should be banned. Intuitive toxicology does not easily make room for issues of degree. It does not accommodate the judgment that low levels of admittedly carcinogenic substances should sometimes be tolerated because the risks are low and the costs of eliminating them are high. It does not show an understanding of the different imaginable dose–response curves and the possibility of safe thresholds, or even benefits from low exposure levels.

Drawing on the work of Paul Slovic and his coauthors, we have also seen that as part of intuitive toxicology, people rely on the "affect heuristic," through which their judgments about risks are greatly affected by rapid, even automatic responses.[17] Consider, for example, the remarkable fact that stock prices increase significantly on sunny days, a fact that is hard to explain in terms that do not rely on affect.[18] With respect to risks, people's affect often operates as a kind of mental shortcut, substituting for a more careful inquiry into consequences. Something very much of this sort has happened with the Bush Administration's suspension of the arsenic standard, partly because of skepticism about President Bush, but above all because of the associations of arsenic. "If there is one thing we all seem to agree on is that we do not want arsenic in our drinking water. It is an extremely potent human carcinogen. . . . It is this simple: Arsenic is a killer."[19]

Indeed, we could easily imagine public outrage over any decision to allow arsenic in drinking water, even if the permissible level was exceedingly low. The outrage is likely to be promoted by cascade effects, in which people's concern is heightened by the fact that other people are concerned. Indeed the Bush Administration's suspension of the arsenic rule seems to have created a cascade effect, in which many people objected to the suspension because other (reasonable) people seemed to have objected. In fact, one of the most compelling arguments, within the House of Representatives and the public at large, was that other countries regulated arsenic at the level of stringency proposed in the Clinton Administration.[20] The practices of other countries seemed to operate

---

[17] See Paul Slovic et al., The Affect Heuristic, in Intuitive Judgment: Heuristics and Biases, Thomas Gilovich et al., eds. (Cambridge: Cambridge Univ. Press, forthcoming). Related arguments can be found in the discussion of outrage in Daniel Kahneman et al., Shared Outrage and Erratic Awards, 16 J. Risk & Uncertainty 49 (1998), also in Cass R. Sunstein et al., supra note 20 in Chapter 4.

[18] See David Hirschleifer & Tyler Shumway, Good Day Sunshine: Stock Returns and the Weather, available at *papers.ssrn.com/sol3/results.cfm.*

[19] Cong. Rec. H4744 (remarks of Rep. Waxman).

[20] See, for example, Cong. Rec. H4743 (July 27, 2001) (remarks of Rep. Bonior).

as a kind of mental shortcut, showing what it is right to do — notwithstanding the reasonable questions that might be asked about the scientific bases for those practices.

There is a deeper point here. The problems in intuitive toxicology and the crudeness of the affect heuristic strongly support the use of CBA, understood not at all as a way to stop regulation but as a way to ensure that when government acts, it does so with some understanding of the likely consequences. CBA might well be understood as a way of moving beyond "intuitive toxicology" toward a form of toxicology that is actually supported by the data.

STATUTORY BACKGROUND

Regulatory statutes often require agencies to require as much as "feasible,"[21] or to "protect the public health."[22] Only a few such statutes expressly require agency decisions to turn on cost–benefit balancing.[23] The SDWA is an intriguing hybrid, combining an analysis of public health and feasibility with reference to CBA as well. Indeed, the cost–benefit provisions of SDWA go as far as any other federal statute in requiring close attention to costs and benefits. Because Congress has been quite interested in imposing more general cost–benefit requirements, the SDWA might well be a harbinger of the future. For that reason alone, the implementation of the statute is worth careful attention.

More particularly, the SDWA asks the EPA to proceed in three steps. First, the EPA is asked to set "maximum contaminant level goals" for water pollutants.[24] The goals must be set "at the level at which no known or anticipated adverse effects on the health of persons occur and which allows an adequate margin of safety." In practice, this statutory standard will frequently call for a maximum contaminant level goal (MCLG) of 0 because many contaminants cannot be shown to have safe thresholds, and because the "adequate margin of safety" language will, in these specific circumstances, seem to support a 0 MCLG. Second, the EPA is told to specify "a maximum contaminant level [MCL] . . . which is as close to the maximum contaminant level goal as is feasible." The statute defines feasible (not terribly helpfully) to mean "feasible with the use of the best technology, treatment techniques, and other means which" the EPA

---

[21] See, for example, 29 USC §655(b)(5) ("feasible"); 42 USC §7521 (A)(3)(A) ("will be available"); 42 USC §7412(d)(2) ("achievable"); 42 USC §6411(a)(1) ("has been adequately demonstrated").

[22] 42 USC §7409(b).

[23] See, for example, 15 USC §2601 et seq. (Toxic Substances Control Act); 7 USC §136 et seq. (Federal Insecticide, Fungicide, and Rodenticide Act).

[24] 42 USC §300g-1(b)(4)(A).

finds "are available." Third, the EPA is required to undertake a risk assessment for pollutants, discussing the level of the danger and the costs of achieving the requisite reduction. The risk assessment is supposed to give an account, for the MCL being considered and for all alternatives levels being considered, of the "quantifiable and nonquantifiable health risk reduction benefits for which there is a factual basis in the rulemaking record"; the quantifiable and nonquantifiable costs; the "incremental costs and benefits associated with each alternative"; and any increased health risk that may occur from compliance, "including risks associated with co-occurring contaminants."[25]

The risk assessment is no mere disclosure provision. The EPA is expressly permitted (not required) to set a maximum contaminant level at a level other than the feasible level if it determines that the benefits of that level "would not justify the costs of complying with the level." On the basis of that determination, the EPA is permitted to set a maximum level "that maximizes health risk reduction benefits at a cost that is justified by the benefits." Courts are authorized to review the EPA's judgment about whether the benefits of a certain level justify the costs, but only by asking whether that judgment is "arbitrary and capricious."[26]

ARSENIC AND THE FEDERAL GOVERNMENT

Arsenic is commonly found in nature, as a part of the mineral compound "arsenopyrite." As a result of soil and rock erosion, it is released into the water supply, where it can be found in New England, eastern Michigan, and the southwest United States. It has long been known that arsenic is toxic, and for years, the EPA has had in place an arsenic regulation calling for an MCL of 50 micrograms per liter. But in the past decades, some evidence suggests arsenic may have significant adverse effects at levels well below the 50-micrograms-per-liter standard. The principal evidence comes from epidemiological studies in Chile, Argentina, and above all Taiwan, finding that exposure levels of 300–600 micrograms cause significant increases of various cancers and other adverse effects.[27]

In 1996, Congress directed EPA to propose a new standard for arsenic by January 1, 2000. At the same time, Congress told the National Academy of Sciences and EPA to study the health effects of arsenic in order to assist the rulemaking effort. In 1996, the EPA requested that the National Research Council (NRC) of the National Academy of Sciences conduct an independent review of arsenic toxicity data and recommend changes to EPA's arsenic criteria.

[25] 42 USC 300g-1 (3)(C)(I)(VI).
[26] 42 USC 300g-1 (1)(b)(D).
[27] See 66 Fed. Reg. at 7001–3.

In its 1999 report, the NRC located few studies that examined arsenic effects at low-level concentrations and even fewer studies in agreement. A 1995 Japanese study found cancer mortality near or below expectation among persons exposed to arsenic in drinking water at less than 50 micrograms per liter. Domestic research in the same year revealed no association between bladder cancer risk and arsenic exposure, where 81 of 88 Utah towns (92 percent) had concentrations below 10 micrograms, and only one town exceeded the 50-micrograms-per-liter standard. A 1999 assessment of Utah mortality rates, which the EPA described as "the best U.S. study currently available," found no increased bladder or lung cancer risks after exposure to arsenic levels of 14 to 166 micrograms per liter.[28] More recent studies in Finland and Taiwan, however, linked increased risks of bladder cancer and cerebrovascular disease to groundwater arsenic consumption as low as 0.1 to 50 micrograms per liter.[29] The Taiwan study, with its large population base, seemed especially impressive.

These results could have led the NRC in several different directions. It would not have been entirely shocking for the NRC to find that the evidence was too inconclusive to support a new rule. Nonetheless, the NRC concluded that the Taiwan studies, examining larger doses, provided the best available evidence on human health effects of arsenic. NRC used linear extrapolations from these data to obtain cancer risks at exposure levels below 50 micrograms per liter and subsequently recommended the EPA significantly lower its current standard.[30] Indeed, the NRC concluded that "considering the data on bladder and lung cancer noted in the studies ... a similar approach for all cancers could easily result in a combined cancer risk on the order of 1 in 100" from exposure at 50 micrograms.[31] The 1 in 100 risk figure is a special source of concern, because EPA is usually attentive to environmental risks at or above 1 in 1,000,000.

Critics challenged the recommendation on the grounds that Taiwanese cooking and health practices put citizens at greater risk for arsenic toxicity than Americans, as demonstrated by the absence of a single report of U.S.

[28] The EPA discounted these results in its final MCL report, based upon the already low cancer rates of the subject population when compared to the entire state. 66 Fed. Reg. at 7004; D. R. Lewis et al., Drinking Water Arsenic in Utah: A Cohort Mortality Study, 107(5) Envtl. Health Perspectives 359 (1999).

[29] P. Kurttio et al., Arsenic Concentrations in Well Water and Risk of Bladder and Kidney Cancer in Finland, 107(9) Envtl. Health Perspectives 705 (1999); H. Y. Chiou et al., Arsenic Methylation Capacity, Body Retention, and Null Genotypes of Glutathione S-transferase MI and TI Among Current Arsenic-Exposed Residents in Taiwan, 386 Mutat. Res. 197 (1997).

[30] National Research Council, supra note 4 in chapter 7, at 8–9.

[31] Abt Associates, Inc., Arsenic in Drinking Rule Economic Analysis 1–13 (Washington, D.C.: GPO, 2000).

arsenic-induced cancer.[32] The Taiwanese population is much poorer than the American population, suffering from a number of dietary and nutritional deficiencies, including a higher intake of arsenic from food, and a deficiency in selenium, zinc, and vitamin B12, all of which can reduce the toxicity of arsenic. In fact, animal studies even suggest that arsenic may be a nutritional requirement, though there is insufficient data to indicate any nutritional role in human health.[33] Despite these criticisms, the EPA relied heavily upon the NRC's scientific conclusions when redeveloping its current MCL.

In 2000, the EPA issued a proposed regulation, setting an MCLG of 0 because no safe level could be identified; an MCL of 3, on the ground that this was the lowest feasible level; and a regulatory ceiling of 5, on the ground that the CBA justified this approach, but not any more stringent mandate. It also requested comments on regulatory ceilings of 3, 10, and 20 micrograms per liter, for which it provided accounts of both benefits and costs. On January 22, 2001, the EPA issued a final rule, essentially embodying the same analysis as the proposal, but with a crucial change, to a regulatory ceiling of 10 micrograms per liter rather than 5. The EPA urged that its assessment of costs and benefits, for four different levels of stringency, justified the 10-micrograms-per-liter level.

COSTS

The new regulation would have required several thousand water systems, serving about 10 million people, to install new equipment. The overall cost of the 10-micrograms-per-liter standard would have been about $210 million. But the aggregate figure is not entirely informative; across the nation, the additional payments would vary considerably. For most households, the annual increase in water bills would be in the range of $30. But water systems with 500 or fewer customers would face significantly higher costs, ranging up to $325 per household. These water systems represent a small fraction of the total number of people affected by arsenic; they tend to involve rural communities.

As it was required to do, the EPA also calculated the costs of alternative levels of regulation. A 20-micrograms-per-liter standard would cost about $70 million; a 5-micrograms-per-liter standard, $440 million; and a 3-micrograms-per-liter standard, $720 million. Here too the disaggregated figures are important. The most stringent standard, of 3 micrograms per liter, would cost an

---

[32] See Sue E. Umshler, When Arsenic Is Safer in Your Cup of Tea Than in Your Local Water Treatment Plant, 39 Nat. Resources J. 565, 589–592 (1999); see also 66 Fed. Reg. at 7003–4.

[33] Id. at 587.

Table 7.1 Mean annual costs of arsenic regulation per household (in 1999 dollars)

System Size	3 micrograms	5 micrograms	10 micrograms	20 micrograms
Less than 100	317	318.26	326.82	351.15
101–500	166.91	164.02	162.50	166.72
501–1,000	74.81	73.11	70.72	68.24
1,001–3,300	63.76	61.94	58.24	54.36
3,301–10,000	42.84	40.18	37.71	34.63
10,001–50,000	38.40	36.07	32.37	29.05
50,001–100,000	31.63	29.45	24.81	22.64
100,001–1,000,000	25.29	23.34	20.52	19.26
More than 1,000,000	7.41	2.79	0.86	0.15
All categories	41.34	36.95	31.85	23.95

average of $41 per affected household; the 20-micrograms-per-liter standard would cost about an average of $24. At the high end, the 20-micrograms-per-liter standard is actually more expensive (at $350) than the 3-micrograms-per-liter standard ($317) because of the particular control technologies that would be involved. Consider Table 7.1.

EPA did not offer a population-wide breakdown to show the numbers of people served by the various system sizes and to see whether the people who would bear the costs could do so easily or with difficulty. But one analysis suggests that almost nine out of ten people (87 percent) who consume arsenic at a significant level in their tap water (over 1 microgram per liter) are served by systems serving more than 10,000 customers.[34] This means that 87 percent of the people who will have to pay for water technology would face annual increases of less than $30 — not trivial, perhaps, but certainly not a huge expenditure.

BENEFITS

Within the EPA, the much harder issues involved the benefits of the 10-micrograms-per-liter requirement. (I emphasize that I am dealing here with the evidence at the time of the decision and that subsequent evidence appears to have strengthened the case for stringent regulation.) The most easily quantified benefits involve prevented cases of bladder and lung cancer; here the

[34] Natural Resources Defense Council, Arsenic and Old Laws: A Scientific and Public Health Analysis of Arsenic Occurrence in Drinking Water, Its Health Effects, and EPA's Outdated Arsenic Tap Water Standard, Chapter. 3, p. 5 (2001), available at www.nrdc.org/water/drinking/arsenic/exesum.asp.

epidemiological data, mostly from Taiwan, allowed quantitative estimates to be made. For two reasons, however, even these estimates should be taken with many grains of salt. The first reason is that there are differences, noted earlier, between the population of Taiwan and that of the United States. The second reason is that a great deal turns on the nature of the dose–response curve. If the curve is "linear," meaning that cancer cases do not drop sharply at low exposure levels, many more cancers will be predicted than if the curve is "sublinear," meaning that after exposure declines to a certain level, the number of cancer cases drops off. Lacking any data on the question, the EPA decided to assume that the dose–response curve is linear, noting that "the use of a linear procedure to extrapolate from a higher, observed data range to a lower range beyond observation is a science policy approach that has been in use by Federal agencies for four decades."[35] The EPA added that the policy objectives are to avoid underestimating risk in order to protect public health and be consistent across risk assessments. From these remarks, it seems clear that the default assumption of linearity is not based on science, which cannot produce a standard default assumption, but on a policy judgment, designed to err on the side of protecting health by ensuring against underestimation of the risks.

Armed with the assumption of linearity, the EPA thought that estimates were feasible for bladder and lung cancers. The EPA calculated bladder and lung cancer risks/benefits using the analysis of the NRC. The NRC used the Taiwan data to calculate a 1 to 1.5 per 1,000 lifetime risk of male fatal bladder cancer at the current 50-micrograms-per-liter standard; it also examined the Chile and Argentina studies and concluded the rates of cancer were comparable to the Taiwan data. The EPA assessed lung cancer risks, which are known to be about 2.5 times greater than bladder cancer risks. But for many of the health effects from arsenic, the EPA concluded that quantification was impossible.

I. Lives and Health: Quantities. The EPA estimated that the 10-micrograms-per-liter requirement would prevent 21 to 29 cancer deaths and 16 to 26 cases

---

[35] 66 Fed. Reg. at 7004. In selecting its dose–response model, the EPA examined a 2000 study by Morales that presented ten potential dose–response models based upon interpretations of the original Taiwan data. Morales et al., Risk of Internal Cancers from Arsenic in Drinking Water, 108 Env. Health Perspectives 655 (2000). The EPA rejected those models with a comparison population because these resulted in supralinear dose–response relationships (higher than a linear response). The EPA concluded that there was no basis for this type of relationship because the NRC report had concluded that the dose–response relationship for arsenic at low levels should be either linear or less than linear (not more). 66 Fed. Reg. at 7006. The EPA then chose a linear model based upon these policies.

Table 7.2 Annual total bladder and lung cancer cases avoided

Arsenic Level	Reduced Mortality Cases	Reduced Morbidity Cases	Total Cancer Cases Avoided
3	32.6–74.1	24.6–64.2	57.2–138.3
5	29.1–53.7	22.0–46.5	51.1–100.2
10	21.3–29.8	16.1–25.9	37.4–55.7
20	10.2–11.3	8.5–8.8	19.0–19.8

of curable cancer. By comparison, a 20-micrograms-per-liter requirement would prevent 11 deaths and 9 curable cancers; a 5-micrograms-per-liter requirement, 20 to 54 deaths and 22 to 47 curable cancers; and a 3-micrograms-per-liter requirement, 32 to 74 cancer deaths and 24 to 64 curable cancers. Consider Table 7.2.

2. Lives and Health: No Quantities. The EPA also concluded that the 10-micrograms-per-liter standard would produce "important non-quantified benefits." "Chief among these are certain health effects known to be caused by arsenic, though, while they may be substantial, the extent to which these impacts occur at levels below 50 [micrograms per liter] is unknown."

The relevant effects include several kinds of cancer: skin, kidney, liver, prostate, and nasal passages. They also include pulmonary effects, cardiovascular effects, immunological effects, neurological effects, and endocrine effects. To this the EPA added that there would be other benefits that would defy quantification. Among these is "the effect on those systems that install treatment technologies that can affect multiple contaminants." Some of the technologies that would reduce arsenic levels would also remove "many other contaminants that EPA is in the process of regulating or considering regulating."

3. Converting Quantities To Dollars. To compare the quantified benefits of regulation with the $200 million cost, EPA was required to engage in several exercises in conversion. With respect to lives saved, the EPA used a value of a statistical life of $6.1 million. That figure was derived by calculating the average of over two dozen studies, mostly in the 1970s, generally designed to show how much an employer had to pay employees to compensate for a statistical risk of death. By multiplying the number of expected mortalities by $6.1 million, EPA obtained most of the "dollar value" of the arsenic regulation.

As noted, however, many of the cancers caused by arsenic are not fatal. For a nonfatal cancer, the EPA used a figure of $607,000. This figure does not actually come from measurements of people's willingness to pay to reduce a statistical risk

Table 7.3 Estimated benefits from reducing arsenic in drinking water

Arsenic Level (micrograms per liter)	Total Quantified Health (Benefits $ millions 1999 – lower and upper bounds)	Potential Nonquantified Health Benefits (all levels)
3	213.8–490.9	Skin cancer, kidney cancer,
5	191.1–355.6	cancer of nasal passages, liver cancer,
10	139.6–197.7	prostate cancer, cardiovascular effects,
20	66.2–75.3	pulmonary, neurological, endocrine effects

of cancer but instead (and somewhat astonishingly) from shoppers' responses to hypothetical questions about how much they would be willing to pay to reduce a statistical risk of chronic bronchitis. Apparently the EPA thought that this was the closest available analogue to a nonfatal cancer. This, then, was the EPA's basic analysis, captured in Table 7.3.

It should be clear that the monetized costs of the 10-micrograms-per-liter standard are between $60 million and $2 million higher than the monetized benefits – and also that overall benefits are in line with overall costs only at the 20-micrograms-per-liter level. EPA was well aware of this point. Nonetheless, it concluded that once the nonquantified benefits of the 10-micrograms-per-liter standard were included, the costs would be well justified. The cost per cancer case avoided for the final rule would be between $3.2 million and $4.8 million – hardly an extraordinary price to pay, and far lower than the $5 million to $12.2 million range produced by a 3-micrograms-per-liter standard.

PEER REVIEW? ARSENIC AT AEI-BROOKINGS

The EPA's conclusion was sharply disputed by a widely reported paper from the American Enterprise Institute(AEI)–Brookings Joint Center for Regulatory Studies.[36] The authors, Jason Burnett and Robert Hahn, concluded that the costs of the rule would exceed the benefits by about $190 million each year – and

[36] See Jason K. Burnett & Robert W. Hahn, EPA's Arsenic Rule: The Benefits of the Standard Do Not Justify the Costs, American Enterprise Institute-Brookings Joint Center for Regulatory Studies, available at *www.aei.brook.edu/publications/abstract.asp?pID* = *115* (January 2001).

hence that the rule deserved membership in the Joint Center's "$100 million club," including regulations that cost at least $100 million more than they promise to deliver. For two reasons, the Burnett–Hahn study is worth close attention. First, the AEI–Brookings Joint Center is highly respected for its careful work on CBA, and Hahn is an especially able and influential observer of the regulatory process. Second, the disagreements between EPA and the Joint Center provide a great deal of information about the nature of CBA itself – and about the likely nature of legal challenges to such analysis by federal agencies.

Burnett and Hahn raised no questions about EPA's finding of a $200 million cost to the arsenic rule. Instead, they made several key adjustments to the EPA's calculation of benefits. The first set of adjustments involved the actual number of cancer cases to be prevented. The second set involved the translation of that figure into a dollar amount.

To calculate cancer cases, Burnett and Hahn made two changes. First, they attempted to quantify the "nonquantifiable benefits" by multiplying EPA's estimate of twenty-eight lives saved by two, for a total of fifty-six. "Our reasoning is that including 'nonquantifiable risks' would increase the lives-saved estimate by some factor between one and four." This number came in turn from the report of the National Research Council, which suggests that the risk of death from all kinds of cancer might be eight times the risk of bladder cancers. Recognizing that EPA's quantified figure represents both bladder and lung cancers, Burnett and Hahn took a multiple of four as producing a "reasonable upper bound" of 112; but fifty-six seemed more reasonable.

Second, Burnett and Hahn divided their chosen number of fifty-six by five, to reflect their judgment that the risk of arsenic is not linearly related to arsenic concentrations. "This assumption is not realistic because the human body can metabolize arsenic at low levels, rendering it nontoxic." (Note that the EPA concluded that recent research has drawn into doubt the claim that the metabolized forms of arsenic are any less toxic.) For Burnett and Hahn, the upshot is that the new regulation would save about eleven lives annually.

To translate this amount into dollar terms, Burnett and Hahn adjusted the $6.1 million figure downward. They emphasized that cancer follows exposure to arsenic not immediately but only after a latency period, ranging from between ten and forty years. Burnett and Hahn use a 7 percent discount rate, on the theory that "future benefits should be discounted just as future costs are."[37] As a result of the adjustment, the value of a statistical life fell to $1.1 million. Sharply disagreeing with the National Research Council and the EPA, with their projected risk of 1 in 100, Burnett and Hahn added that "the risk reduction is about one in 1 million, which is so small as not to be worth

[37] Id. at 8.

Table 7.4 AEI–Brookings Joint Center estimates of costs and benefits of arsenic regulation

	Lives Saved	Benefits ($ million)	Costs ($ million)	Net Costs ($ million)
EPA's Model Without Accounting for Latency	28	170	210	40
EPA's Model Accounting for Latency	28	50	210	160
Our High Estimate	110	200	210	10
Our Best Estimate	11	23	210	190
Our Low Estimate	5.5	10	210	200

addressing, given the uncertainties in the data and the EPA's limited resources to develop regulations." In fact, Burnett and Hahn concluded that no plausible version of the arsenic proposal, going beyond the existing 50-micrograms-per-liter standard, could be justified on cost–benefit grounds. Table 7.4 presents their overview.

Burnett and Hahn go further still. They urge that the arsenic regulation would be likely to produce a net loss in life, rather than a gain. The reason, explored in Chapter 6, is that expensive regulations have been found to have mortality effects, in part because they make less money available for health-care expenditures. According to a plausible estimate, a statistical life is lost for every $15 million expenditure, so that a regulation that costs $15 million per life saved results in no net mortality reduction.[38] If this is correct, a regulation that costs $190 million on net is likely to result in a loss of over ten lives, on balance, every year. This, in fact, is the Burnett–Hahn conclusion.

QUESTIONS AND DOUBTS

Many questions should be raised about the analysis by both EPA and Burnett and Hahn. The first set of questions involves the judgment about the likely benefits in terms of mortality and morbidity. The second set involves the translation of those benefits into dollar equivalents.

My goal here is not to take sides on the disagreement between EPA and Burnett and Hahn. It is to suggest instead that the state of scientific knowledge

---

[38] See Randall Lutter et al., supra note 9 in chapter 6.

is such as to justify only benefit ranges, not specific benefit numbers. This point might easily be taken as a challenge to CBA in general, and it is properly so taken if CBA is justified as a way of giving specific bottom lines to resolve hard cases. But if CBA is justified more modestly, as a way of getting a sense of the potential consequences of various courses of action, nothing I say here should be seen as a challenge to the basic method. Indeed, a virtue of CBA is that it helps to explain why the arsenic question is hard, not easy, and why competing judgments of value could lead in competing reasonable directions. I will say more about all this later.

LIFE AND HEALTH AGAIN

The Dose–Response Curve, in General and in Particular

In calculating health effects, EPA assumed a linear dose–response curve for arsenic. In so doing, it followed its usual practice, which is to assume a linear, nonthreshold model for Class A carcinogens in drinking water. In the EPA's words, this is a "conservative mathematical model for cancer risk assessment.... It is consistent with a no-threshold model of carcinogenesis, i.e., exposure to even a very small amount of a substance is assumed to produce a finite increased risk of cancer."[39] Note in this regard that the EPA's Science Advisory Board, which consisted of prominent scientists who issued a report advising the agency, also recommended linear extrapolation based upon the Taiwan data.

But Burnett and Hahn are correct to urge that this was not an inevitable decision. It is quite possible that, at low levels, the effects of arsenic dwindle. There are many complexities here, for dose–response curves come in many shapes and sizes. "It has long been recognized that a number of different mathematical models can fit a given set of dose–response data reasonably well, but produce vastly different predictions of risk when extrapolated to doses below the data range. Thus, extrapolated doses corresponding to 'de minimis' risk levels can differ by several orders of magnitude, depending on the shape of the dose–response curve at low doses."[40]

Often there is no evidence about the relationship between adverse effects and low doses, and hence a great deal of guesswork is involved. An overview suggests;

[39] 40 CFR Pt. 132, App. C (West 2001).
[40] Ralph L. Kodell, U-Shaped Dose–Response Relationships for Mutation and Cancer, Human and Ecological Risk Assessment (forthcoming).

that a number of models have been proposed, and there is active debate on which of these is most appropriate. One that is widely used by regulatory agencies because it is "conservative" is a linear no-threshold extrapolation. As noted, proof has not been provided for any carcinogen that no threshold exists, and in fact, thresholds have been observed in many studies, particularly with weak carcinogens. The assumption of linearity at low doses is also not well founded. Indeed, even for the less complicated process of chemical mutagenesis *in vivo*, a drop below linearity at low doses has been demonstrated. Therefore, a "hockey stick"-shaped curve would appear to best fit current data and concepts on carcinogenic mechanisms at low levels of exposure."[41]

Here are the basic possibilities (see Appendix C for details).

I. Supralinearity. For some forms of radiation, the curve is actually "supralinear," in the sense that with lower doses, deaths fall at relatively lower rates than a linear curve would predict.[42] If a dose–response curve is supralinear, of course, the death rate will be higher than if it is linear. Agencies do not assume supralinearity, apparently because it is an unusual pattern. No one has urged supralinearity in the context of arsenic.

2. Linearity. It has long been assumed that linear curves are appropriate for "genotoxic" carcinogens, that is, carcinogens that work directly on DNA to produce mutations that give rise to tumors.[43] For a long time, arsenic has been assumed not to be genotoxic, a point that draws the EPA's assumption of linearity into some doubt; sublinearity is the ordinary assumption for nongenotoxic carcinogens. But a recent paper suggests that arsenic might be genotoxic after all.[44]

---

[41] Casarett and Doull's Toxicology: The Basic Science of Poisons, 4th ed., 154, Mary O. Amdur, John Doull, & Curtis D. Klaassen, eds. (New York: Pergamon 1991). See also D. G. Hoel et al., The Impact of Toxicity on Carcinogenicity Studies: Implications for Risk Assessment, 9 Carcinogenesis 2045 (1988); E. M. Laska & M. J. Meisner, Statistical Methods and the Application of Bioassay, 27 Annu. Rev. Pharmacol. Toxicol. 385 (1988); D. B. Farrar & K. S. Crump, Exact Statistical Tests for Any Carcinogenic Effect in Animal Bioassays, 15 Fund. Appl. Toxicol. 710 (1990).

[42] John W. Gofman, Radiation-Induced Cancer from Low-Dose Exposure: An Independent Analysis (1990).

[43] See Kodel, supra note 40 in chapter 7.

[44] M. A. Mass et al., Trivalent Methylated Arsenic Species Are Genotoxic, 14 Chemical Research in Toxicology 355 (2001).

3. Sublinearity. According to a standard text, the typical dose–response curve is "sigmoidal" in shape and thus sublinear at low doses.[45] Though there is some dispute about the issue, evidence suggests that this is the shape of the dose–response curve for benzene.[46] As noted, scientists generally assume sublinearity for substances that are nongeotoxic, that is, that do not work directly on DNA.[47]

4. Thresholds. Sometimes there is a threshold below which exposure produces no adverse effects, as is apparently the case for basal cell carcinoma and exposure to the sun.[48] This is the extreme case of sublinearity. It is generally agreed that thresholds exist "for all toxicities other than cancer.... Conceptually, a threshold makes sense for most toxic effects."[49] But government agencies tend to treat carcinogens as lacking safe thresholds. Taken purely as a scientific judgment, this is disputed: "It is a fact that most of the identified human carcinogens induce cancer only after exposure to high doses."[50]

5. U-Shapes. Some dose–response curves (such as those for flouride) actually show desirable effects at low levels so that what is harmful to health at high doses turns out to produce beneficial effects at low doses.[51] There appears to be increasing reason to believe that U-shapes are common. "In recent years, the concept of hormesis, the phenomenon whereby a toxic substance elicits a beneficial effect at doses below its observed range of toxicity, has been gaining popularity among scientists engaged in toxicology and risk assessment."[52]

---

[45] Encyclopedia of Toxicology 509, Philip Wexler, ed. (New York: Academic Press, 1998).

[46] See O. Wong & G.K. Raabe, Cell-Type-Specific Leukemia Analyses in a Combined Cohort of More than 208,000 Petroleum Workers, 21 Regul. Toxicol. Pharmacol. 380 (1995).

[47] I. Purchase and T. Auton, Thresholds in chemical carcinogenesis, 22 Regul. Toxicol. Pharmacol. 199–205 (1995).

[48] See Anne Kricker et al., A Dose Response Curve for Sun Exposure and Basal Cell Carcinoma, 60 Internat. J. Cancer 482 (1995).

[49] Williams et al., supra note 3 in Chapter 7.

[50] Toxicology, supra note 2 in chapter 7, at 176.

[51] Ralph Kodell & Qi Zheng, U-Shaped Dose–Response Curves for Carcinogenesis, unpublished manuscript (1999).

[52] See id. The author's conclusion is worth quoting: "For carcinogens that may exhibit U-shaped dose-response curves, traditional linear, low-dose extrapolation truly is conservative in the sense of public-health protection. However, this 'default' procedure cannot be justified simply on the basis of either presumed genotoxicity or additivity to background. If definitive data on low-dose behavior of specific carcinogens should indicate U-shaped behavior, then relaxing the default procedure to accommodate substantially lower-than-linear estimates of risk seems justified, without fear of seriously underestimating risk.... However, it will require strong data, of a nature and quality not customarily available, to warrant a regulatory agency's

The possibility of varying shapes suggests many possible projections of the health consequences of exposure to low doses of arsenic. Without having any direct evidence for arsenic in particular, the National Research Council suggested, "Of the several modes of action that are considered most plausible, a sub-linear dose response curve in the low-dose range is predicted, though linearity cannot be ruled out."[53]

This statement should be taken as exceptionally speculative. It ought not to be read to suggest a reliable scientific judgment about the true dose–response curve. In fact the NRC offered no evidence that would justify its "prediction" for arsenic. It appears to have been generalizing from the more typical patterns. If a specific judgment is required, this approach is as sensible as any other; but it is not much more than a hunch. Nonetheless, we can reach some more definite conclusions. First, when agencies generally assume linearity, it is not because anything in the science solidly justifies this assumption, but because they take a "conservative" approach to uncertain data.[54] This is a policy choice, not a technical one – a point with implications for judicial review, as we shall see. Second: Rather than setting forth a specific number, it seems best to acknowledge the uncertainty about the dose–response curve and, hence, to identify a range of benefits, capturing a low end and a high end.

What is the upshot? For arsenic in particular, the high end emerges from a linear curve and would therefore be 28. The low end is 6, which is what emerges from dividing 28 by 5. That division is essentially arbitrary, so we should not credit the Burnett–Hahn suggestion that it is likely to be accurate.

NONQUANTIFIED BENEFITS

What about the nonquantified benefits? Here it is certainly responsible to say, with the EPA, that the data do not allow numerical judgments of any kind. But it would also be responsible to attempt to specify an upper and lower bound. Burnett and Hahn estimate the "nonquantified" benefits by multiplying EPA's expected lives saved by 2. But this seems arbitrary. As they note, the National Research Council estimated the risk of all types of cancer as *eight* times greater

---

acceptance of a dose–response relationship that predicts less-than-background risk at low doses. The modeling exercise presented here provides additional support and encouragement for investigators to pursue the gathering of biologically definitive data other than typical tumor incidence data when hormesis is strongly suggested or conjectured."

[53] National Research Council, supra note 4 in this Chapter at p. 153.

[54] But see Adam M. Finkel, A Second Opinion on an Environmental Misdiagnosis, 3 N. Y. U. Env. L. J. 295, 341–5 (1995), for some evidence that linearity is a scientifically plausible assumption.

than the risk from bladder cancer alone. Because EPA's figure of 28 came from both bladder and lung cancer, it would have been sensible to posit a range, with an upper bound of 112 (multiplying 28 times 4). If the lower bound (from the analysis of possible sublinearity) is 6, the upper bound, from that assumption, would be 24.

PROBLEMS IN TAIWAN

I have suggested that there are many reasons to question the Taiwan data, which involved a poorer population, with a worse diet, and at risk of arsenic from multiple sources other than drinking water. Another criticism of the Taiwan data is that it measures arsenic exposure by overall exposure to village wells and not individual exposure. There is an additional problem. Wells within each village had varying arsenic levels (so that people using certain wells had much higher exposures than others in the same village), but not all village wells were measured, and villagers were assigned a single median concentration (the data also did not account for villagers who moved, since it assumed a lifetime exposure to the levels of a subject's present village). Thus the principal data on which the EPA relied was "noisy," and unavoidably so.

On the basis of EPA's data, the best conclusion is that with reasonable assumptions, the number of lives saved by the regulation would range between 6 and 112. To say the least, that is an exceedingly wide range. If the regulation were expected to cost $6 million, it would seem reasonable to proceed; almost no one denies that a cost per life saved of $1 million is worthwhile. If the regulation were expected to cost $10 billion, it would seem reasonable not to proceed. But what if the cost fell between $6 million and $10 billion? What if the cost were $200 million (as the EPA estimated)? To make progress on that question, it is necessary to discuss the question of monetization.

MONETIZING

With respect to money, the principal disagreement between EPA and Burnett–Hahn involves the appropriate discount rate. I will return to that issue shortly; for the moment let us put it to one side. As the EPA acknowledges in its "sensitivity analysis," there are good reasons, in fact, to adjust EPA's monetized estimate upward rather than downward.

1. Arsenic versus the Workplace. As I have noted, the EPA's $6.1 million comes from workplace risks, not involving cancer, but generally involving dangers to which workers expose themselves voluntarily, in the sense that they receive compensation in return. In fact, many questions might be raised about the

Table 7.5 Values of-life studies

Study	Method	Value of Statistical Life ($ million)
Kneisner and Leith (1991)	Labor market	0.7
Smith and Gilbert (1984)	Labor market	0.8
Dillingham (1985)	Labor market	1.1
Marin and Psacharopoulos (1982)	Labor market	3.4
V.K. Smith (1976)	Labor market	5.7
Viscusi (1981)	Labor market	7.9
Leigh and Folsom (1984)	Labor market	11.7
Leigh (1987)	Labor market	12.6
Garen (1988)	Labor market	16.3

workplace risk studies. One problem is the sheer variety of the numbers in those studies, ranging from $0.7 million, in 1997 dollars, to $16.3 million. Consider Table 7.5.[55]

The wide range of the outcomes raises questions about the reliability of the $6.1 million figure. EPA updated the relevant numbers for inflation, but it did not otherwise make adjustments. On reasonable assumptions, the EPA appears to have produced a significant undervaluation of the monetary value of the lives at stake.

2. Income Growth. The EPA acknowledged that the $6.1 million figure reflects no adjustment to account for changes in national real income growth. In principle, the failure to undertake an adjustment seems to be a serious mistake. Of course people with more money would be willing to pay more, other things being equal, to reduce statistical risks. As the EPA also noted in its sensitivity analysis, the appropriate adjustment would increase a value of statistical life (VSL) from $6.1 million to $6.7 million.

3. Distinctive Risks. The risk of cancer from drinking water is qualitatively different from the workplace risks that EPA used to generate its VSL. The risks from drinking water seem peculiarly involuntary and uncontrollable, and a great deal of literature suggests that involuntary and uncontrollable risks produce an unusually high willingness to pay. Now it is important not to think that there is a rigid dichotomy between the involuntary/uncontrollable and the voluntary/controllable. This is a continuum, without sharp divisions

---

[55] See EPA, Guidelines for Preparing Economic Analyses 89 (Washington, D.C.: GPO, 2000).

among various points. As we saw in Chapter 3, the underlying issues seem to be whether those exposed to the risk are exposed knowingly and whether it is costly or otherwise difficult for people to avoid the risk. But as compared to workplace risks, the risk of arsenic from drinking water might seem worse along the relevant dimensions. For this reason, it makes sense to ask whether people would be willing to pay a premium to avoid the risks associated with arsenic.

There are some related points. People seem to have a special fear of cancer, and they seem to be willing to pay more to prevent a cancer death than a sudden unanticipated death or a death from heart disease. The "cancer premium" might be produced by the "dread" nature of cancer; it seems well-established that some risks are particularly dreaded, and that dreaded risks produce special social concern, holding the statistical risk constant. There is a continuing dispute about whether the evidence is sufficient to justify a change in the willingness to pay figure. But some studies suggest that people are willing to pay twice as much to prevent a cancer death as an instantaneous death (see Chapter 3).

The EPA was alert to these points. Hence its own sensitivity analysis suggests the need for an upwards revision of 7 percent, because of the involuntariness and uncontrollability of the risk. With this revision, along with the revision for income growth, the value of a statistical life would rise to about $7.2 million. In fact, there are reasons to suggest that this might be too low. One study suggests that "the value of avoiding a death from an involuntary, carcinogenic risk should be estimated as four times as large as the value of avoiding an instantaneous workplace fatality."[56] If we take this approach, the value jumps from $6.7 million to $26.8 million, at least as an upper bound.

4. One More Wealth Effect. There is a final point. The studies that produced the $6.1 million figure involved the workplace, and the people involved were poorer than most workers. Because the median salary of all wage earners is 23 percent higher than the median salary of most workers involved in the willingness-to-pay studies, a further adjustment seems appropriate, producing a VSL of $33 million.

Now it would be foolish to claim that this figure has a unique claim to accuracy. But with different assumptions, none of them entirely implausible, the value of a statistical life can range from $1.1 million to $33 million – and the number of lives saved from 6 to 112. That produces a lower bound, in terms of dollars, of $6.6 million and an upper bound, in terms of dollars, of $3.15 billion!

---

[56] See Richard Revesz, Environmental Regulation, Cost–Benefit Analysis, and the Discounting of Human Lives, 99 Col. L. Rev 941, 982 (1999).

5. Life-Years As Opposed To Lives. Would the arsenic rule protect young people or old people? The question seems to matter, for in principle, it is better for the government to devote resources toward saving many years rather than simply a few. If the government can prevent a death at 75 that would otherwise occur at 80, surely it should attempt to do so; but if resources are limited, it would do better to prevent a death at 20 that would otherwise occur at 80. In part because of the long latency period involved, the average age of the victims of arsenic-induced cancer would be relatively high, probably above retirement age. Nonetheless, the EPA treated each life involved as worth $6.1 million. This number might well be inflated.

6. Nonfatal Cancers. As we have seen, the EPA valued a nonfatal cancer at $607,000, based on shopping mall studies involving answers to hypothetical questions with respect to chronic bronchitis. There are obviously many problems with this approach; chronic bronchitis simply is not nonfatal cancer. In fact another study, also with serious methodological problems, produced a $3.6 million figure for nonfatal cancers.[57] This amount seems quite odd, because it suggests that preventing a nonfatal cancer is valued at well over 50 percent of the value of preventing a fatal cancer ($6.1 million). But suppose that this number is taken to be accurate or a reasonable upper bound. If so, the monetized value of reductions in nonfatal cancers, from the 10 ppb standard, rises in value to about $92 million – a sizeable jump over the $15 million produced by the $607,000 figure.

7. Discounting. It does seem sensible to say that a discount rate should be applied to latent harms. A cancer thirty years from now is not as bad as a cancer tomorrow. It is less bad partly because it allows a number of years of cancer-free life, and partly because people usually prefer current health to future health. Now this point does not take a stand on the controversial question whether harms to future generations should be discounted.[58] The only suggestion is that reasonable people today would be willing to pay less to prevent a cancer in decades than a cancer in weeks. To be sure, it would be possible to respond that arsenic regulation is designed to prevent risks of harm, not actual harms, and that the risks, unlike the harms, will occur immediately. The suggestion is correct, but not responsive. People would pay more to prevent a risk-of-a-harm in a month than a risk-of-a-harm in two decades; and that claim is sufficient to justify discounting here.

But to make an assessment, it is not enough to decide to discount. We also have to decide on (a) the appropriate discount rate and (b) the latency period.

---

[57] See Arsenic Rule Benefits Analysis: An SAB Review 17 (Washington, D.C.: GPO, 2001).

[58] See (Revesz, n.56, this Chapter) for a helpful treatment, separating the two questions.

Table 7.6 Cost–benefit ranges for arsenic regulation

	Lives	Benefits	Costs	Net Benefits or Costs
EPA	28 (plus unquantified)	$170 million (plus unquantified)	$210 million	not specified
AEI–Brookings "Best Estimate"	11	$23 million	$210 million	−$190 million
(Very) High Estimate	112	$3.4 billion	$210 million	$3.25 billion
High Estimate	112	$650 million	$210 million	$430 million
My Best Estimate	None; too speculative	None; too speculative	$210 million	No estimate
Low Estimate (based on fundamental acceptance of EPA conclusions)	6	$13 million	210 million	−$197 million
(Very) Low Estimate (based on external criticisms of EPA conclusions)	0	0 million	$210 million	−$210 million

Hahn and Burnett choose a 7% figure, which comes from the discount rate for money. But there is no reason to think that the same discount rate is sensible for latent harms, and considerable reason to think the opposite. In fact some evidence supports a discount rate of 2%–3%, which would result, not in a figure of $1.1 million per life saved, but a figure closer to $4.5 million. (See chapter 8 for more details.) And if the latency period is chosen to be twenty years rather than thirty, the number increases still further, approaching $5 million. Table 7.6 is my own summary of possible cost–benefit assessments.

One final point about Table 7.6. It might be suggested that some effort should be made to identify a "best estimate," and that analysis would be greatly improved by trying to assign probabilities to the various outcomes, with the "best estimate" consisting of the most probable one. The goal of this suggestion is correct. When the underlying science and economies allow analysts to come up with a best estimate and to assign probabilities to the alternative outcomes, this indeed should be done. In terms of monetizing the relevant values, it seems correct to say that the cancer risk deserves a premium, as compared to workplace risks, but also to insist on discounting the monetary value of the risk to take account of the latency period and the fewer life-years saved. Hence rough estimates of $4.5 million per life saved, and $1.5 million per nonfatal cancer prevented, seem as reasonable as anything else, even if somewhat arbitrary. At the very least, the EPA's $6.1 million figure appears too high in light of the long latency period, and the AEI-Brookings $1.1 million figure appears too low in light of the high discount rate that it reflects and the various factors suggesting that the workplace studies understate the monetary value of the risk involved here.

But with respect to health benefits, science does not allow best estimates to be provided here. It would be reasonable to suggest that the high estimate of 112 is unrealistically high in light of the problems in the Taiwan data and the possibility that the dose-response curve is sublinear. The estimate of 0 lives saved is highly improbable. But it does seem to me sensible to move to concern with life-years saved, rather than lives saved, and because of the long latency period, the quantified benefits are most unlikely to be much higher than the $210 million price tag.[59] On the other hand, they might well be higher whether or not they are much higher, and for reasons to be elaborated shortly, the bottom-line numbers need not be dispositive.

LESSONS

Does all this suggest that CBA is, in cases of this sort, unhelpful? It would not be hard to imagine an affirmative answer to that question. A skeptic might conclude that because the range of uncertainty is so large, any number at all could be justified, and the ultimate decision is essentially "political" or based on "values." This view is not exactly wrong, but it should not be taken as a convincing challenge to CBA.

An analysis of benefits and costs cannot resolve the ultimate judgment, but it can certainly inform it. Once we understand the potential effects of different arsenic regulations, and see where the uncertainties come from, we are in a much better position to know what to do. Of course a decision on that count will be a product of "values"; how could it be otherwise? The point is that the values should be identified as such, so that when government acts, its reasons are transparent and explicable. If what I have said thus far is correct, the choice of a new arsenic rule is a genuinely hard question. It is a tribute to CBA that we know exactly why it is hard.

[59] This judgment is based on the information before the EPA when it initially decided to issue the new regulation. New data suggest that the monetized benefits may indeed be much higher than the monetized costs.

CBA IN COURT

We are now in a position to see the multiple possible challenges to any agency decision that involves cost–benefit balancing. Because such balancing has become a staple of regulatory practice, it is important for people to have some understanding of the underlying ideas and of how agencies might be said to have gone wrong. There are lessons for courts as well, mostly involving the need for deference to agencies.

HOW TO MAKE BENEFITS GO WAY UP OR WAY DOWN

With respect to the regulation of social risks, the legal culture is increasingly required to pay close attention to both science and economics, and here legal understanding remains in a primitive state. If we keep in mind the arithmetic of arsenic, we can see how creative citizens and lawyers, representing water systems or environmentalists, might be able to mount reasonable challenges to EPA's decisions, regardless (almost) of the content of those decisions. There are several points to keep in mind.

- A great deal depends on the dose–response curve, and at low levels, the scientific evidence will often be inconclusive. With the assumption of a linear curve, the benefits of regulation will seem far higher than they might otherwise be. But from the scientific point of view, that assumption might well be vulnerable. In the case of arsenic, the most striking point is that the independent entities on which EPA relies actually split on the issue, with the Scientific Advisory Board supporting linearity, and the National Research Council tentatively favoring sublinearity. Note too that there is mixed evidence on the crucial question whether metabolized arsenic is dangerous. A decision to assume linearity, in the face of scientific uncertainty, is best seen as a reasonable policy judgment. For a lawyer objecting to a regulation that seems too stringent, the best claim is that sublinearity is more likely, given the body's ability to metabolize at low levels. For a lawyer objecting to a regulation that seems inadequate, the best claim is that, in the absence of specific data, linearity is the standard default assumption on policy grounds.
- When regulating a pollutant, EPA will often have to rely on evidence from other times and areas, and it will not be difficult to suggest that there are relevant differences between the population at issue and the population from which the evidence derives. In the case of arsenic, the Taiwan data could certainly be challenged as inadequate, certainly in

light of the absence of data from the United States that confirms the basic results.

- For a lawyer on either side, it is not hard to argue that nonquantified benefits should be quantified, if this is at all possible. Without quantification, how can agency decisions be evaluated? Once a decision is made to quantify benefits that had formerly been unquantified, agency judgments are subject to challenge, because the judgment about how to quantify will be so speculative. If the agency has not specified a range, but has relied on a fairly specific projection, it will be extremely vulnerable.

- If cancer risks are involved, the agency's decision to use its ordinary VSL can be criticized on the ground that solid evidence shows a higher VSL for risks that are dreaded and uncontrollable (as cancer risks are likely to be). Lawyers objecting to insufficiently aggressive regulation should use this evidence to suggest that the numbers that come from workplace studies are simply too low. Lawyers objecting to overaggressive regulation should insist that the only reliable data come from the workplace studies, and that any effort to produce higher numbers are too speculative.

- Agencies frequently lack good data on morbidity risks and use crude substitutes. These are easily subject to challenge. An environmental lawyer could easily urge, in the arsenic case, that the chronic bronchitis numbers are too low because a cause of cancer is highly likely to produce higher willingness to pay (WTP) than a case of chronic bronchitis. For their part, industry lawyers could easily urge that chronic bronchitis is comparable or perhaps worse, simply because it is chronic. A case of cured cancer, even if it is entirely cured, is not much more serious than a case of any other curable disease. In either case, it would be easy to challenge the actual numbers used for chronic bronchitis as unreliable because they were generated through responses by shoppers, in North Carolina, to hypothetical questions. Even if well designed, that study is not likely to produce reliable numbers.

- If an agency uses lives rather than life-years, there may be a serious problem, at least if the regulation would protect a large number of children or elderly people. For protection of children, the $6.1 million figure is arguably far too low. For protection of elderly people, that same figure is arguably far too high.[60]

- The level of benefits will differ dramatically in accordance with the chosen discount rate. It would be easy to challenge any agency's decision

---

[60] It is not clear, however, how to think about willingness to pay in this context. Older people tend to be wealthier, and they might well be willing to pay large amounts to protect relatively few life years.

not to discount a risk that will come to fruition in the future. A monetary loss, or a loss to health, is worse today than years hence. And once the agency has chosen to discount, any particular discount rate might well be challenged. Economists disagree about the proper approach. If the agency chooses a discount rate for health in the vicinity of the discount rate for money (7 percent to 10 percent), its choice might well be challenged, on the ground that no good evidence supports the view that health problems averted should be discounted at the same rate as financial losses averted. But if the agency chooses a discount rate below 7 percent, it would not be hard to challenge that choice as essentially arbitrary and unsupported by evidence.

AGAINST SCIENCE COURTS

Notwithstanding the availability of countless legal challenges, the basic lesson for courts is simple: Hands off. This means that when courts are reviewing an agency's judgments about health benefits, and about how to monetize them, they should give agencies the benefit of every reasonable doubt.

The reasons are twofold. First, the issues are exceedingly complex, and judges are not specialists in the area at hand. Like everyone else, they are prone to error. There is no systematic reason to think that a firm judicial hand will make things better rather than worse. Second, any judicial judgment will perpetuate the status quo and make rulemaking more difficult. Because it is extremely time-consuming to make rules, and because a clever advocate, on one or another side, is highly likely to be able to produce a plausible challenge to whatever an agency does, an aggressive judicial posture will essentially freeze whatever rule is currently in place. In many domains, people have expressed concern with the "ossification" of rulemaking. When a statute calls for cost–benefit balancing, any nondeferential posture, from courts, will magnify the risk of ossification.

This does not mean that agencies should be permitted to do whatever they want. We can easily imagine genuinely arbitrary decisions. But so long as the agency has not done something outlandish, its efforts to quantify health benefits, and to monetize them, should be held acceptable.

POLICY ANALYSTS: WHAT SHOULD BE DONE?

No Obviously Best Choice

1. **Puzzles.** On the analysis thus far, it should be clear that, on the evidence before it at the time, there was no obviously best choice for EPA. Of the options

considered, the most dramatic would be the two poles: to retain the existing 50-micrograms-per-liter standard or to select the 3-micrograms-per-liter standard, which the EPA deemed feasible. Neither of these choices would be entirely ludicrous. Notwithstanding the NRC report, it would not be irrational to conclude that the existing data, most of it from Taiwan, simply does not justify further restrictions, especially in light of studies suggesting no adverse effects from low levels of arsenic in drinking water. And notwithstanding the AEI–Brookings study, it would not be impossible to produce numbers suggesting that the 3-micrograms-per-liter standard might well be justified, at least if the nonquantified benefits are taken into account, and pegged at the higher points in the range.

2. Tiebreakers. Might it be possible to resolve the controversy through some general background considerations? Where individuals and governments are not sure what to do, they often invoke "second-order" principles, designed to simplify inquire in the event of difficulty.[61] There are several possibilities here.

One solution would be to invoke the "precautionary principle," which says that reasonable doubts should be resolved in favor of protecting safety, health, and the environment.[62] But recall here the discussion in Chapter 5. If the precautionary principle is meant to suggest that significant investments are worthwhile to prevent speculative harms, it is certainly correct. But everything depends on the size of the investment and the speculativeness of the harm. Taken seriously, the precautionary principle would lead to huge expenditures, exhausting the relevant budget before the menu of options could be thoroughly consulted. Indeed, the precautionary principle would lead to paralysis because there are risks on all sides of the equation.

To see this point, recall that some households would be required to spend more than $300 per year for water. EPA Administrator Christine Whitman expressed a concern that the increased expenditure will lead many people to use small, local wells, which have heavily polluted water. In these circumstances, the precautionary principle suggests that new arsenic regulation is undesirable, because it might sacrifice lives. Recall too that expensive regulations can have adverse effects on life and health – and hence that the $200 million expenditure for arsenic regulation has, as a worst case scenario, significant adverse health effects, with perhaps as many as thirty to forty lives lost. If this is so, the precautionary principle seems to argue against new regulation. It seems clear

---

[61] See Cass R. Sunstein & Edna Ullmann-Margalit, Second-Order Decisions, in Behavioral Law and Economics, Cass R. Sunstein, ed. (New York: Cambridge Univ. Press, 2000).

[62] Carolyn Raffensberger & Joel Tickner, eds., Protecting Public Health & the Environment: Implementing the Precautionary Principle (Washington, D.C.: Island Press, 2001).

that precaution, by itself, can be taken as an argument for no regulation, much regulation, and every point in between. On reflection, the idea is insufficiently unhelpful.

Perhaps a more refined argument is better. For most of the country, the incremental cost of the arsenic regulation is low – less than $30 per year. If the vast majority of people would receive additional protection at a cost that is rather high in the aggregate ($210 million) but extremely low for each affected family, shouldn't government proceed, perhaps with exemptions or subsidies for those who would have to pay more? The argument is not implausible, but it proves too much. In many cases, it would be possible to do some good by asking everyone to pay, say, $2 per year. Should the EPA ask every American to pay, $2 year, so as to create a $500 million fund to be used to pay for additional reductions in sulfur dioxide emissions? Carbon monoxide emissions? Benzene emissions? Clean up of lead paint? Antitobacco advertising? Childhood immunizations? Relief of poverty? Because the list of possibilities is endless, it is unhelpful to treat small per-family costs as if they were zero or its moral equivalent; we do better to ensure that those funds are used for purposes that would do more good than harm, or for the most possible good. This does not mean that a regulation imposing small per-family costs (say, $30 per family, for 200 million people) should be treated as identical to a regulation imposing the same aggregate but higher per-family costs (say, $300 per family, for 20 million people). High per-family costs do raise particular concerns. But a regulation that badly fails cost–benefit balancing should not be accepted on the ground that each family or person will pay little. (Imagine a program that would require every American to pay $1 per year for little or no return.)

Yet another tiebreaker is possible. Perhaps the EPA should refrain from further regulation on the theory that government should not act unless there is a clear demonstration that regulation is desirable, all things considered. Perhaps we should adopt a presumption against regulatory controls unless the CBA shows that they are justified, or unless there are special reasons – perhaps distributional in character – that support them. Perhaps the government should not require costly expenditures here, in view of the fact that the same expenditures might be used for other goals, such as crime reduction and automobile safety, where they could do more good.

The problem is that the same kind of argument could have been used against a wide range of environmental regulations, even though those regulations have, on balance, been vindicated by history.[63] In the context of air quality regulation, a contemporaneous assessment of costs and benefits would, in many cases, have

---

[63] Paul Portnoy, supra note 19 in chapter I, at 77, 101–5.

given rise to the same kind of uncertainty found here. Note that, this is not to suggest that, in such cases, the costs would have been found to outweigh the benefits. The problem is instead that the most that could have been done was to identify a "benefits range" leaving a great deal of uncertainty about what to do. If the past is any guide, it suggests that inaction, in such circumstances, would be a foolish course.

3. Between the Poles. While no particular approach would be obviously best, or obviously unreasonable, the more reasonable approaches would be between the poles. On the existing numbers, the 3-micrograms-per-liter standard seems hard to justify. No data supports the view that there would be significant health gains from moving from a 10-micrograms-per-liter ceiling to one of 3 micrograms per liter. In view of the significant expense of the restriction, 10 micrograms per liter seems better. At the same time, the data do raise questions about the existence of significant risks at the 50-micrograms-per-liter level. A new regulation might be seen as a kind of insurance policy, one without an enormous price tag. A choice of a 10- or 20-micrograms-per-liter ceiling would seem to be best – especially if it would be possible to relieve the high burdens imposed on some households.

This last point raises a more general one, overlooked thus far: The EPA's menu of alternatives has been relatively narrow and has lacked much creativity. The EPA discussed four different permissible exposure levels, without thinking more imaginatively about how to minimize the costs of arsenic regulation. The blame for the narrow focus lies not with EPA but with Congress. I now discuss several other approaches, designed to show more flexibility toward those burdened by drinking water regulation.

ARSENIC TARGETING AND ARSENIC WAIVING

A possible approach would involve "targeting," that is, imposing regulation on water systems when the cost–benefit ratio is especially good. Recall that for much of the country, the cost of compliance with the 10-micrograms-per-liter standard is quite low. On plausible (which is not to say certainly correct) assumptions, the cost–benefit ratio for those systems is adequate to justify the regulation. These points suggest a simple alternative: Impose a targeted rule, with a sliding scale of regulations, ensuring that the cost–benefit ratio supports the outcome in each area. Where, for example, the annual cost of regulation is less than $50 per household, government might impose a 5-micrograms-per-liter standard; where the annual cost is less than $150, it might impose a 10-micrograms-per-liter standard; where it is less than $350, it might impose a 20-micrograms-per-liter standard.

An approach of this kind would undoubtedly be controversial. Critics would ask: Why should people in some parts of the country be subject to more arsenic in their drinking water than others? The question might seem especially difficult to answer if, as seems likely, many of those subject to the more lenient standard would be relatively poor. Why should poor people, and especially poor children, face levels of arsenic found unacceptably dangerous in other parts of the country? But these questions have more rhetorical force than they deserve. If acceptable levels of risk are a function of both cost and benefit, it makes perfect sense to say that such levels will vary depending on the costs and benefits of controls in different localities. In some areas of the country, it will be worthwhile to "purchase" an additional increment of safety; in other areas, it will not be. This point seems sufficient to suggest that EPA should have the authority to impose national standards that are not uniform. But the SOWA forbids any such nonuniform standards. In keeping with its cost–benefit focus, the statute should be amended so as to allow EPA greater flexibility.

If EPA cannot adopt a targeted regulation, might it allow waivers for areas in which the benefits do not justify the costs? Once the data are disaggregated, it seems reasonable to consider the following option: Adopt the 10-micrograms-per-liter regulation for most water systems, where the per-family cost of compliance is low, but offer a variance for water systems where the per-family cost is high. In fact, this approach would be quite close to one involving targeted regulation. The SDWA does allow waivers, but only for short periods of time, and hence waivers are a less satisfactory outcome than targeting.

Within the same domain of solutions, EPA might ask for "point-of-use" solutions, such as tap water filters.[64] According to some data, significant human exposure to arsenic comes from less than 15 percent of the water supplied by public water systems that would be subject to regulation. The remainder goes down the drain after cleaning, flushing, and the like or is delivered to commercial and industrial establishments for various uses. Perhaps some systems would find it cheaper to pay for point-of-use treatment than to treat the entire water supply. Here too, however, the law appears to stand in the way, denying the EPA the flexibility to permit solutions of this sort.

ARSENIC MARKETS

In all of contemporary environmental law, some of the most dramatic developments have involved the rise of market instruments for pollution control. These instruments take many forms, but among the most popular are "cap-and-trade" systems, in which the total level of emissions is capped at a certain level, and

---

[64] I am grateful to A. M. Freeman for this suggestion.

polluters are allowed to trade licenses, so long as the cap is respected. A chief advantage of cap-and-trade systems is that they ensure the lowest cost means of achieving regulatory goals. Those who can eliminate pollution cheaply will do exactly that. Those for whom reductions are expensive will purchase additional permits (for details, see Chapter 10).

Why not create a system of tradeable emissions rights, involving the right to subject people to arsenic? The idea might seem macabre, but if so, the reason is likely to be a belief that arsenic is a poison, seriously dangerous at any level. This is a form of intuitive toxicology. If we suppose that within the range under discussion (say, 3 to 20 micrograms per liter), dangerously high exposure levels will not occur, and the issue is one of appropriate degrees of safety, we could easily imagine a cap-and-trade system. Government could create an overall cap on arsenic and give licenses to subject people to, say, 15 micrograms per liter, but also allow trading, so that companies that can reduce at low cost will do so, whereas those that can do so at only high cost will stay at 15 micrograms per liter or perhaps buy licenses to subject people to higher levels. Because of the familiar "hot spots" problem, government would, under this regime, take steps to ensure that no one is subjected to unacceptably high levels – say, 25 or higher.

As compared with a system of national command and control, it is likely that a system of this kind would produce much lower costs. Indeed, a system of tradeable rights would likely spur considerable innovation in arsenic control technology. To evaluate it, we would want to know the aggregate cost of the system and also compare the likely benefits to those that would be enjoyed under the alternatives. It is not unimaginable that properly designed, a cap-and-trade system would produce both lower costs and higher benefits than the command-and-control alternative. Note in this regard that the Clinton Administration proposed a 10-micrograms-per-liter ceiling, to be applied nationally, but that a cap-and-trade system might ensure that in much of the country, people would have levels well below 10 micrograms per liter.

As compared with a system of arsenic targeting, the chief advantage of a cap-and-trade system is that it imposes less of an informational demand on the government – allowing the market, rather than EPA, to ascertain the costs of arsenic reduction. Under arsenic targeting, the EPA would have to decide, in every area of the country, the real costs of reduction to various points – a difficult determination for which error is inevitable. Under a cap-and-trade system, those with low costs will trade their licenses, whereas those with high costs will attempt to acquire more in the way of arsenic rights. Of course, the same objections that might be made to arsenic targeting might be made to a cap-and-trade system. Perhaps poor people will be subject to unusually high arsenic levels. But if these objections are not convincing there, they are also unconvincing in this context.

Under SDWA, however, the EPA lacks the authority to implement a trading system for arsenic. This is a serious gap. The statute should be amended to allow the EPA to permit trading if the evidence justifies that step. Of course trading should not be allowed to create what are, under existing science, unacceptable "hot spots."

ARSENIC SUBSIDIES

It might be suggested that the EPA should impose a stringent regulation of arsenic, but that the federal government should subsidize communities for which the annual cost is high. Of course, the EPA cannot offer subsidies on its own. But perhaps Congress should do so. In fact, Congress has made federal financial assistance available for water systems, and while the relevant programs contain a degree of discretion, it is certainly possible for financially strapped water systems to receive a degree of federal help. Recall that the total cost of the 10-micrograms-per-liter regulation would be about $210 million each year. To say the least, this would not be a large sum in the federal budget. If the federal government restricted itself to paying the cost of compliance in areas in which the annual per-household cost exceeds $100, its total taxpayer bill would be about $10 million – hardly a large sum to pay. In short, the EPA might impose aggressive regulation but provide relief to those communities that would bear a high financial burden.

Clearly this would not be a foolish approach to the arsenic problem. The difficulty is that we do not know, from the numbers, whether this is the best way, or even a good way, to spend limited taxpayer dollars. Suppose that the health risks that the regulation is reducing are quite small, so that the regulation will save somewhere between 0 and 0.5 lives. Is it really worthwhile to spend $10 million to save between 0 and 0.5 lives? Many government programs are designed to decrease risks to life and health; some of those programs attempt to reduce violent crime. Perhaps the $10 million would be better spent on those programs. Now it would be possible to respond that, as a practical matter, any $10 million subsidy is more likely to come from some other, less valuable use, and that by using it to protect people against the health hazards of arsenic, we would not really be diverting resources from a more valuable use. Among the universe of imaginable government expenditures, a $10 million subsidy to reduce arsenic levels is hardly the worst. But in light of existing data, we cannot be sure that it is the best. The same considerations that justify cost–benefit balancing in the first place suggest that the hard issues cannot be avoided by arguing for an across-the-board 10-micrograms-per-liter standard, accompanied by a federal subsidy for those who face a difficult financial burden.

Arsenic Disclosure

An alternative possibility would be to rely less on regulation and more on information. In many domains of regulatory policy, government has moved to replace command and control with efforts to require companies to disclose their activities, and relevant risks, to the public (see Chapter 10). In the context at hand, the suggestion would be simple: Require companies to meet some statutory requirement so that people are not exposed to clear harm (30 ppb?) but, beyond that point, require companies to disclose the level of arsenic in their drinking water, perhaps with information that would put the numbers into some context. Perhaps the disclosure requirement would not apply if companies reached some low level (10 ppb?). We could thus imagine a kind of three-tiered rule, with a minimal mandate that all communities must meet (30 ppb, for example), a disclosure requirement for arsenic levels within a certain range, and a "floor" (10 ppb, for example) below which companies would have no disclosure duties.

For arsenic, this strategy would have both advantages and disadvantages. One advantage is that it could spur companies to reduce arsenic levels on their own, without facing the most draconian governmental requirements.[65] For companies chosing that route, it is likely that the reductions would not be terribly expensive. Public pressure might produce low-cost reductions in some areas, while also allowing companies to maintain certain levels of arsenic if the public, in those areas, was not so concerned in light of the mix of health benefits and water costs. In this way, disclosure might even produce a kind of "drinking water federalism." Another advantage of disclosure is that it might perform an important educative role – ensuring that people will learn that some carcinogenic substances are not especially dangerous and also alerting people to the need for tradeoffs (in the form of a higher water bill).

But there are pitfalls as well. We have seen that the very idea of arsenic in drinking water seems to cause serious public alarm, in part because of the operation of intuitive toxicology. For a certain percentage of the population, mandatory disclosure of arsenic levels could itself signal that there is good reason for public concern. Perhaps mandatory disclosure could produce excessive fear, even panic. Many people might ask why, exactly, companies are disclosing this fact, and whether disclosure means that they are, in some sense, being poisoned. The point suggests that sometimes disclosure will not really inform people, because their background beliefs will lead them to read the information badly. The question remains whether it is possible to give some contextual information,

---

[65] See Bradley Karkkainen, Information As Environmental Regulation, 89 Georgetown L. J. 257 (2001).

so that people have an accurate sense of what the disclosure actually means. In this context, we should probably be skeptical of the likelihood that the contextual information would really help.

As a legal matter, the issue is simple, for EPA has no authority to use information disclosure as a substitute for regulation. In the particular context of the SOWA, Congress's choice for regulatory mandates may even make sense. But in the future, it would be useful to allow agencies to experiment in this vein, to see if disclosure will, in some cases, do more good than alternative approaches.

A MISSING QUESTION: DISTRIBUTIONAL ISSUES

There is one significant gap in the discussion thus far: a full account of the distributional effects of different arsenic regulations. To have an adequate sense of whether and how to proceed, it would be most valuable to have an account of the income and wealth of those who will be subject to the relevant costs. If, for example, those who would bear $300 or more in increased annual costs are disproportionately poor, government should hesitate before imposing the regulation. It is easy to imagine a situation in which water quality regulation is "regressive," in the sense that its costs come down especially hard on poor people. Now that is not a decisive objection to the regulation. But it is certainly an important point to consider.

Of course, it would be easy to imagine the following sort of rejoinder: Shouldn't poor people have water that is as safe as that of rich people? Why should poor people, including poor children, have water quality inferior to that enjoyed by rich people? The simplest answer is that safety is a matter of degree, and if safer water quality is very expensive, then poor people are better off without it than with it. Cars should certainly be safe, but rich people are more likely than poor people to buy Volvos. It would not be sensible for government to force poor people to buy Volvos, and the reason is that if you are poor, you might reasonably use what money you have on something other than adding an additional bit of safety to your car. Perhaps you will use that money on food or medical care or shelter. The same is true for water quality. If the consequence of decreasing (small) risks significantly decreases family income for poor people, then it is perfectly legitimate for the government to refuse to act. Of course, it is possible that the benefits of environmental regulation will be enjoyed disproportionately by poor people, and that they will bear disproportionately few of the costs.

The more general suggestion is that whenever an agency is producing a regulatory impact analysis, it should attempt a distributional analysis as well. It is important to know who will bear both the benefits and the burdens of regulation. One study shows, for example, that the benefits of pollution control in California have gone, disproportionately, to poor people and minority group members.[66] It would be extremely desirable to assemble similar information for drinking water regulation.

LESSONS

It would be possible to take this chapter as an attack on CBA, on the ground that a specification of benefits and costs tells us little that we did not know before. And if CBA is justified as a way of actually producing decisions in hard cases, CBA has indeed been criticized by the analysis here. But this would be the wrong lesson. As a substitute for intuitive toxicology, an effort to trace both costs and benefits can inform inquiry, making decisions less of a stab in the dark. This is a substantial gain. Once the range is specified, a judgment of value, and not of fact, will be involved in the ultimate decision whether or not to proceed. But the judgment of value will be easier to identify once we know what we know and what we do not know. A real virtue of CBA is that it helps to explain exactly why the choice of regulation, in the case of arsenic, is genuinely difficult. In this way, CBA is a large improvement over "intuitive toxicology."

I have also discussed the underlying policy issues. EPA could make many reasonable decisions here, though its best choice would probably be as it was: level 10 micrograms per liter. But my principal claims have involved broadening the agencies' viewscreen. First, agencies should have the flexibility to produce variable standards, targeting regulation to areas where it would survive cost–benefit balancing and also adopting economic incentives to ensure low-cost solutions. Second, agencies should be required to identify the winners and losers produced by regulation – to show where poor people, or rich people, are disproportionate losers or gainers. A distributional analysis should not be taken as conclusive, but it will help to inform analysis. An effort to increase agency flexibility, and also to identify both winners and losers, would be natural steps, not toward placing regulatory judgments in an arithmetic straightjacket, but toward ensuring that when government acts, it does so in a way that is informed by a full account of the consequences.

[66] See Matthew E. Kahn, The Beneficiaries of Clean Air Act Regulation, 24 Regulation 34 (2001).

8

Of Courts and Law:
Cost–Benefit Default Principles

Consider the following cases:

1. The Clean Air Act requires the Environmental Protection Agency to issue standards controlling any substance that "contributes significantly" to pollution problems in certain areas. The EPA issues regulations governing relevant pollutants, but without considering the cost of compliance. Industries challenge the regulations on the ground that cost is a statutorily relevant factor.

2. The National Highway Traffic Safety Administration is asked to promote fuel economy in automobiles "to the extent feasible." The NHTSA issues fuel economy standards that are admittedly feasible, in the sense that no one doubts that they are technologically and economically possible. But the Coalition for Automobile Safety, a public interest organization, contends that the effect of the standards will be to lead manufacturers to produce smaller and more dangerous cars. The coalition contends that NHTSA acted unlawfully in failing to take this effect into account.

3. A federal statute requires the Occupational Safety and Health Administration to regulate toxic substances "to the extent feasible." OSHA interprets this language to require it to consider whether the regulation is technologically feasible and whether it is "practicable," economically speaking, for the industry to comply. OSHA imposes a regulation that is admittedly "feasible" under this test, but the regulation cannot pass a cost–benefit test because the benefits are low and the costs are high. Insisting that costs should be compared with benefits, industries subject to the regulation complain that it is unlawful.

In which of these cases has the agency acted unlawfully? The question is of immense importance, both for regulatory policy and for the relationship between courts and agencies. My main purpose in this chapter is to demonstrate that federal law has now built a novel set of rules for statutory construction: the *cost–benefit default principles*. In the face of statutory uncertainty, cases provide support for each of the following principles. For some of the principles, the law is more developed than for others, but each of the principles is an identifiable part of contemporary public law.

- Unless Congress has clearly said otherwise, agencies will be permitted to make de minimis exceptions to statutory requirements by exempting small risks from regulatory controls.
- Unless Congress has clearly said otherwise, agencies will be permitted to take costs into account in issuing regulations. In its current form, this principle means that where statutes are ambiguous, agencies will have the authority to consider costs as well as benefits.
- Unless Congress has clearly said otherwise, agencies will be permitted to balance the health risks created by regulation against the health benefits created by regulation.
- Unless Congress has clearly said otherwise, agencies will be permitted to decline to regulate past the point where regulation would be economically or technologically feasible.
- Unless Congress has clearly said otherwise, agencies will be expected to balance costs against benefits in issuing regulations.

It should be immediately apparent that these principles help counteract many of the difficulties faced by individuals and societies in thinking about risks. Suppose, for example, that the availability heuristic is making people fear a risk that is, in fact, trivial. If agencies are permitted to exempt insignificant risks, they will have the legal power to resist availability cascades. Or imagine that intense emotions are producing public concern about a risk that has a trivial probability of materializing. Here as well, the authority to exempt insignificant risks gives the agency a healthy degree of insulation. Or suppose that the public is neglecting tradeoffs, in the form of substitute risks or costs in general. If so, the agency is authorized to consider health–health tradeoffs in particular and indeed tradeoffs as a whole. We might even say that the cost–benefit default principles show an *implicit behavioral rationality*, in the sense that they are the kinds of principles that judges would have chosen if they were alert to the problems stressed here. I do not suggest that judges have self-consciously adopted the principles for these particular reasons. But I do urge that an understanding of human cognition helps to justify their existence.

Even when thus defended, however, the default principles raise many questions. For the most part, the cost–benefit default principles say what agencies are *permitted* to do. It is not clear whether the default principles also mean that where statutes are ambiguous, agencies will be *required* to do any of these things. Nor do the principles give much indication of how agencies permitting "acceptable" risks, or engaging in cost–benefit analysis, might be expected to proceed. What does it mean to say that agencies are permitted to "consider" costs? Would it be unlawful for an agency to say that even very high costs are worth incurring? In what way should the monetary valuation of human life be constrained? What counts as an acceptable or de minimis risk? How should agencies deal with the interests of future generations? Among my largest purposes here is to understand the nature of the cost–benefit default principles, their legitimacy, and their future content.

Let us begin by exploring the default principles.

DE MINIMIS EXCEPTIONS

THE BASIC IDEA

In a series of cases, the courts have developed a principle authorizing agencies to make de minimis exceptions to regulatory requirements. In other words, agencies are allowed not to regulate trivial risks. The initial case was *Monsanto Company v. Kennedy.*[1] There the agency banned acrylonitrile on the ground that it counts as a "food additive," migrating in small amounts from bottles into drinks within bottles. The FDA concluded that the ban was justified on safety grounds, a conclusion that the court found inadequately justified. But what is more important here is the general language with which the court remanded the case to the FDA. The court stressed that the agency had discretion to exclude a chemical from the statutory definition of food additives if "the level of migration into food . . . is so negligible as to present no public health or safety concerns."

A related case presented the question whether the EPA was permitted to make categorical exemptions under the Prevention of Significant Deterioration program of the Clean Air Act.[2] Here the court spoke in more ambitious terms, showing considerable enthusiasm for de minimis exemptions. It announced that "[c]ategorical exemptions may be permissible as an exercise of agency power, inherent in most statutory schemes, to overlook circumstances that in context may fairly be considered de minimis. It is commonplace, of course, that the law does not concern itself with trifling matters, and this principle has often found application in the administrative context. Courts should be reluctant to apply the literal terms of a statute to mandate pointless expenditures."[3] In fact,

---

[1]   613 F.2d 947 (DC Cir., 1979).

[2]   *Alabama Power Company v. Costle,* 636 F.2d 323 (DC Cir., 1979).

[3]   Id at 359.

the court expressly connected this principle with the idea that the court should "look beyond the words to the purpose of the act" to avoid "absurd or futile results." Thus the court concluded, in its broadest statement on the point, that "most regulatory statutes, including the Clean Air Act, permit" de minimis exemptions upon an adequate factual showing.

Here, then, is an explicit recognition of agency authority to exempt small or de minimis risks from regulatory controls. The authority operates as a clear statement principle, no less but also no more: Where Congress has unambiguously banned such exceptions, agencies are bound and may not create de minimis exemptions even in compelling circumstances.[4] There are many decisions in the same vein.[5]

The OSHA Variation: Requiring De Minimis Exceptions

A noteworthy variation on the basic idea of permitting de minimis exceptions can be found in the plurality opinion in *Industrial Union Department, AFL-CIO v. API*, known as the Benzene Case.[6] The central issue in the case was whether OSHA had to show a "significant risk" in order to regulate a toxic substance (benzene in the case itself). In arguing that it did not, the government pointed to the central provision, which said (and says) that in promulgating the relevant standards, the Secretary "shall set the standard which most adequately assures, to the extent feasible, on the basis of the best available evidence, that no employee will suffer material impairment of health or functional capacity, even if such employee has regular exposure to the hazard dealt with by such standard for the period of his working life."[7] The statute's general definition of occupational safety and health standards said (and says) that these are standards "reasonably necessary or appropriate to provide safe or healthful places of employment."[8]

A straightforward interpretation of the statutory terms, urged by four justices on the Supreme Court, would seem to suggest that no significant risk need be shown. The key statutory language is the "no employee will suffer" phrase,

---

[4] *Public Citizen v. Young*, 831 F.2d 1108 (DC Cir., 1987).

[5] See, for example, *Sierra Club v. EPA*, 992 F.2d 337, 343–5 (DC Cir., 1993); *EDF v. EPA*, 82 F.3d 451 (DC Cir., 1996); *Public Citizen v. FTC*, 869 F.2d 1541, 1556–7 (DC Cir., 1989); *Ohio v. EPA* 997 F.2d 1520, 1535 (DC Cir., 1993) (suggesting that "the literal meaning of a statute need not be followed where the precise terms lead to absurd or futile results, or where failure to allow a de minimis exemption is contrary to the primary legislative goal").

[6] 448 US 607 (1980).

[7] 29 USC 655(b)(5).

[8] 29 USC 652(8).

which indicates that even if a toxic substance places only one or a few workers in jeopardy, OSHA must act to provide protection. Whatever the meaning of the obscure general definitional clause ("reasonably necessary or appropriate"), the more specific provision, dealing with toxic substances, would appear to trump any contrary indications in the more general one. Nonetheless, a plurality of the Court rejected OSHA's argument to this effect and hence rejected OSHA's interpretation of the statute.

In holding that a "significant risk" must be shown, the plurality contended that a contrary interpretation would defy common sense: "In light of the fact that there are literally thousands of substances used in the workplace that have been identified as carcinogens or suspected carcinogens, the Government's theory would give OSHA power to impose enormous costs that might produce little, if any, discernible benefits."[9] Though the plurality left undecided the question whether the agency must also show a reasonable proportion between costs and benefits, it is clear, from the passage just quoted, that the "significant risk" requirement was motivated partly by the desire to ensure some kind of proportionality between benefits and costs, on the theory that the requirement serves to protect against the most egregious disproportions.[10]

A HAZARDOUS WASTE WRINKLE: NO BENEFITS, NO REGULATION

In an important case involving hazardous wastes, the court of appeals interpreted the Clean Air Act aggressively so as to prohibit EPA from imposing regulation without a showing that the regulation would actually clean the air. *Chemical Manufacturers Association v. EPA*[11] involved an unusual rule requiring hazardous waste combustors to comply with new emissions standards. The EPA established a bifurcated compliance schedule. Combustors would have three years to modify existing facilities and processes to come into compliance with the standards. But if combustors decided on "early cessation," and found that it was not cost-effective to make the required changes, they would be required to cease burning hazardous waste entirely within two years.

At first glance, the EPA's program seems to make a great deal of sense. Those attempting to make expensive changes should receive a longer period for compliance than those refusing to make such changes. But EPA itself acknowledged

---

[9] 448 US at 617.

[10] Id. In a later case, the Court held that OSHA was not required to engage in cost–benefit balancing because of what it saw as the clarity of the statutory text. See *American Textile Manufacturers Institute v. Donovan*, 452 US 490 (1981).

[11] 217 F.3d 861 (DC Cir., 2000).

that those who chose "early cessation" would actually redirect hazardous waste to other "facilities to be burned under essentially the same conditions."[12] Thus the early cessation rule would have no significant beneficial effects on hazardous waste or on hazardous waste pollution. "It will instead merely reallocate which combustion facilities process the same hazardous waste under the same conditions."[13] The court held that in these circumstances, the rule was unlawful because it would not promote the purpose of the act, which was to clean the air. In the court's view, it is simply unreasonable "to impose costly obligations on regulated entities" without showing that those obligations would help to promote the act's environmental goals. "Given the absence of environmental benefits – indeed, the possibility of environmental harm," the rule could not be valid.

Chemical Manufacturers Association v. EPA is a striking application of the principle that regulation should be expected to deliver significant benefits. The court seems to be urging that agencies will not be permitted to require expensive activity without a showing that the expense will produce nontrivial environmental benefits. An issue involving interest-group pressure seems to lurk in the background here: Commercial waste incinerators, intervenors in the case, stood to gain a great deal from the rule (because it would transfer business to them), and we may speculate that the court feared that the EPA was issuing a regulation, nominally based on environmental grounds, that would favor a well-organized private group with an economic stake in the outcome.

SUBSTITUTE RISKS

In Chapter 6, I discussed the problem of risk–risk or health–health tradeoffs, which arise when regulation of one health problem gives rise to another health problem. Recent cases suggest an emerging principle of interpretation, in the form of a strong presumption in favor of permitting (and even requiring) agencies to take account of substitute risks, and hence to undertake health–health tradeoffs. In *American Trucking Association v. EPA*, for example, it was argued that while ground-level ozone creates certain health risks, it also produces certain health benefits, above all because it provides protection against skin cancer and cataracts.[14] The EPA responded that it lacked authority to consider the risks created by regulation or (to put the point slightly differently) the health benefits of an air pollutant.

Taken on its own, the statutory text seemed to support the EPA's view, or at least to make that view a reasonable interpretation of ambiguous terms. The

---

[12] Id. at 864.

[13] Id.

[14] *American Trucking Association v. EPA*, 175 F.3d 1027, 1051 (DC Cir., 1999).

statute provides that ambient standards must be based on "criteria" documents, which are supposed to include "the latest scientific knowledge useful in indicating the kind and extent of all identifiable effects on public health or welfare which may be expected from the presence of such pollutant in the ambient air, in varying quantities."[15] EPA urged, plausibly, that the phrase "identifiable effects" of "such pollutant" was meant to refer to the adverse effects of the "pollutant," not to its beneficial effects. But the court concluded that the statute could not be interpreted in that way. In a passage that suggests a strong presumption in favor of health–health tradeoffs, the court said that the statute was unambiguous, and (more convincingly) that "EPA's interpretation fails even the reasonableness standard . . . ; it seems bizarre that a statute intended to improve human health would . . . lock the agency into looking at only one half of a substance's health effects in determining the maximum level for that substance."[16] What is most striking about this suggestion is that the court seems to have gone beyond the view that the agency is permitted to engage in health–health tradeoffs if it chooses and to require the EPA to do so even if it would chose otherwise.

Or return to *Competitive Enterprise Institute v. NHTSA*,[17] where the plaintiffs challenged fuel economy standards precisely on the ground that the agency had failed to take account of the adverse effects of such standards on automobile safety. In the face of an ambiguous statute, the court insisted that a full explanation was required for a decision that, in the abstract, would seem to create serious substitute risks. As a result of this decision, it is now the law that NHTSA must taken into account any evidence of adverse safety effects in the process of setting fuel economy standards. On remand, NHTSA confronted the evidence and concluded that the alleged effect could not be demonstrated – a conclusion that the court upheld on appeal.[18] What is important for present purposes is the clear holding that the agency is permitted and even obliged to consider health–health tradeoffs in setting fuel economy standards.

In some cases, judicial permission to consider substitute risks has done real violence to statutory language. Consider, for example, the EPA's approach to lead contamination in water. As we saw in Chapter 7, the Safe Drinking Water Act requires the EPA to produce maximum contaminant level goals for water contaminants. These goals are required to "be set at the level at which no known or anticipated adverse effects on the health of persons occur," with an adequate margin of safety. For lead, the EPA's MCLG was zero, because no safe threshold had been established. After an MCLG is established, EPA is required to set a

[15] 42 USC 7408(aq)(2).

[16] 175 F.3d at 1052.

[17] 956 F.2d 321 (DC Cir., 1992).

[18] 45 F.3d 481, 484–86 (DC Cir., 1995).

maximum contaminant level, to be set "as close to the maximum contaminant level goal as is feasible."[19] The EPA is also authorized not to set a maximum contaminant level, and to require "the use of a treatment technique in lieu of establishing" that level, if it finds "that it is not economically or technologically feasible to ascertain the level of the contaminant."[20]

The EPA is thus required to set a standard of performance, and not to require a "technique" for achieving the desired performance, unless it is not feasible to monitor water quality. For lead, then, we would expect EPA to set its MCL as close as "feasible" (economically and technologically) to the MCLG of zero, except if it was not "feasible," to ascertain the level of lead contamination. But this is not what EPA did because of some distinctive features of the lead problem. Source water is basically lead-free; the real problem comes from corrosion of service lines and plumbing materials. With this point in mind, EPA refused to set any MCL for lead, on the ground that an MCL would require public water systems to use extremely aggressive corrosion control techniques, which, while economically and technologically "feasible," would be counterproductive because they would increase the level of other contaminants in the water. What appeared to be the legally mandated solution would make the water less safe, not more so. The EPA therefore chose a more modest approach. Instead of issuing an MCL, it required all large water systems to institute certain corrosion control treatment and required smaller systems to do so if and only if representative sampling found significant lead contamination.

Did the EPA violate the Safe Water Drinking Act? At first glance, it seems clear that it did. The EPA did not contend that an MCL was not "feasible" to implement, nor did it argue that it was not "feasible," in the economic or technological sense, to monitor lead levels in water. Nonetheless, the court upheld the agency's decision.[21] The court accepted the EPA's suggestion that the word "feasible" could be construed to mean "capable of being accomplished in a manner consistent with the Act." The court said that "case law is replete with examples of statutes the ordinary meaning of which is not necessarily what the Congress intended," and it added that "where a literal meaning of a statutory term would lead to absurd results," that term "has no plain meaning."[22] Because an MCL would itself lead to more contamination, "it could lead to a result squarely at odds with the purpose of the Safe Drinking Water Act." The court therefore accepted EPA's view "that requiring public water systems to design and implement custom corrosion control plans for lead will result in optimal

---

[19] 42 USC 300g-1(b)(4)(2).
[20] 42 USC 300g-1(b)(6)(D).
[21] *American Water Works v. EPA*, 40 F.3d 1266, 1271 (DC Cir., 1994).
[22] Id.

treatment of drinking water overall, i.e. treatment that deals adequately with lead without causing public water systems to violate drinking water regulations for other contaminants."

It should be plain that the court permitted a quite surprising interpretation of the act. The statutory terms seem to make no room for the EPA's refusal to issue an MCL. Nonetheless, the EPA's refusal made good pragmatic sense in light of the risks that would be introduced by any such regulation. The court's decision is probably the clearest example to date of an aggressive default principle, allowing agencies to ensure that regulation does not introduce problems equivalent to those that it is attempting to solve.

CONSIDERATION OF COST

The presumption that agencies may "consider costs" has also emerged in a series of important cases within the District of Columbia Circuit. Consider three examples.

At issue in *Grand Canyon Air Coalition v. Federal Aviation Administration*[23] was an FAA regulation designed to reduce noise from airplanes over the Grand Canyon. The statute required "substantial restoration" of the "natural quiet," which the FAA understood to mean that the relevant area must achieve 50 percent of the natural quiet at least 75 percent of the day. In refusing to impose stricter controls, the FAA explained that it took into "consideration of the needs of the air tour industry."[24] Those challenging the rule said that the FAA's task was to ensure "substantial restoration" of the "natural quiet," and that the needs of the air tour industry could not lawfully be taken into account. The court responded by invoking something like a presumption in favor of considering cost, noting that nothing in the statute "forbids the government from considering the impact of its regulation on the air tour industry."[25] The court's passage appears to be a recognition that in the face of congressional silence, at least one kind of cost – that involving the air tour industry – will be within agency discretion to consider.

In the same vein is *George Warren Corporation v. EPA*,[26] where domestic companies challenged the EPA's implementation of the reformulated gasoline provisions of the Clean Air Act. A central question for the EPA was how to treat foreign refiners and importers. In resolving that question, the EPA considered not only air quality benefits but also the comments of the Department of Energy (DOE). That agency expressed concern that certain approaches could increase the price

[23] 154 F.3d 45 (1998).
[24] Id. at 48.
[25] Id.
[26] 159 F.2d 616 (DC Cir., 1998).

and decrease the quantity of gasoline, by making it more difficult for foreign refiners to divert production to the United States in periods of increased demand.
The EPA took this point expressly into account in its rule. The result was an
outcome more favorable to foreign refiners, and less favorable to environmental
protection or domestic competitors, than EPA might otherwise have chosen.
Nonetheless, the court upheld the agency's decision, emphasizing the absence
of an explicit legislative ban on consideration of these economic factors. The
court appeared to suggest that an express congressional preclusion of economic
factors would be necessary to make them irrelevant as a matter of law.

By far the most explicit statement on point, however, comes from *State of
Michigan v. EPA.*[27] At issue there was an EPA decision to approve a state implementation plan (SIP) for the regulation of ozone. The statutory terms provided
that SIPs must contain provisions adequately prohibiting "any source or other
type of emissions activity within the state from emitting any air pollutants in
amounts which will . . . contribute significantly to nonattainment in, or interfere
with maintenance by, any other State with respect to any such national primary
or secondary ambient air quality standard."[28] At first glance, this provision might
well be read as a kind of absolute ban on "significantly contributing" pollutants.
But the EPA did not understand it that way. Instead, the EPA reached a more
subtle conclusion: The "significant contributors" would be required to reduce
their ozone, but only by the amount achievable via "highly cost-effective controls," meaning those that could produce large reductions relatively cheaply. In
states with high control costs, then, relatively low reductions would be required.

Apparently because of the clarity of the statutory language on the particular point, no one in the case argued that EPA was required to balance costs
against benefits before issuing regulations. Challenging the EPA's interpretation,
environmental groups urged that the statute banned any consideration of costs
at all. The court rejected the argument, finding no "clear congressional intent
to preclude consideration of costs."[29] But the court obviously had a difficult
time with the statutory terms "contribute significantly," which seem to refer to
environmental damage, not to environmental damage measured in light of cost.
In upholding the EPA's decision, the court insisted that significance should not
"be measured in only one dimension," that of "health alone." In fact in some settings, the term "begs a consideration of costs."[30] In the court's view, EPA would
be unable to determine " 'significance' if it may consider only health," especially
in light of the fact that ozone causes adverse health effects at any level. If adverse

[27] 213 F.3d 663 (DC Cir., 2000).
[28] 42 USC 7410(a)(2)(D)9I)(I).
[29] Id. at 678.
[30] Id.

effects exist on all levels, how can EPA possibly choose a standard without giving some weight to cost? In any case, "the most formidable obstacle" to a ban on consideration of cost "is the settled law of this circuit,"[31] which requires an explicit legislative statement to preclude consideration of cost. Here, then, is an express judicial endorsement of a cost–benefit default principle, permitting agencies to consider costs if they seek to do so.

FEASIBILITY

Many statutes expressly require regulation to be "feasible." But what if the statute is silent or ambiguous on the question whether agencies may impose regulations beyond the point of "feasibility"? Sometimes statutes are "technology forcing," in the sense that they require companies to innovate, and thus to do more than what current technology permits.[32] Often, however, the technology that is "forced" by statutory requirements is entirely feasible, indeed that is part of the reason that Congress requires it. In fact, technology-forcing can be justified by cost–benefit principles themselves – if the benefits of forcing technology outweigh the costs, as they sometimes do. Companies might fail to innovate with respect to pollution control simply because they do not internalize all the benefits of the innovation. But technological innovation is sometimes neither feasible nor justified by cost–benefit principles. Because of large costs, regulation will sometimes raise serious questions from the standpoint of feasibility, in the sense that it will drive many companies out of business or require technologies that are not now and cannot soon be made available. Here the question is how to handle legislative silence.

The question arose most prominently in *NRDC v. EPA*,[33] involving the toxic substances provision of the Clean Air Act. That provision, since substantially revised,[34] required EPA to issue regulations that would provide "an ample margin of safety to protect the public health." The principal question was whether cost was relevant to the EPA's judgment. On its face, the statute might seem to block any consideration of cost and indeed to require regulations that would reduce risks to zero, especially because for many toxic substances, safe thresholds simply do not exist. Alert to this point, the EPA urged that it should be allowed to take feasibility into account in setting regulations. The court accepted this conclusion by suggesting that regulations could avoid "zero risk" in two ways. First, the

---

[31] 213 F. 3d at 678.

[32] For general discussion, see Bruce LaPierre, Technology-Forcing and Federal Environmental Protection Statutes, 62 Iowa L. Rev. 771 (1977).

[33] 824 F.2d 1146 (DC Cir., 1987).

[34] See 42 USC 7412.

EPA was required to make an initial, benefits-based, cost-blind determination of what is "safe"; but citing the Benzene Case, the court said that "safe" did not mean "risk-free."[35] Thus "the Administrator's decision must be based upon an expert judgment with regard to the level of emission that will result in an 'acceptable' risk to health." Of course, there is a degree of arbitrariness in any particular judgment here, especially if the judgment is cost-blind. But the court was apparently attempting to ensure a degree of visibility and consistency in agency decisions, by ensuring that the "acceptable risk" judgment would be made publicly and would be adhered to in a range of cases.

Second, the court said that in deciding how far to go beyond "safety," in order to provide an "ample margin," the Administrator was permitted to consider both costs and feasibility.[36] It is clear that the court engrafted these ideas onto a statute that did not expressly include them. In this sense, the decision suggests an interpretive principle to the effect that a statute that is silent or ambiguous on the point will ordinarily be taken to permit the agency to take account of the feasibility of statutory commands.

COSTS AND BENEFITS

If the statute is ambiguous or silent on the point, will an agency be permitted to decide in accordance with cost–benefit balancing? Is an agency authorized to make such balancing the basis for decision?

In General

An affirmative answer was given in *NRDC v. EPA*[37] (the same title, but not the same case, as that just discussed). At issue there was the EPA's decision whether to classify a source of fugitive emissions as "major" within the meaning of a statutory provision calling for regulation of "major emitting facilities."[38] The EPA concluded that it would not add certain industrial sources, including surface coal mines, on the ground that the social and economic costs of regulation would outweigh the environmental benefits.[39] The statutory language did not require cost–benefit analysis, and the court emphasized that an alternative construction was not barred by statutory language and legislative history.[40] Nonetheless,

[35] 824 F.2d at 1149.
[36] Id. at 1150–51.
[37] 937 F.2d 641 (DC Cir., 1991).
[38] 42 USC 7475.
[39] 937 F.2d at 643.
[40] Id. at 645.

the court said that it would accept the agency's interpretation in the face of legislative silence.

Interpretation of OSHA has showed identical thinking. Outside of the area of toxic substances, the statute (with its opaque "reasonably necessary or appropriate" language) is ambiguous on whether cost–benefit analysis may be made the basis for decision. Here a prominent court went out of its way to say that OSHA is permitted to decide on the basis of cost–benefit balancing if it wishes.[41] On remand, the agency appeared to decline the court's invitation, choosing a test based largely on a mixture of the "significant risk" and "feasibility" requirements, a test that the court upheld.[42] But the story does not end there. The agency has continued to say – perhaps to insulate itself from a court challenge – that it finds a "reasonable relationship" between costs and benefits, and in its most recent pronouncement on the issue, the court treated this as an authoritative constructive of the statute.[43] It remains to see whether an OSHA regulation that fails to show such a reasonable relationship might be challenged as unlawful.

THE TSCA WRINKLE

A more aggressive ruling, with a statutory text more favorable to cost–benefit balancing, is *Corrosion Proof Fittings v. EPA.*[44] What makes this a wrinkle is that, as in the Benzene Case, the court said not merely that the agency is permitted to follow an interpretive principle, but that it is required to do so. At the same time, the *Corrosion Proof Fitting v. EPA* court's decision is the most elaborate statement to date of the emerging federal common law of cost–benefit analysis.

At issue was the EPA's attempted ban on asbestos, an admittedly carcinogenic substance, under the Toxic Substances Control Act (TSCA).[45] TSCA allows EPA to regulate "unreasonable risks,"[46] and it therefore invites some kind of cost–benefit balancing. But the court went far beyond what the statute unambiguously invited. In addition to allowing EPA to engage in cost–benefit balancing, the court required a high degree of quantification from EPA, including explicit comparisons of the cost–benefit ratios for different degrees of regulation, and also separate discussions of how regulation would affect different

---

[41] International Union, *UAW v. OSHA*, 938 F.2d 1310 (DC Cir., 1991).

[42] International Union, *UAW v. OSHA*, 37 F.3d 605 (DC Cir., 1994).

[43] See *State of Michigan v. EPA*, supra note 317.

[44] 947 F.2d 1201 (5th Cir., 1991).

[45] 15 USC 2600 et seq.

[46] The term appears no less than thirty-five times in thirty-three pages of the statute. See William Rodgers, The Lesson of the Owls and the Crows, 4 J. Land Use & Env. L. 377, 379 (1989). See, for example, 15 USC 2605(a).

industries using asbestos. The court thus insisted that the EPA go beyond a comparison of "a world with no further regulation" and "a world in which no manufacture of asbestos takes place" to include as well cost–benefit comparisons under different approaches to regulation.[47]

At the same time, the court objected, not to the overall cost–benefit ratio, but to the cost–benefit ratios for some areas in which asbestos was to be banned: "[T]he agency's analysis results in figures as high as $74 million per life saved. For example, the EPA states that its ban of asbestos pipe will save three lives over the next thirteen years, at a cost of $128–277 million (343–76 million per life saved) ...; that its ban of asbestos shingle will cost $23–34 million to save 0.32 statistical lives ($72–106 million per life saved); that its ban of asbestos coatings will cost $46–181 million to save 2.22 lives ($14–54 million per life saved)"[48] With evident incredulity, the court said that the "EPA would have this court believe that Congress ... thought that spending $200–300 million to save approximately seven lives (approximately $30–40 million per life) over thirteen years is reasonable."[49] All in all, this is an exceptionally aggressive use of the interpretive principle in favor of cost–benefit balancing. The court not only construes statutory text in a way that mandates such balancing but also requires a demonstration that particular parts, and subparts, of the relevant regulation satisfy a cost–benefit inquiry.[50]

A NOTE ON AMERICAN TRUCKING

In a sense, the cost–benefit default principles were tested before the Supreme Court in *Whitman v. American Trucking Association*.[51] In that case, the Court was asked to say that the EPA could consider costs in setting national ambient air quality standards. The Court refused the invitation, concluding that such standards must be set without regard to cost. The Court emphasized the evident clarity of the statutory provision at issue, which defined national standards as those "requisite to protect the public health."[52] In context, the reference to "public health" seemed to require a cost-blind judgment, based on health alone.

---

[47] Id. at 1208.

[48] Id. at 1209.

[49] Id.

[50] See also *American Dental Association v. Martin*, 984 F.2d 823 (7th Cir., 1993) (upholding OSHA regulations designed to protect against hepatitis and AIDS, and noting that the "rule's implicit valuation of life is high – about $4 million – but not so astronomical certainly by regulatory standards, as to call the rationality of the rule seriously into question, especially when we consider that neither Hepatitis B nor AIDS is a disease of old people").

[51] 121 S. Ct 903 (2001).

[52] 42 USC 7409(b)(1).

Does *Whitman v. American Trucking Association* throw the cost–benefit default principles into doubt? The simple answer is that it does not. The Court concluded that the Clean Air Act was unambiguous; it did not by any means suggest that an ambiguous statute would be taken to disallow consideration of costs. In his separate opinion, Justice Breyer was careful to say that courts "should read silences or ambiguities in the language of regulatory statutes" to permit consideration of "all of a proposed regulation's adverse effects," at least where those effects would clearly be serious and disproportionate." Justice Breyer is clearly saying that, in the face of statutory ambiguity, agencies should be allowed to consider costs, if only because that approach would increase the likelihood of rational regulation. It is most unlikely that the Court would disagree with him. This is especially so in light of the fact, emphasized by both the Court and Justice Breyer,that the Clean Air Act allows EPA to consider costs at numerous stages in the implementation process. Indeed, in *Whitman v.* American Trucking *Association*, the Court went out of its way to refer, with approval, to lower court decisions creating cost–benefit default principles.[53]

UNDERLYING CONSIDERATIONS

What are the foundations of the cost–benefit default principles? What is their rationale? Though the various default principles should be evaluated separately, there are common concerns in the background. We begin with statutory interpretation in general.

AMBIGUITY, ABSURDITY, AND EXCESSIVE GENERALITY

Three Kinds of Default Principles. There is nothing new or unusual about default principles for statutory interpretation. They are ubiquitous. In fact, they are inevitable.[54] Language has no meaning without default principles of many kinds; everyone uses them every day. Generally such principles are agreed-upon, so much so that they do not seem to be principles at all. They are part of what it means to understand the relevant language. They need not even be identified, much less defended. But sometimes the principles are contested, or at least are subject to contest, and in such cases, they must certainly be identified and defended, and the fact that they are being used is obvious to all.

[53] 121 S. Ct. at 910.

[54] For discussion from different perspectives, see William Eskridge, Dynamic Statutory Interpretation (Cambridge: Harvard Univ. Press, 1994); Cass R. Sunstein, Interpreting Statutes in the Regulatory State, 103 Harv. L. Rev. 415, 420–35 (1989).

We might distinguish three circumstances here.

- The simplest cases involve genuine ambiguity, in the sense that without resort to an identifiable default principle, courts really do not know what the statutory term means. Here the default principle will operate as a tie-breaker, authorizing an agency to act when the case is otherwise in equipoise. The use of default principles is uncontroversial in such cases; without some such principles, cases cannot be decided.
- Less simple cases involve texts that are most naturally or easily taken to forbid the agency action, but when there is nonetheless ambiguity. Here the default principles are serving as "clear statement" principles – suggesting that the statute will be understood to allow the agency to do what it seeks unless Congress expressly says otherwise. This is, of course, a more aggressive use of default principles, pushing statutes away from the disfavored terrain. It appears to be the law, for example, that agencies will be allowed to consider costs unless Congress expressly prohibits them from doing so; this is a clear statement principle, used not just when courts are in equipoise.
- The third and most complex cases involves the sort of interpretive problem that might be understood to involve *excessive generality*. This is the kind of problem found when, for example, a statute saying "no vehicles in the park" is applied to a war memorial consisting of a tank used in World War II, or when a nephew who has murdered his uncle seeks to inherit under a will that has not been revoked.[55] In many legal systems, courts will look behind the language of the statute to prevent an outcome that makes no sense and that could not possibly have been intended.[56] This was the court's suggestion about the de minimis exception in *Alabama Power Company v. Costle*,[57] and the court's requirement that EPA consider health–health tradeoffs was clearly understood in similar terms, as an effort to prevent an outcome that would be "bizarre" and hence that Congress could not have wanted.[58]

Sense Versus Nonsense. These are the circumstances for using default principles. But what is the appropriate content of such principles? This is a large question, and it makes sense to begin with established understandings.

[55] See *Riggs v. Palmer*, 22 N.E. 188 (1889).
[56] See Neil McCormick & Robert Summers, Interpreting Statutes: A Comparative Study (Aldershot, England: Dartmouth, 1991).
[57] 636 F.2d 323, 360–61 (DC Cir., 1979).
[58] *American Trucking Association v. EPA*, 173 F.3d 1027, 1052 (DC Cir., 1999).

Where meaning is not clear, many time-honored principles are designed to give sense and rationality the benefit of the doubt. An old interpretive principle, with roots in almost all legal systems,[59] counsels courts to avoid "absurdity"; sometimes this principle has been taken to override statutory language. More particular principles, of considerable current importance, disfavor retroactivity[60]; require Congress to speak clearly if it seeks to create exemptions from the antitrust law; give the benefit of the doubt to Native Americans; and say that agencies will not, on their own, be taken to have the authority to apply statutes outside the territorial boundaries of the United States.[61] It was probably inevitable that, confronted with a wide range of regulatory enactments, courts would eventually develop a set of analogues for the regulatory state – principles that give rationality and sense the benefit of the doubt in the particular context of contemporary regulatory law.

Each of the cost–benefit default principles is best defended on just this ground – that they do give sense and rationality the benefit of the doubt and that Congress should not be taken to have mandated irrationality or absurdity. On this count, some of the default principles should be less controversial than others. At the very least, it seems sensible to say that agencies are permitted to ignore trivial risks and to balance the health benefits of regulation against the health costs of regulation. Where Congress has left things unclear, agencies should have discretion to move statutes away from the domain of senselessness.

Consider the idea that agencies may make de minimis exceptions, which is an outgrowth of the old idea, *de minimis non curat lex*. If the risk at issue is tiny, the agency is not required to eliminate it. Much of the rationale here is a kind of implicit cost–benefit balancing. If regulation occurs, both private and public resources must be expended to ensure compliance. When the benefits of regulation are trivial, the agency is permitted to refuse to regulate, on the ground that the costs are likely to outweigh any benefits. When the benefits of regulation are trivial, no one is likely to have anything to complain about if regulation is foregone. Those who are attempting to complain are likely to be well-organized private groups with a self-interested agenda, unrelated to the purposes for which the statute was enacted.

In a way, the idea of health–health tradeoffs is simpler still. If agencies are imposing health risks at the same time that they are protecting health, they should, at the very least, be permitted to take this fact into account. What most matters, after all, is whether risks are being reduced on balance. Other things

---

[59] See McCormick & Summers, supra note 56 in this Chapter.

[60] *Bowen v. Georgetown University Hospital*, 488 US 204, 208–9 (1988).

[61] See Cass R. Sunstein, Nondelegation Canons, 67 U. Chi. L. Rev. 315 (2000).

being equal, it is hardly desirable for government to reduce the respiratory risks of ground-level ozone if ground-level ozone also provides significant protection against cancer and cataracts. The agency should be permitted to ask whether this is what it should do, subject to review for reasonableness. In any case, permission to engage in health–health balancing helps counteract the constant risk of tunnel vision on the part of regulators.

Why are agencies presumptively entitled to consider costs? The basic idea must be that a "benefits only" approach also reflects a kind of tunnel vision, a myopic focus on only one of the variety of things that matter. Suppose, for example, that one approach to regulation would produce a certain level of air quality benefits, but it does so at a cost of $800 million, and that another competing approach would produce a very slightly lower level of air quality benefits, but it does so at a cost of $150 million. If costs can be made relevant, the agency is permitted to do what seems quite sensible: to save the $650 million on the ground that the benefits of the expenditure would not be high enough to justify the expenditure.

Of course, it would be necessary to know a great deal more to know how to evaluate the particular problem. If the $650 million would mean a significant loss of jobs, and if the lower air quality benefits would not result in significant mortality or morbidity effects, it seems most sensible not to expend the resources. But if the $650 million would mean slightly reduced profits for producers, or slightly increased prices for a dispensable good, and if the air quality benefits would mean a nontrivial reduction in respiratory problems for tens of thousands of asthmatics, the case for more stringent regulation is far stronger. The point is not that a bare accounting of costs and benefits tells officials all of what they need to know.[62] It is only that a sensible agency is entitled to, and does, "consider" the costs of regulation. Congress should not be understood to have banned agencies from doing this. If Congress has a particular reason to require otherwise, it is permitted to do exactly that. Ideas of this sort help support the closely related idea that agencies are presumptively permitted to compare costs against benefits and also to consider whether compliance is feasible.

AGENCY PERMISSION VERSUS AGENCY REQUIREMENTS

Thus far, we have seen what agencies are *permitted* to do, if Congress is silent on the point. But it is necessary to distinguish between cases in which an agency attempts to do what cost–benefit principles permit and cases in which an agency refuses to do what courts are permitting. We know that, for the agency, no legal

---

[62] See Matthew Adler & Eric Posner, Rethinking Cost–Benefit Analysis, 109 Yale L. J. 165 (1999) (arguing that cost–benefit analysis is only a decision procedure).

problem will arise in the first set of cases. What about the second? Might the default principles sometimes require agencies to follow a particular course?

THE FRAMEWORK

To answer this question, some brief background is in order. *Chevron v. NRDC*,[63] the dominant case in the area, sets out a two-step inquiry for judicial review of agency decisions. The first question ("step one") is whether Congress has "directly decided the precise question at issue" – more simply, whether Congress has unambiguously banned what the agency proposes to do. Under *Chevron*, agencies are generally permitted to construe ambiguous statutes as they see fit. It follows that even without a cost–benefit default principle, agencies should be permitted to consider costs so long as the statute is ambiguous on the point. When *Chevron* is combined with the default principle, the overall lesson is exceedingly straightforward: Agencies are permitted to consider costs when Congress has not said that they may not.

Under *Chevron*, however, the issue is not finished upon a finding that Congress has not directly addressed the precise question at issue. It remains to ask whether the agency's interpretation of the statute is reasonable ("step two"). When the *American Trucking Associations v. EPA* court held that the EPA was required to consider the benefits as well as the risks of a pollutant, it did so partly on the ground that the agency's interpretation to the contrary was not reasonable (because it was, in the court's view, "bizarre"). It is therefore possible that even if an agency's decision does not violate *Chevron* step one (because the statute is ambiguous), it will nonetheless violate step two, if the decision can be shown to be arbitrary or bizarre.

THE FRAMEWORK APPLIED

Suppose that the agency has refused to allow a de minimis exemption, to engage in health-health comparisons, or to consider costs when the statute allows it to do so. If the agency has refused to do what the cost–benefit principles permit it to do, the analysis would proceed in the following steps.

I. The first question would involve *Chevron* step one: Has EPA violated unambiguous congressional instructions or transgressed some judgment made "directly" by Congress? At first glance, the answer, by hypothesis, will be No. The statute is ambiguous rather than clear. The only possible response is that the cost–benefit default rule now operates as a kind of canon of construction, serving as part of the inquiry in *Chevron* step one.

[63]   467 US 837 (1984).

The argument is unquestionably adventurous, but not as much so as it might appear. Many canons of construction now work in precisely that way. Consider, for example, the following canons: Statutes will not be understood to apply outside the territorial borders of the United States[64]; statutes will not be understood to apply retroactively[65]; statutes will not be taken to raise serious constitutional questions.[66] In all these cases, agency interpretations do not prevail under *Chevron* step one, not because Congress has expressed its will clearly, but because Congress is required to speak with clarity if it wishes agencies to act in the way that they seek. Perhaps the cost–benefit default principles should be understood in similar terms.

This is indeed possible, but it would require a significant stretch from existing law. The canons discussed above have a degree of longevity, indeed a straightforward justification from longstanding traditions. The cost–benefit default principles have not yet acquired the status of the canons of construction that operate as part of *Chevron* step one. It is therefore exceedingly doubtful that an agency's refusal to proceed in the manner suggested by the cost–benefit default principles would be struck down under step one.

2. The second question would involve *Chevron* step two: Is the agency's interpretation of the statute "reasonable"? I suggest that the foregoing considerations, supporting the default rules in general, suggest the basis for a particular presumption: The agency's interpretation is to be presumed unreasonable if it interprets the statute to fail to make de minimis exemptions, to disallow health–health tradeoffs, not to consider costs or feasibility, to regulate insignificant risks, or to ban cost–benefit balancing. Of these various possibilities, the presumption of unreasonableness is strongest when the agency is attempting to regulate a de minimis risk or refusing to consider health–health tradeoffs. In such cases, the agency's decision seems most obviously unreasonable. Why should expenditures be required for trivial risks? Why should the agency be permitted to increase overall risks? These questions do not have obvious answers.

The argument that agencies would be unreasonable to reject the other default principles is less clear. But even in such cases, any reasonable judgment will ordinarily be based on some kind of weighing of costs and benefits, and not on an inquiry into benefits alone. Return to *State of Michigan v. EPA*, and suppose that, in some states, the costs of reducing the "significant contribution" would be exceedingly high, whereas the benefits would be low, in light of the fact that the risks associated with the relevant concentrations of ozone are not severe. If

[64] *EEOC v. Arabian American Oil*, 499 US 244, 248 (1991).

[65] *Bowen v. Georgetown University Hospital*, 488 US 204, 208–9 (1988).

[66] *DeBartolo v. Florida East Coast*, 485 US 568 (1988).

the costs would be high and the benefits low, on what rationale should be the EPA refuse even to consider the former? Here too there appears to be no good answer.

Notice that what is involved here is a presumption only, and it is rebuttable. It is possible to imagine agency explanations that would show why its view – to reject one or another of the cost–benefit default principles – is reasonable. It is that question to which I now turn.

Rebutting the Presumption

In several contexts, Congress, as well as agencies and courts, could reasonably find the default principles inapplicable. The following catalogue is intended to identify circumstances in which agencies might sensibly decide not to go in the direction suggested by the default principles – and also in which a reasonable legislature might ban agencies from going in that direction.

I. **Regulating De Minimis Risks: The Case of Low Benefits and Administrative Difficulties.** Suppose that an agency has discretion to interpret the relevant statute so as to allow exemptions of de minimis risks for (as an illustration) carcinogenic color additives in food. Suppose that the agency refuses to interpret the statute this way because (a) the benefits of color food additives are generally low (noncarcinogenic color additives will do about as well), (b) as a matter of science, it is not always simple to distinguish between weak and strong carcinogens, and (c) a flat rule will be simpler to administer. At least at first glance, this sort of explanation seems fully reasonable. It would distinguish the case from one in which the agency attempts to interpret the OSHA statute in such a way as to call for costly regulation of insignificant risks.

2. **Regulating Risks That Might or Might Not Be De Minimis: The Case of Scientific Ignorance.** Suppose that the agency attempts to regulate risks that (it agrees) cannot be shown to be significant. Suppose that it contends, not that it will understand the statute to cover demonstrably insignificant or demonstrably de minimis risks, but instead to cover instead risks that, in light of existing scientific information, might be small but might be large – a distinction that cannot be made with existing tools and in light of existing scientific understandings. In other words, the agency interprets the statute to allow regulation where the benefits might be significant, but cannot be shown to be significant given existing knowledge. This, in short, is a case where there is a wide range of expected benefits, from quite low to quite high, and where science cannot choose a probable "point" along the range (not an uncommon situation, as the discussion of arsenic suggests). This does not seem to be an unreasonable interpretation

of an ambiguous statute. But even so, the agency should be required to identify the range of potential benefits so as to ensure that the possible gains, discounted by the probability that they will be realized, is sufficient to make regulation worthwhile.

3. Disregarding Costs at One Stage of a Multistage Inquiry. Might it be reasonable for an agency to interpret a statute not to allow consideration of costs? In some cases, this would indeed be reasonable. Recall that under the Clean Air Act, the EPA is supposed to set standards at the level that, with an "adequate margin of safety," is "requisite to protect the public health."[67] Suppose that the EPA urges (as it has for a number of years, and as the Supreme Court has approved in *American Trucking Association v. EPA*) that costs will be considered not in setting standards in the first instance (where health is the sole consideration), but at other, later stages, in the development of state implementation plans and in insistence on deadlines for compliance. In such a system, the EPA would say that national ambient air quality standards are based only on an inquiry into issues of health, that this is a benefits-based judgment, but that the decision how and when to meet those standards, made through complex procedures at the state and federal levels, will consider costs as well as benefits.

In fact, this is how the Clean Air Act now operates.[68] National standards are issued in what is at least nominally a cost-blind manner, but costs emphatically and openly play a part at other stages of the process, in the design and enforcement of state implementation plans. Whether or not it is ultimately convincing, this kind of procedural defense of "health only" judgments seems at least plausible. Whether it would be better for costs to be considered throughout is an issue on which reasonable people can differ. This is a highly pragmatic question, on which general enthusiasm for cost–benefit balancing is not decisive.

4. Disregarding Particular Costs As Statutorily Irrelevant. There are other arenas in which costs might reasonably be disregarded; at least agencies might disregard costs of a certain kind. Suppose, for example, that the FAA concluded that the needs of the air tour industry were entitled to no weight in issuing regulations controlling noise at the Grand Canyon. Under a different administration, the FAA might believe that the statute is best understood to ensure that those who enjoy the Grand Canyon can do so with a minimum of noise – and that the adverse effects on the air tour industry are irrelevant, even if this means that fewer people will be able to enjoy the Grand Canyon. At first glance, this is an entirely

---

[67] 42 USC 7409(b).

[68] See 42 USC 7410; Portney, supra note 19 in Chapter I.

reasonable judgment. Where Congress has been unclear, administrations and administrators might make different decisions on that question.

5. Disregarding Feasibility As Part of Overall Balancing. Is it ever reasonable for an agency to ignore the question whether regulation is feasible for the industry? Might the FAA choose to interpret an ambiguous statute so as to impose an air quality regulation that would not be feasible for the air tour industry over the Grand Canyon, so that the relevant companies could not stay in business? At first glance, feasibility seems relevant, but it is possible to imagine cases in which an agency might reasonably choose to interpret a statute to allow rules that are not feasible. The agency might believe that it is more important to reduce noise levels than to allow the continued operation of the air tour industry. When judgments of this kind are made, the agency is effectively engaging in a kind of cost–benefit balancing, one that justifies regulation that is not feasible. Of course, an agency might engage in technology-forcing, though usually this approach depends on a judgment that regulation is indeed feasible because more advanced technologies are possible to develop.

6. Rights and Irreversibility. Thus far the discussion has emphasized pragmatic or instrumental considerations. But are there contexts in which the cost–benefit default principles are inapplicable in principle? In many domains, of course, cost–benefit balancing fails to describe the operation of law; rights-based thinking often "blocks" resorts to costs, or at least costs of a certain kind.[69] Ordinarily ideas of this sort play a role in constitutional law,[70] where certain "costs" are off limits. For example, the costs undoubtedly associated with politically controversial speech are not a legitimate basis for regulating such speech. Those costs are entitled to no weight at all.

Such thinking is not foreign to regulatory policy. The most vivid example is the Endangered Species Act,[71] which forbids agency from engaging in action that would threaten members of endangered species even if a balancing test would appear to justify the action.[72] Can this be explained in a legal system pervaded by cost–benefit default principles? Perhaps it can be. The Endangered Species Act is concerned with preventing genuinely irreversible losses, and at least in the context of human activities that cause extinction, perhaps the statute

---

[69] See the discussion of exclusionary reasons in Joseph Raz, Practical Reason and Norms, 37–45 (Princeton: Princeton University Press, 1990).

[70] See Richard Pildes, Why Rights Are Not Trumps, 27 J. Legal Stud. 725 (1999).

[71] 16 USC 1531 et seq.

[72] *TVA v. Hill,* 437 US 153 (1978).

is best taken to be rooted in a theory of rights, one that rebuts the presumption in favor of cost–benefit balancing. Now it is possible that some kind of "meta" balancing justifies a flat prohibition on actions that would destroy members of an endangered species. Perhaps that higher form of cost–benefit balancing calls for a refusal to engage in cost–benefit balancing in particular cases. The benefits might be thought to be so high, and the costs usually so low, as to support such a prohibition, disallowing balancing each time. But this way of understanding the statute seems to misconceive its foundations, which lie in a judgment that human beings should not knowingly bring about the extinction of other species, at least in the absence of truly extraordinary circumstances.

It is possible to generalize from this example. Where regulatory policy is designed to ensure against irreversible damage, or otherwise to prevent the violation of rights, the cost–benefit default principles might well be displaced. In most domains of regulatory policy, however, what is involved is not the danger of irreversible loss, but instead issues of degree, and hence the presumption remains intact.

UNSETTLED QUESTIONS: SPECIFYING THE PRINCIPLES

The cost–benefit default principles leave many open questions. They are abstract and general. It is here that a great deal of law will be made in the next decades. I offer a few remarks on the crucial issues.

THE INCIPIENT COMMON LAW OF ACCEPTABLE RISKS

What makes a risk significant or de minimis? We might be able to find some agreed-upon standards. If the risk is less than that created by eating a moderate number of peanuts with legally permitted aflotoxin levels, or from living in Denver rather than New York for a week every year, the case might seem relatively easy. Risks of this little are the kind that people ignore each day. But how should we evaluate a cancer risk from, say, a lifetime exposure to a certain carcinogenic substance of one in 1,000,000? One in 100,000? One in 10,000,000? Does it matter if the exposed population is large or small?

These are the pivotal questions. For guidance, recall that the International Commission on Radiological Protection recommends that environmental factors should not be allowed to cause an incremental cancer risk, for those exposed over a lifetime, of 3 in 1,000 or more[73] – but that the practice of American agencies is highly variable, with the EPA's acceptable range varying, under different

---

[73] Sadowitz & Graham, supra note 6 in Chapter 6.

programs, from I in 10,000 to I in 1,000,000.[74] In the Benzene Case, the plurality of the Supreme Court attempted to provide some clarification, making a distinction between two quantitatively different levels of risk. If the risk of getting cancer from drinking a glass of water is one in a billion, the plurality said, it could not possibly be considered significant.[75] By contrast, a fatality risk of I/1,000 from regular inhalation of gasoline vapors "might well" be considered significant. OSHA has built on this simple idea in issuing its own regulations. Thus the agency has said that a lifetime risk of 1.64/1,000 will be counted as significant, whereas a lifetime risk of 0.6 in 100,000 "may be approaching a level that can be viewed as safe."[76]

The effort to look at the statistical risk faced by members of the exposed population is certainly a nice start, and in light of the Supreme Court's statements, perhaps OSHA's approach is sufficient to survive judicial scrutiny, while the EPA's one-in-one-million standard might be questionable. An effort at quantification is a helpful way of clarifying the basis for the agency's decision, especially laudable in light of the slipperiness of the idea of "significance." But many questions might be asked. In deciding whether a risk is trivial or significant, it would seem important to ask not only about the level of the risk faced by each person but also about the size of the exposed population.[77] If two people in the United States face a lifetime risk of 2/10,000, perhaps the risk should not be deemed significant in light of the fact that it is overwhelmingly likely that no fatalities will be suffered. We could easily imagine a challenge to a decision to treat such a risk as significant as a matter of law. Certainly the agency should explain any failure to take account of the small number of exposed people.

At the same time, a statistically small risk, if faced by large numbers of people, might well be deemed significant. If 20 million people face a lifetime risk of 1/200,000, one hundred people are expected to die – far from a trivial number. If 200 million people face a risk of one in one million, 200 people are also expected to die; is this number insignificant merely because the statistical risk, for each person, is small? We could easily imagine a challenge to an agency decision to treat the latter risks as insignificant; indeed that challenge might even be convincing. The point raises serious doubts about the Supreme Court plurality's confidence that a risk of one in a billion, from drinking a glass of water, could not be deemed significant. If each person drinks five glasses of water per day, and if there are 260 million Americans, the one-in-a-billion risk no

[74] Id.

[75] See 448 US at 655.

[76] 52 Fed. Reg. 46,168, 46, 234 (1987).

[77] Agency attention to the size of the exposed population is strongly urged in Hamilton & Viscusi, supra note 14 in Chapter 2.

longer seems so small, converted into expected annual fatalities (474.5, hardly an insignificant number). We should conclude that it is at least reasonable for agencies to consider risks to be significant, and not de minimis, if the probability is very low but the exposed population quite large. It is also reasonable to suggest that if the probability is very low but the exposed population sufficiently large, a high number of expected fatalities should require the agency to consider the risk "significant" as a matter of law.

There is an additional problem. Both OSHA and the Supreme Court seem to focus on the "lifetime" risk – that is, the risk that would come from being exposed to a substance for all of one's working life. Under OSHA, it does seem that this focus is required by the statute, at least for toxic substances, for which the relevant provision is expressly drawn in terms of lifetime exposure. But in the abstract, and under other provisions, we should not be focusing on the risk, of fatality or anything else, that would come from a lifetime of exposure, *except to the extent that all, most, or many people actually have a lifetime of exposure*. Imagine, for example, that almost all workers in the relevant industry are exposed, not for their lifetimes, but for five years or less. What risk do they face? This is the crucial question. Perhaps the risk, for them, is a small fraction of the lifetime risk. Sensible policy requires the government to reduce the risks that people actually face, not the risk that people fancifully face. When an agency has discretion, the agency should look not at lifetime risk, but at actual risk.

What all this suggests is that when agencies are asking whether risks are significant, they ought to move in the direction of setting out a range of "expected benefits," in terms of mortality, morbidity, and other relevant variables (see Chapter 9 for details). These variables could be aggregated into some sort of total number, below which a risk would be treated as insignificant. Of course, there will be a large degree of guesswork in generating the relevant numbers. Of course too, there will be a degree of arbitrariness in choosing the precise point at which risks are no longer significant. But without movement in the direction of quantification, it will not be possible to produce informed, transparent, and consistent policy. Thus an effort to quantify the level of risk that would be deemed acceptable would replace the current system, with its high degree of inconsistency and guesswork, with something like a common law of acceptable risks.

THE MEANING OF FEASIBILITY: NO ON–OFF SWITCH

What does it mean to say that regulation must be "feasible"? In the abstract, a requirement that regulation be feasible might seem to invite cost–benefit balancing. But as we have seen, a feasibility requirement involves no balancing of costs and benefits. It offers instead a cost-only inquiry into whether achievement of the regulatory goal is practicable.

But there is a problem here as well. Feasibility is not an on–off switch. Any significant increase in costs is likely to prove not feasible for at least some companies. As the costs increase, the number of companies for whom the regulation proves not feasible will increase, too. In these circumstances, it seems extremely artificial to say that, at a certain point, regulation becomes not feasible. Perhaps there is a set point at which regulation, by virtue of its stringency, establishes a sudden, large-scale increase in the number of companies who cannot bear the cost of regulatory controls while continuing in business. But it is more likely that as the costs grow, the number of companies who cannot bear the cost grows too, perhaps with several specific points at which that number spikes upward. In these circumstances, what sense is made by a feasibility constraint? At first glance, very little.

Perhaps there is an intelligible answer here. Perhaps Congress wants to say that for most regulations, companies must comply, unless a large number of them can show that they cannot comply and continue. And certainly this is a relatively simple inquiry in most cases. What makes little sense is the suggestion that agencies can pick a single point that is feasible, and go to, but not beyond, that point.

In these circumstances, how can we account for the evident popularity of legal requirements that regulation be feasible or achievable? There are several possibilities, suggesting that the feasibility standard might be justified by reference to institutional considerations. From the standpoint of those concerned with safety and the environment, a cost–benefit standard might be thought to introduce undue opportunities for industry to stall the process, perhaps because of the prospect and actuality of judicial review. A requirement that regulation must be feasible greatly improves the agency's chances in court. Though the evidence is limited, this conclusion is supported by the record of agencies on appeal; no agency has lost a challenge to the feasibility of its regulation, but cost–benefit requirements have proved troublesome for agencies in court.

This is a point about the goals of supporters of environmental regulation. From the standpoint of Congress, there is a separate point. A statute that expressly refers to cost–benefit balancing seems to invite complaints about the decision to trade off lives for dollars; for this reason, statutes that embody CBA are unpopular in many circles. (It is noteworthy here that *none* of the actual and seriously considered enactments involving cost–benefit balancing has *ever* set out numbers for valuing regulatory benefits.) Legislators who seek to avoid complaints about CBA, while also seeking to impose a constraint on excessive regulation, might naturally be drawn to feasibility requirements. From the standpoint of industry, perhaps feasibility statutes are not so troublesome if it is possible to maintain control over the agency's docket and over appropriations, so as to ensure that draconian statutes are, in practice, far less than that.

These points help explain the appeal of feasibility constraints. But they still do not tell us what such constraints mean. The best answer, which is not entirely satisfactory, is that a regulation becomes infeasible if it results in significant dislocations in the industry, in the form of large numbers of business failures, substantial losses of jobs, or the equivalent.[78] Ideas of this sort are qualitative, rather than quantitative, and in implementation, they leave a great deal of discretion to agencies. What might be expected in the future is a more quantitative account from agencies implementing regulations that are said to be feasible or refusing to impose regulations said to be infeasible.

CONSIDERING COSTS

What of principles (or statutes) that ask agencies to "take into consideration" costs (and other relevant factors)? Statutes of this kind typically include an "achievability" constraint as well, one that operates, in practice, in the same way as a feasibility requirement. What is added by the idea that agencies should also take costs into consideration?

The answer seems to be that such provisions give agencies the discretion not to go to the full extent of feasibility if the costs of doing so are disproportionately high. Suppose, for example, that a regulation would cost $800 million and that it would save ten lives annually. Suppose too that it is entirely feasible. If the agency is permitted to take costs into consideration, presumably it is permitted to impose a less intrusive regulation, or perhaps not to regulate at all. The foregoing sentence is qualified because the idea that costs must be taken "into consideration" does not say how much *weight* costs must have; it does not say, by itself, to what extent agencies must treat costs as relevant to the ultimate decision. Presumably it would be unlawful for an agency to ignore costs altogether. At a minimum, then, the agency must discuss cost and explain its decision in light of that factor.

This is a procedural understanding of the "consideration" requirement, one that has precedent under other statutes. But is there a substantive requirement as well? Must an agency give some kind of weight to costs, in addition to discussing them? The best answer is "yes" to both questions. An agency decision would be unlawful if it gave no weight whatsoever to costs, as, for example, through the choice of a regulation that would do only trivially more good than one that

---

[78] See, for example, *United Steelworkers v. Marshall*, 647 F.2d 1189 (5th Cir., 1980); *Building and Construction Trades v. OSHA*, 838 F.2d 1258 (DC Cir., 1988); *NCP v. Brock*, 825 F.2d 482 (DC Cir., 1987).

would be 50 percent less costly. An agency decision would also be doubtful if it made costs an overriding factor as, for example, by choosing a regulation that is slightly less expensive (say, $1 million annually) but also much less effective (say, because it would leave 30 additional deaths annually). On this view, a requirement that an agency take costs into consideration falls short of cost–benefit analysis, in the sense that the agency is expected to give principal weight to the initially identified factor, and from there to make adjustments because of costs.[79] An agency would run into difficulty if it transformed costs into the overriding statutory factor *or* if it gave costs no substantive consideration at all. These are the polar cases for administrative illegality. Cases that fall between the poles should present hard line-drawing questions, but no serious conceptual issues.

OF COSTS AND BENEFITS

It remains to discuss the largest problem of all. If cost–benefit balancing is required, what is an agency permitted to do? What is it prohibited from doing? Of course, there are hard issues of valuation here. If an agency values a life at $10 million, it will produce outcomes very different from those that would be follow if it valued a life at $500,000. Is an agency permitted to value a life at, say, $100 million, or at $50,000?

BASIC ISSUES OF VALUATION: THE STANDARD APPROACH

For several decades, agencies have undertaken cost–benefit analysis of major regulations. But how are costs and benefits to be calculated? In principle, the issue is often easier to resolve on the cost side, though the practical problems here can be very serious, especially in light of industry's incentive to overestimate costs. With respect to benefits, the now-standard approach involves an effort to calculate people's willingness to pay for the various goods at stake. Sophisticated (though still controversial) methods are available for this purpose.[80]

There remains a good deal of variation across agencies, with statistical lives being valued at between $1.5 million and $6.1 million. With respect to statistical lives, consider Table 8.1.[81]

---

[79] See *API v. EPA*, 52 F.3d 1113, 1119–20 (DC Cir., 1995), holding that the factors that follow the "taking into consideration" language must be treated as secondary.

[80] See W. Kip Viscusi, Fatal Tradeoffs (Cambridge, Mass.: Harvard Univ. Press, 1992).

[81] Borrowed from Matthew Adler & Eric Posner, Implementing Cost–Benefit Analysis When Preferences Are Distorted, in Cost–Benefit Analysis, Matthew Adler and Eric Posner, eds. (Chicago: Univ. Chicago Press, 2001).

Table 8.1 Valuations of life

Agency	Regulation	Citation	Value ($ million)
Department of Transportation – Federal Aviation Administration	Proposed establishment of the Harlingen Airport Radar Service Area, TX	55 FR 32064 August 6, 1990	1.5
Department of Agriculture – Food Safety and Inspection Service	Pathogen reduction: hazard analysis and critical control point systems	61 FR 38806 July 25, 1996	1.6
Department of Health and Human Services – Food and Drug Administration	Regulations restricting the sale and distribution of cigarettes and smokeless tobacco to protect children and adolescents	61 FR 44396 August 28, 1996	2.5
Department of Transportation – Federal Aviation Administration	Aircraft flight simulator use in pilot training, testing, and checking and at training centers	61 FR 34508 July 2, 1996	2.7
Environmental Protection Agency	Protection of stratospheric ozone	53 FR 30566 August 12, 1988	3
Department of Health and Human Services – Food and Drug Administration	Proposed rules to amend the food-labeling regulations	56 FR 60856 November 27, 1991	3
Department of Transportation – Federal Aviation Administration	Financial responsibility requirements for licensed launch activities	61 FR 38992 July 25, 1996	3
Department of Agriculture – Food and Nutrition Service	Proposed national school lunch program and school breakfast program	59 FR 30218 June 10, 1994	1.5, 3.0

Agency	Regulation	Citation / Date	Value
Environmental Protection Agency	National ambient air quality standards for particulate matter	62 FR 38652 July 18, 1997	4.8
Environmental Protection Agency	National ambient air quality standards for ozone	62 FR 38856 July 18, 1996	4.8
Department of Health and Human Services – Food and Drug Administration	Medical devices: current good manufacturing practice	61 FR 52602 October 7, 1996	5
Department of Health and Human Services – Public Health Service, Food and Drug Administration	Quality mammography standards	62 FR 55852 October 28, 1997	5
Environmental Protection Agency	Requirements for lead-based paint activities in target housing and child-occupied facilities	61 FR 45778 August 29, 1996	5.5
Environmental Protection Agency	National primary drinking water regulations: disinfectants and disinfection by-products	63 FR 69390 December 16, 1998	5.6
Environmental Protection Agency	Radon in drinking water health risk reduction and cost analysis	64 FR 9560 February 26, 1999	5.8
Environmental Protection Agency	Arsenic in drinking water	66 FR 7014 January 22, 2001	6.1

Table 8.2 Willingness-to-pay estimates (mean values)

Health Endpoint	Mean WTP Value Per Incident (1990 $)
Mortality	
Life saved	4.8 million
Life year extended	120,000
Hospital admissions	
All respiratory illnesses, all ages	12,700
Pneumonia, age <65	13,400
COPD, age >65	15,900
Ischemic heart disease, age <65	20,600
Congestive heart failure, age >65	16,600
Emergency visits for asthma	9,000
Chronic bronchitis	260,000
Upper respiratory symptoms	19
Lower respiratory symptoms	12
Acute bronchitis	45
Acute respiratory symptoms (any of 19)	18
Asthma	32
Shortness of breath	5.30
Sinusitis and hay fever	Not monetized
Work loss days	83
Restricted activity days (RAD)	
Minor RAD	38
Respiratory RAD	Not monetized
Worker productivity	$1 per worker per 10% change in ozone
Visibility Residential	$14 per unit decrease in deciview per household
Recreational	$7.30–11 per unit decrease in deciview per household
Household soiling damage	$2.50 per household

Source: Environmental Protection Agency, Regulatory Impact Analysis for Ozone and Particulates (Washington, D.C.: Government Printing Office, 1996).

Notwithstanding these variations, willingness to pay is the general basis for undertaking calculations. It is on the basis of this sort of analysis that the EPA compiled Table 8.2,[82] which can be taken as representative.

To become intelligible, of course, these numbers must be combined with an assessment of the problems that would be averted with various approaches

[82] Technically, the compilation was produced by the "Innovative Strategies Group" within EPA, working with a private consultant.

Table 8.3 Proposed PM_{10} standard $(50/150 \ \mu g/m^3)$ 99th percentile national annual health incidence reductions[a]

Endpoint		Partial Attainment Scenario
	Annual $PM_{2.5}$ $(\mu g/m^3)$	50
	Daily $PM_{2.5}$ $(\mu g/m^3)$	150
1. Mortality: Short-term exposure		360
Long-term exposure		340
2. Chronic bronchitis		6,800
Hospital admissions		
3. All respiratory (all ages)		190
All respiratory (ages 65+)		470
Pneumonia (ages 65+)		170
COPD (ages 65+)		140
4. Congestive heart failure		130
5. Ischemic heart disease		140
6. Acute bronchitis		1,100
7. Lower respiratory symptoms		10,400
8. Upper respiratory symptoms		5,300
Shortness of breath		18,300
Asthma attacks		8,800
9. Work loss days		106,000
10. Minor restricted activity days (MRADs)		879,000

[a]Estimates are incremental to the current ozone and PM NAAQS: (year = 2010)

to regulation. As an example of such an assessment, consider the numbers in Table 8.3, designed for the EPA's regulation of ozone and particulates (discussed in more detail in Chapter 9).

A simple exercise of multiplication, putting the two tables together, will generate monetized benefits, which can then be compared with monetized costs. Of course it is possible to challenge the numbers in both tables. In fact, evidence suggests that prospective estimates are bound to contain serious errors. The Office of Technology Assessment, asked in 1992 to evaluate the accuracy of OSHA's prospective estimates, found many mistakes.[83] But the basic method increasingly dominates administrative practice.

---

[83] See OMB, 1999 Report to Congress, at 40–3. A table, id. at 41, contains an illuminating summary.

LEGAL FLOORS AND CEILINGS

When would a given cost–benefit ratio be held to be unlawful? The simplest answer is that when the costs significantly exceed the benefits, if these are properly measured. A reasonable agency might begin with numbers near the middle of both market valuations and government valuations – in the case of a statistical life, somewhere between $4 million and $8 million. If an agency seeks to deviate from those numbers, it should explain why.

In Chapters 5 and 7, we saw several possible grounds for making adjustments. For example, an agency might make a reasonable upward adjustment if it believes that children are largely at risk – perhaps because more life-years are at stake, perhaps because children are unable to protect themselves and hence have a special equitable claim to government resources. A downward adjustment would similarly be lawful if the agency finds that mostly old people are at risk, so that any extensions of lives would produce a low level of savings in terms of life-years. Or the agency might reasonably conclude that special attention should be given to risks faced by poor people or African Americans, on the ground that existing injustice is compounded in a situation in which health and environmental dangers are thus concentrated. A distributional analysis, suggesting that the costs can easily be borne by those who are being ask to bear them, might also support the regulation. As we have seen, the government might make upward adjustments for uncontrollable, involuntary, and dread risks. While these points give agencies a degree of flexibility, they do not give them carte blanche because they operate in limited domains, and because they come with a duty of reasoned explanation. This duty is procedural, but it is far more than that. In the *Corrosion Proof Fittings v. EPA* case, for example, it is hard to see how the agency could have justified the extreme cost–benefit ratios that applied to certain bans on asbestos.[84]

THE DISCOUNT RATE

Perhaps the most difficult issue here, from the theoretical point of view, involves the selection of the appropriate discount rate. How should the agency value future gains and losses? In terms of ultimate outcomes, the choice matters a great deal. If an agency chooses a discount rate of 2 percent, the outcome will be very different from what it would be if an agency chooses a discount rate of 10 percent; the benefits calculation will shift dramatically as a result. If a human life is valued at $8 million, and if an agency chooses a 10 percent discount rate,

[84] 947 F.2d 1201 (5th Cir. 1991).

a life saved 100 years from now is worth only $581.[85] "At a discount rate of five percent, one death next year counts for more than a billion deaths in 500 years."[86] OMB suggests a 7 percent discount rate, but this is highly controversial. A key question is therefore: What legal constraints should be imposed on the agency's choice?[87]

My basic conclusion is that it is much harder to untangle the theoretical issue than to identify the appropriate posture of reviewing courts. In this highly technical area, courts should generally adopt a posture of deference, requiring agencies only to produce a reasonable explanation for their choice and to show a degree of consistency. Part of the reason for deference is the extreme complexity of the underlying issues. Part of the reason is the risk that an aggressive judicial posture would contribute to the "ossification" of rulemaking[88] – a particular problem in this setting because any particular discount rate will be easy to challenge, with reasonable arguments suggesting that it is too low or too high. To understand these points, some details are in order.

Usually statutes are silent on the question of appropriate discount rate. In fact, I have been unable to find *any* statute that specifies a discount rate for agencies to follow. On judicial review, the question will therefore involve a claim that the agency's choice is arbitrary. Here the national government shows strikingly (and inexplicably) variable practices. As noted, the Office of Management and Budget suggests a 7% discount rate,[89] departing from a 10% rate in the 1980s. But agencies are not bound by OMB guidelines, and they have ranged from as low as 3% (Food and Drug Administration, Department of Housing and Urban Development) to as high as 10% (EPA).[90] In fact, the same agency sometimes endorses different discount rates for no apparent reason – with EPA, for example, selecting a 3% rate for regulation of lead-based paint as compared to 7% for regulation of drinking water and 10% for regulation of emissions from locomotives.[91] Here government practice seems extremely erratic.

---

[85] See Michael Gerrard, Demons and Angels in Hazardous Waste Regulation, 92 NW L. Rev. 706, 742–3 (1998).

[86] Derek Parfit, Reasons and Persons 357 (Oxford: Oxford Univ. Press, 1984).

[87] Valuable treatments include Richard Revesz, Environmental Regulation, Cost–Benefit Analysis, and the Discounting of Human Lives, 99 Col. L. Rev. 941 (1999); Comment, Judicial Review of Discount Rates Used in Regulatory Cost–Benefit Analysis, 65 U. Chi. L. Rev. 1333 (1998).

[88] Thomas McGarity, Some Thoughts on "Deossifying" the Rulemaking Process, 1992 Duke L. J. 1385.

[89] See OMB, Benefit–Cost Analysis of Federal Programs, 57 Fed. Reg. at 53520 (1992).

[90] See Comment, supra note 87 in this chapter, at 1336–7.

[91] Id. at 1337.

From the purely economic standpoint, there are serious conundrums here. The impetus for discounting future effects stems from the judgment that, in the context of money, discounting future benefits and losses is entirely rational: A dollar today is worth more than a dollar tomorrow. There are two reasons for this: investment value (or opportunity cost) and pure time preference.[92] A dollar today can be invested, and for this reason it is worth more than a dollar a year from now. An emphasis on the investment value of money yields a discount rate of roughly 5 to 7%. Quite apart from this point, people generally seem to have a preference for receiving money sooner rather than later. People value current consumption more than they value future consumption; for this reason alone, $1,000 is worth more today than in a decade. An inquiry into pure time preference produces discount rates of roughly 1 to 3%. Though they lead to different numbers, both points justify discounting future income gains and losses.

So far, so good. The problem is that notwithstanding conventional wisdom among economists, these points are not easily taken to justify a discount rate for the nonmonetary benefits of regulation, such as fatalities averted. If a regulation will save ten lives this year, and ten years annually for the next ten years, it cannot plausibly be urged that the future savings are worth less than the current savings, on the ground that a current life saved can be immediately "invested." The point about investment value, or the opportunity cost of using capital, seems utterly irrelevant here. With time preference, things are less clear. Perhaps people would rather save ten lives today than ten lives in a decade. But it is unclear that this is so; and even if it is, what moral status would such a time preference have? Almost certainly it makes sense to say that it would be worse for you to lose your limb now than to lose it in ten years; in the latter case, you will have ten more years of use of the limb. And probably it makes sense to say that agencies should attend to life-years saved, not just lives saved. But holding all this constant, the death of a thirty-five year old in 2004 does not seem worth more than the death of a thirty-five year old in 2044. And since different people are involved, the moral problem is serious: The preference of the chooser in 2002 is certainly relevant to determining that chooser's own fate, and the timing of risks that might come to fruition for that chooser; but the chooser's preference cannot easily be used to determine the fate of someone not yet born.

These points suggest that, as Richard Revesz suggests, it is important to distinguish two issues that go under the name of "discounting" and that have yet to be separated in administrative practice: (a) latent harms, in the form of exposures whose consequences will occur later in someone's lifetime; and (b) harms to future generations.[93] It is reasonable to say that latent harms

---

[92] Id. at 1341–6.

[93] See Revesz, supra note 87 in this chapter.

should count for less than immediate ones because they remove fewer years from people's lives, and because people do seem to prefer, other things being equal, a harm in the future to a harm in the present. For latent harms, some kind of discount rate is sensible. Return, for example, to the case of arsenic. In its regulation, the EPA treats an arsenic death in the future as equivalent to an arsenic death in the present, even though an arsenic death is likely to come, if it does come, many years after exposure.[94] On this count, the EPA's judgment seems wrong, even arbitrary; some kind of discount rate is clearly appropriate here. On the other hand, OMB's 7 percent figure, based on the investment value of money, is probably too high. There is no reason to believe that the discount rate for future health harms is equal to the discount rate for future income effects, but there is considerable reason to believe otherwise. Indeed, the use of a 7 percent discount rate, if it decisively affects the ultimate decision, would seem to be legally doubtful – arbitrary in its own way.

But the case of harms to future generations, or people not yet born, is altogether different, and in that case the usual grounds for discounting monetary benefits are quite inapplicable. For this reason, some people think that no discounting is appropriate for the nonmonetary benefits of regulation.[95] On this view, a life-year saved is a life-year saved, and it does not matter, for purposes of valuation, when the saving occurs.

But there is a major objection to this way of proceeding: It would appear to require truly extraordinary sacrifices from the present for the sake of the (infinite) future. Perhaps the "failure to discount would leave all generations at a subsistence level of existence, because benefits would be postponed perpetually for the future."[96] On the other hand, it is not clear that the assumption behind this objection is convincing. Technological and other advances made by the current generation benefit future generations as well, and hence impoverishment of the current generation would inevitably harm those who will come later.[97] In any case, there is a hard ethical question here – how much the current generation should suffer for the benefit of the future – and a judgment against discounting would not answer that question unless we were sure that as a matter of policy, we should be engaging in maximizing some aggregate welfare function.[98]

---

[94]   66 Fed. Reg. at 7013.

[95]   Revesz, supra note 87 in this Chapter, at 987–1009 (offering a qualified version of this view).

[96]   See David Pearce & R. Kelly Turner, Economics of Natural Resources and the Environment 223–4 (Baltimore: Johns Hopkins Univ. Press, 1990).

[97]   Revesz, supra note 87 in this chapter, at 994.

[98]   Tyler Cowen & Derek Perfit, Against the Social Discount Rate, in Justice Between Age Groups and Generations 149, Peter Laslett & James Fishkin, eds. (New Haven, Conn: Yale Univ. Press, 1992).

It is not at all clear that this form of maximization is the appropriate choice to make.

At this point it should be clear that these issues are exceedingly complex and that agencies asked to engage in cost–benefit analysis have no clear path to an appropriate choice of discount rate for future generations. In the face of the underlying conundrums, the most that a reviewing court can require is a rationale for the agency's choice that is both articulated and reasonable.

CONCLUSION

In this chapter, I have attempted to identify the cost–benefit default principles, to defend their use, and to explore their meaning for the future. At their least intrusive, the cost–benefit default rules *allow* the agency to go in the suggested direction when the statute is unclear. At their most intrusive, the principles *require* the agency to act in the way they suggest unless Congress has unambiguously said otherwise. I have argued on behalf of both the least and most intrusive version of the cost–benefit default rules, by suggesting that they are likely to give sense and rationality the benefit of the doubt. At the same time, I have urged that the argument on their behalf is presumptive only, and that in certain contexts, agencies have good reasons for embarking on a different course. The question is whether agencies have been able to suffer a reasonable defense of their decision to that effect.

I have also attempted to set out some guidelines for the future, both under the cost–benefit default principles and under statutes that point in the same direction. It is necessary for agencies to particularize the idea of significant and de minimis risks through quantitative guidelines. A large point here is that the statistical probability of harm is not all that matters; the size of the exposed population is important as well. Feasibility is not an off–on switch, and here too agencies should specify what they understand the term to mean, beginning with the admittedly vague notion that massive dislocations would be both necessary and sufficient to show that regulation is not feasible. We have seen that with respect to valuation of life and health, market measures can provide a good start, from which agencies are entitled to make reasonable adjustments. We have also seen that the most difficult issue involves selection of the appropriate discount rate. Reviewing courts should not require agencies to apply the same discount rate to life and health that they apply to money; with respect to discounting, there are good reasons to distinguish money from other goods. The most that courts can do is to impose ceilings and floors on agency judgments, by requiring a good rationale for whatever discount rate is chosen.

9

Cleaning the Air

In issuing and revising a national ambient air quality regulation under the Clean Air Act, the Environmental Protection Agency should provide a detailed "benefits analysis." To this end, it should undertake two tasks. First, it should specify the range of benefits that it believes will result from the regulation, along with a specification of the range of benefits that it believes would result from at least two reasonable alternative approaches, one stricter and one more lenient. In the process, EPA should identify the *residual risk* left under the competing regulatory regimes; it should also acknowledge scientific uncertainty, to the extent that uncertainty exists and requires guesswork. This proposal is an effort to strengthen the role of sound science in environmental protection. Second, the EPA should explain why it believes that the chosen rule is preferable to the less and more stringent alternatives – why the set of benefits to be received from the selected rule justify that rule, whereas the set of benefits to be received from the less and more stringent rule do not. In the process it should explain why the residual risk left by the selected rule is acceptable, while the residual risk left by the less stringent rule is not. This proposal is an effort to strengthen the role of democratic forces in environmental protection.[1]

If necessary, reviewing courts should require the EPA to perform these tasks. Taken together, the two proposals should increase the level of consistency across regulations, reducing the power of well-organized private groups and also diminishing the risks associated with both insufficient and excessive environmental regulation. If the EPA has undertaken the two tasks, and carried them out in a reasonable way, judicial review is at an end; courts should uphold the EPA's decision.

---

[1] Of course, costs are important, too; the two proposals are based on the current understanding that benefits, but not costs, may be taken into account in issuing primary standards. The question of costs is taken up later.

Ideas of this kind have potentially broad implications, extending well beyond the Clean Air Act and even the EPA, to the work of the Occupational Safety and Health Administration, the Consumer Product Safety Commission, and the National Highway Traffic and Safety Administration as well. They would mark a key moment in the movement toward a system of environmental protection that is at once more democratic and better informed. At the same time, they would accelerate the continuing shift from 1970s environmentalism and indeed 1970s regulation in general, away from recognizing the existence of problems of safety and health and toward assessing their magnitude, in such a way as to reduce both regulatory paranoia and regulatory neglect, and to put a premium on the acquisition of information. These are the claims that I will attempt to defend in this chapter.

A note at the outset: With respect to ambient air quality standards, I am making a plea for "benefits analysis" – not for cost–benefit analysis, for which I have been arguing throughout. There are two reasons for limiting my plea to the analysis of benefits. The first is narrowly legalistic: The relevant provisions of the Clean Air Act simply do not permit the EPA to consider costs. The second reason, mentioned in Chapter 8, is pragmatic: When the EPA sets national standards, it merely initiates a process, and costs are indeed pertinent when states actually implement those standards. Now it is possible to think that the relevant provisions of the Clean Air Act should be amended so as to allow the EPA to engage in cost–benefit balancing when setting standards in the first instance; I shall discuss this issue later. My basic argument here is that even if the EPA is focusing on "public health" alone, it should try to be as quantitative as possible, so as to ensure sense, and transparency, in government's decision to regulate to one point rather than another. In this way, we shall see that quantitative risk analysis – more simply, benefits analysis – is appropriate even under statutes that ban consideration of cost.

THE CLEAN AIR ACT

The Clean Air Act may well be the most important of all environmental statutes. Its effects include a wide range of beneficial consequences for human health and well-being and extremely high costs on the private sector. The Environmental Protection Agency estimates overall compliance costs at $0.5 trillion.[2] The act's claim to success rests on enormous improvements in ambient air quality and

---

[2] J. Clarence Davies & Jan Mazurek, Pollution Control in the United States: Evaluating the System 130 (Washington, D.C.: Resources for the Future, 1998).

corresponding health benefits. The EPA estimates that the act prevents at least 45,000 deaths annually and that it also prevents a minimum of 13,000 heart attacks and 7000 annual strokes.[3] On a standard (though not undisputed) view, the benefits of the act, ranging between $5.6 trillion and $49.4 trillion, far exceed its costs.[4]

The act has nonetheless been subject to telling criticism. The foundation of clear air regulation consists in the EPA's issuance of nationally uniform ambient air quality standards. But in light of the extraordinary diversity of the fifty states, it is not clear that the idea of national standards can be rationally defended. As a matter of law, it is generally agreed that the standard-setting process does not and cannot involve consideration of costs. But does it make sense, or is it even feasible, to say that national standards will be founded on an assessment of benefits alone, conducted in a cost vacuum? If an improvement in ambient air quality would produce health benefits that are small but not trivial, isn't it clear that the improvement is justified if compliance costs are trivial, but perhaps not if the costs are very high? There is reason to think that at least in some cases, an understanding of costs has affected the EPA's decision about appropriate standards – but that the cost–benefit balancing has been left implicit and free from public scrutiny and review.[5]

Perhaps the largest question involves the criteria by which EPA decides whether one or another level of regulation is (in the statutory phrase) "requisite to protect the public health." For most pollutants, air quality at various levels is not either "safe" or "not safe"; there are diminishing degrees of risk associated with diminishing degrees of exposure. On what basis is a particular level of residual risk said to be the appropriate one? What judgments do, or should, enter into that conclusion? The EPA has been criticized for sometimes suggesting, in

---

[3] Id. Judgments about benefits, nonmonetized but especially monetized, are highly sensitive to contentious assumptions; hence, the "bottom line" numbers should be taken with many grains of salt. See Randall Lutter, An Analysis of the Use of EPA's Benefit Estimates in OMB's Draft Report on the Costs and Benefits of Regulation (October 1998), available at *aei.brookings.org*, urging the use of plausible alternative assumptions and that EPA's benefit calculations are inflated. See also Heinzerling, supra note 5 in Chapter 2 (urging that cost per lives saved are inflated, also because of contentious assumptions). Though coming from different directions, Lutter and Heinzerling both argue, convincingly, that characterization of both benefits and costs can shift dramatically with small changes in assumptions, an argument that much bears on the central claims of this Chapter.

[4] See Davies & Mazurek, supra note 2 in this chapter, at 130, 147.

[5] See id; see also Boyden Gray, The Clean Air Act Under Regulatory Reform, 11 Tul. Env. L. J. 235 (1998).

an unhelpful and conclusory fashion, that it chooses the "safe" level, as if this were solely a technocratic judgment and as if "safety" were an on–off switch,[6] when its decision about permissible levels rests instead on a series of political, scientific, and economic judgments and compromises.

There are two problems with this state of affairs. The first involves democratic deliberation. If the EPA does not give a clear sense of the range of adverse effects, and if it does not say why one set of such effects calls for regulation and another does not, the public and its representatives are not informed of the nature of the underlying questions, and people are unable to evaluate the choices actually made. Under the EPA's articulated position, a purely technical issue (Would a certain level be safe?) is sometimes substituted, at least publicly, for the real and more complicated ones (What level of safety is appropriate in light of all the relevant factors? Why should one level of regulation be preferred to another?).

The second problem involves sound regulatory policy. Any proposed national standard could be loosened or tightened, and the question is whether the agency has chosen the optimal, or at least a reasonable, regulatory "point." Without a clear and (to the extent possible) quantified presentation of the expected environmental benefits of the various alternatives, there can be no assurance that the agency has chosen that point, rather than one that is too strict or too lenient.

SETTING NATIONAL STANDARDS

THE KEY PROVISIONS

The Clean Air Act was enacted in 1970. Though many hundreds of pages in length, some of them mind-numbingly specific and detailed, the act offers two remarkably brief provisions designed to set the statutory program in motion.

The first of these provisions, and the central focus here, involves primary national ambient air quality standards.[7] Here the EPA is asked to set standards "the attainment and maintenance of which in the judgment of the Administrator," based on air quality criteria documents "and allowing an adequate margin of safety, are requisite to protect the public health." The second of these provisions involves secondary national ambient air quality standards, which the EPA must set at levels "requisite to protect the public welfare from any known or anticipated adverse effects associated with the presence of such

---

[6] See Landy et al., supra note 3 in Chapter 4, at 379–83. The criticism is not sound as applied to the particulates and ozone regulations, but here too, the EPA's explanation leaves many open questions.

[7] 42 USC 7409 (b).

air pollutant in the ambient air."[8] "Welfare" is defined to include "effects on soils, water, crops, vegetation, manmade materials, animals, wildlife, weather, visibility, and climate, damage to and deterioration of property, and hazards to transportation, as well as effects on economic values an on personal comfort and well-being."[9] For secondary standards, involving welfare rather than health, there is no provision for an "adequate margin of safety." But the secondary standards are anticipated to be more stringent than the primary ones; notice in particular the statutory emphasis on plant and animal lfe.

These provisions have three especially noteworthy features. First, they seem not to contemplate any consideration of cost in the standard-setting process. Primary standards are based on health, apparently to be assessed in a cost vacuum, while secondary standards are based on welfare, also apparently to be assessed without regard to cost. Second, the standards are fully national – even though political judgments about air quality vary greatly from state to state, and even though the effects of improved air quality (on the cost and benefit sides) are highly variable from one state to another. Finally, both provisions appear to contemplate the existence of "safe thresholds." The basic idea is that the EPA should ensure that air is "safe" and that public welfare is "protected." What makes this idea distinctive is its artificiality. To be sure, we could imagine pollutants for which the evidence indicated a point of "no risk" or "de minimis risk." It is possible to construct a dose–response curve for which risks effectively vanish at a certain defined point (see Appendix D). But for many pollutants, there are diminishing degrees of risk, associated with diminishing degrees of pollution. Safety is not an off–on switch; it is a matter of degree. When it is said that a certain level of pollution is safe, what is really meant is that the residual risk is acceptable or tolerable – not that there is no risk at all. Consider, for example, this commendably direct testimony from the Chair of EPA's Scientific Advisory Committee's panel on ozone and particulates, unambiguously confessing the impossible nature of the task imposed on the EPA by the act:

> Based on information now available, it appears that ozone may elicit a continuum of biological responses down to background concentrations. It is critical to understand that a biological response does not necessarily imply an adverse health effect. Nevertheless, this means that the paradigm of selecting a standard at the lowest-observable-effects-level and then providing an "adequate margin of safety" is not

[8] 42 USC 7409(b)(2).
[9] 42 USC 7602(h).

possible. It further means that risk assessments must play a central role in identifying an appropriate level.[10]

How might we explain the enactment of provisions that seem at once so vague, rigid, and artificial? Much of the answer lies in the distinctive political dynamic of environmental debates in the late 1960s and early 1970s, in which citizens wanted air to be safe and politicians who failed to respond were at great risk. In the 1970s in particular, politicians would proceed at their peril if they asserted that safety could be compromised by other goals. At the same time, politicians were affected by, and doubtless catered to, the pervasive psychological urge for certainty, as confirmed by evidence that people are willing to pay a great deal for "no risk" and much less for "substantially less risk."[11] The idea that the Clean Air Act would produce absolute safety rather than merely reduced risk made it far easier to support, and far harder to challenge.

Undoubtedly Congress believed that it was delegating to EPA the power to be reasonable rather than unreasonable, and in any case the act allowed various safeguards in the event that compliance proved to be excessively costly. As we will see, the most important safeguard consisted in a form of (implicitly authorized) civil disobedience on the part of all relevant actors, including the EPA, which was simply not prepared to shut down automobile traffic in Los Angeles, a step that would have been necessary to produce compliance with national air quality standards.

PROBLEMS AND PUZZLES

All these points have created serious difficulties for the EPA in practice. For nonthreshold pollutants, it seems both natural and sensible to assess further reductions in terms of their cost. If, for example, the expense of reducing sulfur dioxide from 0.3 to 0.2 ppm is trivial, then the reduction is almost certainly worthwhile (unless the dose–response curve has a most peculiar shape). Even if there is little direct evidence of adverse human health effects at 0.2 ppm, this is likely to be a result of the limited data rather than an absence of such effects. But matters look very different if the cost would run into the tens of billions of dollars. When benefits are highly uncertain, it is peculiar to say that EPA cannot consider cost, especially since health gains are almost inevitable as permissible exposure levels decline.

[10] Prepared Testimony of George T. Woolf, Chair, EPA's Clean Air Scientific Advisory Committee's Panel on Ozone and PM, Before the House Judiciary Committee, July 29, 1997.

[11] See Daniel Kahneman and Amos Tversky, Prospect Theory: An Analysis of Decision Under Risk, 47 Econometrica 263 (1979). George Loewenstein et al., Risk As Feelings.

In light of this point, some critics have suggested that some kind of cost–benefit balancing inevitably occurs at EPA.[12] At least publicly, EPA denies this claim. Consider Administrator Carol Browner's suggestion:

> Costs of meeting the standards and related factors have never been considered in setting the national ambient air quality standards themselves.... [T]he focus has been entirely on health, risk, exposure and damage to the environment.... And the American public deserves to know whether the air in its cities and counties is unsafe or not; that question should never be confused with the separate issues of how long it may take or how much it may cost to reduce pollution to safe levels. Indeed, to allow costs and related factors to influence the determination of what levels protect public health would be to mislead the American public in a very fundamental way.[13]

Only insiders know for certain whether EPA does in fact consider costs in issuing national ambient air quality standards. But consider, by way of contrast and as a possible clue, the Administrator's explanation of the 1979 revision of the ozone standard:

> The Clean Air Act, as the Administrator interprets it, does not permit him to take factors such as cost or attainability into account in setting the standard; it is to be a standard that will adequately protect public health. He recognizes that controlling ozone to very low levels is a task that will have significant impact on economic and social activities. This recognition causes him to reject as an option the setting of a zero-level standard.... However, it is public health, and not economic impact, that must be the compelling factor in the decision.[14]

This explanation, difficult to follow though it is, is most naturally taken as suggestion that despite the nominal irrelevance of cost, costs do matter in the context of standard-setting for nonthreshold pollutants.

With respect to state-by-state variations, there is little question that the exceedingly high costs of attainment will, for many states, produce frequent violations of national requirements – and this has, in fact, turned out to be the case. Several decades after the initial issuance of ambient air quality standards

---

[12] See George Eads, The Confusion of Goals and Instruments: The Explicit Consideration of Cost in Setting National Ambient Air Quality Standards, in To Breathe Freely: Risk, Consent, and Air, Mary Gibson, ed. (New York: Bowman & Little Field, 1985).

[13] Testimony of Carol Browner before the Senate Environment and Public Works Committee, February 12, 1997.

[14] See 45 Fed. Reg. 55,066, 55072 (1980).

for ozone, for example, over 50 million people live in areas that are frequently in violation of national standards. Smaller numbers — but still many millions — of people live in nonattainment areas for other pollutants (see Appendix B for details). Indeed it is contemplated, by the 1990 revision of the act, that one of the nation's largest urban areas, Los Angeles, will not be in compliance until 2010 at the earliest.

The upshot is that in theory, the act requires nationally uniform standards; but in practice, it authorizes an enormous amount of variation among states. National standards have mostly served not as real law, but as targets or *aspirations* — flexible goals to which the federal government can point without, however, insisting on compliance unless or until it is reasonable. The aspirational quality of national standards has led Congress to enact an increasingly complex set of provisions for nonattainment areas, provisions that anticipate compliance in certain areas over a period of many years and that, in practice, therefore recognize the existence of reasonable variations across states.

This point leads to a more general one, bearing on cost–benefit balancing as well as federalism. The EPA's official position that standard-setting is cost-blind is complemented by explicit statements to the effect that cost, efficiency, and feasibility are relevant in making choices about compliance. In a way, these statements are puzzling, for the Supreme Court has held that cost, and infeasibility, are irrelevant to the EPA's decision whether to approve state implementation plans.[15] But the EPA appears to acknowledge that state implementation plans will themselves consider control costs, and also that cost will be relevant in setting schedules for compliance.

Finally, EPA must make hard choices about how safe is safe enough — choices that involve not merely the facts but also evaluative judgments about acceptable degrees of risk. A central question has to do with the ingredients of any judgment that a certain risk is too high; there are many important questions here. These include

- the *size* of the population at risk (whether 100,000, a million, or tens of millions of people are at risk);
- the *nature* of the population at risk (whether it involves a large number of children, whether only elderly people are affected, whether those affected have a preexisting condition such as asthma);
- the *likelihood of harm* for particular members of the affected population (whether the likelihood of incurring harm is 1 in 1,000, 1 in 10,000, or 1 in 1,000,000. Thus, for example, the plurality of the Supreme

---

[15] See *Union Electric v. EPA*, 427 US 246 (1976).

Court held, in the Benzene Case,[16] that OSHA was to regulate only "significant risks," and that a risk of one in a billion could not count as significant. OSHA now concludes that a lifetime annual risk over 1 in 1,000 counts as significant,[17] but undoubtedly the importance of addressing such a risk will depend on other factors, notably including the size of the affected population.);

- the *severity of the risk* (whether it involves cancer or mortality risks, or increased hospital admissions, bronchitis, respiratory symptoms, lost work days, or what the EPA calls minor restricted activity days).

EPA considers all these questions in issuing national standards. But EPA has developed no clear guidelines to discipline its judgment about when one or another level of regulation is appropriate. It has not said, for example, that if 100,000 people face a cancer risk of 1/1,000, regulation is presumptively desirable, but if 10,000 face a 1/1,000 chance of minor respiratory problems, regulation is presumptively not desirable. A reading of EPA's voluminous documents on the major air pollutants provides an enormous amount of data, but little information on the answers that would trigger a decision to increase or decrease regulation. As we will see, all the various points noted here might reasonably be turned into a kind of global figure, "quality-adjusted life years," attempting to quantify the various benefits from regulation.[18]

One final note: As we have seen throughout, an obvious and important question has to do with the *distributional* effects of national ambient air quality standards. Who bears the costs? Who receives the benefits? Full information is not available. An early study found that, under the act, poor people and African Americans are net gainers, whereas wealthy people and whites are net losers[19] – perhaps not a shocking finding in light of the fact that many of the adverse effects of air pollution are concentrated in large cities. This finding has been confirmed by more recent work, showing that economically disadvantaged people have been the big beneficiaries of the Clean Air Act.[20]

---

[16] *Industrial Union Department v. American Petroleum Institute*, 448 US 607 (1980).

[17] See *Building and Constructions Trades v. Brock*, 838 F.2d 1258, 1265 (DC Cir. 1988).

[18] Richard Zeckhauser & Donald Shepard, Where Now for Saving Lives?, 40 L. & Contemp. Probs. 5 (1976).

[19] See Henry M. Peskin, Environmental Policy and the Distribution of Benefits and Costs, in Current Issues in Environmental Policy, Paul Portney, ed. (Washington, D.C.: Resources for the Future, 1978).

[20] Matthew E. Kahn, The Beneficiaries of Clean Air Act Regulation, 24 Regulation 34 (2001).

REVISING NATIONAL STANDARDS – AND THE TYRANNY OF THE STATUS QUO

In 1971, EPA issued six national standards, governing ozone, particulates, carbon monocide, nitrogen oxides, and particulates 2.5. In 1978, EPA issued a seventh standard, involving lead; it did so as a result of a court order. These seven regulations amount to the centerpiece of EPA's regulatory system for the control of national ambient air quality.

Of course, it would be extremely surprising if the standards originally adopted in 1971 and 1978 turn out to survive new scientific evidence, and many people have urged that adjustments are desirable, in the direction of both tightening and loosening existing requirements. Congress has thus created an "agency-forcing" mechanism designed to require EPA reconsideration of primary and secondary standards. Under the act, EPA is required to review the relevant criteria and standards at least once every five years and to revise them "as appropriate" under the statutory guidelines. EPA is specifically required to consider, and to explain any significant departures from, the recommendations of CASAC, an independent committee established specifically to advise the administrators on air quality criteria and standards.

So much for the statutory requirements; the possibility of litigation raises further complexities. The EPA is highly vulnerable to suits by those seeking more stringent controls and new regulations based on apparent evidence of hazards at existing levels. If EPA does not act within the statutory period, or if it decides not to impose more stringent controls, it will predictably be faced by a suit from environmental organization – one that, in view of likely scientific evidence, has a nontrivial chance of success. This is so especially in light of a judicial suggestion that the administrator may be barred from declining "to establish a margin of safety in the face of documented adverse health effects."[21] But the EPA is also highly vulnerable to challenges by industry whenever it tightens a standard. Creative lawyers have a quite good chance of successfully challenging an EPA regulation whether it has tightened, or refused to tighten, existing standards.

It is therefore possible to venture a prediction: The day will eventually come when the same court of appeals holds that the EPA has behaved unlawfully both for regulating *above* a certain level and also for not regulating *below* that level! The basic point is that the centrality of litigation to environmental protection creates a new form of tyranny of the status quo – a great deal of inertia in favor

---

[21] *American Lung Association v. EPA*, 134 F.3d 388, 393 (DC Cir. 1998).

of the existing regulatory framework, whatever its content. The general problem for modern administrative law is that because of the complexity of the scientific evidence, skilled advocates are highly likely to be able to find a serious problem in the agency's rationale, a factor that makes rulemaking extremely cumbersome and increasingly encourages agencies to avoid it altogether.

THE RECORD

Thus far, it might be tempting to be quite skeptical of the Clean Air Act – to think that it rests on false assumptions, that it foolishly ignores costs and state-by-state variations, that it invites excessive litigation, and that it is an extremely crude foundation for regulatory policy. There is considerable sense in these skeptical reactions. But it must also be acknowledged that the act has done a great deal of good – indeed, that reductions in air pollution can plausibly be counted among the substantial success stories in regulatory government in the last half-century. The good news is that for all of the pollutants, there have been large improvements in ambient air quality (see Appendix B for details). Even the cost–benefit ratio appears to be quite good, at least according to most studies. A general review contains many criticisms of American efforts at environmental protection but concludes that "the benefits of the Clean Air Act seem clearly to outweigh the costs."[22] Thus a study of EPA rule between 1990 and 1995 found that the costs outweighed the benefits by no less than $70 billion.[23]

On the other hand, better tools could have produced similar results at a far lower expense (a point to which I return in Chapter 10). Thus there is evidence that with better tools, especially economic incentives, EPA could have achieved that same benefits at one-quarter of the costs.[24] There is also a problem of poor priority-setting. EPA's own studies suggest that it is not devoting resources to the most serious problems and indeed that inadequate priority-setting is a particular problem for clear air regulation, where large problems (such as indoor air pollution) receive relatively little attention. An important task for the future is to ensure that EPA devotes limited public and private resources to the most serious environmental hazards. Under the Clean Air Act, we often do not know if the EPA is tackling serious problems or little ones. With respect

---

[22] J. Clarence Davies & Jan Mazuerk, Regulating Pollution: Does the US System Work? 31 (Washington, D.C.: Resources for the Future, 1996).

[23] Id.

[24] See Tom Tietenburg, Emissions Trading: An Exercise in Reforming Pollution Policy (Washington, D.C.: Resources for the Future, 1985).

to national standards, it seems possible, in the abstract, that the EPA should be more stringent in some cases and less stringent in others. The only way to tell is to ensure more in the way of quantification.

PARTICULATES AND OZONE AT EPA: A CASE IN POINT

These issues are hard to understand in the abstract; it will be useful to specify them by reference to the EPA's efforts to revise its regulations governing particulates and ozone. The final rules for particulates and ozone were based on a massive amount of evidence, involving thousands of pages of documents. A general review of the evidence suggests that there would be both high benefits and high costs from the new particulates standard. For the new ozone standard, both costs and benefits would be significantly lower. EPA offered a great deal of detail about the harms apparently caused by particulates and ozone at existing levels. It also acknowledged uncertainties in the evidence. There are extensive discussions of the scientific literature. EPA ultimately chose a standard of 15/65 for particulate matter (PM) – more specifically, an *annual* standard, for $PM_{2.5}$, of 15 mg/m^3, based on the three-year average of annual arithmetic $PM_{2.5}$ concentrations; it also set an *hourly* standard of 65 mg/m^3, based on the three-year average of the ninety-eighth percentile of twenty-four-hour $PM_{2.5}$ concentrations.

EPA set a 0.08 ppm standard for ozone averaged over an eight-hour period, replacing the previous 0.12 ppm standard, averaged over a one-hour period. In an illustrative comment, Administrator Browner publicly defended the 0.08-ppm standard for ozone "because, though it is in the middle of the range recommended for consideration by CASAC and the EPA staff paper, as a policy choice it reflects the lowest level recommended by individual CASAC panel members and it is the lowest level tested and shown to cause effects in controlled human-exposure health studies."[25] In its explanation of the final rules, the EPA did not defend these selections against plausible alternatives. The Regulatory Impact Analysis (RIA) did better; it also discussed a more stringent and a less stringent alternative – particulates standards of 16/65 and 15/50, and ozone standards of 0.08 5th max and 0.08 3rd max.

The EPA's own public justification was extremely long and detailed but in important respects vague and conclusory. The heart of the EPA's analysis was as follows. (I discuss particulates as an illustration.) The EPA began by referring to "the greatly expanded body of community epidemiological studies." This evidence showed a range of adverse health effects, including premature mortality;

---

[25] See Browner testimony, supra note 13 in Chapter 9. The quotations below are taken from EPA's amount at 62 Fed. Reg. 38, 652 (1997).

and there was also evidence that children, the elderly, and asthmatics are most vulnerable to these effects. More particular evidence emerged from quantitative risk estimates from two example cities, estimates that included a judgment that existing standards create residual risks of "hundreds of premature deaths each year, hundreds to thousands of respiratory-related hospital admissions, and tens of thousands of additional respiratory-related symptoms in children." (In an inadvertently hilarious qualification, the EPA added that the "epidemiological findings cannot be wholly attributed to inappropriate or incorrect statistical methods, misspecification of concentration-effect models, biases in study design or implementation, measurement errors" and the like.) But the EPA noted that the results "should be interpreted cautiously" and should be taken to "provide ample reason to be concerned that there are detectable health effects attributable to PM at levels below the current standards."

The EPA's basic claim was that "the increase in relative risk is small for the most serious outcomes" but "significant from an overall public health perspective, because of the large number of individuals in sensitive populations that are exposed to ambient as well as the significance of the health effects involved." International evidence, and evaluations by over 1,000 experts, supported the view that the existing standard was insufficiently protective. Much of the EPA's discussion involved the fact that existing evidence does not reveal mechanisms to explain the range of reported adverse effects. And frequently the EPA repeated what appeared to be a key phrase, almost a mantra, to the effect that the data "provides the basis for decisions on standard levels that would reduce risk sufficiently to protect public health with an adequate margin of safety, recognizing that such standards will not be risk-free."

To the EPA's credit, it did offer some discussion of both less stringent and more stringent alternatives. But the discussion is quite brief, especially considering the centrality of the comparative question. As against the less stringent possibilities, EPA said that "despite well recognized uncertainties, the consistency and coherence of the epidemiological evidence and the seriousness of the health effects require a more protective response." As against those who argued for more stringent regulation, EPA said that "the inherent scientific uncertainties are too great" and also that such regulation "might result in regulatory programs that go beyond those that are needed to effectively reduce risks to public health." Studies "provide some suggestion of risks extending to lower concentrations, but they do not provide a sufficient basis for establishing a lower annual standard level."

Hence any reader is likely to be puzzled about exactly why EPA chose the particular regulations it did—about why it did not regulate either somewhat more or somewhat less. A special puzzle is why the EPA did not impose more stringent controls on particulates; the RIA shows that a more stringent regulation would have produced $4 billion in increased health benefits. The problem is not that the EPA was careless or off-hand; its exhaustive documentation was anything but that. The problem is that, in the explanation accompanying the final rules, EPA did not attempt to quantify the risks under competing standards, nor did it show the basic value judgment that would deem one risk too high, another risk acceptable, and another risk too low (that is, below the level requisite to protect the public health.)

In many ways, the most informative document was, in fact, the RIA. It was the most informative document because it provided actual numbers on the benefits (including nonmonetized and monetized quantities) and cost sides. The problem was that in its justification, EPA made little use of this document. Indeed, the RIA was written by a contractor, not by EPA personnel, and it had little or no influence on the ultimate decision. Some of the benefits calculations appear to have been rejected by EPA itself. Nonetheless, the RIA provided the only systematic discussion of the consequences of the approach chosen and of alternative approaches. Here are some of the principal conclusions:

(a) The new particulates regulation would prevent 350 annual mortalities; 6,800 cases of chronic bronchitis; 1,100 cases of acute bronchitis; about 1,200 hospital admissions averted from, for example, congestive heart failure (130) and respiratory problems (470); 106,000 lost work days; and 879,000 minor restricted activity days.

(b) The new ozone regulation would prevent 0 to 80 deaths; 130 emergency department visits for asthma; 29,840 acute respiratory symptoms; 0 to 530 chronic bronchitis cases; 0 to 20 hospital admissions for congestive heart failure; 0 to 50,440 lost work days; and 0 to 420,300 minor restricted activity days. (Note that in both cases the RIA specifies a range, which is a tribute to candor in the midst of scientific uncertainty.)

(c) All these benefits are monetized: $4.8 million per life saved; $120,000 per life-year saved; $12,700 per respiratory illness; $16,600 per congestive heart failure for those over 65; $9,000 for emergency department visits for asthma; $260,000 for chronic bronchitis; $83 per lost work day; and $38 per minor restricted activity day.

(d) For the health regulation of ozone, the overall analysis shows, by 2010, benefits of $0.4 billion (low-end estimate) to $2.1 billion (high-end estimate), and costs of $1.1 billion. For particulates, the benefits range from $19 billion to $104 billion, whereas the costs are anticipated to be $8.6 billion. A noteworthy point is that the ozone rule might have negative net benefits of −$0.7 billion, if the low-end estimate is correct.

(e) The RIA also suggests the costs and benefits of the two alternatives. The more stringent particulates standard would have high-end benefits of $108 billion and costs of $9.4 billion; the less stringent particulates would have high-end benefits of $90 and costs of $5.5 billion. The less stringent ozone standard would have high-end benefits of $1.6 billion and costs of 0.9 billion; the more stringent ozone standard would have high-end benefits of $2.9 billion and costs of $1.4 billion. The most noteworthy point here is that, by the EPA's own accounting, the more stringent particulates standard would have produced $4 billion in greater benefits (on the high-end estimate). This would seem to count as a substantial improvement in public health, especially considering the fact that each life is valued at $4.8 million; translated into lives, the more stringent regulation would prevent more than 200 additional deaths each year. EPA did not square this conclusion with its decision not to choose more stringent regulation. Indeed, it seems clear that EPA's own calculations showed that a tighter particulates standard would have produced far greater health benefits than the ozone standard; this leaves a serious unexplained anomaly in the two standards taken together.

(f) A serious gap in the RIA is that it does not give low-end estimates for the benefits associated with the alternatives; only high-end estimates are given for these. For the options actually chosen, a range is specified, which greatly assists assessment of the EPA's judgment. But without the range, it is hard to compare the options not chosen. An additional problem, reflected in the EPA's explanation as a whole, is the absence of a detailed assessment — even a wholly benefits-based assessment — of why the options that were chosen were deemed superior to those that were not chosen.

In this light, what overall evaluation would be reasonable? If the EPA's conclusions are correct, the particulates regulation promises significant benefits, while the ozone regulation promises relatively small benefits at best. The basic problem is that the agency has not explained, in concrete terms, why it chose one level of regulation rather than another. What, then, should the agency do?

WHAT THE CLEAN AIR ACT BASICALLY MEANS

To approach this question, we must start with the law, which, it will be recalled, requires EPA to set standards at levels that, with an "ample margin of safety," is "requisite to protect the public health." The most reasonable interpretation is that the EPA must call for regulation of risks that are serious and substantial. At the same time, EPA cannot call for regulation of small or trivial risks, for such regulation would not be "requisite to protect the public health."

Thus if the residual risk of a pollutant is trivial or de minimis — if, for example, the risk involves minor respiratory problems but no more than that – then EPA is not obligated to regulate it. Indeed, EPA regulation of a trivial or de minimis risk should be held unlawful, on the ground that such regulation is not requisite to protect the public health, even with an adequate margin of safety. If EPA seeks to reduce exposure to ground-level ozone below a level that already ensures protection against all serious risks faced by substantial numbers of persons, it is acting unlawfully. (Indeed, there is a plausible argument that this is the case for EPA's new regulation of ozone.) On the other hand, EPA is required (not merely permitted) to regulate any substantial or significant risk. If, for example, 10,000 people are likely to die each year as a result of exposure to a certain level of lead, EPA must act; it is not authorized to allow that level of risk.

These points go a long way toward establishing EPA's basic responsibilities. Suppose, for example, that existing evidence shows increased mortality risks from sulfur dioxide at levels above 0.8 ppm, and increased hospital admissions at levels about 0.6 ppm, but no mortality risk from sulfur dioxide levels below 0.4 ppm and no increase in hospital admissions below 0.4 ppm, that there is chronic plant injury at 0.1 ppm, and also that respiratory problems increase among a small, sensitive subpopulation at 0.15 ppm. On the facts as stated, EPA's discretion is confined. It could not issue a primary standard above 0.6 ppm or so, and it could not issue a standard below 0.5 ppm or so – unless it could make extrapolations from the evidence that would suggest a substantial risk at lower levels. Of course, this is a stylized and artificial example, and often the evidence will allow a range of reasonable judgments (see Chapter 7). But that is an inevitable product of the uncertain science.

CEILINGS, FLOORS, AND BENEFITS ANALYSIS

I have emphasized that notwithstanding its commendable detail about the underlying evidence, the EPA's explanation of its rule leaves much to be desired. The agency's extensive discussion is abstract and conclusory on the key points. It does provide evidence that ozone and particulates can have adverse effects at current levels. But it does not give a sufficiently clear sense of the level of those adverse effects, nor does it explain why the particular, selected regulation was optimally suited to new information about health effects. This is a serious failure.

BENEFITS ANALYSIS

By way of response, I suggest that in issuing national ambient air quality standards, EPA should provide a detailed "benefits analysis." To improve the role of science, the benefits analysis should attempt to describe, in both qualitative and quantitative terms, the various savings from the selected regulation and at least two alternatives, one more stringent, the other less so. This is an effort to strengthen the role of technocratic forces by ensuring that EPA is acting pursuant to a clear understanding of the health and welfare effects of reasonable options. In the process, EPA should identify the residual risk left, under alternative approaches, by the pollutant in question and explain why that residual risk is not above the level "requisite to protect the public health." The EPA should thus take steps to identify the size of the population affected, the severity of the various risks, and the likelihood that members of any particular group will suffer the relevant effects. To the extent possible, it should attempt to quantify each of these items. It might say, for example, that 40 million people are at risk, that 10 million of these people are under the age of eighteen, that 5 million are over the age of sixty, that there is a 1/1,000 chance of cancer as a result of exposure, and that the relevant risks range from respiratory problems to hospitalization and missed work-days to cancer (each of which might be quantified).

The EPA should also explain why one set of savings, thus quantified, justifies regulation, whereas other sets of savings do not. Here there is an inevitable judgment of value, and no purely technocratic exercise. The EPA might conclude, for example, that one approach leaves an excessive risk to health because it would result in between 500 and 1,500 annual deaths as compared with the chosen approach, whereas another initiative would go beyond the level required to protect the public health because it would result in between 0 and 150 annual deaths, most of them involving the elderly. This is an effort to strengthen democratic forces in regulation, by ensuring that the relevant value judgment is made publicly and exposed to democratic view.

EPA should also attempt to reduce its own discretion by showing that at least as a presumption, risks above a certain level will not be tolerated ("risk ceilings") and that risks below a certain level ("risk floors") will be acceptable. It should, in short, explain why a standard for ozone of 0.08 ppm is to be preferred to a standard of 0.09 or 0.07 ppm, and do so by reference to generalizable criteria. If, as seems clear, the risks prevented by the new ozone regulation are far smaller than the risks that would be prevented by more stringent regulation of particulates, EPA should explain the apparent anomaly. A chief advantage of this approach is that it should ensure interregulation consistency, in such a way as to combat, simultaneously, interest-group power, public torpor, and public overreaction with respect to certain pollutants.

Of course, any analysis of expected benefits will depend on contentious assumptions. The most serious problem here is that, in many cases, scientific uncertainty will confound any attempt to quantify with anything like precision. In Chapter 7, we saw this point in great detail. In these circumstances, one of EPA's real questions involves timing: Does it act now, or does it wait until the scientific information provides more clarity with respect to health effects? Inaction would create potential problems, possibly even a significant number of preventable deaths; but action could create problems too, in the form of high costs for trivial health benefits. This is certainly a plausible reading of the situation with respect to both particulates and (especially) ozone; in both cases, we do not know enough to assign specific numbers to different exposure levels. When existing evidence does not justify any particular number, then EPA should do the best that it can to specify a reasonable range.

In terms of intergovernmental design, it makes sense to ensure that the analysis of the rule, and the alternatives to the rule, is developed in conjunction with another institution in the executive branch, such as the Office of Management and Budget, which already plays a role of this sort. The purpose of intergovernmental review of this kind would be to ensure a form of internal "peer review," designed to overcome possible biases and errors on the part of any particular bureaucracy. An external check is well-suited to accomplishing this goal.

AN ANALOGY: FROM HEALTH TO THE ENVIRONMENT

A promising approach to the evaluation of benefits comes from the health field, where much attention has focused on evaluating preferences for healthy conditions (or aversion to unhealthy ones) in terms of what are called quality-adjusted life years (QALYs).[26] A QALY is a measure of health based on people's attitudes toward various conditions. It rejects the concept of monetary evaluation of health; instead, it focuses on how people value various health states. It seeks to generate a means of comparing various states of health through a single metric so that comparisons and tradeoffs can be made for public policy purposes. The measure attempts to take into account both quantitative benefits of health improvement, such as increase in life expectancy, and more qualitative improvements, such as quality-of-life benefits.

The QALY approach works by asking people through interview techniques to express their strength of preference for various health states. The most advanced methods disaggregate the process by asking people to describe how they would value a health improvement along several dimensions: mobility, physical activity, social activity, and the kinds of symptom effects involved. The answers to these questions are combined into a single scale, ranked 0.0 (for death) to 1.0 (for optimum functioning). The result is an index of utility for health states measured on an interval (or cardinal) scale. By independently determining the cost of various treatments and their likely outcomes, reseachers can suggest a cost per QALY of various public programs. Alternative programs can be ranked in what is essentially a utility-based cost-effectiveness scale.

[26] The measure was first described by Zeckhauser and Shepard, supra note 18 in Chapter 9.

In the context of the Clean Air Act, it makes little sense to engage in surveys about how people rank various health risks. In the governing RIA, EPA has already attempted to measure willingness to pay to reduce various risks, and it could easily adapt these figures to generate numbers for overall risk reductions, defined in terms of quality-adjusted life-years. Lives saved might, for example, be converted into a life-years saved number, and EPA could add to this various numbers representing the other health gains to be brought about by the regulation. The approach to particulates might be compared to, and squared with, the approach to ozone, and these approaches might also be rationalized with existing regulation of lead, sulfur dioxide, nitrogen oxides, and carbon monoxide.

TOWARD A (NEW) COMMON LAW
OF REGULATORY PROTECTION

Through such a route, EPA could begin to develop what it should have provided long ago: a common law of public health protection. This would reflect a system of judgments indicating when a given set of harms is sufficient to trigger additional regulation, and also when a set of harms is too trivial to count as a legally cognizable public health problem. And eventually it should be possible to have quite disaggregated data, showing the geographical areas in which health problems are most concentrated. For example, the health risks of lead were concentrated in the inner city[27]; the same may well be true of particulates. If this is so, a careful benefits analysis could pave the way toward an understanding of where regulatory activity would accomplish the most good, in a way that would diminish some of the problems associated with a nationally uniform policy. Such an approach could also help to invigorate local processes for environmental protection, so as to allow a higher degree of coordination between the national government and states and localities.

This final point raises a general question about the content of any such common law: the status, for purposes of law and policy, of *interregulation inconsistency*. Suppose, for example, that the EPA leaves a much higher residual risk for particulates than for ozone, as indeed it plainly appears to have done here. Is this indefensible, or even unlawful? As we have seen, one of the virtues of the approach suggested here is that it attempts to promote consistency in the rule-making process, in such a way as to reduce the power of well-organized private groups. It might seem to follow that if EPA allows a much higher residual risk for one substance than for another, it should be vulnerable on judicial review — just as it would be open to attack if it allows a much lower residual risk for a particular pollutant. This does indeed follow. The question is whether EPA can

[27] See Kahn, supra note 20 in this Chapter.

defend apparent interregulation inconsistency in statutorily relevant terms (as, for example, by showing that children are at particular risk from one or another problem). If it cannot, it has acted unlawfully.

CONGRESS: SAFETY AND ITS COST

Should Congress amend the national ambient air quality provisions of the Clean Air Act? This is not the place for an extended discussion of that question; but the analysis thus far suggests three possibilities.

HOW SAFE IS SAFE ENOUGH?

As emphasized throughout, a crucial defect of the national ambient air quality provisions is that they seem to assume that whether air is safe can be assessed solely on the basis of the facts. The truth is that the facts might be able to show the degree of risk (at least within a range), but they cannot show whether any particular degree of safety is safe enough. The result of the statutory framework is to misframe the key question and also to give EPA little guidance for answering and asking that question. As we have seen, EPA has greatly struggled with the resulting difficulties.

Congress should amend the statute to identify the factors for EPA to consider in making the judgment about appropriate national standards. Congress might offer substantive guidance by saying, for example, that the EPA must consider risk severity, size of affected population, and likelihood of adverse effects at various exposure levels. On the procedural side, it might require EPA to identify, to the extent possible, the nature of the risks that it is reducing, and at the same time to attempt to quantify the relevant risk reductions. The strongest argument against an amendment to this effect is that it is unnecessary; if the EPA moved in the directions suggested earlier, it would essentially be interpreting the current statute as if it contained instructions of exactly this sort. But an amendment of this kind would at least provide a clear legislative signal and move EPA judgments in the direction of greater transparency.

MORE FLEXIBLE TOOLS

We now know that significant cost savings can be achieved by using more flexible, market-oriented instruments.[28] Sometimes, however, the EPA does not choose such instruments even when it is legally authorized to do so. It would make sense to amend the statute to require the EPA, wherever feasible, to

[28] See generally National Academy of Public Administration, The Environmental Goes to Market (Washington, D.C.: National Academy of Public Administration, 1994).

use economic incentives rather than a command-and-control approach. It is clear that an approach of this kind could save substantial resources, and if the instruments are properly chosen, it should do so without at the same time compromising air quality goals. An effort to encourage the EPA to select less-burdensome alternatives could send a desirable signal to attempt the least-cost methods of obtaining regulatory goals, and might in addition spur creative experimentation. I will return to this question in Chapter 10.

COSTS AND BENEFITS

A possible lesson of EPA experience with national standards is that EPA should be required or at least permitted to consider costs when setting such standards. The basic reasoning here is straightforward. If a reduction from 0.8 to 0.7 ppm would be a trivial expense, surely it should be required; if it would cost trillions of dollars, there had better be good grounds to believe in very substantial health benefits. A possible argument to the contrary is that national standards operate as aspirations, not ordinary law, and aspirations, at least, should be set on a health-only basis – not because there is a magic place where air quality is "safe," but because it is valuable to obtain, and use, a technocratic judgment that people should have air quality of a certain specified sort. The problem is that it is impossible to assess "safety" in a cost vacuum.

A better argument against an amendment to require cost–benefit analysis is that the statute, complex as it is, actually embodies a better accommodation of costs and benefits than would a statute that required cost–benefit analysis at the level of standard-setting. On this view, the optimal system is one in which EPA makes an initial, purely health-based judgment, and then the process of implementation allows costs to play a role at various stages, emphatically including an expectation that implementation will not be immediate. It will, in fact, be a product of a continuing inquiry into whether compliance is worthwhile, all things considered. A possible virtue of this state of affairs is precisely the aspirational quality of the health-based standard, setting a target against which various state performances can be measured. The aspirational quality can also contribute to technology-forcing, an important and often highly desirable phenomenon in environmental protection[29] and a phenomenon to which cost–benefit analysis is, at least in practice,[30] unlikely to contribute.

---

[29] Technology-forcing is not desirable if the costs of the forcing greatly exceed the benefits – if, for example, the new technology contributes little to air quality but substantially increases prices and diminishes wages.

[30] In principle, a competent cost–benefit analysis would include the costs of new technological developments. The problem is that government is likely to have very little information

In the abstract, it is hard to know whether this argument is valid. What is clear is that the statutory scheme, pragmatically defensible as it may be, is far from transparent and provides a set of confusing signals to the American public.

PAINTING WITH NUMBERS

Whenever an agency issues a regulation designed to diminish risks to health, safety, or the environment, it should attempt to identify the gains sought by the particular regulation it has chosen, and it should compare these gains to those under at least two reasonable alternative regimes, one stricter and one more lenient. In this light, the most serious problem with the EPA's performance in issuing national air quality standards is that it usually fails to explain, in simple, concise terms, its decision to require a particular level of ambient air quality. Sometimes the EPA acts as if it were pursuing safety and ensuring safe levels, without sufficiently acknowledging that, for most pollutants, the serious question is what degree of safety. To its credit, the EPA invariably offers extensive discussions of the underlying data, demonstrating that there is a genuine health risk at current levels. To the extent that it provides an explanation of its particular choices, the discussion often involves little more than evidence of nontrivial adverse effects at those current levels – evidence that may well argue for a reduction from current levels but that does not by itself call for any particular regulatory standard.

In this chapter, I have argued that EPA (and other agencies involved in similar tasks) should offer a detailed benefits analysis. The central goal of this approach would be to create a kind of federal common law of environmental protection, generated in the first instance by administrative agencies and designed to promote consistency and rationality in the protection of health and safety. I have also claimed that ordinary judicial review should require any national ambient air quality standard to be accompanied by an adequate explanation of why that level, rather than one more or less stringent, has been selected. By itself, this requirement calls (to the extent feasible) for a high degree of quantification from EPA. It also bears on the performance of other regulatory agencies entrusted with the task of promoting health, safety, and the environment.

about the cost of technological innovation, and industry is likely to overstate those costs by a significant amount.

10

Tools

What is the problem we wish to solve when we try to construct a rational economic order? On certain familiar assumptions, the answer is simple enough. *If* we possess all the relevant information, *if* we can start out from a given system of preferences, and *if* we command complete knowledge of available means, the problem which remains is purely one of logic.... This, however, is emphatically *not* the economic problem which society faces.... The reason for this is that the "data" from which the economic calculus starts are never for the whole society "given" to a single mind which could work out the implications and can never be so given.[1]

The tools by which government attempts to reduce risk are as important, in their way, as the goals that government has chosen. In this chapter, I urge a large-scale shift in the law of risk reduction, away from government commands and toward four alternative strategies: (1) disclosure of information, (2) economic incentives, (3) risk reduction contracts, and (4) free market environmentalism.

One of the purposes of this shift is to reduce the burdens on government, even or especially a government that aspires to engage in cost–benefit balancing. As we have seen, it is exceedingly difficult to come up with accurate numbers. Centralized planning by government is unlikely to work well, even if government is asking the right questions. Any effort to relieve government of its burdens is likely to have major advantages. Strategies that try to take advantage of market forces and to use the information that such forces provide are likely to be much better.

There is an additional point. All these strategies promise, in many settings, to produce regulatory benefits at a lower cost, potentially saving billions of dollars. The promise of equal gains at lower cost is important because it reduces

---

[1] Hayek, supra note 42 in Chapter 5.

the potentially adverse effects of expensive regulation, including higher prices and lower employment. It is also important because it helps to weaken political resistance to efforts to protect people against risks. A strategy that imposes lower costs will make the targets of regulation less skeptical of it. For this reason, the movement toward "cheaper tools" should be seen not just as an effort to help businesses and others subject to regulation but also as an indispensable means of promoting sensible regulation.

As we will see, the Toxic Release Inventory, a mere disclosure requirement, ranks as one of the greatest success stories in all of environmental law, producing large, cost-effective reduction in toxic emissions. The acid deposition program of the Clean Air Act, based on economic incentives and rejecting government mandates, ranks as another great success story, with annual costs of $870 million and annual benefits of $15 billion or more, including reductions in premature deaths (nearly 10,000 annually) and reduced cases of chronic bronchitis (more than 14,500 annually).[2]

The two programs offer exceptional models for the future. I will be urging far more ambitious programs in this vein. In particular, I suggest that government should move toward a "national warnings system," designed to ensure that people have a good sense of the risks that they are encountering from products and activities. I will also suggest that government should use economic incentives far more, partly by allowing a great deal of trading among pollution sources, so as to ensure that those who can reduce risks cheaply will do exactly that. In the particular area of global warming, emissions trading is indispensable to real progress. Sources of carbon dioxide should be given tradable emissions rights so that global reductions will be as cheap as possible. But trading is desirable in many domains. As we shall see, governments all over the world should be creating more and bigger "bubbles," allowing pollution sources to trade emissions rights so as to ensure that reductions will be made by those who can do so most cheaply. "More bubbles, and bigger bubbles" is a sensible slogan for the future, as I shall explain in some detail.

RIGID COMMANDS AND DIFFICULT CALCULATIONS

In controlling risk, governments often rely on command-and-control regulation, by which public officials allow people little flexibility in promoting risk reduction goals. Command-and-control regulation sometimes takes the form of technological mandates, through which government effectively requires particular

---

[2] See Robert Percival, Environmental Regulation, 3d ed., 596 (Boston: Aspen Law & Business 1999).

technologies that it prefers; consider catalytic converters for cars. More often, government does not specify technologies, but requires across-the-board reductions in emissions – saying, for example, that in ten years, all cars must emit 90 percent less carbon monoxide, on average, than they now do. Requirements of this kind are more flexible than technological mandates because they allow people to choose the least expensive means of acquiring risk reduction goals. But they have a rigidity of their own. How does government know what level of risk reduction is appropriate? Why 90 percent, rather than 70 percent, or 95 percent?

The same questions raise some serious problems with cost–benefit balancing as a whole. How can government possibly collect the information that would enable it, well in advance, to know the costs and benefits of various approaches to reduce risks? To know about costs, government must depend on regulated companies, which themselves lack some crucial information. In addition, regulated companies have a huge incentive to exaggerate the costs of regulation – to say that whatever government wants them to do, they cannot possibly do, without expending truly extraordinary amounts of resources. As a result, they overstate the actual numbers. In fact, overstatement has been common in the law of environmental protection. In retrospect, regulations that appeared to be extremely expensive, even to be infeasible, have often proved to cost a mere fraction of what was assumed. Consider the acid deposition program. Expected to cost $2 billion to $3 billion annually, the program has cost only $870 million per year.[3] One of the reasons is that companies are able to innovate – to produce cheaper methods of obtaining regulatory goals. The government is in a poor position to know whether and how much innovation is sensible or feasible.

In fact, a skeptic might say that, by itself, a requirement of cost–benefit analysis allows legislators to take credit for "getting the regulators under control" without forcing them to make hard choices, which remain with agencies and the president. This credit-claiming device can hardly substitute for fundamental reform. Imagine – to take a rough analogy – if the Soviet Union had decided (in, say, 1986) to replace an "absolutist" five-year plan for producing wheat with another five-year plan, one that better recognized the need for balancing the competing variables. This step would have been an improvement; a five-year plan based on governmental balancing is no less a five-year plan than one based on governmental absolutism. I have suggested the value of what I will call a "Hayekian turn" in risk regulation, one that would substitute, to the extent possible, market forces for government mandates. Governmental dictation of outcomes rooted in cost–benefit analysis is better than governmental dictation based on absolutism, but neither is ideal.

[3] See id.

In this light, we can easily imagine a generation of dreary cycles with respect to reform. In those cycles, conservatives might require more cost–benefit balancing, more procedures, more "sound science," and fewer deadlines for administrators; liberals might then argue against cost-benefit analysis and for solely health-based or solely technology-based standards, fewer procedures, and stricter deadlines; conservatives, a few years later, might seek greater procedural requirements and more attention to costs; liberals might respond with the familiar litany; and so on until, say, 2050. Something of this kind is not a bad description of regulatory debates since 1980. But its continuation would represent an enormous failure of imagination and creativity. It would fix American policy in outmoded debates of the early 1970s, before the outpouring of learning that makes the "more" or "less" debate seem increasingly unhelpful.

A state that is determined to control risks in a sensible way ought not to content itself with governmental specification of outcomes after governmental cost-benefit judgments. It ought instead *to encourage nongovernmental actors to generate information and to produce cost–effective outcomes on the basis of restructured incentives.* For example, a great advantage of economic incentives and disclosure remedies is that they reduce the informational burden on government and shift that burden to people who know relevant costs and benefits. Instead of requiring a certain technology for cars – a question that government is ill-equipped to answer – government might impose a fee or a tax on high-polluting vehicles. The latter strategy imposes a far less severe information-gathering burden on government, which no longer need choose among technologies. That choice would be made by the newly structured market.

RISK INFORMATION

Many people are unaware of the risks that they face in day-to-day life. Often workers do not know about toxic substances in the workplace or about the risks that such substances cause. Consumers of ordinary foods are usually unable to evaluate the dangers posed by fats, calcium, sugar, and salt. Ignorance of this sort is especially likely in light of the difficulties, stressed throughout this book, that ordinary people face in obtaining information about risk. Causation is extremely complex here, and accurate inferences are extremely difficult to draw. Often risks take many years to materialize. Individual susceptibility varies, and changing technology makes learning from the past a hazardous enterprise. Often companies are not asked to disclose the amount of pollution, or harm, that they impose; if they were asked to do so, they would almost certainly impose less pollution and less harm.

There are two large reasons for ensuring more disclosure of risk-related information. The first involves economic efficiency. The second involves democracy.

EFFICIENCY

From the economic point of view, there are several reasons why the market for information might fail. First, information is a public good in the technical sense that once it is available at all, or to anyone, it is likely to be available to everyone or to many people. People can thus capture the benefits of information without having to pay for its production. Once created, a report discussing the risks posed by carcinogens in the workforce may well benefit employees a great deal, but no individual employee has the right incentive to pay his proportional share for the report. Each employee has the incentive to "free ride" on the efforts of others. The result is that too little information will be forthcoming. The point applies to materials about shared risks in general.

Second, manufacturers sometimes have poor incentives to provide information about hazardous products. Competition over the extent of danger may decrease total purchases of the product rather than help any particular manufacturer to obtain greater sales. The phenomenon has sometimes played a role in discouraging competition over safety among manufacturers of tobacco products. At least in principle, the phenomenon should occur frequently, though there are certainly many cases in which companies compete to show that their products are safe.

Information asymmetries may produce a "lemons" problem, in which dangerous products drive safe ones out of the market.[4] Imagine, for example, that producers know which products are safe, but that consumers cannot tell. Sellers of safe products may not be able to compete if such products sell for no higher price than dangerous ones, if safe products are more expensive to produce, and if consumers are unable to tell the difference. In that case, the fact that sellers have information, while buyers do not, will ensure that lemons – here dangerous products – will dominate the market. Regulation designed to provide information is the proper remedy.

This remedy might take the form of governmentally provided information, education campaigns, or disclosure requirements. Such remedies may cost more than they are worth. But if they work, and if they are not too expensive, they should be favored on economic grounds. They may fortify the operation of

---

[4] See George Akerlof, The Market for "Lemons": Quality Uncertainty and the Market Mechanism, 84 Q. J. Econ. 488 (1970).

the marketplace. They may be a precondition for free choice, the background assumption of free markets.

We now have a good deal of empirical information about disclosure of risks. Studies suggest that disclosure can often be a helpful and cost-effective strategy.[5] Workers do indeed respond to new information about risks, quitting or demanding higher salaries. Consumers can react well to the disclosure about danger levels. In general, there is every reason to think that governmentally mandated disclosure, if suitably designed, is an effective mechanism for promoting economic efficiency. I will discuss these points in more detail later.

Democracy

Suppose that we wanted to increase the democratic character of contemporary government, by promoting citizen participation in and control over governmental processes. A good initial step would be for government to provide enough information so that people can make knowledgeable judgments. Government might itself supply information or require disclosure by private citizens and companies. Return, for example, to the matter of expenditures per life saved. As we have seen, what emerges is a crazy-quilt. At the very least, the American public should be informed of these disparities so that it can evaluate them. Provision of information about the content and expense of regulatory programs should be high on the governmental agenda.

More generally, people appear not to have a clear sense of the relationships among different risks that are confronted in everyday life. The resulting ignorance creates a large obstacle not only to informed decisions but also to citizenship. The problem appears in the private sector, in local government, and at the state and national levels. Workers uninformed of risks are unable to participate usefully in the process of deciding among different possible levels of workplace safety. Local communities, seeking to decide whether to allow toxic waste sites or plants that produce sulfur dioxide, need to be in a position to make informed choices. Instead they tend to react to sensationalistic anecdotes or to scare tactics.

A large virtue of a federal system is that it permits different states, having different values, to make different choices about social arrangements. In the context at hand, many decisions about the relations among industrial development,

---

[5] See W. Kip Viscusi & Wesley A. Magat with Joel Huber et al., Learning About Risk: Consumer and Worker Response to Hazard Information (Cambridge, Mass.: Harvard Univ. Press, 1987); Joel Huber, Informational Regulation of Consumer Health Risks, 17 Rand J. Env. 351 (1986); W. K. Viscusi & Charles J. O'Connor, Adaptive Responses to Chemical Labelling, 74 Am. Econ. Rev. 942 (1984).

employment, pollution, and risk must be made at the state level. An absence of information is a severe obstacle to this process. The same is true at the national level, where sensational anecdotes displace reasoned analysis of the alternatives. The most general way to put the point is to note that on the framers' view, America was supposed to be a deliberative democracy, in which representatives, accountable to the people, would make decisions through a process of deliberation uncontrolled by private factions. Without better information, neither deliberation nor democracy is possible. Legal reforms designed to remedy the situation are a precondition for democratic politics. The earlier discussion of a website providing risk information was designed to provide a start (see Chapter 5).

The national government has taken a number of steps in the right direction. Mandatory messages about risks from cigarette smoking, first set out in 1965 and modified in 1969 and 1984, are of course the most familiar example. The FDA has long maintained a policy of requiring risk labels for pharmaceutical products. The EPA has done the same for pesticides and asbestos. Congress requires warnings on products with saccharin. There are numerous other illustrations. Indeed, the effort to provide information counts as one of the most striking, if incipient, developments in modern regulatory law. Several initiatives are especially noteworthy.

In 1983, the Occupational Safety and Health Administration issued a Hazard Communication Standard (HCS), applicable to the manufacturing sector. In 1986, the HCS was made generally applicable. Under the HCS, chemical producers and importers must evaluate the hazards of the chemicals they produce or import; develop technical hazard information for materials safety data sheets and labels for hazardous substances; and, most importantly, transmit this information to users of the relevant substances. All employers must adopt a hazard communication program – including individual training – and inform workers of the relevant risks. There is empirical work suggesting that the HCS is bringing about good results in the labor market.[6]

As I have noted, some disclosure statutes are designed to trigger political rather than market mechanisms; here consumers are not directly involved. The most famous of these statutes is the National Environmental Policy Act (NEPA). Enacted in 1972, the principal goal of NEPA is to require government to compile and disclose environmentally related information before government goes forward with any projects having a major effect on the environment. NEPA does not require government to give environmental effects any particular weight, nor is there judicial review of the substance of agency decisions. The purpose of disclosure is principally to trigger political safeguards, coming from the

---

[6] See id.

government's own judgments or from external pressure. Hence any governmental indifference to adverse environmental effects is perfectly acceptable under NEPA: The idea behind the statute is that if the public is not indifferent, the government will have to give some weight to environmental effects.

In 1986, Congress enacted an ambitious statute, the Emergency Planning and Comunity Right to Know Act (EPCRA).[7] Under this statute, firms and individuals must report, to state and local government, the quantities of potentially hazardous chemicals that have been sorted or released into the environment. Users of such chemicals must report to their local fire departments about the location, types, and quantities of stored chemicals. They must also give information about potential adverse health effects. EPCRA has had important beneficial effects, spurring innovative, cost-effective programs from the EPA and from state and local government.[8] In fact, the requirement of disclosure has been one of the most unambiguous success stories in modern environmental law. The apparent reason is that environmentally concerned groups, and the media in general, tend to target the worst offenders, producing a kind of "environmental blacklist."[9] Companies that end up on the list are likely to take steps to reduce their emissions, and companies are also likely to take steps to ensure that they do not end up on the list.

The Food and Drug Administration (FDA) has also adopted informational strategies. In its most ambitious set of initiatives, the FDA (a) compelled nutritional labeling on nearly all processed foods, including information relating to cholesterol, saturated fat, calories from fat, and fiber; (b) required compliance with government specified serving sizes; (c) compelled companies to conform to government definitions of standardized terms, including, "reduced," "fresh," "free," and "low"; and (d) allowed health claims only if these (1) are supported by scientific evidence and (2) communciate clear and complete information about such matters as fat and heart disease, fat and cancer, sodium and high blood pressure, and calcium and osteoporosis.

Many other statutes involving health, safety, and the environment fall in this general category. The Animal Welfare Act is designed partly to ensure publicity about the treatment of animals. Covered laboratories are required to file reports with the government about their conduct,[10] with the apparent thought that the reports will deter noncompliance and also allow continuing monitoring. In addition to its various command-and-control provisions, the Clean Air Act

[7] 42 USC 9601 et seq.

[8] See GAO, Toxic Chemicals, Report to the Congress (Washington, D.C.: GPO, 1991).

[9] See Archon Fung & Dara O'Rourke, Reinventing Environmental Regulation from the Ground Up, 25 Environmental Management 115 (2000).

[10] Animal Welfare Act, 7 U.S.C. §§2131–59 (1994).

Table 10.1 Examples of informational regulation

	Trigger Market Reactions	Trigger Political Reactions
Duties imposed on private sector	Tobacco warnings legislation; nutrition regulation; warnings for television programming; hazardous warning regulation; Telecommunications Act of 1996 (ratings system)	EPCRA (annual reports); proposed broadcasters code; Animal Welfare Act; Clear Air Act's "risk management plans"; Age Discrimination Act
Duties imposed on government	Warnings about the use of drugs	EPCRA (Toxic Release Inventory); NEPA; Safe Drinking Water Act; FECA

requires companies to create and disclose "risk management plans" involving accidental releases of chemicals; the plans must include a worse case scenario.[11] President George W. Bush has sought to reduce greenhouse gas emissions in part by compiling information about who does what, with the hope that public disclosure will promote voluntary reductions. The Office of Information and Regulatory Affairs has asked the Food and Drug Administration to disclose trans-fatty acids in the Nutrition Facts panel of food, urging that disclosure could, at relatively low cost, prevent up to 17,000 cases of coronary heart disease each year. The Safe Drinking Water Act was amended in 1996 to require annual "consumer confidence reports," to be developed and disseminated by community water suppliers.[12] Statutes governing discrimination and medical care also seem committed partly to the idea that "sunlight is the best of disinfectants"[13]; thus they require covered institutions to compile reports about their conduct and compliance with applicable law. As noted, the Federal Election Committee Act (FECA) requires political committees to disclose a great deal of information about their activities. In the same category is a proposed code for television broadcasters, which is designed partly to ensure publicity about the public service activities of various stations; the goal is to ensure more in the way of such activities indirectly and simply by virtue of the fact that there will be a public accounting. For an overview, consider Table 10.1.

These initiatives are simply a beginning. Broader and more ambitious programs, coordinating the general communication of social risks, are very much in

[11] 42 USC 7412(r).
[12] 42 USC 300g-3 (c)(4) (1996).
[13] The phrase comes from Louis Brandeis, Other People's Money 62 (New York: St. Martins Press, 1995).

order. It has been suggested that government might eventually develop a "national warnings system" containing a systematized terminology for warnings.[14] Such a system could apply to all contexts and risks, and give a uniform sense of risk levels. The existence of a uniform language would make it possible to assess risks across a wide range of social spheres. Most important of all, such a system would perform a vital educative function, one that could complement the functioning of markets and provide a necessary precondition for democratic choice.

WHEN INFORMATION IS TOO MUCH – OR ISN'T ENOUGH

Notwithstanding the potential for much progress here, there are two problems with informational strategies. First, the provision of information can be expensive. Second, the provision of information can be ineffectual or even counterproductive. Information strategies can fail cost–benefit balancing.

Consider, for example, the fact that the government estimated the cost of the FDA disclosure rules as no less $1.7 billion over twenty years. The president of the National Food Processors Association claimed that the first year costs alone would exceed $2 billion.[15] In either case, the cost is significant. OSHA's hazard communication policy is estimated to save 200 lives per year – a lot – but at an annual cost of $360 million. The expenditure per life saved is therefore $1.8 million – far better than a large number of regulations, and an amount well worth spending, but more than many agencies spend for life-saving regulations. It is therefore not the case that the OSHA rule stands out as a means of saving lives especially cheaply. When informational strategies are costly, there are two possible responses from government. The first is to do nothing. If the savings – in terms of health, life, informed choice – are relatively low, costly strategies, even informational ones, make little sense. There will therefore be circumstances in which a government remedy for an absence of information is unwarranted.

The second possibility is to impose a regulatory strategy rather than to require disclosure. By a regulatory strategy, I mean a mandatory outcome, such as a flat ban on the materials in question or governmental specification of a particular outcome, as in a mandated maximum level of carcinogens in the workplace. Sometimes the regulatory strategy will be cheaper because the price of disclosing information – changing packaging and so forth – is so high. This is likely to be the right response when most or all people would respond to the information in the same way. In that case, it is unnecessary to provide information

[14] See W. K. Viscusi, Reforming Products Liability, 155 (Cambridge, Mass.: Harvard Univ. Press, 1991).
[15] The Chicago Tribune, November 7, 1991, p. 2.

and better simply to dictate an outcome that, by hypothesis, is generally or almost universally preferred. For an especially dangerous substance, one that reasonable people would not choose to encounter, a flat ban is appropriate. Even when informational strategies are not prohibitively expensive, they may be ineffectual and thus have low benefits. This is so for various reasons.

INFORMATION PROCESSING

I have emphasized that people have limited ability to process information. They have a notoriously difficult time in thinking about low-probability events. Sometimes they discount such events to zero; sometimes they treat them as much more dangerous than they actually are. If people are told, for example, that a certain substance causes cancer, they may think, as in the case of arsenic, that it is far more dangerous than it is in fact. (Recall the discussion of intuitive toxicology in Chapter 2.) But some carcinogenic substances pose little risk.

For example, California's Proposition 65, an initiative designed to promote citizen awareness of risk levels, requires warnings for exposure to carcinogens. At first glance, the requirement seems unexceptionable, indeed an important advance. But it has in some cases been counterproductive. Consumers appear to think that twelve of every 100 users of a product with the required warning will die from cancer. This estimate exceeds reality by a factor of 1,000 or more.[16] With respect to information, less may be more. If information is not provided in a clear and usable form, it may actually make people less knowledgeable than they were before.

Or consider the questions raised by genetically modified foods. There is now an effort, both national and international, to require such foods to be labeled as such, so that consumers will know that food contains genetically modified organisms. At first glance, it seems right to say that consumers should know what they are eating, and that the labels are justified as a way to ensure that people can choose genetically modified food or not. But things are not so clear. In fact, I believe that it would be a big mistake to require labels for genetically modified food. There is no evidence that genetically modified organisms are dangerous to eat as such, nor is there clear evidence that such organisms will create environmental hazards.[17] In fact, many kinds of food, including organic food, seems to create dangers more serious than those associated with genetically modified organisms. Should organic food carry its own labels and warnings? If

---

[16] See W. Kip Viscusi, Predicting the Effects of Food Cancer Risk Warnings on Consumers, 43 Food Drug Cosmetic Law J. 283 (1988).

[17] See Alan McHughen, Pandora's Picnic Basket: The Potential and Hazards of Genetically Modified Foods (Oxford: Oxford Univ. Press, 2000), for an outstanding treatment.

not, why should genetically modified food be singled out? The general difficulty is that, for some products, labels and warnings would in a sense make people less informed, not more so. To the extent that warnings on genetically modified food make people think that they are eating something unhealthy, the warnings will cause unnecessary fear and even confuse people.

HEURISTICS AND INTUITIVE TOXICOLOGY

We have seen that people are intuitive toxicologists who tend to use heuristic devices that produce systemic errors. Recall the availability heuristic, in accordance with which people tend to think an event is more probable if they can readily bring to mind memories of its occurrence. People overestimate risks from highly visible or sensational causes but underestimate risks from less dramatic ones. In the face of these heuristics, public disclosure might be ineffective in improving people's awareness. At the very least, disclosure requirements should be made with people's background beliefs firmly in mind.

MOTIVATIONAL DISTORTIONS

People often believe themselves to be immune from risks that they acknowledge are significant and real with respect to others. In one study, for example, 97 percent of those surveyed ranked themselves as average or above average in their ability to avoid both bicycle and power mower accidents.[18] Disclosure of information may be an unhelpful tool when people do not internalize the new data. In the same vein, the desire to reduce cognitive dissonance may prevent people from recognizing that risks are real even when information is provided. Creative approaches to disclosure might reduce the problem. Consider the ingenious advertising campaign, "drive defensively; watch out for the other guy" – a campaign that attempts to respond to people's optimism and self-confidence.

OVERLOAD

People face a pervasive risk of information overload, causing consumers to treat a large amount of information as equivalent to no information at all.[19] Certainly

---

[18] Paul Slovic et al., Informing the Public About the Risks from Ionizing Radiation, in Judgment and Decision Making: An Interdisciplinary Reader 118, Hal R. Arkes & Kenneth R. Hammond, eds. (Cambridge: Cambridge Univ. Press, 1986).

[19] See Jacob Jacoby et al., Corrective Advertising and Affirmative Disclosure Statements, 46 J. Mktg. 61, 70 (Winter 1982).

this is true when disclosure campaigns are filled with details that cannot be easily processed.

TENACITY OF INITIAL BELIEFS

Initially held beliefs are not easy to modify. This is so even when new information, undermining those beliefs, has been presented.[20]

STRATEGIC RESPONSES

Companies may respond to disclosure requirements by refusing to provide information at all (if this is an available option). The result will be the removal from the market of information that is useful overall. If industry responds to a requirement of evidentiary support for scientific claims with mere "puffing," consumers may have less information than they did to begin with. If advertisers must conduct extensive tests before they are permitted to make claims, they will be given a strong incentive to avoid making claims at all.[21]

PUBLIC GOOD ISSUES

Information may be an inadequate strategy when greater safety is a public good. Imagine, for example, that the replacement of carcinogen X with safe product Y would benefit all workers simultaneously because all of them would simultaneously be exposed to Y rather than X. Imagine too that each worker is bargaining separately with the employer. In that case, no individual employee may have a sufficient incentive to decrease his demand for wages and other benefits to obtain increased safety. Because the benefits of the new substance are provided to everyone, no individual employee will "pay" enough to obtain them, preferring instead to take a free ride on the efforts of others.[22] The result will be too little safety on conventional economic criteria. Here a regulatory response is appropriate.

DISCLOSURE AND THE DISADVANTAGED

Disclosure strategies may also have disproportionately little effect on people who are undereducated, elderly, or poor. If this is so, the risks that

---

[20] Id. at 118.

[21] See Richard Craswell, Interpreting Deceptive Advertising, 65 B. U. L. Rev. 657 (1985).

[22] If labor were completely mobile, the problem would be greatly reduced.

such strategies are aimed to counteract may continue to be faced by the disadvantaged.[23]

These points suggest that there are real limitations to informational strategies. They should be taken seriously but used productively, providing helpful guidance to those seeking to design effective information requirements. Indeed, some of these very limitations can be overcome through more and better information. Well-tailored programs would minimize the relevant risks by putting the information in its most understandable form. Instead of labeling a substance a "carcinogen," a uniform system of risk regulation could give better awareness of risk levels. While informational strategies are no panacea, they would accomplish considerable good, at least if the possible obstacles are kept firmly in mind.

MORE EFFECTIVE COMMUNICATION OF RISK INFORMATION[24]

Studies of risk communication[25] have emphasized that information becomes relevant to people through their specific background assumptions, knowledge, and systems of value. Unfortunately, many government-sponsored risk communications take the form of highly generalized and often inscrutable recommendations. Effective information disclosure requires knowledge of the beliefs on which citizens are likely to draw. If these background frameworks are incomplete or error-filled, factually accurate information may well be ignored or misunderstood. More information might even make people less informed.

Risk-communication specialists have developed a general approach to discovering the most effective forms of information disclosure.[26] Applying this approach in 1987, experts were able to generate a highly effective brochure for addressing the recent radon scare, a brochure that was far more effective than the widely distributed EPA brochure on that topic. The process revealed that, in addition to holding many accurate beliefs about radon exposure, people also held many inaccurate beliefs: that radon contamination of surfaces is permanent (39%), that radon affects plants (58%), that it contaminates blood (38%), and that it causes breast cancer (29%). Few people understood that radon decays

---

[23] See George Schucker et al., The Impact of the Saccharin Warning Label, 2 J. Pub. Policy & Mktg. 46 (1983).

[24] This section was originally coauthored with Richard Pildes and appeared in Pildes & Sunstein, supra note 15 in Chapter 1.

[25] Slovic, supra note 12 in Chapter 2, at 675.

[26] The discussion that follows is based on Granger Morgan et al., Communicating Risks to the Public, 26 Env. Sci. Technol. 2048 (1992).

quickly (13%).[27] The combination of some of these beliefs would make the radon problem seem severe and unsolvable; consider the lack of knowledge of the fact that radon decays quickly. On the basis of this information, brochures were designed that specifically addressed the flaws and gaps in people's background beliefs.

The unsuccessful EPA brochure had been prepared through traditional methods: scientific experts were asked what information was relevant, and it was then packaged attractively. The initial version of the EPA's "Citizen's Guide to Radon," for example, did not discuss whether radon contamination is permanent. When empirically tested, this EPA brochure performed significantly worse than the brochures prepared through the alternative method. When people were asked to recall simple facts, they did equally well with all the brochures. But when faced with tasks requiring inference, the new brochures dramatically outperformed the EPA material. For example, when asked what a homeowner could do to reduce high radon levels in the house, 43% of EPA readers answered "don't know" and 9% said "there is no way to fix the problem." In contrast, 100% of the readers of the brochure designed on the basis of risk communication studies, and 96% of another, answered "hire a contractor to fix the problem."[28]

Informational remedies should also respond to various heuristics and anomalies that affect how people "hear" warnings. For example, it matters a great deal whether a health effect is framed as a loss or a gain. People are far more willing to forego gains than to accept equivalent losses. Real-world experiments show that pamphlets describing the positive effects of breast self-examination (for example, women who undertake such examinations have a greater chance of finding a tumor at a treatable stage) are largely ineffective – but that there are significant changes in behavior from pamphlets that stress the negative consequences of a refusal to undertake self-examinations (women who fail to perform such examinations have a decreased chance of finding a tumor at a treatable stage).[29] Similar results were found for efforts to inform people of the advantages of energy insulation: an emphasis on the gains from insulation produced far less change than an emphasis on the losses from noninsulation.[30] If, in sum, government wants to alter behavior, it is much better to say, "if you do not take preventative steps, you are 10 percent more likely to get cancer," than to say, "if you take preventative steps, you are 10 percent less likely to get cancer."

[27] Id.

[28] Id. at 2054.

[29] See Beth Meyerowitz & Shelly Chaiken, The Effect of Message Framing on Breast Self-Examination, 52 J. Personality & Soc. Psych. 500 (1987).

[30] Marti Galzales, Elliot Aronson & Mark Costanzo, Using Social Cognition and Persuasion to Promote Energy Conservation, 18 J. Appl. Soc. Psych. 1049 (1988).

Vivid and personal information is also more effective than statistical evidence. So too, people tend to be risk optimists, thinking that they are less subject to hazards than most other people (see Chapters 1 and 10); for this reason, information can be ignored. Efforts to convey information about AIDS, for example, appear to be adversely affected by people's tendency to assume that the risk does not apply to them.[31] Those concerned about the spread of AIDS should attempt to convey information not merely by stating the facts but also by doing so in a way that is intentionally targeted at the negative (and by no means inevitable) social image of condom use. This point raises a larger one, to which I now turn.

A NOTE ON ADVERTISING CAMPAIGNS – AND SOCIAL MEANING

Suppose that people are engaging in conduct that carries risks; what is the best way to discourage them? Some of the most helpful evidence comes from the domain of antismoking campaigns, where we know a great deal about what works and about what does not. An intriguing study,[32] for example, tested the effectiveness, within focus groups, of the following antismoking advertisements:

- romantic rejection, meaning an effort to show that smoking decreases popularity with members of the opposite sex;
- addiction, emphasizing that smokers find it hard to quit;
- cessation, showing that it is important to quit and emphasizing how quitting might be assisted;
- second-hand smoke, emphasizing the adverse effects of smoking on others, including children;
- industry manipulation, showing that tobacco companies intentionally plot to manipulate people to get them to smoke;
- long-term health effects, emphasizing that smokers are subject to dangers of heart disease and lung cancer late in life;
- short-term health effects, emphasizing that smokers incur a set of risks more or less immediately.

The most striking finding was that, of all these advertisements, two were judged most effective: the advertisements involving second-hand smoke and industry manipulation. In contrast, the advertisements involving romantic rejection and long-term health effects were deemed least effective. Notably, the

[31] See Elliott Aronson, The Social Animal, 7th ed., 91–2 (New York: W. H. Freeman, 1995).
[32] Lisa Goldman & Stanton Glantz, Evaluation of Antismoking Advertising Campaigns, 279 JAMA 772 (1998).

most effective advertisements appealed to people's self-conception, rather than their self-interest, narrowly defined. Evidently people do not want to be the source of harm to innocent third parties, particularly if the innocent parties are children. At the same time, people do not want to be manipulated by industry, and some of the most effective advertisements made smokers feel like puppets. Indeed the industry manipulation advertisements were particularly ingenious because they worked directly against the preferred self-image of most smokers, as rebels, independent of authority. Many people start to smoke, or continue to smoke, less because they like smoking than because they like the social image of the smoker. If an informational campaign can change that image in the minds of smokers themselves, it is likely to work.

Why, then, did the romantic rejection advertisement fall flat? To say the least, most people want to be popular with members of the opposite sex. The likely problem is that these advertisements were not found credible. Apparently it was hard to find people who believed, before they saw the advertisement, that smoking would not undermine one's popularity with members of the opposite sex, but who were also convinced, after seeing the advertisement, that this was, in fact, a danger. Government campaigns are either not helpful or not trusted on this point. In any case, many viewers found these advertisements offensive.

It might seem still more surprising that the advertisements emphasizing long-term health consequences were quite ineffective, and that those emphasizing short-term health problems were only slightly more effective. Here one problem may be that many young people believe that they smoke too little to face adverse health consequences, or in any case that they will quit smoking before it can really harm them.[33] For this reason alone, an emphasis on the long-term effects of smoking is unlikely to change behavior. Advertisements involving adverse health effects also fail to tell people anything that they did not already know — and new information is necessary to alter behavior.

Compare some of the public relations thinking of cigarette companies. An executive for Philip Morris wrote that among experts within tobacco companies, "there is general agreement on [why people begin to smoke]. The 16 to 20 year-old begins smoking for psychosocial reasons. The act of smoking is symbolic, it signifies adulthood, he smokes to enhance his image in the eyes of his peers."[34] Thus companies seek to promote a general impression (in the words of an advertising agency for Philip Morris) "that it is acceptable to smoke" and that certain brands "offer this age group a peer group which feeds their need to

---

[33] See Smoking: Risk, Perception, and Policy, Paul Slovic, ed. (New York: Russell Sage, 2001).
[34] Quoted in Jon Hanson & Douglas Kysar, The Joint Failure of Economic Theory and Legal Regulation, in Smoking, Id. at 229, 255.

belong."[35] With risk to minority communities, Brown & Williamson was quite explicit: "[T]his relatively small and often tightly knit community can work to B & W's marketing advantage, if exploited properly. Peer pressure often plays a more important role in many phases of life in the minority community. Therefore, dominance of the marketplace and the community environment is necessary to successfully increase market share."[36]

We can draw some general lessons here. For a risk-related educational campaign to work, it should (a) be trustworthy, (b) contain new information, and (c) be vivid. These are the minimal preconditions for a significant reduction in risk. At the same time, those who run risks often do so because their actions seem rebellious or independent; thus the "social meaning" of the action is often what drives behavior. Any educational effort will do well if it can change that social meaning. Hence a risk reduction campaign is especially likely to work if it can convince those who run risks that, in doing so, they are being manipulated by a group of greedy people rather than expressing their own free will. In addition, people who run risks often like to think that they are not thereby harming others. An educational campaign is more likely to be effective if it can convince people that their own conduct is hardly self-regarding but imposes harms on innocent third parties as well. In sum, people do not want to be dupes, subject to the manipulations of others. But they also do not want to be bad, imposing dangers on other people.

These ideas have broad implications. In the area of drunk driving, for example, it is easy to emphasize that people who drink and drive are imposing danger on others, emphatically including children. Vivid accounts, emphasizing actual people who have lost their lives at the hands of drunk drivers, work better than remote statistical demonstrations. With respect to the risks of poor diet, it might well be useful to stress that those who sell fast foods, or candy, are interested in "hooking" young people, in part through highly manipulative advertising campaigns. In the context of use of guns, it might be helpful to emphasize that the National Rifle Association is funded in large part by gun manufacturers, and that manufacturers of guns are often behind efforts to claim that the Constitution guarantees rights of gun ownership. It is noteworthy in this connection that in encouraging Americans to fly, in the aftermath of the terrorist attacks of September 11, 2001, President George W. Bush emphasized, not that there was a low statistical risk of death, or even that flying was basically safe, but that flying was an act of patriotism, one that would help ensure that terrorism had not fundamentally affected the nation's economy.

[35] Id. at 256.
[36] Id.

For reasons discussed in Chapter 4, it is also true that people generally like to do what (relevant) others do. If people overestimate the number of people who engage in risk-related activity, public disclosure of the true numbers can further decrease the activity in question. This approach has been highly successful in efforts to discourage binge drinking on college campuses.[37] It is also been found to work in producing more compliance with the tax laws: When people are informed of the high level of voluntary compliance, more of them tend to comply. In many domains, this approach would prevent people from taking excessive risks, at least when they are doing so because they think that large numbers of other people are too.

ECONOMIC INCENTIVES

We have seen that command-and-control regulation can be highly dysfunctional. Sometimes relevant statutes forbid agencies from choosing incentive-based strategies even if agencies know that such strategies would work better. This is unfortunate because economic incentives are often more effective than governmental commands, and when they are equally effective, they are usually much cheaper. On cost–benefit grounds, incentives should often be the regulatory tool of choice.

By economic incentives, I mean to emphasize two major ideas: financial penalties imposed on harm-producing behavior ("polluters pay") and trading systems by which people who pollute or cause certain kinds of harm may trade their "rights" to do so ("tradable emissions rights"). The category of economic incentives also includes subsidies to those who agree to reduce harm-producing activity. Consider, for example, tax credits for those who use low-pollution technologies, or payments to those who agree to take old, high-polluting vehicles off the road ("cash for clunkers"). Though I will spend little time on subsidies here, they too are worth considering, especially because they might be favored on distributional grounds (as, for example, when poor people, or poor nations, receive economic help in return for conferring a benefit on others). In many contexts, such incentives should supplement and even displace command-and-control regulation.[38]

---

[37] See H. Wesley Perkins, College Student Misperceptions of Alcohol and Other Drug Norms among Peers: Exploring Causes, Consequences, and Implications for Prevention Programs, in Designing Alcohol and Other Drug Prevention Programs in Higher Education 177–206 (Washington, DC: The Higher Education Center for Alcohol and Other Drug Prevention, U.S. Department of Education, 1997).

[38] In most ways, the analysis of subsidies should be similar to the analysis of penalties.

Efficiency

It is inefficient for government to prescribe the means for achieving social objectives. Ordinarily it would be far better, on economic grounds, for government (a) to create incentives to engage in socially desirable conduct and (b) to permit the market to decide how companies respond to those incentives. I outline the key ideas briefly here, and turn to some complexities below.[39]

Polluters Pay. At least as a general rule, it is especially inefficient for government to dictate technology. A "performance standard," telling people (for example) to reduce sulfur dioxide emissions to a certain level, is better than a technology requirement simply because it is more flexible and allows companies to meet the standard as they choose. The American government has learned to appreciate this point. Under the Clean Air Act, Congress and the EPA have moved steadily away from technological requirements and toward performance standards, aware that this is a far cheaper way of achieving air quality goals. But much of the time, a still better approach is to impose a tax on harmful behavior and to let market forces determine the response to the increased cost. In many settings, the best approach is for government to impose fees on those who put pollutants into the atmosphere. Consumption of the harm-producing good will decline. People will, for example, be less likely to use high-polluting gasoline; emissions of carbon dioxide, the leading contributor to global warning, will decline. Producers will shift to less harmful methods of production. They might, for example, substitute clean for dirty coal.

An idea of this kind might be made part and parcel of a system of "green taxes." With such a system, nations might tax people who impose harms on others — users of dirty automobiles, coal-fired power plants, gasoline that produces air pollution, or products that contribute to destruction of the ozone layer or the greenhouse effect. Tax levies of various sorts are used by many nations already, though they have been slow in coming to the United States. These levies have had, or are projected to have, excellent results. Thus a higher tax on leaded gasoline in Great Britain increased the market share of unleaded gas from 4 to 30 percent within less than a year.[40] It is estimated that a doubling of pesticide prices would cut pesticide use in half.[41] With respect to global warming, it is

---

[39] There are many discussions of this topic; Robert Stavins has been an especially valuable contributor. See Robert N. Stavins, Environmental Economics and Public Policy: Selected Papers of Robert N. Stavins, 1988–1999 (Cheltenham: Elger Publishing, 2001).

[40] Lester Brown et al., Saving the Planet: How to Shape an Environmentally Sustainable Global Economy 143 (New York: Norton, 1991).

[41] Id. at 146.

estimated that a fee of $110 per ton on carbon would decrease carbon dioxide emissions by 20 percent within ten years.[42] An important advantage of such strategies is that they would dramatically increase government revenues. The suggested carbon tax would generate over $130 billion.[43] Other such taxes on polluting activity could produce billions of additional dollars in revenue.[44] Of course taxes of this kind – if meant to raise revenue – have to be designed so that they are not so high as to eliminate the revenue source.

The same idea could be applied in other areas as well. Workers' compensation plans, for example, operate as effective guarantees of workplace safety. According to a careful study, "If the safety incentives of workers' compensation were removed, fatality rates in the United States economy would increase by almost 30 percent. Over 1200 more workers would die from job injuries every year in the absence of the safety incentives provided by workers' compensation."[45] This contrasts with a mere 2 to 4 percent reduction in injuries from OSHA, an amount that links up well with the fact that annual workers' compensation premiums are more than 1,000 times as large as total annual OSHA penalties. The tax system could be used to provide better incentives to employers who furnish dangerous workplaces. The Consumer Product Safety Commission might experiment with a system in which producers of harm-producing products must pay a fee into the federal treasury. Ultimately, we might hope for a coordinated system of risk regulation, one that imposed specified fees for harm-producing activities.

Tradeable Permits. Thus far I have been discussing the "polluters pay" principle. But in many contexts, it make sense to consider a system of tradeable permits, in which polluters, or other creators of risk, are given licenses to engage in the relevant behavior and are then authorized to trade their "licenses" with other people. In the pollution context, this would mean that people who reduce their pollution below a specified level could trade their "pollution rights" for cash. In one stroke, such a system would create market-based disincentives to pollute and market-based incentives for pollution control. Such a system would also reward rather than punish technological innovation in pollution control, and do so with the aid of private markets. In the context of global warming, for example, much attention has been given to the possibility of creating markets in greenhouse gas emissions rights, with caps on national emissions. The Kyoto Protocol, designed

---

[42] Id. at 148.

[43] Id. at 145.

[44] Id.

[45] W. Kip Viscusi, Reforming Products Liability 178 (Cambridge, Mass.: Harvard Univ. Press, 1991).

to reduce global warming, creates a series of mechanisms for emissions trading; it is estimated that the trading system would radically reduce the total cost of the program.[46] A central advantage of such a system is that it would ensure that reductions would be made by those who could do so most cheaply – and that those with a real need for emissions would pay people, perhaps especially in poor nations, who would prefer to have the money. Very generally, and quite outside the environmental area, it makes sense to think about programs of this sort for regulation of harmful behavior. Of course, many people object to the idea that polluters and other risk creators might be given a "right" to create harm. I will turn to that objection in due course.

DEMOCRACY

Thus far, we have seen that a shift to economic incentives would be efficient and effective. What consequences would such a shift have for democratic government? The answer is that it would have significant consequences, and that these would be a extremely beneficial.[47] The current system puts public attention in the wrong places. Imagine, for example, that Congress and the citizenry – following the contemporary model – are focusing on the question whether ethanol, or some other gasoline substitute, should be required in new cars. It is perfectly predictable that in answering this question, well-organized groups with a significant stake in the outcome will bring their influence to bear. It is also predictable that ethanol producers may seek and actually obtain regulatory benefits, and for reasons bearing absolutely no relationship to environmental protection. At the same time, the underlying substantive question – whether ethanol is actually an environmentally superior product – will have to be resolved on the basis of technological complexities not easily addressed by the public or its representatives. If this is the issue on which the political process focuses, we are therefore likely to have a series of laws that represent, not public-spirited deliberation with a measure of broad accountability, but instead tradeoffs among well-organized private groups, or government by faction. By directing attention to means, this system creates strong incentives for interest groups to ensure that they are favored in the legislature or the bureaucracy. To be sure, a performance standard, not looking at particular means, is a great deal better. But in thinking about performance, it is highly likely that well-organized groups will be asking about the means to achieve that performance, and here interest group maneuvering is inevitable.

[46] See Bjorn Lomborg, The Skeptical Environmentalist 303 (Cambridge: Cambridge Univ. Press, 2001).

[47] I draw here on Bruce Ackerman & Richard B. Stewart, Reforming Environmental Law: The Democratic Case for Market Incentives, 13 Colum. J. Env. L. 171 (1988).

Compare a system of economic incentives. In a system of cap-and-trade, the issue is not one of means, or even of performance of particular enterprises, but the amount of sulfur dioxide that will be allowed into the atmosphere – an issue to be resolved in the process of deciding how many licenses to be given out and for how much pollution. A large advantage of this shift is that it would increase the likelihood that citizens and representatives would focus on how much pollution reduction there should be and at what cost. The right question would be put squarely before the electorate. No longer would it be possible to pretend that environmental protection is costless. No longer would the central issue be displaced by the question of largely incidental question of means. A system of polluters pay has similar advantages, especially insofar as it allows the market to decide on appropriate means of achieve reductions.

Moreover, a system of financial incentives allows far less room for interest-group maneuvering. The large question – how much environmental protection at what cost – does not easily permit legislators to favor a well-organized, narrow group, such as the agricultural lobby or the coal lobby. Special favors cannot readily be provided through a system of economic incentives. The very generality of the question will work against narrow favoritism. To be sure, the ultimate question of pollution reduction may be answered in a way that reflects sustained political pressure, or a stab in the dark, rather than democratic deliberation. In the 1990 acid deposition program, Congress' chosen "cap" on overall emissions did seem to be fairly arbitrary. But the relevant risks are minimized, certainly as compared with a command-and-control system.

There are other democratic advantages. Economic incentives should simultaneously promote coordination and rationality in regulation, by giving government an incentive to attend closely, and for the first time, to how other risks are treated. This should bring a salutary measure of structure and sense to risk regulation in general. As an important byproduct, the new system should create a powerful incentive to obtain information about the actual effects of pollution and pollution control. If members of Congress are deciding on the level of risk reduction, they will not want to do so in a vacuum, especially in light of the significant costs of large reductions. Affected groups will therefore be encouraged to engage in research about real-world consequences. Information about consequences frequently remains in its most preliminary stages. The new premium placed on information should be a particularly important gain. There is every reason to design regulatory strategies that put a premium on greater research so that when a nation acts, it knows what it is getting, and at what price.

All these considerations suggest that economic incentives – favored so firmly on economic grounds – have as one of their principal justifications a series of democracy-reinforcing, faction-limiting characteristics.

INITIATIVES

The movement toward economic incentives is real. Thus far, it has occurred mostly in the environmental area. In the 1980s, an important series of administrative initiatives brought about "emissions trading," especially under the Clean Air Act.[48] Under the EPA's policy, a firm that reduces its emissions below legal requirements may obtain "credits" that can be used against higher emissions elsewhere. Through the "offset" policy, which is formally codified in the Clean Air Act, a company may locate in an area not in compliance with national air quality standards if and only if it can offset the new emissions by reducing existing emissions, either from its own sources or from other firms. Through the "banking" policy, firms are permitted to store emission credits for their own future use. Companies may also engage in "netting," by which a firm modifies a source but avoids the most stringent emissions limits that would otherwise be applied to the modification by reducing emissions from another source within the same plant. And through "bubbles," existing sources may place an imaginary bubble over their plants, allowing different emissions levels by each emitting device so long as the total emissions level is in compliance with aggregate requirements.

We now have a good deal of evidence about the emissions trading program. For various reasons, the use of the program has been quite limited.[49] An early study showed 42 federal bubbles; 90 state bubbles; 2,000 federal offsets; between 5,000 and 12,000 acts of netting; and 100 acts of banking.[50] Despite this limited activity, there is considerable evidence that this policy has been successful. Overall, the program has produced savings of between $525 million and $12 billion.[51] By any measure, this is an enormous gain. On balance, moreover, the environmental consequences have been beneficial. Offsets must, by definition, produce environmental gains. The preliminary evidence shows favorable effects from bubbles as well. There may be modest beneficial effects from banking and modest adverse effects from netting. The overall environmental effect is therefore good.

As part of the process for eliminating lead from gasoline – a decision that was, not incidentally, strongly supported by a cost–benefit study – the EPA

---

[48] See EPA, Emissions Trading Policy Statement: General Principles for Creation, Banking, and Use of Emission Reduction Credits, 51 Fed. Reg. 43,814 (1986).

[49] See David Dudek & Palmisano, Emissions Trading: Why is This Thoroughbred Hobbled?, 13 Colum. J. Env. L. 217 (1988).

[50] Robert Hahn & Gordon, Hester, Marketable Permits: Lessons for Theory and Practice, 16 Ecol. L. Q. 361, 374 table 2 (1989).

[51] See id.

also permitted emissions trading. Under this policy, a refinery that produced gasoline with lower than required lead levels could earn credits. These could be traded with other refineries or banked for future use. Until the termination of the program in 1987, when the phasedown of lead ended, emissions credits for lead were widely traded. The EPA concluded that there had been cost savings of about 20 percent over alternative systems, marking total savings in the hundreds of million of dollars. There have been similar efforts with water pollution and ozone depletion.[52]

In the United States, the most dramatic program of economic incentives can be found in the 1990 amendments to the Clean Air Act.[53] The act now explicitly creates an emissions trading system for the control of acid deposition. In these amendments, Congress made an explicit decision about aggregate emissions level for a pollutant. Whether the particular decision is the correct one may be disputed. But surely there are large democratic benefits from ensuring that public attention is focused on that issue. There are other beneficial features to the acid deposition provisions. Congress has said that polluters may obtain allowances for emissions avoided through energy conservation and renewable energy. In this way, avoidance of this kind is turned into dollars, in the form of an increased permission to pollute. This provision creates an incentive to shift to conservation and renewable sources, without providing further environmental degradation. Polluters are explicitly permitted to trade their allowances; this is a first in national legislation. In this way, people who are able to reduce their pollution below the specified level receive economic benefits. Again incentives are created for environmentally beneficial behavior. An especially intriguing provision allows spot and advance sales of sulfur dioxide allowances, to be purchasable at $1,500 per ton. Through this route, polluters must – for the first time – pay a fee for their pollution. Even more intriguing is a provision calling for auction sales of specified numbers of sulfur dioxide allowances. Here the market is permitted to set the price for polluting activity.

The acid deposition program has turned out to be a terrific success.[54] Compliance with the program has been nearly perfect. Considerable trading has occurred; an effective market in permits developed, just as anticipated. As compared with a command-and-control system, the trading mechanism is estimated to have saved $357 million annually in its first five years. For the next

---

[52] On ozone depletion, see 53 Fed. Reg. 30,566 (Aug. 11, 1988); on water pollution, see Robert Hahn & Robert Stavins, Incentive-Based Environmental Regulation: A New Era from an Old Idea, 18 Ecol. L. Q. 1, 18–19 (1991).

[53] 42 USC 7651 et seq.

[54] See generally A. Denny Ellerman et al., Markets for Clean Air (Cambridge: Cambridge Univ. Press, 2000).

fifteen years, the mechanism is predicted to save $2.28 billion annually, for an overall savings in excess of $20 billion. Since enactment of the program, the price of transporting coal has been reduced dramatically because of deregulation, and the program proved able to handle this surprise, with permits trading for far less than anticipated. Indeed it is fair to say that the acid deposition program ranks among the most spectacular success stories in all of environmental regulation. Because the costs of the program have been so much lower than anticipated, the cost–benefit ratio seems especially good, with compliance costs of $870 million compared to annual benefits ranging from $12 billion to $78 billion – including reductions of nearly 10,000 premature deaths and over 14,500 cases of chronic bronchitis. We may hope that in the future Congress will build on the acid deposition model, using economic incentives to control environmental harms.

OBJECTIONS AND REJOINDERS

There are several possible objections to the use of economic incentives. The clearest problems arise when the appropriate response to a harm-producing activity is a flat ban. With an especially dangerous pollutant, or a deadly killer, an increased price is, of course, inadequate. The pollutant should be eliminated from the market, at least if (a) its social benefits do not outweigh the relevant danger and (b) less dangerous substitutes are available. The government has banned lead in gasoline and the use of CFCs, which help to destroy the ozone layer; both of these bans were strongly justified on cost–benefit grounds.

Another objection is that economic incentives might be thought to operate as a regressive tax, in the sense that they raise prices in general, and the rise in prices will come down especially hard on the poor. An increase in the price of gasoline, or in the cost of high-polluting vehicles, will make things more difficult for poor people in particular. Indeed, any effort to require manufacturers and sellers to "internalize" the costs of their production might seem objectionable insofar as it increases prices in a way that is especially hard on the indigent. For this reason, many people ordinarily disposed to support environmental protection are skeptical of "green taxes." Environmental protection is certainly important, but shouldn't the government avoid strategies that hurt the poor far more than the rich?

In general, I do not believe that this objection to economic incentives is persuasive. *Any* regulatory solution will increase prices; economic incentives are not distinctive in this regard. A government mandate will increase prices no less than an economic incentive. And if the solution is otherwise sensible, it ought not to be rejected as a "regressive tax," any more than the price system itself is a regressive tax. In any case, a failure to require enterprises to bear the social costs of their risk-creating activities is hardly an effective way of benefiting the poor. The class of people burdened by this failure includes a numerous people, many of them not poor at all; the failure to impose the right incentives burdens a variety of people, many of them quite poor, who will continue to face risks, including the risks created by pollution. It is not sensible to reject economic incentives on the ground that they hurt poor people. It is certainly sensible, of course, to worry about the consequences of price increases, produced by either market forces or by government, for poor people. The point suggests that the taxes or fines produced by economic incentives might be accompanied by subsidies or transfer payments to people who are needy. Some of these subsidies might be funded from the very revenues produced by the program itself. And when the distributive concern seems most serious, government might use subsidies for harm-reducing behavior rather than penalties for harm-producing behavior. Rich countries, for example, might pay poor countries to reduce their greenhouse gas emissions, just as rich countries now participate in "debt for nature" swaps, agreeing to pay poor nations who agree to preserve globally important assets, such as rain forests.

Some people object to economic incentives on moral grounds. It is sometimes argued, as against economic incentives, that they improperly "commodify" certain interests. Certainly some human interests ought not to be traded on markets at all. Perhaps such trading debases and diminishes the interests in question, with harmful consequences for social attitudes. In some settings, this objection seems plausible. Thus there may be reason to question a decision to allow prostitution, or the trading of body parts; I do not mean to resolve these issues here.[55] But in the contexts I am discussing here, it is doubtful that the argument takes one very far. It is odd to suggest that social attitudes would really be changed by a system in which polluters and others who cause harm must pay for what they do. Indeed, a shift of this kind, requiring polluters to pay, might even have desirable effects on social attitudes. In any case, it seems far better to require people who cause harm to pay, rather than to allow them to do so for free. There is no evidence that the acid deposition program has, by allowing trading, made people less concerned about the harms of pollution, or less troubled by polluting activity.

Of course, any incentive-based system must confront a range of practical problems. In the environmental context, for example, there is a risk that polluters will cluster in a particular area, thus subjecting people in that area to unacceptably high danger. The problem of "hot spots" calls for careful design of economic incentive programs. We have seen that this problem requires caution in any emissions trading system for arsenic.

---

[55] For discussion, see Anderson, supra note 4 in Chapter 3.

In addition, determination of the amount of any tax or fine is not a simple scientific exercise. It entails a judgment about appropriate risk levels, and that decision will pose great difficulties. In the context of global warming, there are formidable problems in designing an effective system for permit trading.[56] But these sorts of questions should be treated as matters of design and detail. They do not bear fundamentally on the shift to economic incentives.

LITTLE BUBBLES OR BIG BUBBLES? WHY BIGGER IS BETTER

One of the most important issues in risk regulation involves the size of the bubbles within which trading may occur. In the context of global warming, the issue has become highly salient. Almost everyone seems to favor a system in which the right to emit carbon dioxide can be traded freely, so as to ensure low-cost attainment of any global cap. But it would be possible to go much further. The 2001 climate change agreement in Bonn became possible not only because (1) emissions trading was generally permitted, but also because (2) industrialized nations could be given credits for paying to reduce carbon dioxide emissions in poor nations, and also because (3) Japan was able to obtain an agreement to receive credits for reductions attributable to reductions obtained not from carbon dioxide emissions but from forest growth, because forests act as carbon "sinks." The example shows that it is possible for imaginative trading systems to include "big bubbles," in which polluters, or risk creators, are allowed to choose any effective means of reducing the problem to which they have been contributing.[57]

Consider how bubble size might grow. At a minimum, the EPA might allow trading within any plant. A plant with a dozen smoke stacks might be authorized to add new smoke stacks, so long as any increase in, say, sulfur dioxide pollution is offset by decreases in such pollution from other stacks. On this approach, now standard within environmental policy, the plant would be treated as if it were encased in a single bubble. But consider a more ambitious alternative: All sulfur dioxide in a locality, or even a state, might be treated as if encased in a big bubble so that sulfur dioxide trading could occur from all sources within that big bubble. Within the United States, there has been considerable experimentation

---

[56] See David Victor, The Collapse of the Kyoto Protocol and the Struggle to Slow Global Warming (Princeton, N.J.: Princeton Univ. Press, 2001).

[57] See E. Donald Elliott & Gail Charnley, Toward Bigger Bubbles: Why Interpollutant and Interrisk Trading Are Good Ideas and How We Get There from Here, 13 F. for Applied Res. & Pub. Policy 48 (Winter 1998), from which I have learned a great deal.

in this direction. Indeed, the acid deposition program goes still further. It creates a very big bubble, containing the entire nation and allowing sulfur dioxide to be traded among all power plants within it.

But we need not stop there. Many air pollutants come from cars as well as power plants. It would be easy to imagine a fleetwide bubble for motor vehicle pollution, requiring producers of new cars to ensure, not per-vehicle reductions, but fleetwide reductions, designing to meet some aggregate goal for pollution from new cars. Congress has been moving in this very direction. But why stop with new cars? Companies might be authorized to meet pollution reduction goals *either* by producing cleaner new fleets *or* by retiring old, high-polluting vehicles from the road. One manufacturer might not participate in the "old car retirement program" and might pay instead for clean new cars. But another manufacturer might meet its overall obligations by retiring older vehicles. Full trading might be permitted. It would be possible to imagine a program that would effectively cover all vehicles, both old and new, in an effort to ensure the cheapest and most effective way of controlling pollution from cars and trucks.

But we could go much further. Why not allow car companies to trade with power plants? If a power plant would find it cheaper to pay a car company to reduce emissions of sulfur dioxide, perhaps it should be permitted to do exactly that. If a motor vehicle company would find it cheaper to subsidize pollution reduction from power plants, why not allow it to do so? Congress might even enact a particular provision to allow very big bubbles. It might say, for example, "Notwithstanding any other provision of law, an agency shall be permitted to regulate with economic incentives, if it can show that these methods will produce the same benefits in a more cost-effective manner."[58] Of course, such a provision would involve risks. It could create further litigation, perhaps initiated by self-interested private groups seeking to stall desirable regulation. It could allow agencies unenthustiastic about regulatory mandates to proceed with less effective means of achieving compliance. But the problems with existing processes – excessive costs, insufficient regulatory benefits – are sufficient to make it worthwhile to move in this direction.

We could go further still. The discussion thus far has involved bubbles involving the same pollutant; but it is easy to imagine cross-pollutant trading. Suppose, for example, that one company would find it expensive to reduce sulfur dioxide emissions but not terribly expensive to reduce carbon dioxide emissions, whereas another company would find it much easier to reduce carbon dioxide

---

[58] I borrow here from Statement of Jonathan Wiener, Before the Committee on Governmental Affairs, United States Senate, March 8, 1995.

than sulfur dioxide. Should the two be allowed to trade? Current law generally forbids them from doing so. But we should welcome the trade if a given unit of sulfur dioxide can be "translated" into a given unit of carbon dioxide so as to create a common currency. In principle, the translation should certainly be possible. In fact the Kyoto Protocol attempts to do something of just this sort, allowing translation of many greenhouse cases into a single currency. The approach could be expanded. If carbon dioxide emissions are generally more harmful, per unit, than sulfur dioxide emissions, per the same unit, then the trade should be allowed only on terms that recognizes the disparity in harm. For example, someone who proposes to "trade" a right to emit ten tons of carbon dioxide might be able to buy (say) fifteen tons of sulfur dioxide in return.

It is even possible to imagine a system that places a wide range of pollutants under a single bubble, allowing cross-pollutant trading in accordance with the chosen translation formula. In light of the success of more modest trading programs, an ambitious initiative along these lines should save many billions of dollars. Of course there are risks. If a particular pollutant is expensive to reduce, people might take few steps to reduce it, and the result could be to create a serious problem of hot spots. In the course of ordinary administration, however, it would be possible to monitor the problem and to resort to governmental commands if the risk becomes real.

As a thought experiment, we could even imagine a system in which each individual is given a permit, containing the right to contribute to a certain level of pollution each year, through the use of electricity, motor vehicles, municipal services, and more. In such a system, individuals would have the right to choose the activities that would lead to the permitted contributions. Some people would fall below the permitted level; if they chose, they could "retire" the unused portion of their permits, or instead trade their remaining rights to the highest bidder. If the proposal seems exotic or ludicrous, it is, I think, because of the obvious administrative burden it would impose on individuals and on governments. But we could imagine a less ambitious system of this kind, reflected in user fees for activities that impose social costs. It is not implausible to predict that government will venture more experiments in this direction in the future.

In this light, we can see that cost–benefit analysis involves the biggest bubble of all. When cost–benefit balancing is at work, it is as if a huge bubble is placed over the entire nation, allowing all effects to be aggregated as such.

POLLUTERS PAY OR TRADEABLE PERMITS?

I have not yet explored an important and somewhat technical question: How should government choose between the two possible systems of economic incentives? In theory, the two approaches should be equally good. If polluters are forced to pay, and if government chooses the right payment, the market will provide the right amount of pollution. (Recall that the right amount is unlikely to be zero; pollution reduction can cause various harms, including risks to life itself.) Similarly, if the government "caps" pollution and chooses the correct cap, the market will ensure that people are paying the right price for polluting activity. But the theory oversimplifies a great deal.

How should government choose between the two approaches? The conventional answer, which I summarize here, is that the choice between them depends on what the government knows.[59] Consider the potential problems with pollution taxes. If the government sets the tax lower than it should, emissions will be too high. The government might set the tax too low simply because it lacks necessary information; for example, the costs of abatement might be lower than the government anticipated. Hence a key problem with taxes is that they might be set at the wrong level, thus producing excessive pollution (or insufficient pollution if the government sets the tax too high, discouraging desirable activity). Tradeable permits avoid this particular problem because government creates an overall cap and does not have to set a specific tax per unit of pollution (or activity). But the cap itself might be set in the wrong place; it might be too high or too low. In these circumstances, the conventional analysis offers a solution. We need to know how "steep" are the marginal cost and marginal benefit curves. If environmental damages rise more steeply than compliance costs fall, then government should be most concerned about the risk of excessive emissions. If so, marketable permits should be preferred. But if compliance costs fall more steeply than environmental damages rise, then the most serious problem is excessive compliance costs, and government should choose a tax, not a cap.

As I have said, this is the conventional analysis; but I am not sure that it is correct. At first glance, a system of pollution taxes seems to require much less information than a system of marketable permits. To set up taxes, government needs to know only the harm produced by each unit of emission, and to establish a price accordingly. How much harm is done by a ton of sulfur dioxide? This is not easy to know, but it is less demanding than the alternative, which involves knowledge of the appropriate "cap" throughout a region. To choose such a cap, the government needs to know all the costs and benefits of emissions at various imaginable levels. Should the national cap on sulfur dioxide be set at eight million tons, or ten million tons, or twelve million tons? In the abstract, that question is very hard to answer. If a cap-and-trade system is better than one

---

[59] For a good summary, see Jonathan Wiener, Global Environmental Regulation, 108 Yale L. J. 677, 728–9 (1999).

of polluters pay, it is because the government can calculate the aggregate figure more easily than it can calculate the per-unit level of harm. Perhaps this is true in the cases of acid deposition and global warming. My principal purpose here, however, is not to sort out these complexities but simply to show the advantages of economic incentives over command-and-control.[60]

RISK REDUCTION CONTRACTS

Sometimes government has responded to its own lack of information through "environmental contracting."[61] Through environmental contracting, the government tells polluters about its basic goals and enters into an agreement by which polluters contract to achieve those goals. The advantage of this system is that the means of compliance are left to the private sector, so long as environmental goals are actually met.

In the Netherlands, for example, government has experimented with comprehensive, multimedia environmental targets for pollution reduction, accompanied by agreements from industry groups to achieve overall targets. In return for these agreements, government agrees to eliminate otherwise applicable pollutant-by-pollutant regulations and to reduce any changes in requirements during the length of the contract period. The European Community has made good use of environmental agreements, as have a number of nations within Europe.[62] Such agreements have been developed to regulate disposal of spent batteries in Germany, the metal industry in the Netherlands, and pollution by the cement industry in Belgium. In 2000, the European Community reached an agreement with European automobile manufacturers, calling for substantial reductions in carbon dioxide emissions from new cars.

The largest and most important risk reduction contracts have occurred in Europe and Japan. But in the United States, the EPA and other agencies have taken modest steps in the same direction. Under the 1990 Clean Air Act, companies can, in essence, "contract out" of technology-based controls for five years if they achieve a 90 percent reduction in toxic pollutants before EPA promulgates relevant regulations.[63] Under most federal statutes, however, EPA

---

[60] See id. for an excellent, detailed discussion.

[61] See Peter Mennell & Richard B. Stewart, Environmental Law and Policy 420–2 (Boston: Little, Brown, & Co., 1995); Jan M. Van Dunne, Environmental Contracts and Covenants (Rotterdam, Netherlands: Institute of Environmental Damages, 1993).

[62] For an overview, see Richard B. Stewart, A New Generation of Environmental Regulation?, 42 U.S.C. 29 Capitol Univ. L. Rev. 21, 80–6 (2001).

[63] 112(h).

cannot approve private plans as substitutes for public mandates, even if the plans promise better results for less money. Congress should move in the direction of allowing private substitutes so long as government monitoring is maintained. Of course, it remains important to know whether the benefits from the private alternative are higher than the costs; perhaps the private alternative is cheaper but still not worthwhile on balance.

How should government protect endangered species? For many decades, the preferred strategy was simple: Identify endangered species as such, and punish people who kill members of those species. In many cases, however, this approach seemed ineffectual, or at least imperfect, and for one simple reason: Government became involved much too late. More recently, American government has experiment with "habitat conservation plans" (HCPs). These plans are made possible by the fact that the Endangered Species Act authorizes the Department of the Interior to grant "permits" for "incidental" takings of members of listed or endangered species. The department has made creative use of this authority, giving landowners a permit "to take" members of an endangered species in return for creating a habitat conservation plan and ensuring that there will be no serious harm to the species' chance for survival.

To receive a permit, applicants generally prepare a detailed HCP, outlining the effects of the proposed development and proposing ways to mitigate any harms. The plan might, for example, contain a promise to restrict development to certain areas, or to acquire, fund, or preserve alternative habitat for the species. The department reviews the plan to see whether it will provide adequate protection for the species. The result is that government has approved a large number of HCPs, many of them quite large, in which negotiated agreements ensure protection of species. There have been many remarkable developments here. Entrepreneurs have been creating "habitat banks," consisting of habitat sites that are available for purchase by prospective developers.[64] The government has also created a "no surprises policy," assuring landowners that so long as they comply with the terms of the HCP, the government will not alter the levels of regulatory compliance and mandatory mitigation.

An equally ambitious example is Project XL, developed by the EPA. Under Project XL, the EPA allows companies to generate their own preferred ways of achieving regulatory goals. Once those ways are suggested and approved, the government enters into a contract, effectively allowing companies to "opt out" of regulatory requirements. Thus facilities are permitted to use innovative pollution control techniques, promising better environmental performance, in return for relaxed reporting and permitting requirements. The goal of Project

[64] See Stewart, supra note 62 in Chapter 10, at 74.

XL is to allow people to enter into large-scale agreements that promise bigger, multifaceted reductions, going beyond those required by existing law, in return for an agreement by EPA to "waive" that law. Unfortunately, it is not at all clear that this initiative is consistent with existing law. Indeed, EPA staff has adopted an informal slogan: "If it isn't illegal, it isn't XL." But it is clear that in principle, Project XL has a great deal of promise.

Project XL does not give companies complete freedom to design their own programs for improving environmental performance. To qualify, companies must show that the innovative strategy will provide *better*, and not merely equal, environmental protection. In addition, companies must show that they have consulted with stakeholders, including community groups; that the project is feasible; that it sets forth clear objectives and requirements that can actually be measured; and that it will not transfer risks and hazards to poor or minority communities.[65] As an example, consider Georgia-Pacific Corporation's pulp and paper mill in Big Island, Virginia.[66] The mill produces components of cardboard from hardwood pulp; it has traditionally incinerated spent pulping liquor, thus producing significant emissions of hazardous air pollutants. As part of its XL plan, Georgia-Pacific will develop and install a new technology that will transform pulping liquor into clean-burning gases, which can then be used as fuel to create energy for the plant. The new technology will eliminate most of the hazardous air pollution and also reduce the mill's need to purchase energy from elsewhere, thus reducing emissions of greenhouse gases. In return for Georgia-Pacific's agreement to develop and use the new technology, EPA agreed to a slight modification of the legal deadline for ensuring reductions of hazardous air pollutants.

How should government deal with those who have violated environmental laws and are therefore subject to civil and criminal penalties? The traditional answer is: Impose those penalties. But in a creative alternative approach, the EPA has obtained a distinctive form of environmental agreement, designed to require violators to undertake environmental projects in return for a waiver of some part of the financial penalties required by law.[67] These "supplemental environmental project" (SEP) provisions require violators to face some monetary penalties to ensure adequate deterrence, but they also allow a relaxation of penalties so long as violators undertake some environmentally friendly action with a "nexus" to the violations. If, for example, a company has polluted a lake, it might face

---

[65] See the superb overview in Dennis D. Hirsch, Project XL and the Special Case: The EPA's Untold Success Story, 26 Colum. J. Env. L. 219 (2001).

[66] See id.

[67] For the EPA's policy, see *es.epa.gov/oeca/sep/sep.*

reduced penalties if it agrees to help clean up water pollution in a nearby lake. We could easily imagine a far more ambitious approach, building on the idea of "bigger bubbles." Instead of requiring a "nexus" between the violation and the SEP, the government might be authorized to allow violators to face reduced penalties, or perhaps no penalties at all, so long as they proved willing to spend equivalent resources on promoting environmental protection.

In some closely analogous initiatives, the EPA has attempted to encourage companies to promote risk reduction goals voluntarily. Consider, for example, the EPA's Green Lights Program, which is intended to lead companies to use energy-efficient lighting in their facilities. An inspiration for the program is the belief that energy efficiency is good for profits as well as for the environment, and that companies often lack knowledge of what they have to gain. Interested companies sign a memorandum of understanding with the EPA, agreeing to become a Green Lights Partner, calling for improving the energy efficiency of 90 percent of its lighted square footage within five years. In return, the EPA provides technical support and information and also publicizes the company's participation in the program.

The EPA's 33/50 program belongs in the same category. Under this program, the EPA targeted companies emitting certain toxic chemicals in 1988, asking them to produce 33 percent reductions by 1992 and 50 percent reductions by 1995. Of the 10,000 invited companies, 1,300 agreed to participate and hence to commit to the program. By 1994, the program achieved its goal.[68]

Building on these numerous precedents, I suggest that Congress should consider an amendment to existing statutes, designed to authorize agencies to enter into risk reduction contracts. The amendment might say: "Notwithstanding any other provision of law, the EPA [or other agency] shall have the authority to enter into enforceable agreements with regulated persons and institutions, waiving regulatory requirements in return for an enforceable commitment to achieve greater pollution reductions than those otherwise required by law." Such an amendment would promote the central goal of the various initiatives I have been emphasizing here – to deflect governmental attention from means to ends – in the hope of enlisting private creativity in the service of risk reduction policies.

One of the most attractive features of the movement for cost–benefit analysis is that it attempts to reduce the unintended side-effects of risk regulation, including lower employment, reduced wages, and higher prices. One of the (intended) side-effects of cheaper tools is that they make aggressive risk reduction far more

[68] For a review, see *www.epa.gov/opptintr/3350/3350-fnl.pdf.*

feasible and far more attractive, even to people who might otherwise be skeptical of it.

FREE MARKET ENVIRONMENTALISM: BEYOND CALCULATIONS

The three tools discussed thus far retain a substantial regulatory role for government. If government is disclosing risk-related information, it will have to compile that information first. If government is seeking to use economic incentives, it must choose a sensible pollution tax or cap. If government is entering into a risk reduction contract, it must decide on the acceptable degree of risk reduction. But as I have suggested (see Chapter 5), it is possible to imagine a property rights approach, one that restricts government's role to the establishment and protection of the relevant rights. Many environmentalists are deeply skeptical of this approach, thinking that property rights are the problem, not the solution. In some domains they are right, as where people lack the information to bargain to reasonable outcomes; but, in other domains, they are quite wrong. Free market environmentalism should even be seen as a close cousin of economic incentives and information disclosure, one that has significant advantages, because it does not require government to create a cap or to impose a fee, and because it frees government from the obligation to compile and disclose information.

Recall the problem of overgrazing by cattle, a problem that might well be eliminated through the creation of property rights to land.[69] Analogous approaches have been used in many domains. To protect rare songbirds, the Environmental Defense Fund has paid ranchers in Texas to trap and remove cowbirds that invade their nests. The Delta Waterfowl Foundation pays farmers to maintain habitat for duck populations, with excellent results.[70] To protect both ranchers and wolves, Defenders of Wildlife adopted an innovative program, creating a wolf compensation fund from which ranchers could be paid for livestock losses as a result of wolf predation. Indeed, Defenders of Wildlife went so far as to pay ranchers to allow wolves to live on their property, turning a liability into an asset. This approach should be seen as a private analogue to Habitat Conservation Plans, allowing environmentalists to work with ranchers so as to ensure that protection of the environment is profitable, not costly.

In a provocative and illuminating book, Terry Anderson and Donald Leal argue that environmental policy should go much further in this direction.[71]

---

[69] See Anderson and Leal, supra note 43 in Chapter 5, on which I draw throughout this section.
[70] Id. at 173–4.
[71] Id.

They oppose "political environmentalism," in which government imposes mandates or creates incentives. Instead they urge a general system of "free market environmentalism," in which government creates property rights so as to ensure that people have the correct incentives. Consider, for example, the problem of disposing of waste, a problem that creates a number of risks, especially but not only when the waste is toxic. For many decades, governments have ignored the problem and partly made it worse by attempting, at no fee, to dispose of waste on their own. More recently, governments have imposed regulatory mandates for waste disposal and sometimes required individuals and companies to engage in recycling. Anderson and Leal argue that governments should try instead to ensure a functioning market, in which households and companies must pay people to dispose of their waste, and in which those who dispose of waste would be liable for harms that they cause. "A free market solution to the pollution problem would require well-defined and enforced property rights to both the waste and the disposal medium.... At the very least, municipal, state, and federal agencies should raise the price to individuals for using waste disposal systems. Not only will this give people incentives to produce less garbage, it will also provide funds to clean up pollution."[72]

It would be possible to build on this idea in many domains. With respect to fisheries, for example, a system of property rights could create strong incentives against pollution and depleted fish stocks. As Anderson and Leal urge, practices of Native Americans might well provide a model here, for long ago, Native American tribes established systems of property rights to prevent overexploitation of fishing sites. With respect to endangered species, we could imagine property-type approaches designed to give people strong incentives to ensure against capture or killing. It is certainly difficult to use property rights to handle many of the problems that I have discussed, such as global warming. But we should not neglect the possibility of creative solutions even in this domain.[73]

Free market environmentalism is hardly a panacea. In some cases, those who want to reduce social risks might be unable to obtain their goals through market transactions, perhaps because they are poorly organized, perhaps because they lack necessary information, or perhaps because they are simply too poor. Markets depend on the willingness-to-pay criterion, and in some contexts, that criterion may be unacceptable. In some cases, it is simply too difficult to create property rights. In many cases, people lack the information to ensure well-functioning markets, and hence property rights are not enough. For example, it is entirely appropriate to attempt to improve safety at work, especially in light of the fact that workers frequently lack risk-related information. But if

---

[72] Id. at 142.
[73] See id. at 163–7.

free market environmentalism is seen as a pragmatic tool, one that is likely to work in some domains, it will belong in the same family with information disclosure, economic incentives, and risk reduction contracts. The major goal of these tools is to reduce the informational burden on government and to try to reduce risks in a way that minimizes government planning. In this way, an emphasis on cost-benefit balancing should, before long, take government well beyond cost–benefit analysis itself.

Afterword: On Consequences
and Technocrats

A central purpose of this book has been to connect the law of risk regulation to an accurate understanding of how people think about hazards. I have attempted to identify a number of problems in people's risk-related intuitions. Some of these problems produce bad policy and bad law. Well-organized interests, often with selfish motivations, are all too willing to exploit these problems, producing law that is in their own interests. Sometimes the resulting law fails to protect health, safety, or the environment at all. The law should be based on facts, not intuitions, which are unreliable.

COGNITION, EMOTION, NUMBERS

Much of my focus has been on cognition. When confronted with difficult questions, people often substitute easier questions; they rely on mental shortcuts. This is entirely sensible; we all do it every day. But these shortcuts can lead people to make big mistakes. The availability heuristic is a particular case in point, making people think that some risks are much larger, and others much smaller, than they really are. (If the availability heuristic ensures that the availability heuristic will stand out, so be it.) We have also seen that people are "intuitive toxicologists," following a set of simple, misleading rules for thinking about hazards. A particular problem is that people seem to think that products and activities are either "safe" or "unsafe," without seeing that the real questions involve probabilities.

When people lack direct or reliable information, they rely, much of the time, on what other people tend to do or to think. There is a sensible heuristic here as well: Often the judgments and actions of other people should be followed, unless there is particular reason to do otherwise. Reliance on others is frequently rational. But here as well, people may be led to err. When social influences produce informational cascades, people may end up fearing tiny risks simply because they are responding to the signals created by similarly uninformed others. And when like-minded people are talking largely with one another, they tend to move each other toward extremes. At the level of individual behavior, the consequence can be risk-taking behavior, as when people use illegal drugs, drive drunk, or smoke cigarettes; tobacco companies are entirely aware of the influence of peer pressure and seek to exploit it to their advantage. At the level of government action, the result can be a public obsession about trivial problems – or widespread contempt for the "zealotry" of people who are raising legitimate concerns. We have seen that the availability heuristic can interact with social influences, producing "availability cascades" in which particular risks move to the fore, regardless of their actual magnitude. These cascades lead to the "risk of the month" syndrome in both federal and state law.

Often people neglect tradeoffs. They focus on one side of a complicated problem. They fail to see that risks are part of systems, complex ones in fact, and that an effort to control one part of the system will have effects on other parts as well. The most poignant cases arise when an effort to regulate a risk ends up producing other, more serious risks. But there is reason for concern whenever people neglect the costs and burdens associated with risk regulation.

These are mostly points about public cognition. But emotions are important too. A vivid picture of a risk can trigger public concern. By contrast, statistical information often falls on deaf ears. Both insurance companies and state lottery commissions are entirely aware of this. They peddle fear and hope, not by offering data, but by providing images of catastrophe and good fortune. With respect to risks, people often react to such images, rather than to the probability that bad things will actually happen. Vivid images can even "crowd out" sensible assessments of probability. For daily life, as for policy, probability should matter far more than it does. The affect heuristic often ensures that people will evaluate risks and activities on the basis of a rapid, general impression, rather than a good assessment of likely consequences. For busy people, the affect heuristic can make a lot of sense, but it too leads to errors.

All these points bear directly on the law of risk. They help explain why we have the laws that we have. They also suggest sensible reforms. A salient incident, such as the incident at Love Canal, can often drive policy in a particular direction, resulting in the expenditure of hundreds of millions of dollars on relatively small problems. Bandwagon effects can produce widespread public fear about trivial dangers, as in the case of genetically modified food. When a salient incident has not caught public attention, government is likely to neglect serious problems, as in the contexts of skin cancer and indoor air pollution. The key provisions of the Clean Air Act seem written on the (indefensible) assumption that air is either safe or unsafe. The EPA knows otherwise. Too much of the time, government suffers from "tunnel vision" and is not required to take account of the problems that can be created by risk reduction.

In these circumstances, cost–benefit analysis emerges as a natural step, one that can help overcome many of the problems we face in assessing risks. The great virtue of cost–benefit analysis is that it promotes a better understanding of the actual consequences of regulation. When availability bias makes people excessively concerned with trivial risks, cost–benefit analysis is a useful corrective. When the public is becoming fearful of an imaginary danger, but neglecting real dangers in daily life, an effort to tabulate the costs and benefits can overcome both panic and neglect. When regulation actually increases the very risks that it is designed to reduce, an understanding of health–health tradeoffs can be a valuable corrective. I have urged that in attempting to clean the air, the Environmental Protection Agency should be as quantitative as possible. This is not because the numbers tell us nearly everything that we need to know, but because, without the numbers, we do not know nearly enough.

Most generally, I have urged that, to the extent feasible, government should perform cost–benefit calculations for all major regulations and that agencies should generally be required to show that the benefits justify the costs. If an agency seeks to proceed even though the benefits do not justify the costs, it should explain itself, perhaps by showing that the risk at issue is faced disproportionately by children or is especially hard to avoid – or that the benefits of the regulation would be enjoyed mostly by the poor, and the costs imposed mostly on the wealthy.

But it is far from sufficient to ask the government to calculate the numbers. The use of "smarter tools" can help a great deal – for global warming and much more. Information, economic incentives, "environmental contracting," and free market environmentalism provide models for the future. No nation has used these tools nearly as much as it should. We can even venture a prediction: The twenty-first century will be a time when nations, rich and poor alike, move increasingly away from command-and-control programs and increasingly toward methods for reducing risk that rely on disclosing information, creating new markets, and asking people to use their own creativity to find new ways to reduce risk. Of these approaches, disclosure of risk-related information is the most interesting and potentially the most productive strategy, not least because it imposes market pressure on those who subject people to danger.

COST–BENEFIT ANALYSIS AND ITS CRITICS

I have also attempted to understand cost–benefit analysis in a way that is responsive to the legitimate concerns of its many critics. By way of summary, and to bring various strands of the discussion together:

- The magnitude of costs and the magnitude of benefits are not all that matters. Distributional considerations are indeed relevant. I have urged that regulation is not, all of the time, a good way of helping those who are disadvantaged or otherwise needy because the costs of regulation are often borne not by "companies" but by ordinary people — consumers, workers, people who lose their jobs. Nonetheless, it is entirely legitimate for government to take account of the fact — when it is a fact — that the benefits of regulation will be enjoyed mostly by those who need help.

- Cost–benefit analysis can give an illusion of precision, at least if existing knowledge does not permit us to specify benefits or costs. In these circumstances, the best approach is not to reject cost–benefit analysis, but to offer ranges, with a full appreciation of the possibility of uncertainty.

- Some people claim, rightly, that social goods are "incommensurable," in the sense that we do not value all goods in the same way that we value money. A human life is not really equivalent to $6.1 million, or whatever economic amount we choose to spend to prevent a statistical death. Beaches and parks and wolves and seals are not reducible to their economic value. For this reason, cost–benefit analysis, of the sort that I have urged here, should include qualitative as well as quantitative descriptions of the consequences of regulation. We should not think that the monetary "bottom line" is anything magical; it is simply a helpful input into the decision.

- Cost–benefit analysis does not respect "intuitive toxicology," and for this reason it might seem to disregard people's sense of risk and danger. The point is correct, but it is no objection. Policy should ordinarily be rooted in evidence, not baseless fear or unwarranted optimism.

- Cost–benefit analysis might seem to treat human lives cavalierly, simply because it places a monetary value on statistical risks. But any government is required to assign some noninfinite value to statistical risks. It is best for government to be clear about what it is doing and why it is doing it. If the amounts are too low, then government is indeed treating lives cavalierly, and the amounts should be increased.

- Cost–benefit analysis might seem to give insufficient weight to the future and in particular to the interests of future generations. I have urged that a sensible cost–benefit analysis does indeed give weight to the future, though the selection of the appropriate discount rate raises many conundrums.

- Cost–benefit analysis might seem to be undemocratic, especially insofar as it allows policy to be set in large part by experts. I have argued that, on the contrary, cost–benefit analysis is an important tool for promoting democratic goals because it ensures that some account of the likely consequences of regulation will be placed before officials and the public at large. Experts are crucial to sensible policy simply because of their expertise. If public officials want to proceed even though the costs do not justify the benefits, they are permitted to do that, so long as they can generate a good reason for their decision.

- Cost–benefit analysis might be criticized insofar as it relies on private willingness to pay as the basis for calculating both costs and benefits. Sometimes people are poorly informed, and hence are willing to pay little for significant benefits. Sometimes people are unwilling to pay for certain goods simply because their preferences have adapted to the status quo, in which they face real deprivation. Sometimes private willingness to pay will understate benefits, if people are willing to pay more for a good if other people are going to be paying for them too. Poor people might have little willingness to pay simply because they have little ability to pay. In many contexts, these objections have force. There is no special magic in the idea of willingness to pay. I have suggested that government needs some numbers from which to begin its analysis, that private willingness to pay is a good start, but that government can depart from that number if the context shows a sensible reason to do so. Current practice shows considerable good sense on this count.[1]

- Some people fear that, as a practical matter, cost–benefit analysis will simply paralyze government and prevent it from issuing regulations that would do more good than harm. If this is true, then the pragmatic argument for cost–benefit analysis has been defeated. Any effort to ensure cost–benefit balancing should ensure that it does not produce "paralysis by analysis." I have urged that the record suggests that cost–benefit balancing does not, in fact, produce paralysis.

- Cost–benefit analysis might be challenged as a form of centralized government planning, likely to overload government's ability to compile the necessary information. The objection too has much force, especially in light of the fact that government's own incentives are not always to be trusted. The simplest response to this objection relies on the absence of good alternatives: If the government is seeking to regulate arsenic in drinking water, and if it is sensible to do so, how is it going to proceed if it does not compile information about the effects of possible courses of action? A more complex response acknowledges the need for tools that minimize government's burden. Economic incentives, free market environmentalism, and risk reduction contracts are examples.

---

[1] See Adler & Posner, supra note 62 in Chapter 8.

CELEBRATING TECHNOCRATS, AND BEYOND

In many ways, this book has been a celebration of the centrality of science and expertise to the law of risk. Indeed, I have attempted to defend a highly technocratic approach to risk regulation, and given reasons to be sharply skeptical of populism, at least in this domain of the law. But I have also offered two objections to a purely technocratic approach to risk reduction.

First, ours is a deliberative democracy in which reflective public judgment play a large role. Where judgments of value are to be made, they should be made by the citizenry, not by experts. Some deaths are particularly bad, and these deserve unusual attention. It would indeed to obtuse to treat all risks as if they were the same, regardless of context and quality. People are right to insist that it matters whether a risk is voluntarily incurred. When it is especially easy to avoid certain risks, government should not spend a great deal of time and effort in response. People are also right to say that fair distribution of risk matters. Thus I have urged that as part of a cost–benefit analysis, it is important to know who would gain and who would lose – and that government legitimately seeks to mimimize the burdens faced by the most disadvantaged members of society and to maximize the benefits that they receive.

I have also urged that there are qualitative differences among the various goods involved in risk regulation and that the bottom-line numbers should not be decisive. But it remains true that a sensible society is greatly concerned to ensure that people have longer and healthier lives, and that if policies lead government to spend a lot on small problems, and little on large problems, something is amiss. As I have emphasized throughout, a more sensible allocation of resources could save thousands of lives, billions of dollars, or perhaps both.

Second, technocrats tend to ignore the fact that to work well, a regulatory system needs one thing above all – public support and confidence. This is so whether or not a lack of confidence would be fully rational. To the extent that government relies on statistical evidence alone, it is unlikely to promote its own goals. Partly this is because people will assess that evidence in light of their own motivations and their inevitably limited capacities. Regulators who are alert to the importance of both confidence and trust will do what they can to provide information in a way that is well-tailored to how people think about risk – and that tries to educate people when their usual ways of thinking lead them astray. In some circumstances, an understanding of how people think will lead government toward approaches that technocrats will not have on their viewscreen. We might say that good technocrats need to know not only economics and science but psychology as well.

A main goal of this book has been to draw attention to the actual consequences of risk regulation, and to propose methods for ensuring that an accurate
assessment of those consequences plays a larger role than it now does. Some
people think that it is important for law and policy to "make statements" – to
express attitudes that all or most citizens find correct or congenial. And it is
certainly important to allow for the expression of public attitudes through law.
But a well-functioning democracy seeks above all to produce policies that will,
in fact, improve people's lives. Because of predictable features of human cognition, ordinary intuitions provide unreliable guidance about risks, and about
what policies, actual or proposed, will actually do. As we have seen, the resulting
blunders have harmful consequences for regulatory policy. The task for the
future is to develop institutions that will respond to people's values, not to
their errors.

Appendix A

Worldwide Health Statistics

Table A.1 lists the number of deaths by cause across global regions, while Table A.2 indicates that infant mortality rates from selected countries have severely declined in the past decades. At the same time, average life expectancies have risen (see Table A.3); according to the World Health Organization (WHO), Japan retains the longest life expectancy of 75 years among 191 countries, compared with 26 years for the lowest ranking country Sierra Leone.[1] Regionally, Europe has the greatest life expectancy at an average of 75 years, in comparison to a group low of 54 for the African continent (see Figure A.1). In 2000, WHO conducted its first analysis of these countries' health systems and concluded that France provides the best overall health care, followed, among major countries, by Italy, Spain, Oman, Austria, and Japan.[2] Although the United States spent more of its gross domestic product on health care than any other country, it ranked only thirty-seventh out of 191 countries.[3]

Among health concerns, occupational injuries and diseases kill an estimated 1.1 million people worldwide each year, including approximately 300,000 fatalities from 250 million accidents (see Figure A.2 for a breakdown of workplace fatalities).[4] Approximately 30 percent of the workforce in developed countries, and between 50 and 70 percent in developing countries, may be exposed to heavy physical workloads or poor working conditions, which can lead to injuries and musculoskeletal disorders.[5] Those industries most affected include mining,

[1]   WHO, Press Releases, WHO Issues New Healthy Life Expectancy Rankings: Japan Number One in New "Healthy Life" System, available at *www.who.int/inf-pr-2000/en-pr2000-life.html*.
[2]   WHO, Press Releases, World Health Report 2000, available at *www.who.int/whr/2000/en/press_release.htm*.
[3]   Id.
[4]   WHO, Fact Sheets, Occupational Health: Ethically Corect Economically Sound, available at *www.who.int/inf-fs/en/fact084.html*.
[5]   Id.

Table A.I Death estimates by geographic region, 1999 (in thousands)

Cause	Africa	Americas	Eastern Mediterranean	Europe	Southeast Asia	Western Pacific
Total Deaths	10,436	5,687	4,218	9,057	14,270	12,297
Communicable diseases, maternal and perinatal conditions, and nutritional deficiencies	7,360	879	1,496	531	5,599	1,516
Infectious/parasitic	5,223	336	757	177	2,917	577
Respiratory infections	1,086	299	343	275	1,523	514
Maternal conditions	255	18	39	4	158	21
Perinatal conditions	615	153	313	62	851	363
Nutritional deficiencies	180	72	44	14	159	22
Noncommunicable conditions	2,300	4,255	2,318	7,776	7,370	9,462
Malignant neoplasms	523	1,032	274	1,794	1,169	2,273
Other neoplasms	4	21	4	34	15	23
Diabetes mellitus	38	216	54	136	180	153
Nutritional/endocrine disorders	46	92	29	35	17	86
Neuropsychiatric disorders	81	177	62	209	191	191
Cardiovascular diseases	935	1,942	1,369	4,624	4,180	3,919
Respiratory diseases	226	302	156	387	577	1,926
Digestive diseases	210	277	143	364	528	528
Diseases of genitourinary system	120	115	112	121	236	197
Skin diseases	23	9	5	11	9	4
Musculoskeletal diseases	14	21	4	24	15	29
Congenital abnormalities	79	51	106	38	260	119
Injuries	776	552	405	750	1,301	1,317
Unintentional	456	331	292	483	993	857
Intentional	320	221	112	267	308	460

Source: WHO, Statistics, World Health Report 2000, Annex Table 3: Deaths by Cause, Sex and Mortality Stratum in WHO Regions, Estimates for 1999, available at *www.who.int/whr/2000/en/statistics.htm*.

Table A.2 Infant mortality rate trends in Europe and North America, 1965–2000[a]

Country	Years						
	1965–70	1970–75	1975–80	1980–85	1985–90	1990–95	1995–2000
Austria	27	24	17	12	9	7	6
Belgium	23	19	14	11	9	8	7
Canada	21	16	12	9	7	6	6
Czech Republic	22	20	18	15	11	9	6
Denmark	16	12	9	8	8	7	7
France	21	16	11	9	8	7	6
Germany	23	21	15	11	8	6	5
Greece	42	34	25	15	11	9	8
Hungary	37	34	27	20	17	13	10
Italy	33	26	18	13	10	8	7
Norway	14	12	9	8	8	6	5
Spain	33	21	16	11	8	8	7
Sweden	13	10	8	7	6	6	5
United Kingdom	19	17	14	11	9	7	7
United States	22	18	14	11	10	9	7

[a]Rate reflects deaths under 1 year per 1,000 live births.
Source: United Nations Economic Commission for Europe, Statistics, Trends in Europe and North America, 1998 Statistical Yearbook of the UN/ECE, available at *www.unece.org/stats/trend/aut.htm.*

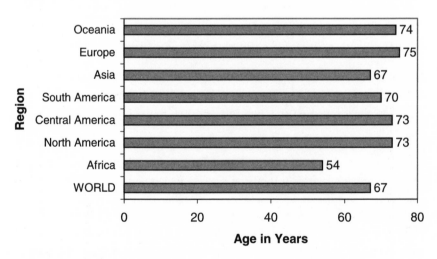

Figure A.1 2001 regional life expectancy
Source: Population Reference Bureau, Publications, 2001 World Population Data Sheet, available at *www.prb.org/pubs/wpds2001/sheet3.html.*

Table A.3 Life expectancy at birth for selected countries, 1950–2005

	1950		1998		2000–2005[a]	
Region/Country	Male	Female	Male	Female	Male	Female
Europe						
Austria	62.0	67.0	74.1	80.7	75.4	81.5
Belgium	62.1	67.4	74.1	80.7	75.7	81.9
Czech Republic	60.9	65.5	70.8	77.7	72.1	78.7
Denmark	68.9	71.5	73.6	79.1	74.2	79.1
France	63.7	69.4	74.6	82.6	75.2	82.8
Germany	64.6	68.5	73.8	80.3	75.0	81.1
Greece	63.4	66.7	75.8	81.0	75.9	81.2
Hungary	59.3	63.4	66.5	75.4	67.8	76.1
Italy	63.7	67.2	75.3	81.7	75.5	81.9
Norway	70.3	73.3	75.4	81.2	76.0	81.9
Spain	59.8	64.3	73.8	81.6	75.4	82.3
Sweden	69.9	72.6	76.5	82.0	77.6	82.6
United Kingdom	66.2	71.1	74.8	80.1	75.7	80.7
Africa						
Congo	37.5	40.6	45.3	48.9	49.6	53.7
Egypt	41.2	43.6	60.1	64.1	66.7	69.9
Ghana	40.4	43.6	54.8	58.9	56.0	58.5
Mali	31.1	34.0	45.7	48.4	51.1	53.0
South Africa	44.0	46.0	53.6	57.8	46.5	48.3
Uganda	38.5	41.6	41.8	43.4	45.3	46.8
Asia/Australia						
Australia	66.7	71.8	77.0	83.0	76.4	82.0
China	39.3	42.3	68.3	71.1	69.1	73.5
India	39.4	38.0	62.1	63.7	63.6	64.9
Japan	59.6	63.1	76.9	83.3	77.8	85.0
Kazakhstan	51.6	61.9	58.1	69.3	59.6	70.7
South Korea	46.0	49.0	70.4	78.0	71.8	79.1
Syria	44.8	47.2	66.5	69.1	70.6	73.1
Thailand	45.0	49.1	65.4	72.8	67.9	73.8
North/South America						
Argentina	60.4	65.1	70.9	78.3	70.6	77.7
Brazil	49.3	52.8	59.4	69.6	64.7	72.6
Costa Rica	56.0	58.6	73.5	78.5	75.0	79.7
Cuba	57.8	61.3	73.0	77.9	74.8	78.7
Mexico	49.2	52.4	68.6	74.8	70.4	76.4
United States	66.0	71.7	72.9	83.3	74.6	80.4
Venezuela	53.8	56.6	69.7	75.9	70.9	76.7

[a]Estimated by Population Division of the United Nations Secretariat.
Source: Infoplease.com, World, World Statistics, Social Statistics, Life Expectancy at Birth for Selected Countries: 1950 and 1998, available at *www.infoplease.com/ipa/A0774532.html*; United Nations Statistics Division, Social Indicators, Indicators on Health, available at *www.un.org/Depts/unsd/social/health.htm*.

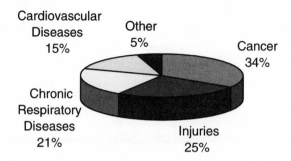

Figure A.2 Estimated global work-related mortality based on 1990–5 data
Source: Fact Sheet, Occupational Health: Ethically Correct, Economically Sound, available at *www.who.int/inf-fs/en/fact084.html.*

farming, fishing, construction, and health-care personnel.[6] Economic losses from occupational injury are devastating; the International Labour Organization (ILO) estimates that, in 1997 alone, the overall economic losses resulting from work-related diseases and injuries were approximately 4 percent of the world's gross national product.[7]

[6] Id.
[7] Id.

Appendix B

Statistical Risks: U.S. General
Mortality Trends

In the past seventy years, regulatory initiatives, technological advances, and behavioral changes have significantly reduced the average level of domestic, occupational, and environmental risks in the United States, as demonstrated by Table B.1. As a result, life expectancy in the United States has catapulted from 47.3 in 1900 to 77.1 in 2000.

Table B.2 presents age-adjusted death rates for selected causes of death across the past two decades. Table B.3 presents mortality rates for leading causes of death in 1998 and 1999.

SPECIFIC MORTALITY TRENDS

TRANSPORTATION ACCIDENTS

Figure B.1 presents fatality statistics for U.S. aircraft transportation since 1987. Globally, the year 2000 ranked as the sixth safest year in terms of fatal airline accidents, registering a death toll of 1,131, well below the average, from 1970 to 1999, of 1,464 casualties per year. Thirty-six fatal accidents were reported in the year 2000, compared to a 1970–99 average of 51 per year and a 1990–9 average of 48.3.

A much larger mortality contributor, motor vehicle accidents, also declined in past decades. Figure B.2 outlines trends in automobile fatalities from 1987. In 1999 alone, an estimated 6,279,000 reported accidents led to 41,611 deaths and 3,236,000 injuries. Although deaths increased 0.3 percent, the fatality rate per 100 million vehicle miles of travel remained at a historic low of 1.6, compared to 1.7 in 1992–6 and 2.2 in 1989. A nationwide safety belt use rate of 67 percent and reduction in alcohol involvement to 38 percent were significant contributors to maintaining fewer casualties.

Table B.1 Principal death risk trends

| Decade | Annual Rate of Change in Death Rates (per 100,000 population) | | |
	Work	Home	Motor Vehicle
1930–1940	−1.8	−0.2	−3.3
1940–1950	−2.3	−2.2	−4.0
1950–1960	−2.8	−2.1	−3.5
1960–1970	−1.2	−1.7	−0.8
1970–1980	−1.6	−2.7	−3.4
1980–1990	−3.2	−2.4	−4.3

[a]Date prior to 1920 includes death-registration states only.
Sources: National Center for Health Statistics, 48(19) National Vital Statistics Report 1, 33–34 table 12 (Feb. 7, 2001); National Center for Health Statistics 47(13) National Vital Statistics Report 1, 17 table 5 (Dec. 24, 1998), at *www.cdc.gov/nchswww/data/nvs47_13.pdf.*
W. Kip Viscusi, Fatal Trade offs 285 (Oxford: Oxford University Press, 1992).

Table B.2 Age-adjusted death rates for selected causes of death from 1979 to 1998

| Cause | Year | | | | | |
	1979	1982	1986	1990	1994	1998
Accidents	47.9	41.4	40.0	37.5	35.7	36.3
Alzheimer's disease	0.2	1.3	4.6	6.4	7.8	8.6
Cancer	204.0	208.3	211.5	216.0	213.1	202.4
Cerebrovascular diseases	97.3	84.4	73.3	65.5	63.3	59.6
Chronic liver disease and cirrhosis	14.8	13.2	11.8	11.1	10.2	9.5
Diabetes mellitus	17.5	17.2	17.2	20.7	22.7	24.2
Heart diseases	401.6	389.0	365.1	321.8	299.7	272.4
Homicide	9.9	9.4	8.6	9.5	9.4	6.7
Hypertension	4.1	4.0	3.8	4.1	4.8	5.4
Infectious and parasitic diseases	1.8	2.1	4.1	13.2	19.0	7.5
Pneumonia and influenza	26.1	26.5	34.8	36.8	33.9	34.6
Suicide	12.6	12.5	13.0	12.5	12.1	11.3
All causes	1,010.9	985	978.6	938.7	920.2	875.8

Source: Center for Disease Control, National Center for Health Statistics, National Vital Statistics System, Mortality, Unpublished table, 1, 10, 15, 16, 27, 32, 43, 44, 52, 63, 80, 83, 84, 87, available at *www.cdc.gov/nchs/data/aadr7998s.pdf.*

Table B.3 Deaths and death-rates for the fifteen leading causes of death from 1998 to 1999

		1998			1999	
Rank	Cause	Death Rate	Number of Deaths	% of Total Deaths	Death Rate	Percent Change from 1998
I	Diseases of heart	272.4	724,915	30.3	267.7	−0.7
2	Cancer	202.4	549,787	23.0	202.6	−0.9
3	Cerebrovascular diseases	59.5	167,340	7.0	61.8	−2.1
4	Chronic lower respiratory diseases	42.0	124,153	5.2	45.8	3.9
5	Accidents (unintentional injuries)	35.0	97,298	4.1	35.7	−1.1
6	Diabetes mellitus	24.2	68,379	2.9	25.2	3.3
7	Influenza and pneumonia	34.6	63,686	2.7	23.5	−2.9
8	Alzheimer's disease	8.6	44,507	1.9	16.5	24.1
9	Nephritis, nephrotic syndrome, and nephrosis	9.8	35,524	1.5	13.1	8.3
10	Septicimia	8.9	30,670	1.3	11.3	6.6
11	Intentional self-harm (suicide)	11.3	29,041	1.2	10.6	−6.2
12	Chronic liver disease and cirrhosis	9.5	26,225	1.1	9.7	−2.0
13	Essential hypertension and hypertensive renal disease	5.4	16,964	0.7	6.3	5.0
14	Assault (homicide)	6.5	16,831	0.7	6.1	−6.2
15	Aortic aneurysm and dissection	6.1	15,806	0.7	5.8	−4.9
	All causes	875.8	2,391,630	100.0	881.9	0.7

Source: Center for Disease Control, National Center for Health Statistics, 49(3) National Vital Statistics Report 1, 5 table D (June 26, 2001), available at *http://www.cdc.gov/nchs/*.

HIV INFECTION

Though no longer ranked among the leading causes of U.S. deaths, HIV infection continues to contribute to American mortality. HIV infection still ranks fifth among 25–44 year olds and is the leading cause of death for black men in this group. Among black women in this age group, HIV ranks third. As indicated by Figures B.3 and B.4, however, HIV-related deaths dropped more than 70 percent between 1995 and 1999, with a reduction in AIDS diagnoses.

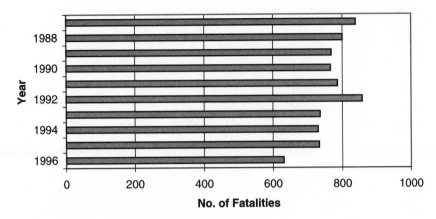

Figure B.1 Aircraft fatalities from 1987 to 1996
Source: National Transportation Safety Board, U.S. General Aviation Flying, 9-9 table 9.10, available at *www.api.faa.gov/handbook96/sh9-996.xls.*

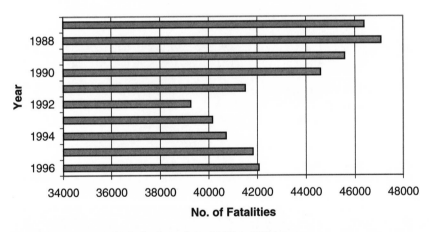

Figure B.2 Motor vehicle fatalities from 1987 to 1996
Source: National Highway Traffic Safety Administration, National Center for Statistics & Analysis, Traffic Safety Facts 1999, 15 table 2, available at *www.fars.nhtsa.dot.gov/pubs/1.pdf.*

OCCUPATIONAL HEALTH AND SAFETY

Since the establishment of the Occupational Safety and Health Administration in 1971, occupational injury and illness rates have declined by 40 percent (see Figure B.5), and workplace fatalities have been cut by 60 percent (see

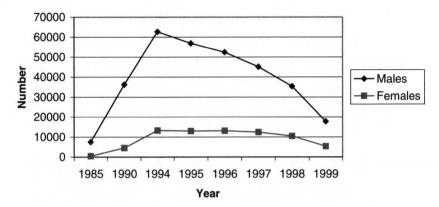

Figure B.3 AIDS cases diagnosed in males and females from 1985 to 1999
Source: Center for Disease Control, National Center for Health Statistics, 49(3) National Vital Statistics Report I, 223 table 53 (June 26, 2001), available at *www.cdc.gov/nchs/data/aadr7998i.pdf.*

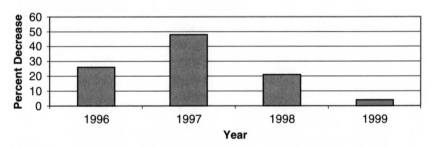

Figure B.4 Reduction in morality rates from HIV infection, 1996–9
Source: Center for Disease Control, National Center for Health Statistics, Mortality Declines for Several Leading Causes of Death in 1999 (June 26, 2001), available at *www.cdc.gov/nchs/releases/01news/declindea.htm.*

Table B.4).[1] At the same time, U.S. employment has nearly doubled from 56 million workers at 3.5 million worksites to 105 million workers at nearly 6.9 million sites in 2001.[2]

According to the National Center for Health Statistics, the number of fatal work injuries in 1999 was 6,023, nearly the same number as the previous year's total despite an increase in employment. Table B.5 presents the leading causes of occupational deaths, with subcategory examples. Decreases in job-related deaths

[1] OSHA, OSHA at 30: Three Decades of Progress in Occupational Safety and Health, available at *www.osha.gov/as/opa/osha-30.html.*
[2] Id.

Table B.4 Occupational fatalities by industry, 1974–1991

Year	Private Industry (Total)	Agriculture, Forestry, & Fishing	Mining	Construction	Manufacturing	Transportation & Public Utilities	Wholesale/Retail Trade	Finance, Insurance, & Real Estate	Services
1974	4,970	—	—	—	—	—	—	—	—
1975	4,570	—	—	—	—	—	—	—	—
1976	3,940	—	—	—	—	—	—	—	—
1977	4,760	—	—	—	—	—	—	—	—
1978	4,590	95	345	925	1,170	835	655	200	365
1979	4,950	110	490	960	1,100	915	930	85	360
1980	4,400	140	460	839	1,080	810	580	150	350
1981	4,370	130	500	800	990	750	730	120	350
1982	4,090	180	440	720	770	970	490	100	420
1983	3,100	80	240	670	730	570	440	70	310
1984	3,740	110	370	660	800	770	440	80	510
1985	3,750	100	260	980	820	730	440	70	340
1986	3,610	110	200	670	770	800	510	190	370
1987	3,400	80	150	820	790	580	460	140	380
1988	3,270	110	220	850	660	650	540	—	—
1989	3,600	110	110	780	690	590	720	—	—
1990	2,900	200	—	700	500	500	500	—	300
1991	2,800	—	100	500	600	400	400	—	600
1992	5,497	808	181	919	765	895	987	122	757
1993	5,643	864	174	932	767	894	1047	118	774
1994	5,959	852	180	1,028	789	949	1079	113	853
1995	5,495	800	156	1,055	709	901	943	125	749
1996	5,597	806	153	1,047	725	970	951	116	776
1997	5,616	833	158	1,107	744	1,008	911	97	727
1998	5,457	840	147	1,174	698	911	799	92	763
1999	5,487	814	122	1,191	722	1,008	751	107	735
2000	5,344	720	156	1,154	668	957	824	79	768

Source: U.S. Department of Labor, Occupational Safety and Health Administration, Statistics & Data, Fatal Workplace Injuries, available at *www.osha.gov/oshstats/privtbl.html*; Bureau of Labor Statistics, Safety & Health Statistics, Census of Fatal Occupational Injuries, tables A-10, A-3, available at *stats.bls.gov/special.requests/ocwc/oshwc/cfoi/cftb0121.pdf* and *stats.bls.gov/special.requests/ocwc/oshwc/cfoi/cftb0003.pdf.*

Table B.5 Fatal occupational injuries by event or exposure from 1994 to 1999

Event or Exposure	1994–8 Average	1999 Number	1999 Percentage
Transportation incidents	2,640	2,613	43
Highway	1,374	1,491	25
Nonhighway	387	353	6
Contact with objects or equipment	984	1,029	17
Struck by object	564	585	10
Assaults and violent acts	1,168	893	15
Homicides	923	645	11
Falls	686	717	12
Fall to lower level	609	634	11
Exposure to harmful substances or environments	583	529	9
Contact with electric current	322	278	5
Fires and explosions	199	216	4
TOTAL	6,280	6,023	100

Source: U.S. Department of Labor, Bureau of Labor Statistics, Census of Fatal Occupational Injuries Summary, table 1 (August 17, 2000), available at *stats.bls.gov/news.release/cfoi.nr0.htm.*

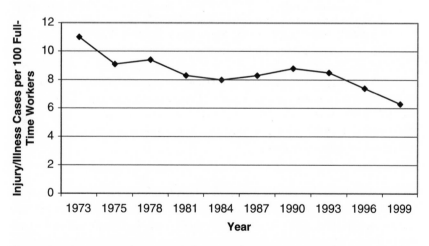

Figure B.5 Occupational injury and illness incidence rates, 1973–99
Source: U.S. Department of Labor, Occupational Safety Health Administration, Statistics & Data, Occupational Injury & Illness Incidence Rates per 100 Full-Time Workers, available at *www.osha.gov/oshstats/bltable.html.*

Table B.6 1999 fatal occupational injuries by occupation

Occupation	Number of Fatalities	Percent of Total Fatalities
Managerial and professional specialty	597	10
Technical, sales, and administrative support	610	10
Service occupations	468	8
Farming, forestry, and fishing	897	15
Precision production, craft, and repair	1,142	19
Operators, fabricators, and laborers	2,194	36
Military	80	1
TOTAL	6,023	100

Source: U.S. Department of Labor, Bureau of Labor Statistics, Census of Fatal Occupational Injuries Summary, table 2 (August 17, 2000), available at *stats.bls.gov/news.release/cfoi.nr0.htm.*

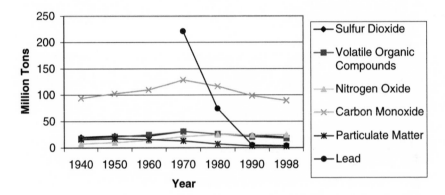

Figure B.6 U.S. emissions of principal pollutants in ten-year intervals through 1998 *Source:* Council on Environmental Quality, Environmental Quality Statistics, tables 5.1–5.7 (1999), available at *ceq.eh.doe.gov/nepa/reports/statistics/air.html*; U.S. Environmental Protection Agency, National Air Quality and Emissions Trends Report, 1–8 (1999), available at *www.epa.gov/oar/aqtrnd981.*

from homicides and electrocutions in 1999 were offset by increases from workers struck by falling objects or caught in running machinery. Homicides fell from the second-leading cause of fatal work injuries to the third, behind highway fatalities and falls.

Table B.6 outlines work fatalities within occupational categories. Construction reported the largest number of fatal work injuries for any industry and accounted for one-fifth of the fatality total. Other industry divisions with large numbers of fatalities relative to their employment include agriculture, forestry, and fishing; transportation and public utilities; and mining.

Table B.7 Percent change in principal pollutant emissions between 1980 and 1999

Pollutant	1980–99	1990–99
CO	−22	−7
Pb	−95	−23
NO_x	+1	+2
VOC	−33	−15
PM_{10}	−55	−16
SO_2	−28	−21

Source: U.S. Environmental Protection Agency, Latest Findings on National Air Quality: 1999 Status and Trends 4 (1999), available at *www.epa.gov/airtrends.*

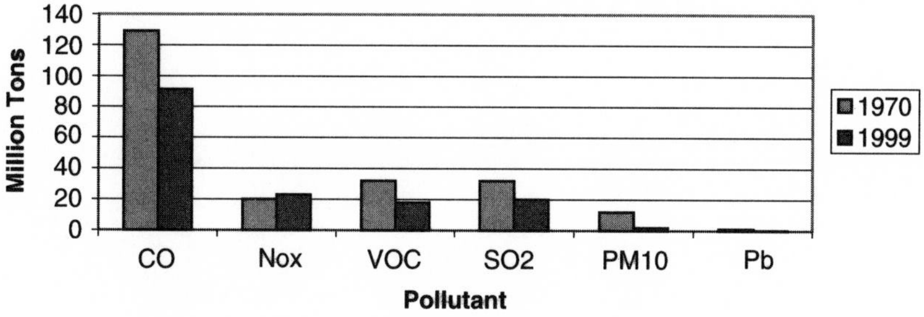

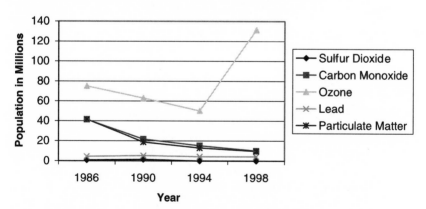

Figure B.7 Comparison of 1970 and 1999 principal pollutant emissions
Source: U.S. Environmental Protection Agency, Latest Findings on National Air Quality: 1999 Status and Trends 2 (1999), available at *www.epa.gov/airtrends.*

Figure B.8 Number of people living in U.S. countries with air quality concentrations above EPA standards
Source: Council on Environmental Quality, Environmental Quality Statistics, table 5.12 (1999), available at *ceq.eh.doe.gov/nepa/reports/statistics/air.html.*

ENVIRONMENTAL TRENDS

The EPA has set national air quality standards for six principal pollutants: carbon monoxide (CO), lead, nitrogen dioxide (NO_2), ozone (O_3, a combination of nitrogen oxide, NO_x, and volatile organic compounds, VOC), particulate matter (PM), and sulfur dioxide (SO_2). Figure B.6 presents emission level trends across the past several decades. Figure B.7 compares emission levels of these pollutants in 1970 to those of 1999; in the past twenty years, estimated emissions have decreased a total of 31 percent. Individual percentage changes are presented in Table B.7 and indicate strong reductions in emissions with the exception of NO_x. Despite great progress in air quality improvement, approximately 62 million people nationwide continue to reside in counties with pollution levels exceeding EPA standards. Figure B.8 presents populations living in these high concentration areas in the past fifteen years.

Appendix C

Cost–Benefit Numbers for Ozone and Particulates

Table C.I Proposed PM_{10} standard $(50/150 \ \mu g/m^3)$ 99th percentile national annual health incidence reductions[a]

Endpoint		Partial Attainment Scenario
	Annual $PM_{2.5}$ $(\mu g/m^3)$	50
	Daily $PM_{2.5}$ $(\mu g/m^3)$	150
I. Mortality: Short-term exposure		360
Long-term exposure		340
2. Chronic bronchitis		6,800
Hospital Admissions:		
3. All respiratory (all ages)		190
All respiratory (ages 65+)		470
Pneumonia (ages 65+)		170
COPD (ages 65+)		140
4. Congestive heart failure		130
5. Ischemic heart disease		140
6. Acute bronchitis		1,100
7. Lower respiratory symptoms		10,400
8. Upper respiratory symptoms		5,300
Shortness of breath		18,300
Asthma attacks		8,800
9. Work loss days		106,000
10. Minor restricted activity days		879,000

[a]Estimates are incremental to the current ozone and PM NAAQS: (year = 2010).

Table C.2 Effects of ozone regulation[a]

Endpoint	Partial Attainment Scenario		
	0.08 5th Max High-end Est.	0.08 4th Max Low-to High-end Est.	0.08 3rd Max High-end Est.
Ozone Health			
1. Mortality	80	0–80	120
Hospital admissions			
2. All respiratory (all ages)	280	300–300	420
All respiratory (ages 65+)	2,300	2,330–2,330	1,570
Pneumonia (ages 65+)	860	870–870	600
COPD (ages 65+)	260	260–260	200
Emergency department visits for asthma	120	130–130	180
3. Acute respiratory symptoms (any of 19)	28,510	29,840–29,840	42,070
Asthma attacks	60	60–60	90
MRADs	620	650–650	920
4. Mortality from air toxics	1	1–1	2
Ancillary PM health			
1. Mortality: Short-term exposure	60	0–80	110
Long-term exposure	180	0–250	340
2. Chronic bronchitis	400	0–530	690
Hospital admissions			
3. All respiratory (all ages)	70	0–90	120
All respiratory (ages 65+)	50	0–60	80
Pneumonia (ages 65+)	20	0–20	30
COPD (ages 65+)	10	0–20	20
4. Congestive heart failure	10	0–20	20
5. Ischemic heart disease	10	0–20	20
6. Acute bronchitis	290	0–400	530
7. Lower respiratory symptoms	3,510	0–4,670	6,190
8. Upper respiratory symptoms	320	0–430	570
Shortness of breath	800	0–1,220	1,660
Asthma attacks	4,210	0–5,510	7,200
9. Work loss days	38,700	0–50,440	66,160
10. Minor restricted activity days	322,460	0–420,300	551,300

[a]Estimates are incremental to the current ozone NAAQS (year = 2010).

Table C.3 Willingness-to-pay estimates (mean values)

Health Endpoint	Mean WTP Value Per Incident (1990 $)
Mortality	
Life saved	4.8 million
Life year extended	120,000
Hospital admissions:	
All respiratory illnesses, all ages	12,700
Pneumonia, age 65+	13,400
COPD, age 65+	15,900
Ischemic heart disease, age 65+	20,600
Congestive heart failure, age 65+	16,600
Emergency visits for asthma	9,000
Chronic bronchitis	260,000
Upper respiratory symptoms	19
Lower respiratory symptoms	12
Acute bronchitis	45
Acute respiratory symptoms (any of 19)	18
Asthma	32
Shortness of breath	5.30
Sinusitis and hay fever	Not monetized
Work loss days	83
Restricted activity days (RAD)	
Minor RAD	38
Respiratory RAD	Not monetized
Worker productivity	$1 per worker per 10% change in ozone
Visibility: Residential	$14 per unit decrease in deciview per household
Recreational	Range of $7.30 to $11 per unit decrease in deciview per household (see U.S. EPA, 1997a)
Household soiling damage	$2.50 per household per $\mu g/m^3$

Table C.4 Proposed PM_{10} standard $(50/150 \ \mu g/m^3)$ 99th percentile national annual monetized health benefits incidence reductions[a]

Endpoint		Partial Attainment Scenario High-End Est.
	Annual $PM_{2.5}$ $(\mu g/m^3)$	50
	Daily $PM_{2.5}$ $(\mu g/m^3)$	150
1. Mortality: Short-term exposure		$1.7
Long-term exposure		$1.6
2. Chronic bronchitis		$1.8
Hospital Admissions		
3. All respiratory (all ages)		$0.002
All respiratory (ages 65+)		$0.006
Pneumonia (ages 65+)		$0.003
COPD (ages 65+)		$0.002
4. Congestive heart failure		$0.002
5. Ischemic heart disease		$0.003
6. Acute bronchitis		$0
7. Lower respiratory symptoms		$0
8. Upper respiratory symptoms		$0
Shortness of breath		$0
Asthma attacks		$0
9. Work loss days		$0.009
10. Minor restricted activity days		$0.034
Total Monetized Benefits		
Using long-term mortality		$3.4
Using short-term mortality		$3.5

[a]Estimates are incremental to the current ozone (0.12 ppm, 1 hour) (billions of 1990 $; year = 2010)

Table C.5 Monetized benefits of ozone regulation

	Partial Attainment Scenario		
Endpoint	0.08 5th Max High-End Est. ($)	0.08 4th Max Low- to High-End Est. ($)	0.08 3rd Max High-End Est.
Ozone Health			
1. Mortality	0.370	0.000–0.380	0.570
Hospital Admissions			
2. All respiratory (all ages)	0.004	0.004–0.004	0.006
All resp. (ages 65+)	0.029	0.029–0.029	0
Pneumonia (ages 65+)	0.014	0.014–0.014	0.010
COPD (ages 65+)	0.004	0.004–0.004	0.003
Emer. dept. visits for asthma	0.001	0.001–0.001	0.002
3. Acute respiratory symptoms (any of 19)	0.001	0.001–0.001	0.001
Asthma attacks	0	0–0	0
MRADs	0	0–0	0
4. Mortality from air toxics	0.003	0.006–0.006	0.011
Ancillary PM Health			
1. Mortality: Short-term exposure	0.300	0–0.400	0.520
Long-term exposure	0.870	0–1.210	1.640
2. Chronic bronchitis	0.110	0–0.140	0.180
Hospital Admissions			
3. All respiratory (all ages)	0.001	0–0.001	0.001
All respiratory (ages 65+)	0.001	0–0.001	0.001
Pneumonia (ages 65+)	0	0–0	0
COPD (ages 65+)	0	0–0	0
4. Congestive heart failure	0	0–0	0
5. Ischemic heart disease	0	0–0	0
6. Acute Bronchitis	0	0–0	0
7. Lower respiratory symptoms	0	0–0	0
8. Upper respiratory symptoms	0	0–0	0
Shortness of breath	0	0–0	0
Asthma attacks	0	0–0	0
9. Work loss days	0.003	0–0.004	0.005
10. Minor restricted activity days	0.012	0–0.016	0.020
Total Monetized Benefits			
Using short-term PM mortality	0.790	0.056	1.300
Using long-term PM mortality	1.400	1.785	2.400

[a]Estimates are incremental to the current ozone NAAQS (0.12 ppm, 1 hour) (billions of 1990 $; year = 2010).

Table C.6 Ozone: summary of national annual monetized health and welfare benefits[a]

Category	Partial Attainment Scenario		
	0.08 5th Max High-End Est. ($)	0.08 4th Max Low- to High-End Est. ($)	0.08 3rd Max High-End Est. ($)
Health benefits	1.4	0.06–1.76	2.4
Welfare benefits	0.25	0.32–0.32	0.5
Total monetized benefits	1.6	0.4–2.1	2.9

[a]Estimates are incremental to the current ozone and PM NAAQS (billions of 1990 $; year = 2010)

Table C.7 Comparison of annual benefits and costs of PM alternatives in 2010[a,b] (1990 $)

$PM_{2.5}$ Alternative ($\mu g/m^3$)	Annual Benefits of Partial Attainment[c] (billion $) (A)	Annual Costs of Partial Attainment (billion $) (B)	Net Benefits of Partial Attainment (billion $) (A − B)	Number of Residual Nonattainment Counties
16/65 (high-end estimate)	90	5.5	85	19
15/65 (low-end estimate, high-end estimate)	19–104	8.6	10–95	30
15/50 (high-end estimate)	108	9.4	98	41

[a] All estimates are measured incremental to partial attainment of the current PM_{10} standard (PM_{10} 50/150, 1 expected exceedance per year).
[b] The results for 16/65 and 15/50 are only for the high-end assumptions range. The low-end estimates were not calculated for these alternatives.
[c] Partial attainment benefits based upon post-control air quality as defined in the control cost analysis.

Table C.8 Comparison of annual benefits and costs of ozone alternatives in 2010[a,b] (1990 $)

Ozone Alternative (ppm)	Annual Benefits of Partial Attainment (billion $)[c] (A)	Annual Costs of Partial Attainment (billion $) (B)	Net Benefits of Partial Attainment (billion $) (A − B)	Number of Residual Nonattainment Areas
0.08 5th Max (high-end estimate)	1.6	0.9	0.7	12
0.08 4th Max (low-end estimate), (high-end estimate)	0.4–2.1	1.1	(0.7)–1.0	17
0.08 3rd Max (high-end estimate)	2.9	1.4	1.5	27

[a] All estimates are measured incremental to partial attainment of the baseline current ozone standard (0.12 ppm, 1 expected exceedance per year).

[b] The results for 0.08, 5th and 0.08, 3rd max. are only for the high-end assumptions. The low-end estimates were not calculated for these alternatives.

[c] Partial attainment benefits based upon post-control air quality estimates as defined in the control cost analysis.

Appendix D

Dose–Response Curves

To evaluate risks associated with toxic substances, and to undertake cost–benefit analysis, it is often important to have a sense of the dose–response curve. Chapter 8 discusses this point in some detail in the context of arsenic. The purpose of this appendix is to give a general overview of the possibilities.

LINEAR RELATIONSHIPS

The dose–response curve can have a variety of shapes, including linear, where response increases proportionally with dose. Figure D.1 displays the linear relationship between dietary dose of organophosphate insecticide dioxathion and inhibition of the enzyme cholinesterase in rats.

Figure D.2 demonstrates another linear relationship, this one between subcutaneous administration of carcinogenic hydrocarbon dibenzanthracene and tumor incidence in mice.

SUBLINEAR RELATIONSHIPS

Chemicals such as benzene, radon, and formaldehyde exhibit sublinear dose–response relationships, where elicited responses are less than proportional. Figure D.3 displays a sublinear relationship for primary pulmonary (lung) tumors in rats following exposure to plutonium dioxide.

Figure D.4 exhibits a sublinear dose–response relationship between the number of female rat liver foci (a precursor to cancer) and the log dose of phenobarbital expressed as picomole per kilogram.

THRESHOLD RELATIONSHIPS

Some chemicals produce no adverse effects below a certain level, resulting in a threshold curve. Threshold-model agents include dioxins and chrysotile asbestos; in addition, nongenotoxic carcinogens are generally assumed to have

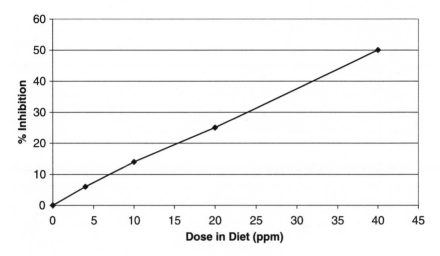

Figure D.I Cholinesterase
Source: S. D. Murphy & K. L. Cheever, Effects of Feeding Insecticides: Inhibition of Carboxylesterase and Cholinesterase Activities in Rats, 17 Arch. Env. Health 749 (1968); reprinted in Casarett and Doull's Toxicology: The Basic Science of Poisons 19, figure 2-2 (Mary O. Amdur et al., eds., New York, Pergamon Press 4th ed., 1991).

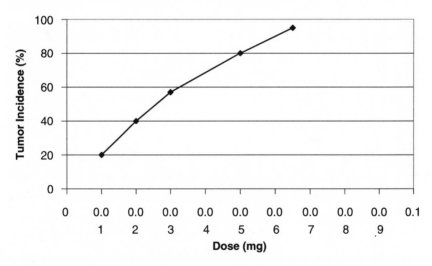

Figure D.2 Dibenzanthracene
Source: Casarett and Doull's Toxicology: The Basic Science of Poisons 23, figure 2-5 (Mary O. Amdur et al., eds., New York, Pergamon Press, 4th ed., 1991), modified from W. R. Bryan & M. B. Shimkin, Quantitative Analysis of Dose–Response Data Obtained with Three Carcinogenic Hydrocarbons in Strain C3H Male Mice, 3 J. Natl. Cancer Inst. 503 (1943).

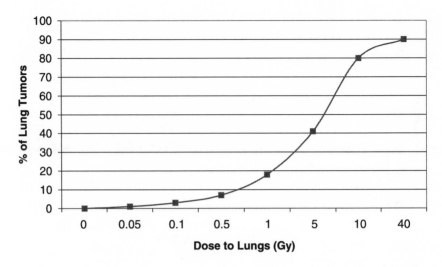

Figure D.3 Plutonium dioxide
Source: C. L. Sanders & D. L. Lundgren, Pulmonary Carcinogenesis in the F344 and Wistar Rat after Inhalation of Plutonium Dioxide, 144 Rad. Res. 206, 212 (1995).

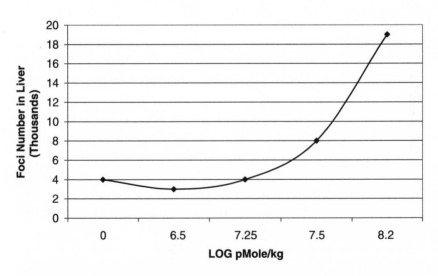

Figure D.4 Phenobarbital
Source: Kirk T. Kitchin et al., Dose–Response Relationship in Multistage Carcinogenesis: Promoters, 102 (Suppl. 1) Env. Health Persp. 255, 257 (1994).

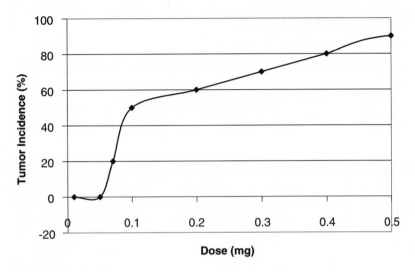

Figure D.5 Benzpyrene
Source: Casarett and Doull's Toxicology: The Basic Science of Poisons 23, figure 2-5 (Mary O. Amdur et al., eds., New York, Pergamon Press, 4th ed., 1991), modified from W. R. Bryan & M. B. Shimkin, Quantitative Analysis of Dose–Response Data Obtained with Three Carcinogenic Hydrocarbons in Strain C3H Male Mice, 3 J. Natl. Cancer Inst., 503 (1943).

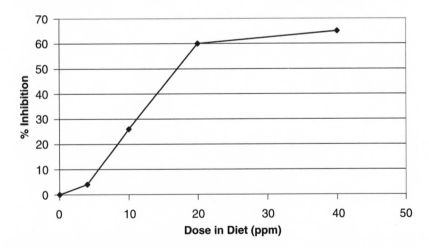

Figure D.6 Carboxylesterase
Source: S. D. Murphy & K. L. Cheever, Effects of Feeding Insecticides: Inhibition of Carboxylesterase and Cholinesterase Activities in Rats, 17 Arch. Env. Health, 749 (1968), reprinted in Casarett and Doull's Toxicology: The Basic Science of Poisons 19, figure 2-2 (Mary O. Amdur et al., eds., New York, Pergamon Press, 4th ed., 1991).

threshold doses. Figure D.5 demonstrates a threshold for the carcinogenic hydrocarbon benzpyrene causing sarcomas in mice.

SUPRALINEAR RELATIONSHIPS

Dose-response relationships exceeding proportionality, such as vinyl chloride, are supralinear. Figure D.6 demonstrates a supralinear curve for the inhibition of

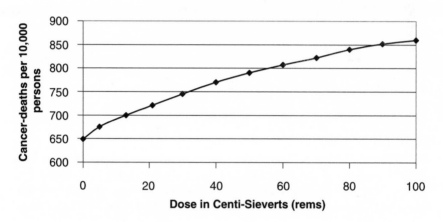

Figure D.7 Atomic bomb radiation
Source: John W. Gofman, Radiation-Induced Cancer from Low-Dose Exposure, figure 14A, 14F (1990), available at *www.ratical.org/radation/CNR/RIC/chp14F.html#fig14e.*

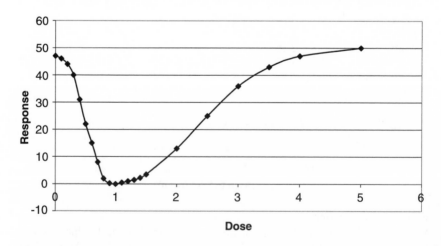

Figure D.8 Fluoride
Source: Gordon A. Fox, EVR 2001: Risk and Toxicity 9–10, figure 2 (2000), available at *chuma.cas.usf.edu/~gfox/EVR2001/risk_and_toxicity.pdf.*

carboxylesterase enzyme activities in rats as a function of insecticide dioxathion dose.

The slight concave-upward pattern in Figure D.7 demonstrates a weaker supralinear relationship between exposure to radiation via an atomic bomb and cancer deaths per 10,000 people.

U-SHAPED RELATIONSHIPS

Hermatic chemicals such as essential nutrients and vitamins exhibit beneficial effects at low doses, coupled with toxic effects at high doses, resulting in a U-shaped curve. The dose–response relationship of fluoride, which exerts positive effects at lower doses, but is toxic at high doses, is outlined in Figure D.8.

Acknowledgments

I am grateful to many people for their help with this book. For teaching me so much about the psychology of risk, and for comments on an early draft, I am especially grateful to Daniel Kahneman. Thanks also to Timur Kuran, my coauthor on "Availability Cascades and Risk Regulation," *51 Stan. L. Rev. 683* (1999). I should add that while Chapter 4 and parts of Chapter 5 grow out of our joint essay, and while Kuran offered generous comments, I substantially revised our previous work, adding new material and some reorientation, and Kuran should not be held responsible for any mistakes that I have made. I owe a more general debt to Kuran for an exceptional collaboration from which I learned a great deal.

For comments on all or parts of the manuscript, I thank Jonathan Baron, Martha Nussbaum, Eric Posner, Richard Posner, and an anonymous referee for Cambridge University Press. Julia Hough was a supportive and encouraging editor. Officials at the Environmental Protection Agency and the Office of Management and Budget provided illuminating discussions. Laura Warren provided truly outstanding research assistance. Special thanks are due to Ellen Ruddick-Sunstein, my daughter, eleven years old as I write. This book is dedicated to her, with love.

I have been working on the topic of risk regulation for two decades, and while this book contains a great deal of new material, it also draws on previous work. Chapter 2 draws on "Cognition and Cost-Benefit Analysis" *29 J. Legal Stud. 1059* (2000); Chapter 3 draws on "Bad Deaths" *14 J. Risk & Uncertainty, 259* (1997); Chapter 4 draws on "Availability Cascades and Risk Regulation" *51 Stan. L. Rev. 683* (1999), as do some sections of Chapter 5; Chapter 6 draws on "Health–Health Tradeoffs" *63 U. Chi. L. Rev. 1533* (1996), which also appeared in my *Free Markets and Social Justice* (New York: Oxford Univ. Press, 1997); Chapter 7 draws on "The Arithmetic of Arsenic" *Geo. L. J.* (forthcoming); Chapter 8 draws on "Cost–Benefit Default Rules" *Mich. L. Rev. 1651* (forthcoming); Chapter 9 draws on "Is the Clean Air Act Unconstitutional"?, *98 Mich. L. Rev. 303* (1999); Chapter 10 draws on "Democratizing America Through Law," *25 Suffolk L. Rev. 949* (1991). Chapters 8 and 9 also draw on my book, *The Cost–Benefit State* (Washington, D.C.: American Bar Association, 2001), which presents some of the arguments here in a way that offers more technical details about law. In all cases, the previous work has been updated and extensively revised. I am most grateful to the journals and publishers just mentioned for permission to reprint previously published material here.

Index

acid deposition, 134–5, 144, 252, 253,
 275–6, 279
acrylonitrile, 193
Administrative Procedure Act (APA),
 114–15, 120, 147, 150, 151
advertisers, 46
advertising campaigns, 266–9
affect, and risk evaluation, 62
affect heuristic, 43–4, 158, 290
affective judgment, 61
affiliation bias, 36
AFL-CIO v. API. See Industrial Union
 Department, *AFL-CIO v. API*
Agent Orange, 97
agricultural practices, regulation of,
 145
AIDS
 communication of information
  about, 266
 deaths from, 56, 65, 111–12
 health care costs and, 133
 new medicines and, 136
 See also HIV infection
air pollutants
 benefits of, 196–7, 209
 nonthreshold, 234
 "significantly contributing", 200
air pollution, 4, 22–3
 effect on other problems, 150–1
 fossil fuels and, 136

from motor vehicles, 2–4
 voluntariness of risk, 23, 69
air quality, 22, 310
 costs and benefits assessment, 183–4
 levels of safety, 231–2
 safety thresholds, 248
air transportation
 accidents, 34, 43, 70, 72–3
 airport security, 97
 deaths from accidents, 56, 65, 67–8,
  301, 304t
 hijackings, 72
Alabama Power Company v. Costle, 205
Alar incident, 82–3, 92, 94, 115
alarmist bias, 45
ambiguity, in statutory interpretation,
 205
American Dental Association v. Martin,
 204n50
American Enterprise Institute
 (AEI)-Brookings Joint Center for
 Regulatory Studies, 166–8
American Trucking Associations v. EPA, 196,
 209, 212
ancillary risks, 134
 consideration of, in law, 146–7
 costs/benefits of investigating, 142–3
 division of labor and, 144
 refusal to consider, 147–50
 regulated vs., 135–6

327

disadvantaged groups (*cont.*)
  information disclosure and, 263–4
  risks faced by, 74–6, 224
disclosure
  of information, 252, 254–60
  of risks, 256
discounting
  of future benefits and losses, 122,
    226
  of latent harms, 176–7
discount rates, 224–8
distribution
  of deaths, 76–7
  government regulation and, 75–6
  regulation of arsenic in drinking
    water and, 189–90
  of risks, 74–6, 114
distributional effects
  Clean Air Act, 237
  of national standards, 237
  of regulation, 156
Domestic Council, 19
Dorner, Dietrich, 1
dose-response curves, 154, 169–72,
  179, 318–23
drugs, regulation of, 136
drunk driving, 268

early cessation, in hazardous waste
  combustion, 195–6
earned income tax credit, 76
Easterbrook, Frank, 137
economic incentives
  command-and-control vs., 248–9,
    269
  democracy and, 272–3
  effect on prices, 276–7
  government regulation and, 269, 273
  as regressive tax, 276–7
  trading systems. *See* trading systems
education
  fear and, 112
  website for, 118–19
  See also information

efficiency
  information markets and, 255–6
  in risk reduction, 270–2
Ehrlichman, John, 19
elderly people, 31, 176, 224, 241
Emergency Planning and Community
    Right to Know Act (EPCRA),
    258
emissions, 308t, 309t
  carbon dioxide, 270–1,
    279–80
  carbon monoxide, 4, 135
  formaldehyde, 3
  greenhouse gas, 259
  levels, 18
  major, 202–3
  nitrogen oxide, 101
  required reductions in, 253
  standards for hazardous waste
    combustion, 195–6
  standards for motor vehicles, 151
  sulfur dioxide, 135, 279–80
  tradeable rights, 252, 269
  trading system, 272, 274–5, 278
  of volatile organic compounds, 4
emotion(s), 43, 44–5, 290
  appeal to, 46–7
  CBA and, 107
  cognition vs., 44–5
  probability neglect and, 51
endangered species, 93, 283, 287
Endangered Species Act, 99, 213–14,
    283
energy insulation, 265
environment
  availability campaigns and, 93
  commitments to, 11, 17–18
  environmental contracting, 282
  Environmental Defense Fund, 286
  environmental impact statements, 15
environmentalism
  free market, 132, 287–8
  political, 287
  1970s, 11–18, 22, 234

ordinary people
  cognition of, 289–90
  communication methods to, 264–5
  experts vs. *See* experts vs. ordinary
    people
  government vs., in risk evaluation, 49
  information about risks for, 256
  information processing by, 261
  pressures from, 32–3
  qualitative judgments of, 55
  richer rationality of, 58–60, 76
  toxicologists' views cf., 35–7
ossification, of rules, 181, 225
overgrazing, 131, 287
ozone, ground-level, 2–3
  benefits and adverse effects of,
    39–40, 123, 149–50, 196, 208,
    210–11
  CBA and, 311–17
  health considerations, 200–1
  risks of, 210–11
  standards for, 245–6
ozone layer, thinning of, 96, 101

pandas, 93
paralysis
  by analysis, 16
  precautionary principle and, 104
parental leave program, 125–6
particulates, 246
  CBA and, 311–17
particulates standards, 240–3
peer review, 115
penalties, for violation of laws, 284–5
performance standards vs. technology
    requirements, 270
pesticides, 12, 14, 40n22, 41–2, 101,
    146, 270
Philip Morris, 267–8
plants, genetically modified, 101–2
point-of-use solutions, 185
pollution
  controls vs. prevention, 101
  effect of flat bans, 276

emissions, 308t, 309t
  fees for, 270–1
  "hot spots" of, 277
  market instruments for control,
    185–6
  market instruments for control
    (*see also* free market
    environmentalism)
  prevention vs. cure, 100–2
  taxes, 270–1, 281
  tradeable permits for, 271–2
  trading among sources, 252
Pollution Prevention Act, 100
poor people
  effects of regulation on, 40
  risk distribution and, 75
  See also poverty
populism
  CBA and, 121
  See also ordinary people
poverty
  mortality and, 138–41
  risks and, 136–41, 175
  See also poor people
precautionary principle, 102–5,
    182–3
Prevention of Significant
    Deterioration program, Clean Air
    Act, 193–4
prices, 125
  economic incentives and, 276–7
priority-setting
  in regulation, 23
probability neglect, 51
Project XL, 283–4
property rights, 287
  environmentalism and, 132
proportionality effect, 47–8
Proposition 65 (California), 261
public discourse, 89, 93, 96
public officials
  pronouncements of, 90
  quest for credit/acclaim, 11,
    15–16